CliffsNotes

AP

U.S. Government and Politics

CRAM PLAN™

Jeri A. Jones, M.A. and Lindsay Reeves

Houghton Mifflin Harcourt
Boston • New York

About the Authors

Jeri A. Jones, M.A., delivered secondary instruction in the Los Angeles Unified School District for 33 years, the last 14 of those teaching AP U.S. History and AP U.S. Government and Politics at an urban medical magnet high school. She received special recognition from her school district as one of only five teachers to achieve a "highly qualified" distinction in all 15 categories of instructional performance (2013) and was also recognized by the City Council of Los Angeles for teaching excellence (2015).

Lindsay Reeves holds a degree in political science, with concentrations in women's studies and sociology. She is an experienced educational content developer who has designed formative assessments, curriculum, and scoring for students taking the AP, Praxis, SAT, and LSAT exams. With extensive experience in education, Common Core Standards, and STEM, her work has been featured in a variety of publications and web-based articles.

Acknowledgments

The authors would like to thank our families and the many great teachers and mentors who have encouraged our personal and educational endeavors. A special thanks to Joy Gilmore and to the outstanding editorial staff at Houghton Mifflin Harcourt, especially Christina Stambaugh.

Dedication

To all my students who, over the course of thirty years, provided me with inspiration, a wonderful laboratory for developing my knowledge about the practice of teaching and the process of learning, and a daily dose of joy! —Jeri A. Jones

I dedicate this book to Daniel and Piper Reeves, Lori and Larry Lewis, and Jeanne Futch. —Lindsay Reeves

Editorial

Executive Editor: Greg Tubach
Senior Editor: Christina Stambaugh
Copy Editor: Lynn Northrup
Production Editor: Jennifer Freilach
Technical Editor: Michael H. Kim
Proofreader: Susan Moritz

CliffsNotes® AP® U.S. Government and Politics Cram Plan™

Library of Congress Control Number: 2018958134
ISBN: 978-0-544-91568-8 (pbk)

Printed in the United States of America
DOC 10 9 8 7 6 5 4 3 2 1

For information about permission to reproduce selections from this book, write to trade.permissions@hmhco.com or to Permissions, Houghton Mifflin Harcourt Publishing Company, 3 Park Avenue, 19th Floor, New York, New York 10016.

www.hmhco.com

Table of Contents

Preface

Congratulations! You've decided to take the Advanced Placement course in U.S. Government and Politics. This book can help you plan your course of study and prepare for the exam. You can use it as a quick reference guide, an in-depth resource, a source for practice, or a refresher of one or more topics in U.S. government and politics. It is packed with information about what to expect on the exam, how to approach the questions, how to plan study time, and how to review the five units. It includes both a diagnostic test and a full-length practice exam, both of which include answers and complete answer explanations.

CliffsNotes AP U.S. Government and Politics Cram Plan is an easy-to-follow study guide that helps you make the most of the time you have to study civic understandings. Although it is not meant to substitute for a formal high school AP class, it provides you with important learning strategies and practice questions to refresh your understanding of the topics outlined in the AP course framework. The skills and concepts defined in this book can help you pass the AP GOV exam by providing you with exam-oriented approaches to real-world scenarios, content knowledge to help you analyze government documents and Supreme Court cases, and practice material to help you evaluate areas in which you excel or those in which you need improvement. If you follow the lessons and strategies in this book, have a sound knowledge of key topics, and study regularly, you will deepen your understanding of U.S. government and politics, which will strengthen your performance on the exam.

Navigating This Book

CliffsNotes AP U.S. Government and Politics Cram Plan is organized as follows:

Introduction to the AP U.S. Government and Politics Exam — A general description of the AP GOV exam, exam format, scoring, question types, essential knowledge about the five units, big ideas, political science disciplinary practices and reasoning processes, frequently asked questions, and test-taking strategies.

- **Chapter 1 — Two-Month Cram Plan:** A study calendar that provides a detailed suggested plan of action for preparing for the AP GOV exam 2 months before your exam.
- **Chapter 2 — One-Month Cram Plan:** A study calendar that provides a detailed suggested plan of action for preparing for the AP GOV exam 1 month before your exam.
- **Chapter 3 — Diagnostic Test:** A shortened version of the AP GOV practice exam in Chapter 9, the diagnostic test introduces you to the AP GOV units, evaluates your areas of strength and weakness to help you focus your study, and provides you with a baseline starting point.
- **Chapter 4 — Unit 1: Foundations of American Democracy**
- **Chapter 5 — Unit 2: Interaction among Branches of Government**
- **Chapter 6 — Unit 3: Civil Liberties and Civil Rights**
- **Chapter 7 — Unit 4: American Political Ideologies and Beliefs**
- **Chapter 8 — Unit 5: Political Participation**
- **Chapter 9 — Full-Length Practice Exam:** Includes answers and in-depth explanations for multiple-choice questions and sample responses and scoring guidelines for the four free-response questions.

- **Appendix — Required Foundational Documents and Supreme Court Cases:** Summarizes the required foundational documents and required Supreme Court cases that you'll need to know for the exam.

How to Use This Book

You determine how you would like to use this study guide. You can decide to read it from cover to cover or just refer to it when you need specific information. Since the review chapters provide terms, study questions, and a summary of each concept outline covered on the exam, many students prefer to gain a broad understanding of U.S. government and politics before they begin an in-depth review of specific key concepts, facts, essential knowledge, founding documents, and Supreme Court cases. Others find it useful to learn general exam information (political science skills and practices and test-taking strategies) before memorizing the specific topics related to U.S. government and politics. It is up to you to choose what best fits your needs.

Here are some of the recommended ways you can use this book.

- Create a customized study "action plan." Pay careful attention to time because your study plan will depend on the total amount of time you have until the exam date. Preview the cram plan calendars in chapters 1 and 2 to organize your study time.
- Read (and then reread) the Introduction to become familiar with the test format, the five units of study, big ideas, political science disciplinary practices and reasoning processes, types of questions, and test-taking strategies.
- Take the diagnostic test (Chapter 3) to assess your strengths and weaknesses.
- Study the government foundational documents and important Supreme Court cases found in the Appendix.
- Get a glimpse of what you'll gain from a chapter by reading through the key concepts, key terms, and the headings referenced at the beginning of each review chapter.
- Follow the recommended sequence of subject matter (chapters 4–8). Within each chapter, take detailed notes on the pages of this book to highlight important facts and topics related to the AP GOV concept outlines.
- If you feel you are familiar with information in a particular chapter, consider attempting to answer the study questions that appear below the concept outlines. Then read through the chapter review section to see if your answers are correct. Note any additional information or connections that you may have missed in your first attempt.
- Look for diagrams, charts, and callout features in chapters 4–8 to enhance your study. The intermingled callout features will allow you to organize information and help you focus on areas of study.
  - **Key Facts** — Lists the significant facts of a topic for a quick study reference.
  - **Did You Know?** — Covers interesting information about scenarios and events on topics to aid in your overall understanding of a topic.
  - **Heads Up: What You Need to Know** — Summarizes details about specific content that will be on the actual AP GOV exam.
  - **TEST TIP** — Offers quick strategies and tips for approaching exam questions.

- Use the "Chapter Review Practice Questions" to gauge your grasp of questions on the AP GOV exam and strengthen your critical reasoning skills. Although it is tempting to look ahead at the answer explanations, try to simulate testing conditions by answering the questions and writing your free-response essays *before* reviewing the explanations. Initially, it may be difficult, but this strategy will reinforce your learning.
- Test your knowledge more completely in the full-length practice exam in Chapter 9.

If you have moments of self-doubt, keep reminding yourself that even though the material is challenging, it is manageable. Take a deep breath, and know that you can do this by using the content, tips, and practice questions offered in this study guide.

The lessons and strategies you are learning in this book will help you throughout your high school and college learning experiences. If you make the commitment to follow them and practice regularly, you will not only be statistically increasing your odds for passing the AP GOV exam, but you will also be learning skills that can help you manage future academic coursework!

Introduction

Welcome to *CliffsNotes AP U.S. Government and Politics Cram Plan*!

Teachers and students alike will find this preparation guide to be a valuable course supplement. The reasons for taking this course may go beyond your test outcome in May. As Thomas Jefferson famously said, "If a nation expects to be ignorant and free…, it expects what never was and never will be." Thus, as Jefferson tells us, an informed citizenry is perhaps the best defense against tyranny. Supporting Jefferson's theory begins with understanding the underpinnings of U.S. government, the Constitution itself, and the heritage of ideas from which it was formulated.

As an American citizen, it is critical to have an informed comprehension of how the institutions of the government operate, how to interact to create public policy, how the role of the citizenry impacts our society, and how the patterns of political behavior impact the policymaking process.

Fortunately for students enrolled in the AP U.S. Government and Politics course, civic understandings are congruent with the more immediate bottom line of passing the exam. This book is designed to familiarize you with the content of the course, the skills you will need to apply to meet the exam expectations, and the format of the exam through a series of practice questions and a full-length practice exam. In the process of studying for the exam, you will develop a deeper appreciation for the design of the government, how public policy is crafted, and your own role in the ongoing evolution of America's experiment with constitutional democracy.

Exam Format

The AP U.S. Government and Politics (AP GOV) exam is divided into two sections, and each section is worth 50 percent of the final score. Section I consists of 55 multiple-choice questions, and Section II consists of 4 free-response questions. The entire test is 3 hours. The chart below summarizes the format of the exam.

Note: Format and scoring are subject to change. Visit the College Board website for updates: https://apcentral.collegeboard.com.

Section	Question Type	Time	Number of Questions	Percent of Total Grade	
Section I **Multiple-Choice Questions**	Multiple choice	80 minutes	55 questions	50%	
Section II **Free-Response Questions**	Concept Application	20 minutes (suggested)	1 question	12.5%	50%
	Quantitative Analysis	20 minutes (suggested)	1 question	12.5%	
	SCOTUS Comparison	20 minutes (suggested)	1 question	12.5%	
	Argument Essay	40 minutes (suggested)	1 question	12.5%	
TOTALS		**3 hours**	**55 multiple choice** **4 essays**	**100%**	

Scoring

Your score on the AP GOV exam will be based on the number of questions you answer correctly for the two separate sections.

> Section I: Multiple-choice questions are 50 percent of your overall score.
>
> Section II: Free-response questions are 50 percent of your overall score.

Based on the combination of the two sections, the scores are converted into a grading scale of 1 to 5. A score of 5 is the best possible score. Most colleges consider a score of 3 or better a passing score. If you receive a passing score, the AP GOV exam can be applied as a college course equivalent—two-semester units will apply toward your college bachelor's degree as a U.S. government course.

As a reference, approximately 50 percent of the students who took the AP GOV in 2018 scored at least a 3 on the exam. If you receive such a score, it can be applied as a one-semester introductory college course equivalent in U.S. government and politics.

AP Score	Score Translation
5	Extremely well qualified
4	Well qualified
3	Qualified
2	Possibly qualified
1	No recommendation

The AP GOV exam is graded on a curve, particularly the multiple-choice questions. Oftentimes, students panic when they get back their first practice exam. "A 65 percent on the multiple choice? I'm failing!" In reality, a 65 percent on the multiple-choice questions can be good enough for a 4 or even a 5 on the entire exam, depending on your score on the free-response section. Note: For multiple-choice questions, no points are deducted for incorrect answers. If you don't know the answer, take an educated guess because there is no penalty for guessing.

Question Types

Knowing what information is covered on the exam provides a significant advantage to students preparing for test day, but equally as important is the ability to anticipate how to approach questions. Knowing how the exam is structured and having a working familiarity with what the questions will look like goes a long way to alleviating testing anxiety.

As you approach each of the questions, consider the following points to receive your best possible score.

- What are the main *constitutional principles, representative policies, and political processes* of each unit?
- What are the broader *big ideas* within each unit?
- What are the important *supporting examples and evidence* of the constitutional principles—significant people, documents, court cases, or laws?
- What are the *implications* of the constitutional principles, political processes, or citizen and/or government official behaviors?

Multiple-Choice Questions

Section I consists of multiple-choice questions that require you to draw reasonable conclusions based on your knowledge of U.S. government and politics.

Key points about multiple-choice questions:

- The exam contains 55 multiple-choice questions—50 percent of your overall score.
- Select one answer from among four choices in each question.
- Questions are drawn from unit content outlines and ask you to identify, define, analyze, explain, or apply course concepts, foundational documents, and Supreme Court cases to real-world scenarios.
- Some questions are grouped into sets. For example, you may find two or more successive questions referencing the same source stimulus (text excerpt or visual graphic, such as a graph, chart, map, or political cartoon, from primary and secondary source documents, or U.S. foundational documents).
- Some questions ask you to compare information presented in a table to match similar course concepts, foundational documents, or Supreme Court cases.
- No points are deducted for incorrect answers; therefore, there is no penalty for guessing.

Free-Response Questions

Section II consists of four free-response questions that focus on knowledge from U.S. government and politics. If you answer all parts of each question and write a response that addresses all points in the scoring criteria as described by the College Board, you can increase your score. Throughout the chapters of this book you will find many opportunities to answer and review a variety of questions similar to those you will encounter on the exam.

Each of the four free-response questions draws from AP GOV unit content outlines and requires you to connect these topics to the big ideas, disciplinary practices, and reasoning processes.

Key points about the free-response questions:

- The four free-response questions comprise 50 percent of your overall score.
- The exam contains at least one free-response question about public policy and at least one question about comparing a required and non-required Supreme Court case.
- Write a response that considers the relationship among the topic question, your thesis, and evidence.
- Each point is earned independently. For example, you can earn a point for a defensible thesis, but fail to earn a point for not providing supporting evidence.
- Essay responses are considered first drafts and may contain some errors.
- Write a response that addresses all points in the scoring criteria as described by the College Board (see the chart below).

Scoring Rubric for Free-Response Questions		
Question Type	**Scoring Criteria**	**Possible Points**
Concept Application	The concept application question will require that you respond to *three* disciplinary practices (1 point each). For example,. ❏ Describe, explain, or compare a political institution, behavior, or process connected with a scenario. ❏ In the context of the scenario, explain or describe how the response above affects a political process, government entity, or citizen behavior. ❏ Explain how the scenario relates to a political institution, behavior, or process.	3 points
Quantitative Analysis	The quantitative analysis question will require that you respond to *four* disciplinary practices (1 point each). For example, ❏ Identify and describe the data presented in a visual graphic. ❏ Describe the patterns, trends, or similarities/differences in the data as prompted in the question. ❏ Draw a conclusion for that pattern, trend, or similarity/difference. ❏ Explain how the specific data implies or illustrates a political principle in the prompt.	4 points
SCOTUS Comparison	The SCOTUS comparison question will require that you respond to four disciplinary practices (1 point each). For example, ❏ Identify a similarity or difference between two Supreme Court cases. ❏ Provide factual information as prompted in the question (describe the facts, reasoning, decision, and opinion) of the required Supreme Court cases. ❏ Explain how or why the reasoning, decisions, and opinion(s) of a required Supreme Court case is relevant to a non-required Supreme Court case. ❏ Describe or explain an interaction between the holding in a non-required Supreme Court case and a relevant political institution, behavior, or process.	4 points
Argument Essay	**THESIS/CLAIM:** Presents a historically defensible thesis that establishes a line of reasoning. (Note: The thesis must make a claim that responds to *all* parts of the question and must *not* just restate the question.) (1 point).	6 points
	EVIDENCE: Uses TWO pieces of specific and relevant evidence to support the argument. (Note: Must be linked to the topic question.) (3 points). OR Uses ONE piece of specific and relevant evidence to support the argument. (Note: Must be linked to the topic question.) (2 points). OR Describes one piece of evidence that is accurately linked to the topic of the question (1 point). (Note: To earn more than 1 point, the response must establish an argument and have earned the point for Thesis/Claim.)	
	REASONING: Uses reasoning to organize and explain how or why the evidence supports the thesis or claim. (Note: To earn this point, you must have earned a point for Evidence.) (1 point).	
	ALTERNATIVE PERSPECTIVES: Responds to an opposing or alternative perspective using refutation, concession, or rebuttal that is consistent with the argument. (Note: To earn this point, your response must have a claim or thesis.) (1 point).	

Units

The AP GOV exam will expect you to understand the essential key topics and concepts outlined in the *AP U.S. Government and Politics Course Framework*. The good news is that the College Board has identified five separate units that give you a clear and detailed description of the course requirements necessary for success.

- Unit 1 (Chapter 4): Foundations of American Democracy
- Unit 2 (Chapter 5): Interactions among Branches of Government
- Unit 3 (Chapter 6): Civil Liberties and Civil Rights
- Unit 4 (Chapter 7): American Political Ideologies and Beliefs
- Unit 5 (Chapter 8): Political Participation

Each of the key concepts encompasses a set of *enduring understandings, essential knowledge, and learning objectives.* You should use these to both guide your studying and predict what will be asked on the exam. Success on the AP GOV exam will depend on the connections that you make between the key concepts and the deeper understandings of U.S. government and politics.

Note: The list of *enduring understandings* for each unit (the key topics and concepts that you should grasp and retain) are listed at the beginning of review chapters 4–8.

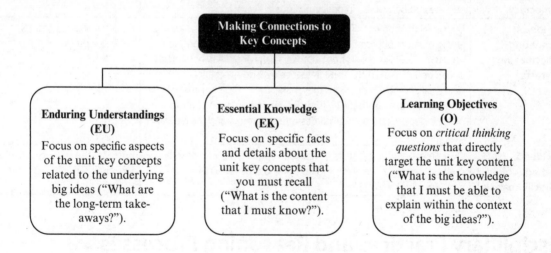

Making Connections to Key Concepts

Enduring Understandings (EU)
Focus on specific aspects of the unit key concepts related to the underlying big ideas ("What are the long-term take-aways?").

Essential Knowledge (EK)
Focus on specific facts and details about the unit key concepts that you must recall ("What is the content that I must know?").

Learning Objectives (O)
Focus on *critical thinking questions* that directly target the unit key content ("What is the knowledge that I must be able to explain within the context of the big ideas?").

Big Ideas

Government and politics are not just about a set of individual principles and processes to be studied in isolation. Political scientists study government and politics by making connections to underlying themes called *big ideas*. Success on the AP GOV exam will depend on the connections that you make between the framework key concepts (*enduring understandings*) and the thematic features described in the big ideas.

Big Idea	Description	Making Connections/Example
Big Idea 1: Constitutionalism	The U.S. constitutional system of government is based on a foundation of central principles; rule of law grounded in the concept of limited government; separation of powers maintained through a system of checks and balances; a federal design dividing sovereignty between the central government (referred to as the "federal government") and the states.	How did interpretations of the Constitution impact the practice of the judicial review?
Big Idea 2: Liberty and Order	Provisions of the Constitution are continually being changed and interpreted to balance laws and liberties.	How have the provisions in the Fourteenth Amendment changed over time?
Big Idea 3: Civic Participation in a Representative Democracy	Various forms of institutional systems like individualism, popular sovereignty, and republicanism influence how people interact with government policymakers and make it possible for citizens to engage and participate in policymaking.	How has the media influenced public opinion and public policy?
Big Idea 4: Competing Policymaking Interests	Ultimately the purpose of the U.S. system of government is to develop and implement public policy, but the policymaking institutions don't do this alone. Policy results from a process involving different interests all competing to exert the most influence over government policymakers and the decisions they make. The competing interests working to impact both the crafting and implementation of public policy include voters, political parties, interest groups, and the federal bureaucracy.	How can interest groups influence presidential elections?
Big Idea 5: Methods of Political Analysis	Over time, political scientists have used various types of research methods to study, measure, and interpret U.S. political behavior, attitudes, and ideologies.	What are the barriers to voting turnout?

Disciplinary Practices and Reasoning Processes

The U.S. Government and Politics disciplinary practices and reasoning processes are the tasks you will apply to each question. If you become familiar with these questions, you can focus on, predict, and respond to all of the questions on the AP GOV exam.

Disciplinary Practices

U.S. Government and Politics Disciplinary Practices	
Practice	**Description**
Practice 1	Apply political concepts and processes to scenarios in context.
Practice 2	Apply Supreme Court decisions.
Practice 3	Analyze and interpret quantitative data represented in tables, charts, graphs, maps, and infographics.
Practice 4	Read, analyze, and interpret foundational documents and other text-based and visual sources.
Practice 5	Develop an argument in essay format.

Reasoning Processes

The AP GOV test-makers want to move away from just reciting facts. You must offer *support* and *reasons* that connect the questions to the course framework. These skills help you to think critically about government and politics.

U.S. Government and Politics Reasoning Processes		
Reasoning	**Description**	**Example**
Definition/Classification	When demonstrating knowledge about political science concepts, describe the characteristics, attributes, traits, and elements of the term or concept; describe patterns or trends; or describe the perspectives of the source.	Describe what it means to have executive privilege.
Process	When explaining political processes, identify the steps or stages in the process, and explain how they relate to each other. Explain the significant relevance or the challenges of the interactions.	Explain the process of how a bill becomes law.
Causation	When explaining the causes and effects of political principles, institutions, processes, policies, and behaviors, explain the reasons and implications for the causes and the changes over time. This involves providing *reasons* for the causes of complex issues or the implications over time. A good way to simplify this skill is to think about the logical sequence: (1) what happened *before*, (2) what happened *during*, and (3) what happened *after*.	Explain the reasons for the Voting Rights Act of 1965.
Comparison	When explaining similarities and differences among political principles, institutions, processes, policies, and behaviors, identify relevant categories of comparison and the reasons and implications for the similarities and differences. To compare and contrast: (1) list similarities and differences of a core issue, (2) group the similarities and differences, and (3) give the relevance of these similarities or differences.	Compare the models of representative democracy.

Required Foundational Documents and Supreme Court Cases

Required foundational documents and Supreme Court cases are an important part of the AP GOV exam, and studying them will help you make civic connections to the U.S. political system, legal precedents, and formal constitutional principles. A summary of each of the required foundational documents and important Supreme Court cases is available in the Appendix for your reference.

Note: Visit the website of the National Constitution Center at: https://constitutioncenter.org/ to view an interactive constitution.

Required Foundational Documents

The philosophies of our Founding Fathers are contained in the foundational documents. It is important that you read and then reread the documents to look for the main points and the political implications. The foundational documents were written in early American history and may be difficult to interpret. Remember to check your understanding of the documents—the main points, the author's political perspective, the document's strengths and challenges, alternative viewpoints, and contemporary viewpoints.

- The Declaration of Independence
- The Articles of Confederation
- The Constitution of the United States
- Bill of Rights
- Federalist No. 10

- Federalist No. 51
- Federalist No. 70
- Federalist No. 78
- Brutus No. 1
- *Letter from Birmingham Jail*

Required Supreme Court Cases

Key elements of landmark Supreme Court cases—the issues, the decisions, and the reasoning behind those decisions—are important to memorize for the AP GOV exam.

- *Marbury v. Madison* (1803)
- *McCulloch v. Maryland* (1819)
- *Schenck v. United States* (1919)
- *Brown v. Board of Education of Topeka* (1954)
- *Baker v. Carr* (1962)
- *Engel v. Vitale* (1962)
- *Gideon v. Wainwright* (1963)
- *Tinker v. Des Moines Independent Community School District* (1969)
- *New York Times Co. v. United States* (1971)
- *Wisconsin v. Yoder* (1972)
- *Roe v. Wade* (1973)
- *Shaw v. Reno* (1993)

- *United States v. Lopez* (1995)
- *McDonald v. Chicago* (2010)
- *Citizens United v. Federal Election Commission* (2010)

Frequently Asked Questions (FAQs)

Q: Who administers the AP U.S. Government and Politics exam?

A: The College Board prepares and scores the AP GOV exam. For further information regarding test administration, contact *Advanced Placement Program (AP)*, P.O. Box 6671, Princeton, NJ, 08541-6671, (888) 225-5427 or (212) 632-1780, e-mail: apstudents@info.collegeboard.org, https://apcentral. collegeboard.com.

Q: Are there prerequisites to taking the AP GOV exam?

A: No. However, you should be able to read college-level textbooks and write grammatically correct and complete sentences.

Q: What is the difference between the AP U.S. Government and Politics exam and the AP Comparative Government and Politics exam?

A: The AP U.S. Government and Politics exam focuses primarily on the United States government. The AP Comparative Government and Politics exam focuses on a global perspective of governments, comparing the policies of Great Britain, Mexico, China, Russia, Iran, and Nigeria.

Q: How do I register for the AP GOV exam?

A: The exam is given in May. If your school offers the AP GOV course, contact your AP teacher or coordinator to register. If your school does not offer the AP GOV course, visit https://apcentral. collegeboard.com for more information.

Q: Can I take the AP GOV exam more than once?

A: Yes, but you may not retake the exam within the same year. If you take the exam again, both scores will be reported unless you cancel one score.

Q: What do I bring to the exam?

A: Bring several no. 2 pencils with erasers for the multiple-choice questions, and bring several pens with black or dark-blue ink for the free-response questions. Bring your 6-digit school code. Bring a watch that does not have Internet access, does not beep, and does not have an alarm. If you do not attend the school where you are taking the exam, bring identification (school-issued photo ID or government-issued ID).

Q: What items am I not allowed to bring to the exam?

A: You cannot bring electronic equipment (cell phone, smartphone, listening devices, cameras, or any other electronic devices). You cannot bring books, scratch paper, highlighters, notes, food, or drinks. Note: You can take notes in the margins of your exam booklet.

Q: **Can I cancel, withhold, or change my report recipient score?**

A: Yes, you can request to cancel your scores at any time before the deadline. Contact AP Services for deadlines and policies.

Q: **How long does it take to receive my score?**

A: Once you sign up for a College Board account at www.collegeboard.org/register, you can receive your scores online sometime in July. You will get an e-mail reminding you how to access your scores. You must enter your AP number (the 8-digit number on the labels inside your AP Student Pack) or your student identifier to access your scores.

Q: **Should I guess on the AP GOV exam?**

A: Yes. Your score is based on the number of questions you answer correctly. If possible, use the elimination strategy (see p. 14) for multiple-choice questions to increase your chances of guessing the correct answer. Don't leave any questions unanswered.

Test-Taking Strategies

To be successful on the AP GOV exam, you must spend time learning about the exam and how best to approach it, study to increase your knowledge, and practice answering simulated questions. This section begins with *general* test-taking strategies and then gives you *specific* information, approaches, and strategies to tackle the questions that relate to real-world scenarios.

General Test-Taking Strategies

Consider the following guidelines as a road map to taking the test:

- Stick to the College Board unit key concepts.
- Know the big ideas.
- Know the required foundational documents and Supreme Court cases.
- Know the disciplinary practices and reasoning processes.
- Know how to link the source to your answer.
- Know political science vocabulary.

Stick to the College Board Unit Key Concepts

The AP GOV course content can seem overwhelming because it has so many political policies, concepts, cases, and outcomes—it is a lot to follow! Take the guesswork out of what to expect on the exam and follow the guidelines in the College Board unit content outlines. Take a deep breath and understand that the College Board has provided key concepts in the *AP U.S. Government and Politics Exam Course Framework* that can help you focus on what is testable.

As you go through the unit reviews in chapters 4–8, focus on constitutional perspectives and important court decisions, as well as significant government leaders, political parties, and popular public opinion. Who did what and why? How can their actions be connected? What were their political views? Were these individuals representative of others or were they separated from the majority? Who would have opposed these individuals and why? How can these people be linked to the broader historical context of other developments, policies, or events? These types of questions will help you connect, organize, and remember the historical narrative of the content outlines.

Know the Big Ideas

Keep your eye on the big picture. Students who are successful on the exam can identify the big ideas of U.S. government and politics (see p. 6). Big ideas are the concepts that clearly delineate main ideas of the U.S. political system. Always keep the connections between big ideas and the unit key concepts in mind to help you organize the information in a way that you can remember it and link it to other political developments.

Know the Required Foundational Documents and Supreme Court Cases

A body of knowledge about required government documents is at the center of all AP GOV questions, especially the U.S. Constitution. Although particular political science developments are certainly a large part of the foundation of America, the College Board will expect you to make connections to the causes, outcomes, and consequences of foundational government documents and U.S. Supreme Court cases. Study these important documents in the Appendix, pp. 335–342.

Know the Disciplinary Practices and Reasoning Processes

To demonstrate critical thinking, students must connect questions to the disciplinary practices and reasoning processes. These skills are applied to every question on the exam (see pp. 6–7).

Know How to Link the Source to Your Answer

One of the objectives of the AP GOV exam is testing your ability to work with document sources in multiple-choice questions and free-response questions. This means that you will have to quickly read over a passage, scenario, or visual source, and then organize your answer based on in-depth critical analysis. For example, as you examine the source stimulus in free-response questions, ask yourself, "Can I show how this source is related to my thesis, and can I provide reasons, evidence, and proof based on this source?"

First, preview the source and circle or underline key points. This will help you match information from the source to your question. For essay responses, think about how each source might fit with your tentative thesis. Write notes in the margins of your test booklet, but remember that you don't have a lot of time to take comprehensive notes. Try to keep notes to one or two words and abbreviate when possible.

Try to think like a political scientist who is conducting research. Researchers don't just look at what a source says, they look for the *context* of the source. Find the context by asking some of the following questions (remember to take notes as you answer these questions):

- Are there headings showing the title, author, case, or date of the source?
- What is the source's main purpose?
- Can I paraphrase the source's main ideas in my own words (for text sources)?
- Can I locate historical trends or patterns (increases or decreases) that will help predict my answer (for visual sources: graphs, charts, tables, and maps)?
- Can I determine one piece of evidence from the source that supports or refutes my argument (for essay responses)?

Note: If you don't have time to read through the entire source, remember to get a gist of what the source is trying to convey.

> **TEST TIP:** Before you approach sources, you should be familiar with the differences between primary and secondary document sources. A *primary source* is an original passage, document, or speech. Primary sources give you a direct "inside view" of the developments from a person who directly witnessed or experienced the historical event. For example, primary sources include government documents, court cases, correspondence, autobiographies, memoirs, diaries, speeches, and letters. A *secondary source* is a "secondhand" account told by a third party who interpreted or wrote about the primary source. For example, a primary source is an argument made in Federalist No. 10 by Madison, who warned of the "mischiefs of factions." A secondary source, on the other hand, is a 21st-century historian who suggests that a representative republic is effective against the "factions" as originally argued by Madison in Federalist No. 10 in the late 18th century.

Know Political Science Vocabulary

The AP Readers of free-response essays are looking for the effective and appropriate use of political science vocabulary that conveys a clear meaning of constitutional, political, and government terms. Refer to the "Important Terms and Concepts Checklist" at the beginning of each review chapter for key terms and where you can find them in the chapter. In addition, when writing your essay responses, avoid slang and informal spoken English. For example, in spoken English one might use the expression *on the flip side*, while in a written essay, *another viewpoint* would be a more appropriate phrase.

Specific Test-Taking Strategies

It's important to consider the types of questions you are being asked and the specific strategies to tackle these questions. Memorization is good for solidifying key terms, cases, documents, and decisions in your long-term memory, but the exam will ask you to analyze questions based on critical reasoning skills. Therefore, if you start to use these strategies before you even take the exam, you are way ahead of the curve.

Strategies for Multiple-Choice Questions

First, let's review the types of multiple-choice questions on the AP GOV exam.

Types of Multiple-Choice Questions		
Question Type	Description	Strategy
Quantitative Analysis	Analyze numerical or statistical data.	Focus on statistical or numerical data presented in information graphics (chart, graph, or table). Analyze and draw conclusions about the patterns, trends, or limitations of the data.
Qualitative Analysis	Analyze text-based sources.	Focus on the text-based primary or secondary source presented in a U.S. founding document, article, speech, correspondence, or book. Read the document carefully to form conclusions about the political outcomes, principles, behaviors, or processes.
Visual Analysis	Analyze visual sources.	Focus on the primary or secondary visual source (political cartoon, map, or image). Draw conclusions about the author's political objective, principles, behaviors, or outcomes.
Concept Application	Explain the context.	Focus on the primary or secondary sources and draw conclusions about the broader historical context of political concepts, events, developments, principles, or processes.
Comparison	Compare and contrast political concepts.	Compare and contrast the similarities and differences to draw conclusions about political concepts.
Knowledge	Define political concepts.	Identify and define political concepts, principles, processes, institutions, and behaviors.

Instructions for multiple-choice questions will appear in your exam booklet, but here are specific strategies to help you work through the multiple-choice questions quickly, accurately, and efficiently.

- Budget your time wisely.
- Use the elimination strategy.
- Mark the answer sheet correctly.
- Read each question and source carefully.
- Watch for "attractive distractors."
- Be on alert for EXCEPT and NOT questions.
- Make an educated guess if necessary.
- Practice, practice, practice.

Budget Your Time Wisely

You have 80 minutes to answer 55 multiple-choice questions. You might calculate that you have about 1½ minutes per question, but this does not include the time it takes to read questions that include a document or visual source. Some questions may take more time, while others may take less time.

Students who spend too much time dwelling on a single question don't get the score they deserve because they leave insufficient time to answer other questions they could get right. With sufficient practice, you will almost automatically know when a question is taking too much time and when to take an educated guess and move on to the next question. There is no penalty for guessing, so make sure you answer every question.

Use the Elimination Strategy

Take advantage of being allowed to mark in your exam booklet. Eliminate one or more answer choices to narrow down your choices to statistically improve your odds of selecting the correct answer.

Keep this marking system very simple and mark your answers in your exam booklet (no need to erase the markings in your booklet because you are allowed to write in your exam booklet). Practice this strategy as you take the diagnostic test and the full-length practice exam in this study guide.

Use a question mark (?) to signify an answer choice as a possible answer, use a diagonal line (/) to cross out an answer choice that is incorrect, and leave the choice blank if you are uncertain. This strategy will help you avoid reconsidering those choices you've already eliminated. Notice that in the example below, you've just narrowed your chances of answering correctly to 50 percent.

> ? **A.**
>   **B.**
>   **C.**
>   **D.**

Mark the Answer Sheet Correctly

Make sure that your marked responses on the bubble answer sheet match your intended responses. When answering questions quickly, it is common to select the wrong answer choice by mistake. Students who skip questions might make the mistake of continuing to mark their answers in sequence and forget to leave a blank space for the unanswered questions. To avoid this mistake, mark your answers (and any other notes) in the exam booklet before you fill in the answer sheet. If necessary, you will be able to double-check your answers.

Read Each Question and Source Carefully

Don't work so quickly that you make careless errors. Read actively and take notes as you read each multiple-choice question and each source. Do not make a hasty assumption that you know the correct answer without reading the whole question, the source (if provided), and all of the answer choices. The hurried test-taker commonly selects an incorrect answer when jumping to a conclusion after reading only one or two of the answer choices in the easy questions. Don't let the easy questions mislead you. You must look at all of the answer choices in order to select the *best* answer.

Watch for "Attractive Distractors"

Watch out for answer choices that look good but are not the *best* answer choice, called *attractive distractors*. Attractive distractors are usually the most commonly selected incorrect answers and are often true statements, but not the best choice. Be aware that facts and concepts presented in answer choices may often contain subtle variations that make it difficult for test-takers to narrow down correct answers. Here are some examples of attractive distractor answer choices that should be eliminated:

- Answer choices that only answer *part* of the question and do not directly answer the entire question
- Answer choices that are not related to the correct foundational document or Supreme Court case
- Answer choices that are not using the correct constitutional context
- Answer choices that are not related to *both* the source and the question

Be on Alert for EXCEPT and NOT Questions

Another common mistake is misreading a question that includes the words *except* or *not.* A negative question reverses the meaning of the question and asks for the opposite to be true in order to select the correct answer. Negative questions can initially be confusing and challenge your thinking. It is helpful to write down brief notes to avoid misreading a question (and therefore answering it incorrectly). To help answer a negative question, treat the answer choices as true or false statements, searching for the answer choice that is false.

Make an Educated Guess If Necessary

Remember, there is no penalty for guessing. If you get stuck on a question, reread it. The answer may become apparent when you take a second look. If not, take an educated guess by eliminating some of the answer choices to increase your odds of choosing the right answer. You have nothing to lose, and quite possibly, something to gain. If you have time, you can always go back to rethink a marked question and change the answer.

If you do not have time to finish the exam, save 1 minute of your exam time to mark the answers for all of your remaining unanswered questions. There is no penalty for guessing, so pick your favorite letter—A, B, C, or D—and fill in all of the blank answer choices with this letter.

Practice, Practice, Practice

The College Board recommends consistent practice to attain a high score. This is why we have included practice questions throughout this study guide: Chapter 3 (diagnostic test), chapters 4–8 (review chapters), and Chapter 9 (full-length practice exam). These practice questions include answers and thorough explanations. Be sure to practice in the exam format as often as possible. To benefit from further practice, you can purchase previously administered AP U.S. Government and Politics exams at https://store. collegeboard.org. Just keep in mind that some exams prior to 2018 may not reflect the most recent format of the exam, but they are still valuable practice.

Strategies for Free-Response Questions

The AP GOV exam contains four free-response questions that ask students to do what historians do—analyze and interpret evidence while providing a reasonable argument. You must be able to construct and support a clear thesis using the provided source documents, scenario, data, or visual graphics and demonstrate that you can provide a line of reasoning, evidence, and support your claims with specific knowledge.

This section will give you strategies for the four types of free-response questions:

- Concept Application Question (1 question)
- Quantitative Analysis Question (1 question)
- SCOTUS Comparison Question (1 question)
- Argument Essay Question (1 question)

Essay Writing

To write effective free-response essays, stay focused on the AP essay-scoring rubric, follow the free-response essay-writing strategies, and practice writing essays.

Use the following checklist when you complete each of the practice free-response essay questions for the AP GOV exam.

- Did I stay focused on *all* parts of the question?
- Did I use prewriting techniques to organize the essay?
- Did I link the broader big idea?
- Did I provide supporting political science evidence and/or examples?
- Did I study verb task skills to apply to essays?
- Did I write a strong thesis statement (argument essay)?

> Note: Sample essays are available at the end of the diagnostic text (Chapter 3), the unit review chapters (chapters 4–8), the full-length practice exam (Chapter 9), and on the College Board website found on the AP U.S. Government and Politics Course Homepage.

Stay Focused on the Question

One of the most important strategies is to keep your essay focused on the question and to address *all parts* of the question prompt. To help you stay focused, underline or circle key words in the question prompt before you start writing. For example, if the question prompt reads, "Describe the characteristics of a bicameral legislature and the different powers held by the <u>Senate</u> and the <u>House</u>," you must respond to *both* parts of the question—the Senate and the House. Too often students lose points because they don't respond to all parts of the question.

Prewrite to Organize Your Essay

Think before you write by brainstorming, planning, and prewriting to organize your thoughts. The technique of brainstorming means that you should write down all ideas and examples that come to your mind. After you brainstorm, organize those ideas in a logical sequence of events. These ideas should emphasize important points, offer evidence, and provide the political science context related to the question prompt.

Link the Broader Big Idea

Remember to keep your eye on the big picture. Identify and connect the question topic to the broader historical context and constitutional principles. If you're stuck and can't think about ideas, reread the question and think of the big ideas: constitutionalism, liberty and order, civic participation in a representative democracy, competing policymaking interests, and methods of political analysis. Remember that free-response questions are generally designed so that you can receive at least partial credit if you have some knowledge of the subject. Partial responses will get partial credit. Even a response that receives 1 point will be added to your total points. One point may not seem like much, but earning 1 point is better than zero.

Provide Supporting Political Science Evidence and/or Examples

To receive the highest score possible, you need to be able to explain the fundamental constitutional principles related to the question with specific supporting evidence, details, and reasoning to support your main thesis. Remember, you are not imposing your own biased opinions, thoughts, or feelings. Think about citing and then describing specific political science facts related to the question prompt—and remember that you must *describe* your evidence with one or more sentences. As you provide this evidence and historical knowledge, you must support the claims in your essay.

It is important to cite historical examples from primary or secondary foundational documents or Supreme Court cases. For example, "The concept of natural rights formed the foundation of the social contract theory and laid the blueprint for the statement, 'life, liberty, and property,' acknowledged by Thomas Jefferson in the Declaration of Independence." Depending on the question, it may also be important to insert the original author's perspective (if known) to support your claims. For example, what influenced or inspired Thomas Jefferson to identify with the concept of "natural rights" written in the Declaration of Independence? (Note: Use quotation marks around direct quotes when citing original content from foundational documents.)

The argument essay question requires that you write about alternative explanations that provide an opposing or alternative perspective that refutes or concedes the argument. Whatever alternative perspective you focus on, remember that your writing should challenge the argument with clearly developed points and an insightful analysis.

Use at least one of the essay-writing skills described in the table below to achieve your highest possible score on free-response essay questions.

Apply Verb Task Skills to Essay Questions

Every essay question targets at least one of the following task verbs from AP Disciplinary Practices and Reasoning Processes. Become familiar with these verbs before your exam date to have an edge on knowing what to expect on free-response essay questions.

- **Identify.** Provide a specific answer that does not require a causal explanation.
- **Define.** Provide a specific meaning for a word or concept.
- **Describe.** Provide the essential details or characteristics of a particular concept or political phenomenon.
- **Explain.** Demonstrate an understanding of how or why a relationship exists by clearly articulating the logical connection or causal pattern between or among various political phenomena.
- **Compare.** Provide an explicit statement that connects two or more concepts.

Skill	Verb Task	Examples
Demonstrate knowledge	Apply knowledge to political concept scenarios by **identifying, defining, describing,** or **explaining** constitutional and political institutions, principles, processes, models, behaviors, and/or beliefs.	**Concept Application Essay** ❑ Can I describe the principles of the Constitution? ❑ Can I describe and compare the interpretations of government policies or perspectives?
Make a connection	Make a connection by **comparing** and **explaining** the similarities or differences among political behaviors, principles, beliefs, cultural factors, and Court decisions.	**SCOTUS Essay** ❑ Can I explain the similarities and differences among related Supreme Court cases? ❑ Can I identify the cause and/or consequence of Supreme Court decisions? **Concept Application Essay** ❑ What are the similarities and differences of political beliefs, ideologies, principles, and models? ❑ Can I reasonably explain how political behaviors, policies, institutions, and constitutional interpretations have changed over time and affected public policy?
Develop a line of reasoning	Develop a line of reasoning to **explain** an argument about political principles, processes, behaviors, and outcomes.	**Argument Essay** ❑ Can I communicate and support a defensible thesis or claim using relevant evidence? ❑ Can I logically organize and analyze evidence to justify my argument? ❑ Can I use refutation, concession, and rebuttal to offer opposing or alternative perspectives? ❑ Can I provide proof that summarizes or supports my argument's conclusion about a political concept?
Analyze data	**Identify**, analyze, and **describe** quantitative data to draw conclusions about political principles, processes, behaviors, and outcomes (e.g., data from tables, graphs, charts, and maps).	**Quantitative Analysis Essay** ❑ Can I describe the data presented? ❑ Can I describe and compare patterns and trends in the data? ❑ Can I draw conclusions about the data?
Interpret text-based sources	**Identify**, interpret, and **explain** text-based qualitative sources from primary and secondary sources (e.g., passages, excerpts, information graphics, and political cartoons).	**Concept Application Essay** ❑ Can I identify the author's perspective, assumptions, claims, implications, and reasoning in a source? ❑ Can I explain how the implications of an author's argument may affect political principles, processes, behaviors, and outcomes? **SCOTUS Essay** ❑ Can I identify Supreme Court decisions and explain the reasoning for concurring or dissenting opinions?

Write a Strong Thesis Statement (Argument Essay)

The introduction of your response should include a convincing thesis statement that tells the AP Reader the main points of your argument within a historical context of government and politics, the question prompt, and the document source (if provided). The thesis statement must be historically defensible. A strong opening paragraph tells the Reader what to expect in the body of your essay and lets the Reader know that you are (1) addressing the central issues of the question prompt, (2) addressing all parts of the question, (3) using multiple pieces of evidence or examples, (4) following a line of logical reasoning, and (5) including pertinent big ideas.

Do not just restate the question in the thesis statement. AP Readers are looking for your own original thinking. After you read the question prompt, what thoughts jump out at you? Can you provide concrete facts to support your ideas? Write down these ideas as you brainstorm to prewrite a tentative thesis. Underline or circle what you will need to locate in the source and use this information to formulate your thesis statement.

The strategic plan of attack on the next page summarizes the strategies for all four free-response question types.

A Strategic Plan of Attack

Read the question TWICE and note the directions, prompt, and sources.

PREWRITE. Gather information from the question and sources by marking and taking notes about the main points. Organize your ideas by prewriting an outline (or list) to prioritize important points and evidence from the question and sources.

WRITING A CONCEPT APPLICATION RESPONSE (Practice 1)

Spend 20 minutes to answer *all* three points of the question, and reference the real-world scenario to receive full credit.

Write a historically accurate essay.

Use historical *context* to describe the *content knowledge* related to the question.

Keep your answers brief, but use a line of reasoning.

Describe or explain how the scenario relates to a political institution, behavior, or process.

WRITING A QUANTITATIVE ANALYSIS RESPONSE (Practice 3)

Spend 20 minutes and answer *all* four points to receive full credit.

Write a historically accurate essay.

Analyze the data to identify patterns and trends to draw a conclusion about the graphic illustration.

Keep your answers brief, but use a line of reasoning to explain how the data demonstrates a political principle in the prompt.

WRITING A SCOTUS COMPARISON RESPONSE (Practice 2)

Spend 20 minutes and answer *all* four points to receive full credit.

Use a line of reasoning to explain the similarities and differences between two Supreme Court cases.

Provide the prompted information from the specified Supreme Court case.

Explain *how* or *why* the information from the required Court case is relevant to a non-required Court case.

Describe or explain an interaction between the holdings in both Court cases while providing supporting facts, reasoning, decisions, and opinions of each case.

WRITING AN ARGUMENT ESSAY RESPONSE (Practice 5)

Spend 40 minutes and answer *all* points to receive full credit of 6 points.

Develop a thesis argument that is a historically defensible claim and establishes a line of reasoning.

Support your claim with at least TWO pieces of specific and relevant supporting evidence (one piece of evidence from a required foundational document, and one from your studies).

Use reasoning to explain why the evidence supports the thesis argument.

For the highest possible score, respond to an alternative perspective using refutation, concession, or rebuttal.

PROOFREAD AND EDIT. Leave yourself a few minutes to correct errors and make minor revisions.

Chapter 1

Two-Month Cram Plan

The calendar below details a two-month action plan for the AP GOV exam. The first step is to determine how much time you have to prepare and then pick the plan that fits your schedule: two-month plan or one-month plan (see pp. 24–26 for a one-month plan). Ask yourself, "How many hours a week can I realistically devote to preparing for the exam?" Be specific. For example, you may be able to study on Tuesdays, Thursdays, and Fridays from 4 to 6 p.m., or you may only have time on Saturdays and Sundays from 8 to 11 a.m. It doesn't matter what plan you pick; what matters is that you stick to the schedule to get your best possible results.

Two-Month Cram Plan	
8 weeks before the exam	**Study Time:** 3 hours ❏ Chapter 3: Take the Diagnostic Test and review the multiple-choice answer explanations. ❏ Compare your multiple-choice responses with topics covered in chapters 4–8. ❏ Compare your essay responses to the free-response essay-scoring criteria and to the sample responses provided. ❏ Browse the AP GOV official website: https://apstudent.collegeboard.org/apcourse/ap-united-states-government-and-politics. ❏ Read the Introduction. ❏ Study the AP GOV exam format (p. 1).
7 weeks before the exam	**Study Time:** 3 hours at least two times a week (or as often as your schedule permits) ❏ Take notes as you study and memorize the AP GOV big ideas (p. 6). ❏ Take notes as you study and memorize the AP GOV disciplinary practices and reasoning processes (pp. 6–7). ❏ Take notes as you study the test-taking strategies (pp. 10–20). ❏ Take notes as you study and memorize the AP GOV required foundational documents and Supreme Court cases (Appendix, pp. 335–342). Use government websites and at least two trustworthy sources to study and take notes about the facts and details regarding foundational documents and Supreme Court cases.
6 weeks before the exam	**Study Time:** 3 hours at least two times a week (or as often as your schedule permits) ❏ Chapter 4: Read and take notes on "Unit 1: Foundations of American Democracy." ❏ Use additional resources to read more about general and specific topics discussed in Chapter 4. ❏ Reread the "AP U.S. Government and Politics Key Concepts" (pp. 51–53), "Study Questions" (p. 54), and "Important Terms and Concepts Checklist" (pp. 54–55) for Unit 1. ❏ Answer the chapter review multiple-choice practice questions and compare your answers to the explanations provided. If you miss a question, be sure to note the logic behind the correct answer.
5 weeks before the exam	**Study Time:** 3 hours at least two times a week (or as often as your schedule permits) ❏ Chapter 5: Read and take notes on "Unit 2: Interactions among Branches of Government." ❏ Use additional resources to read more about general and specific topics discussed in Chapter 5. ❏ Reread the "AP U.S. Government and Politics Key Concepts" (pp. 97–99), "Study Questions" (pp. 99–100), and "Important Terms and Concepts Checklist" (pp. 100–101) for Unit 2. ❏ Answer the chapter review multiple-choice practice questions and compare your answers to the explanations provided. If you miss a question, be sure to note the logic behind the correct answer. ❏ Answer the chapter review free-response question. Compare your response to the scoring criteria and sample response.

Continued

4 weeks before the exam	**Study Time:** 3 hours at least two times a week (or as often as your schedule permits) ❏ Chapter 6: Read and take notes on "Unit 3: Civil Liberties and Civil Rights." ❏ Use additional resources to read more about general and specific topics discussed in Chapter 6. ❏ Reread the "AP U.S. Government and Politics Key Concepts" (pp. 161–162), "Study Questions" (p. 163), and "Important Terms and Concepts Checklist" (pp. 163–164) for Unit 3. ❏ Answer the chapter review multiple-choice practice questions and compare your answers to the explanations provided. If you miss a question, be sure to note the logic behind the correct answer. ❏ Answer the chapter review free-response question. Compare your response to the scoring criteria and sample response.
3 weeks before the exam	**Study Time:** 3 hours at least two times a week (or as often as your schedule permits) ❏ Chapter 7: Read and take notes on "Unit 4: American Political Ideologies and Beliefs." ❏ Use additional resources to read more about general and specific topics discussed in Chapter 7. ❏ Reread the "AP U.S. Government and Politics Key Concepts" (pp. 207–208), "Study Questions" (p. 209), and "Important Terms and Concepts Checklist" (p. 210) for Unit 4. ❏ Answer the chapter review multiple-choice practice questions and compare your answers to the explanations provided. If you miss a question, be sure to note the logic behind the correct answer. ❏ Answer the chapter review free-response question. Compare your response to the scoring criteria and sample response.
2 weeks before the exam	**Study Time:** 3 hours at least two times a week (or as often as your schedule permits) ❏ Chapter 8: Read and take notes on "Unit 5: Political Participation." ❏ Use additional resources to read more about general and specific topics discussed in Chapter 8. ❏ Reread the "AP U.S. Government and Politics Key Concepts" (pp. 243–246), "Study Questions" (pp. 246–247), and "Important Terms and Concepts Checklist" (pp. 247–248) for Unit 5. ❏ Answer the chapter review multiple-choice practice questions and compare your answers to the explanations provided. If you miss a question, be sure to note the logic behind the correct answer. ❏ Answer the chapter review free-response question. Compare your response to the scoring criteria and sample response.
7 days before the exam	**Study Time:** 5 hours ❏ Chapter 9: Take the full-length practice exam and review your answers and the explanations and sample responses. ❏ Based on your performance, identify topics and their corresponding chapters that require further review. ❏ Use additional resources to read more about general and specific topics discussed in the practice exam.
6 days before the exam	**Study Time:** 3 hours ❏ Based on your review, target general and specific topics. ❏ Reread the "Test-Taking Strategies" in the Introduction (pp. 10–20). ❏ Practice writing responses to two free-response questions (at least one should be the argument essay question) using the scoring rubric on p. 4 to score your essays. Note: Previous free-response question topics can be found online at https://apstudent.collegeboard.org/apcourse/ap-united-states-government-and-politics/exam-practice.
5 days before the exam	**Study Time:** 2 hours ❏ Review "AP U.S. Government and Politics Key Concepts" for Unit 1 (pp. 51–53) and Unit 2 (pp. 97–99). ❏ Study and target specific topics as needed.
4 days before the exam	**Study Time:** 2 hours ❏ Review "AP U.S. Government and Politics Key Concepts" for Unit 3 (pp. 161–162). ❏ Study and target specific topics as needed.

3 days before the exam	**Study Time:** 1–2 hours ❑ Review "AP U.S. Government and Politics Key Concepts" for Unit 4 (pp. 207–208). ❑ Study and target specific topics as needed.
2 days before the exam	**Study Time:** 1–2 hours ❑ Review "AP U.S. Government and Politics Key Concepts" for Unit 5 (pp. 243–246). ❑ Study and target specific topics as needed. ❑ Reread any material you feel is necessary.
1 day before the exam	❑ Relax. You have covered all of the material necessary to score well on the exam. ❑ Get plenty of sleep the night before the exam.
Morning of the exam	❑ Eat a balanced, nutritious breakfast with protein. ❑ Keep your usual habits. Don't try something new today. ❑ Bring your photo ID, ticket for admission, watch (that does not have Internet and does not beep), your 6-digit school code, several sharpened no. 2 pencils with erasers, and a few pens with black or dark-blue ink. Note: Cell phones, scratch paper, books, smartwatches, and food/drinks are not allowed at the testing center.

Chapter 2

One-Month Cram Plan

The calendar below details a one-month action plan for the AP GOV exam. The first step is to determine how much time you have to prepare and then pick the plan that fits your schedule: two-month plan or one-month plan (see pp. 21–23 for a two-month plan). Ask yourself, "How many hours a week can I realistically devote to preparing for the exam?" Be specific. For example, you may be able to study on Tuesdays, Thursdays, and Fridays from 4 to 6 p.m., or you may only have time on Saturdays and Sundays from 8 to 11 a.m. It doesn't matter what plan you pick; what matters is that you stick to the schedule to get your best possible results.

One-Month Cram Plan	
4 weeks before the exam	**Study Time:** 5 hours ❏ Chapter 3: Take the Diagnostic Test and review the multiple-choice answer explanations. ❏ Compare your essay responses to the free-response essay-scoring criteria and to the sample responses provided. ❏ Browse the AP GOV official website: https://apstudent.collegeboard.org/apcourse/ap-united-states-government-and-politics. ❏ Read the Introduction. ❏ Study the AP GOV exam format (p. 1). ❏ Take notes as you study and memorize the AP GOV big ideas (p. 6). ❏ Take notes as you study and memorize the AP GOV disciplinary practices and reasoning processes (pp. 6–7). ❏ Take notes as you study the test-taking strategies (pp. 10–20). ❏ Take notes as you study and memorize the AP GOV required foundational documents and Supreme Court cases (Appendix, pp. 335–342). Use government websites and at least two trustworthy sources to study and take notes about the facts and details regarding foundational documents and Supreme Court cases. **Study Time:** 3 hours at least two times a week (or as often as your schedule permits) ❏ Chapter 4: Read and take notes on "Unit 1: Foundations of American Democracy." ❏ Use additional resources to read more about general and specific topics discussed in Chapter 4. ❏ Reread the "AP U.S. Government and Politics Key Concepts" (pp. 51–53), "Study Questions" (p. 54), and "Important Terms and Concepts Checklist" (pp. 54–55) for Unit 1. ❏ Answer the chapter review multiple-choice practice questions and compare your answers to the explanations provided. If you miss a question, be sure to note the logic behind the correct answer.

3 weeks before the exam	**Study Time:** 3 hours at least two times a week (or as often as your schedule permits) ❑ Chapter 5: Read and take notes on "Unit 2: Interactions among Branches of Government." ❑ Use additional resources to read more about general and specific topics discussed in Chapter 5. ❑ Reread the "AP U.S. Government and Politics Key Concepts" (pp. 97–99), "Study Questions" (pp. 99–100), and "Important Terms and Concepts Checklist" (pp. 100–101) for Unit 2. ❑ Answer the chapter review multiple-choice practice questions and compare your answers to the explanations provided. If you miss a question, be sure to note the logic behind the correct answer. ❑ Answer the chapter review free-response question. Compare your response to the scoring criteria and sample response. **Study Time:** 3 hours at least two times a week (or as often as your schedule permits) ❑ Chapter 6: Read and take notes on "Unit 3: Civil Liberties and Civil Rights." ❑ Use additional resources to read more about general and specific topics discussed in Chapter 6. ❑ Reread the "AP U.S. Government and Politics Key Concepts" (pp. 161–162), "Study Questions" (p. 163), and "Important Terms and Concepts Checklist" (pp. 163–164) for Unit 3. ❑ Answer the chapter review multiple-choice practice questions and compare your answers to the explanations provided. If you miss a question, be sure to note the logic behind the correct answer. ❑ Answer the chapter review free-response question. Compare your response to the scoring guidelines and sample response.
2 weeks before the exam	**Study Time:** 3 hours at least two times a week (or as often as your schedule permits) ❑ Chapter 7: Read and take notes on "Unit 4: American Political Ideologies and Beliefs." ❑ Use additional resources to read more about general and specific topics discussed in Chapter 7. ❑ Reread the "AP U.S. Government and Politics Key Concepts" (pp. 207–208), "Study Questions" (p. 209), and "Important Terms and Concepts Checklist" (p. 210) for Unit 4. ❑ Answer the chapter review multiple-choice practice questions and compare your answers to the explanations provided. If you miss a question, be sure to note the logic behind the correct answer. ❑ Answer the chapter review free-response question. Compare your response to the scoring criteria and sample response. **Study Time:** 3 hours at least two times a week (or as often as your schedule permits) ❑ Chapter 8: Read and take notes on "Unit 5: Political Participation." ❑ Use additional resources to read more about general and specific topics discussed in Chapter 8. ❑ Reread the "AP U.S. Government and Politics Key Concepts" (pp. 243–246), "Study Questions" (pp. 246–247), and "Important Terms and Concepts Checklist" (pp. 247–248) for Unit 5. ❑ Answer the chapter review multiple-choice practice questions and compare your answers to the explanations provided. If you miss a question, be sure to note the logic behind the correct answer. ❑ Answer the chapter review free-response question. Compare your response to the scoring criteria and sample response.
7 days before the exam	**Study Time:** 5 hours ❑ Chapter 9: Take the full-length practice exam and review your answers and the explanations and sample responses. ❑ Based on your performance, identify topics and their corresponding chapters that require further review. ❑ Use additional resources to read about general and specific topics discussed in the practice exam.

Continued

6 days before the exam	**Study Time:** 3 hours ❑ Based on your review, target general and specific topics. ❑ Reread the "Test-Taking Strategies" in the Introduction (pp. 10–20). ❑ Practice writing responses to two free-response questions (at least one should be the argument essay question) using the scoring rubric on p. 4 to score your essays. Note: Previous free-response question topics can be found online at https://apstudent.collegeboard.org/apcourse/ap-united-states-government-and-politics/exam-practice.
5 days before the exam	**Study Time:** 2 hours ❑ Review "AP U.S. Government and Politics Key Concepts" for Unit 1 (pp. 51–53) and Unit 2 (pp. 97–99). ❑ Study and target specific topics as needed.
4 days before the exam	**Study Time:** 2 hours ❑ Review "AP U.S. Government and Politics Key Concepts" for Unit 3 (pp. 161–162). ❑ Study and target specific topics as needed.
3 days before the exam	**Study Time:** 1–2 hours ❑ Review "AP U.S. Government and Politics Key Concepts" for Unit 4 (pp. 207–208). ❑ Study and target specific topics as needed.
2 days before the exam	**Study Time:** 1–2 hours ❑ Review "AP U.S. Government and Politics Key Concepts" for Unit 5 (pp. 243–246). ❑ Study and target specific topics as needed. ❑ Reread any material you feel is necessary.
1 day before the exam	❑ Relax. You have covered all of the material necessary to score well on the exam. ❑ Get plenty of sleep the night before the exam.
Morning of the exam	❑ Eat a balanced, nutritious breakfast with protein. ❑ Keep your usual habits. Don't try something new today. ❑ Bring your photo ID, ticket for admission, watch (that does not have Internet and does not beep), your 6-digit school code, several sharpened no. 2 pencils with erasers, and a few pens with black or dark-blue ink. Note: Cell phones, scratch paper, books, smartwatches, and food/drinks are not allowed at the testing center.

Chapter 3

Diagnostic Test

This chapter contains a diagnostic test that will give you valuable insight into the types of questions that may appear on the AP GOV exam. It is for assessment purposes only to help you gauge your understanding of and performance on AP GOV questions. As you take the diagnostic test, try to simulate testing conditions. The time limits for each of the following sections are estimates based on the amounts that are designated by the College Board for the actual exam.

Section	Diagnostic Test	Actual Exam
Section I: Multiple-Choice Questions	25 questions, 40 minutes	55 questions, 80 minutes
Section II: Free-Response Questions		
Concept Application Question	n/a	1 question, 20 minutes (suggested)
Quantitative Analysis Question	1 question, 20 minutes (suggested)	1 question, 20 minutes (suggested)
SCOTUS Comparison Question	n/a	1 question, 20 minutes (suggested)
Argument Essay Question	1 question, 40 minutes (suggested)	1 question, 40 minutes (suggested)

Answer Sheet for Multiple-Choice Questions

1 Ⓐ Ⓑ Ⓒ Ⓓ
2 Ⓐ Ⓑ Ⓒ Ⓓ
3 Ⓐ Ⓑ Ⓒ Ⓓ
4 Ⓐ Ⓑ Ⓒ Ⓓ
5 Ⓐ Ⓑ Ⓒ Ⓓ

6 Ⓐ Ⓑ Ⓒ Ⓓ
7 Ⓐ Ⓑ Ⓒ Ⓓ
8 Ⓐ Ⓑ Ⓒ Ⓓ
9 Ⓐ Ⓑ Ⓒ Ⓓ
10 Ⓐ Ⓑ Ⓒ Ⓓ

11 Ⓐ Ⓑ Ⓒ Ⓓ
12 Ⓐ Ⓑ Ⓒ Ⓓ
13 Ⓐ Ⓑ Ⓒ Ⓓ
14 Ⓐ Ⓑ Ⓒ Ⓓ
15 Ⓐ Ⓑ Ⓒ Ⓓ

16 Ⓐ Ⓑ Ⓒ Ⓓ
17 Ⓐ Ⓑ Ⓒ Ⓓ
18 Ⓐ Ⓑ Ⓒ Ⓓ
19 Ⓐ Ⓑ Ⓒ Ⓓ
20 Ⓐ Ⓑ Ⓒ Ⓓ

21 Ⓐ Ⓑ Ⓒ Ⓓ
22 Ⓐ Ⓑ Ⓒ Ⓓ
23 Ⓐ Ⓑ Ⓒ Ⓓ
24 Ⓐ Ⓑ Ⓒ Ⓓ
25 Ⓐ Ⓑ Ⓒ Ⓓ

Section I

Multiple-Choice Questions

Directions: Read each item and select the best answer.

25 questions

40 minutes

Questions 1–3 refer to the following passage.

Congress has the power "to make all Laws which shall be necessary and proper for carrying into Execution the foregoing Powers, and all other Powers vested by this Constitution in the Government of the United States, or any Department or Officer thereof…"

—Source: United States Constitution; Article I, Section 8, September 27, 1787.

1. Based on your knowledge of U.S. government, which of the following best identifies the constitutional reference in the passage?

    A.   Supremacy Clause
    B.   Elastic Clause
    C.   Vesting Clause
    D.   Qualifications Clause

2. Which of the following Supreme Court cases is most relevant to the passage?

    A.   *McCulloch v. Maryland*
    B.   *Schenck v. United States*
    C.   *Baker v. Carr*
    D.   *Marbury v. Madison*

3. Which of the following statements best describes why the clause above most likely prompted the codification of the Bill of Rights?

    A.   States were emboldened to resist the federal government, and in doing so could override the rights of the individuals.
    B.   The federal government was stripped of its power to safeguard citizen rights.
    C.   Businesses were granted an expansion of state-sponsored power that led to the violation of workers' rights.
    D.   The expansion of the federal government's power required protections for the civil liberties of individuals.

Questions 4–5 refer to the following political cartoon.

Source: Steve Greenberg, "But Where Do You Stand on Abortion?" *Seattle Post-Intelligencer,* July 9, 1989. Cartoon depicts how abortion politics were so divisive that even local elections were being affected.

4. Which of the following best represents the type of voter who asked the question "But where do you stand on abortion?" as depicted in the political cartoon?

   A. Prospective voter
   B. Candidate-centered voter
   C. Single-issue voter
   D. Rational-choice voter

5. Based on your knowledge of U.S. government and politics, the voter who asked the question "But where do you stand on abortion?" most likely belongs to which of the following political parties?

   A. Democratic
   B. Republican
   C. Independent
   D. Progressive

Question 6 refers to the following set of maps.

**Counties That Voted for the Republican or
Democratic Presidential Candidate by 20 Percentage Points or More**

In 1992, 38% of voters lived in landslide counties.

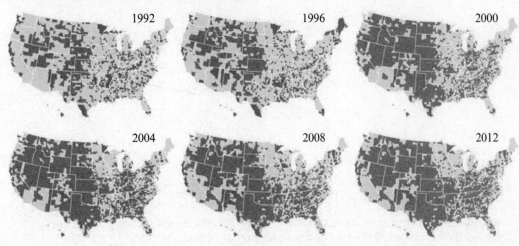

In 2012, 50% of voters lived in landslide counties.

Legend

■ Republicans

☐ Democrats

6. Which of the following conclusions can be drawn from the maps above and your knowledge of U.S. political party voter preferences?

    A. The U.S. is becoming increasingly polarized.

    B. Democrats are winning presidential elections.

    C. Voter turnout is decreasing.

    D. More Republicans are voting.

Questions 7–8 refer to the following graph.

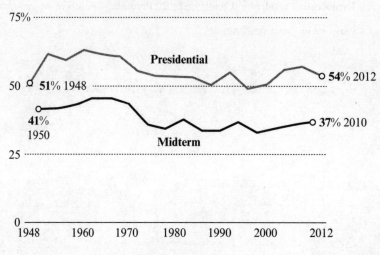

Turnout Rate During Election Years

Note: Turnout rates calculated as total votes cast for president (in presidential election years) or House of Representatives (in midterm election years) divided by voting-age population.

Source: Census Bureau (voting-age population), Office of the Clerk of the House of Representatives (vote totals).

7. Based on your knowledge of U.S. politics and the graph above, which of the following statements most accurately describes voter turnout from 1948 to 2012?

   A. Americans are more concerned about voting for their respective congressional leaders than presidents.
   B. Midterm election turnout is on the rise.
   C. Midterm elections surpass presidential elections in voter turnout.
   D. Presidential elections surpass midterm elections in voter turnout.

8. Based on your knowledge of U.S. politics, what is the most likely reason for increased voter turnout during the 1960s?

   A. The National Organization for Women (NOW) was recruiting more feminists who previously did not vote.
   B. The passage of the Voting Rights Act of 1965 ensured legal protection for previously disenfranchised African Americans.
   C. The Federal Election Commission was established, which successfully persuaded more eligible voters to participate in elections.
   D. The assassination of President John F. Kennedy caused greater voter turnout across the country.

Question 9 refers to the following passage.

Energy in the Executive is a leading character in the definition of good government. It is essential to the protection of the community against foreign attacks; it is not less essential to the steady administration of the laws; to the protection of property against those irregular and high-handed combinations which sometimes interrupt the ordinary course of justice; to the security of liberty against the enterprises and assaults of ambition, of faction, and of anarchy.

—Source: Alexander Hamilton, March 15, 1788.

9. Which of the following U.S. founding documents is most relevant to Hamilton's essay?

   A. The United States Constitution
   B. Brutus No. 1
   C. The Declaration of Independence
   D. Federalist No. 70

Questions 10–11 refer to the following passage.

When in the Course of human events, it becomes necessary for one people to dissolve the political bands which have connected them with another, and to assume among the powers of the earth, the separate and equal station to which the Laws of Nature and of Nature's God entitle them, a decent respect to the opinions of mankind requires that they should declare the causes which impel them to the separation.

—Source: Declaration of Independence; Thomas Jefferson, 1776.

10. Based on your knowledge of U.S. government, which of the following statements best captures the meaning of "the Laws of Nature" referenced in the passage?

   A. The U.S. government's response to natural disasters
   B. The sovereign power of the people to consent to their government
   C. The constitutional principle of individual property ownership
   D. The Articles of Confederation's disapproval of slavery

11. Based on your knowledge of U.S. government, which of the following is the best reason why the author of the *Letter from Birmingham Jail* made reference to "natural rights"?

   A. People were being wrongly imprisoned and subjected to harsh prison conditions.
   B. Segregation statutes contradicted the belief that people retained certain unalienable natural rights.
   C. Peaceful demonstrations were, in theory, legal, but were not permitted.
   D. Minorities wanted to pursue natural rights by forming an independent government.

12. Which of the following legal concepts is associated with the phrase "legislating from the bench," which is sometimes employed by conservatives in response to Supreme Court decisions?

   A. Judicial review
   B. Judicial restraint
   C. Judicial activism
   D. Judicial theory

13. Which of the following Supreme Court cases addresses redistricting and gerrymandering?

    A. *Shaw v. Reno* (1993)
    B. *Engel v. Vitale* (1962)
    C. *Brown v. Board of Education of Topeka* (1954)
    D. *United States v. Lopez* (1995)

14. Which of the following is a defining structural feature of the Constitution?

    A. Legislative terms of 4 years
    B. Electoral limits of one vote per state
    C. Bicameral Congress
    D. Unicameral Congress

15. Based on your knowledge of U.S. government, which of the following Federalist Papers made a rational argument in support of constitutional separation of powers?

    A. Federalist No. 10
    B. Federalist No. 51
    C. Federalist No. 70
    D. Federalist No. 78

16. The Voting Rights Act (1965) authorized all of the following federal actions EXCEPT

    A. Monitoring state voter registration
    B. Prohibiting literacy tests as a voter registration requirement
    C. Appropriating funds to bolster voter turnout
    D. Outlawing poll taxes in federal elections

17. Based on your knowledge of U.S. government, which of the following statements best explains why Shays' Rebellion led to the drafting of the U.S. Constitution?

    A. The central government was ineffective and weak.
    B. An agricultural recession was prompted by property tax increases.
    C. The war debt was demanding greater taxation on merchants.
    D. The federal government had no authority to assist in suppression of revolts.

18. Based on your knowledge of U.S. government and politics, the Pendleton Act (1883) was passed to reform which of the following political institutional practices?

    A. State-sponsored segregation
    B. The patronage system
    C. Congressional gerrymandering
    D. Support of prayer in public schools

19. Which of the following statements clarifies why it is incorrect to assert that "The United States is a direct democracy"?

    A. Individuals do not directly elect congressional leaders.
    B. Individuals do not directly make decisions; decisions are made by elected representatives.
    C. Voter disenfranchisement is widespread.
    D. The eligible voter population is relatively limited.

20. Which of the following was the primary purpose for passing the McCain-Feingold Act in 2002?

    A. To prevent wealthy corporations from overtaking the political process
    B. To suppress negative information about a candidate from being publicly disclosed
    C. To stop political parties and donors from circumventing FECA
    D. To give individuals and corporations equal access to candidates

Questions 21–22 refer to the following graph.

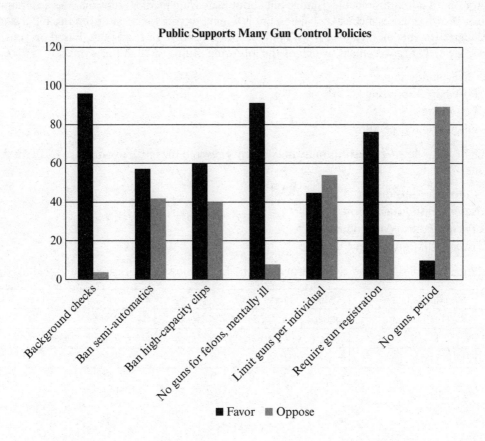

21. Which of the following conclusions best supports the data presented in the graph?

    A. A majority of Americans support a number of legislative options for placing some level of regulation on gun ownership.
    B. While all suggestions for some level of restriction on gun ownership have a degree of support among the public, none is supported by the majority.
    C. A ban on guns for convicted felons and the mentally ill enjoys nearly universal public support, while requiring registration of firearms is opposed by a clear majority.
    D. The public is most closely divided on the question of banning high-capacity clips for automatic weapons.

22. Which of the following government officials would be LEAST likely to be influenced by this public opinion poll in deciding whether to support a more proactive federal role in regulating guns?

    A. The president
    B. A Democratic House member from a marginal district in New York
    C. A Senator from the battleground state of Michigan
    D. A Republican House member from a rural district in Missouri

23. Senator Smith has authored a legislative bill about increasing medical subsidies. As a Republican, Senator Brown opposes medical subsidies, but is willing to vote for Senator Smith's bill if Senator Smith agrees to vote on Senator Brown's bill for lowering corporate tax rates. Based on your knowledge of U.S. government, which of the following is illustrated in this scenario?

    A. Gerrymandering
    B. Pork barrel spending
    C. Logrolling
    D. Discretionary spending

24. Which of the following constitutional amendments lowered the citizen voting age to 18 for American citizens?

    A. Fifteenth Amendment
    B. Seventeenth Amendment
    C. Twenty-Fourth Amendment
    D. Twenty-Sixth Amendment

25. In relation to civil rights and civil liberties, which of the following pairs are accurately linked?

A.	Free Exercise Clause	*Wisconsin v. Yoder* (1972)
B.	Due Process Clause	*Brown v. Board of Education of Topeka* (1954)
C.	Voting Rights Act (1965)	*Tinker v. Des Moines Independent Community School District* (1969)
D.	Second Amendment	*Baker v. Carr* (1962)

IF YOU FINISH BEFORE TIME IS CALLED, CHECK YOUR WORK ON THIS SECTION ONLY. DO NOT WORK ON ANY OTHER SECTION IN THE TEST.

Section II

Free-Response Questions

1 question

20 minutes (suggested)

Directions: Write your response on lined paper. You are not required to develop and support a thesis statement. Use complete sentences—bullet points or outlines are unacceptable. Answer **all** parts of the question to receive full credit.

NOTE: The following quantitative analysis question is for instructional purposes only and may not reflect the format of the actual exam.

Question 1. Use the map below to answer all parts of the question on the next page.

State Medicaid Expansion Decisions, January 2016

Not expanding (19 states)   Expanding–traditional (25 states and DC)   Expanding–waiver (6 states)

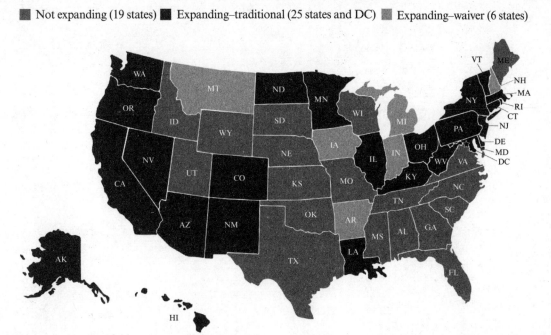

Notes: The governor of Louisiana has issued an executive order to implement a Medicaid expansion effective July 1, 2016. Pennsylvania originally received a waiver to expand its program, but transitioned to a traditional expansion effective September 1, 2015.

Sources: Medicaid State Plan Amendments and Section 1115 Medicaid demonstration waiver documents.

1. Using the map, answer (a), (b), and (c).

   (a) Identify the state Medicaid expansion decision for states in the Northeast.
   (b) Compare the Medicaid expansion decision made by two states or two regions by describing a similarity or difference in the decision and draw a conclusion about that similarity or difference.
   (c) Explain how Medicaid spending and the expansion of Medicaid coverage under the Affordable Care Act (ACA) impacts the federal budget.

IF YOU FINISH BEFORE TIME IS CALLED, CHECK YOUR WORK ON THIS QUESTION ONLY. DO NOT WORK ON ANY OTHER QUESTION IN THE TEST.

1 question

40 minutes (suggested)

Directions: It is suggested that you take a few minutes to plan and outline your essay. Write your response on lined paper. You must demonstrate your understanding of course content, disciplinary practices, and reasoning processes. Your essay is considered a first draft and may contain some grammatical errors that will not be counted against you. However, to receive full credit, your essay must demonstrate defensible content knowledge with substantive examples where appropriate.

Question 2. Develop an argument that explains why racial segregation is incompatible with the Founders' intent to establish a constitutional government by and for a free people.

In your essay, you must:

1. Articulate a defensible claim or thesis that responds to the prompt and establishes a line of reasoning.
2. Support your claim with at least TWO pieces of accurate and relevant information:
    (a) At least ONE piece of evidence must be from ONE of the following foundational documents:
       - *Letter from Birmingham Jail*
       - U.S. Constitution
       - The Declaration of Independence
       - *Brown v. Board of Education of Topeka*
    (b) Use a second piece of evidence from another foundational document from the list or from your study of the evolution of democratic principles across the nation's history.
3. Use reasoning to explain why your evidence supports your claim/thesis.
4. Respond to an opposing or alternative perspective using refutation, concession, or rebuttal.

IF YOU FINISH BEFORE TIME IS CALLED, CHECK YOUR WORK ON THIS QUESTION ONLY. DO NOT WORK ON ANY OTHER QUESTION IN THE TEST.

Answer Key for Multiple-Choice Questions

1. B	6. A	11. B	16. C	21. A
2. A	7. D	12. C	17. A	22. D
3. D	8. B	13. A	18. B	23. C
4. C	9. D	14. C	19. B	24. D
5. B	10. B	15. B	20. C	25. A

Answer Explanations

Section I

Multiple-Choice Questions

1. **B.** This question requires a careful reading of the text to look for context clues. *Necessary and proper* is associated with the term "elastic," choice B. The Elastic Clause is found in Article I, Section 8, of the Constitution. The Supremacy Clause (choice A) is found in Article 6. Vesting clauses (choice C) are found in Articles 1–3, Section 1. Qualification clauses (choice D) can be found in Articles 1–3, Section 1–3.

2. **A.** This question requires knowledge of the constitutional principle of the federal and state powers that are central to the Elastic Clause (Necessary and Proper Clause). The *McCulloch v. Maryland* case was based on the Supremacy Clause and raised the legal question of the federal government having the right to establish and impose taxes on the Second Bank of Maryland. The Elastic Clause gives Congress the power to "make all laws that are necessary and proper." The Supreme Court ruled that the federal government had the right to establish a bank and the state of Maryland could not impose taxes, making choice A correct. *Schenck v. United States* (choice B) was a freedom of speech case that applied to the First Amendment. *Baker v. Carr* (choice C) was centered on the Fourteenth Amendment, forbidding the restrictions of the basic rights of citizens. *Marbury v. Madison* (choice D) was the landmark case that established the precedent for judicial review.

3. **D.** Because the federal government was strengthened under the Elastic Clause, Anti-Federalists advocated for a Bill of Rights, which was ultimately codified as the first 10 Amendments. This guaranteed the protection of the civil liberties of individuals from the absolute power of the federal government, choice D. The Elastic Clause was not included to strengthen the rights of individual states, nor did it unintentionally enable states to revolt against the decisions of the federal government by suppressing the rights of the individuals (choice A). The federal government was not stripped of its power by virtue of the Elastic Clause (choice B), but was instead strengthened, which worried Anti-Federalists. This is not a question of workers' rights (choice C).

4. **C.** The candidate is discussing local issues, and the issue of abortion is not even remotely relevant to the topic. This cartoon demonstrates the mentality of a single-issue voter, choice C, a voter who casts a

ballot strictly on the premises of one overarching issue, even if that issue is not pertinent to the candidate's role. Although prospective voters (choice A) ask questions about the candidate's current platform, including his or her promises, this choice is incorrect because candidates running for a local office do not focus on broader social issues, including abortion. Local candidates focus mostly on community issues. A candidate-centered voter (choice B) prioritizes the candidate, including his or her personality, which is not in view here. Rational-choice voting (choice D) is not relevant because this type of voting focuses on what is the most logical, rational choice of the options available.

5. **B.** Republicans are generally more conservative socially. The ideological views of most Republicans oppose abortion. Many Republicans are known for being single-issue voters who ask particular issue-based questions to determine their candidate's preferences, even if that issue is not particularly salient to the candidate's position, making choice B correct. Democrats (choice A) generally have liberal views on social issues and are more likely to pose a question like "Where do you stand on a woman's right to choose?" Although Independents (choice C) vote on issues, rather than political ideologies, they are least likely to ask this question because they are known to support policies that are different from those of major political parties. Progressive liberals (choice D) seek to eliminate social and economic inequalities. Progressives are ideologically the most liberal on the spectrum, and therefore, are unlikely to be concerned with the question of abortion.

6. **A.** Based on the voting data provided by the maps, it can be concluded that the U.S. is becoming increasingly polarized, choice A. According to the data provided, from 1992 to 2012, the total number of counties that experienced a candidate landslide steadily increased. President George W. Bush was the only Republican candidate to clinch election cycles from 1992 to 2012, with Democratic presidents Bill Clinton and Barack Obama taking four out of the six total election cycles (choice B). Based on the information provided, it is difficult to conclude that voter turnout is either decreasing (choice C) or that more Republicans are voting (choice D).

7. **D.** Presidential elections consistently surpass midterm elections in voter turnout, choice D. According to the graph, eligible voters seem to be far more concerned about the direction of the federal government than they are about their respective state representatives, as illustrated by the deficits between the two elections, eliminating choice A. Midterm election turnout is declining, not rising (choice B), especially since the mid-1970s. Midterm elections have never surpassed presidential elections in voter turnout (choice C).

8. **B.** The passage of the Voting Rights Act in 1965 ensured that African Americans could vote without limitations, especially in the South. As a result, voting turnout soared, choice B. The National Organization for Women (choice A) was formally founded in 1966, and although it certainly contributed to mobilizing women to vote, it is not the best answer from the choices listed, particularly since strong Progressives were merely a fraction of the total eligible voter population. While related, the Federal Election Commission was not established until 1975, eliminating choice C. The assassination of President John F. Kennedy (choice D) did not have a direct impact on voter turnout.

9. **D.** The passage is from Federalist No. 70, an essay by Alexander Hamilton supporting a strong, "energetic," and unified executive branch of government to execute laws, choice D. In Federalist No. 70, Hamilton attempts to develop a formula for a strong, energetic executive branch—unity, duration, good support, and competent powers. You should be familiar with Federalist No. 70 because it is frequently cited on the AP GOV exam when discussing the expansion of presidential power. Based on the date of the passage—1788—you should have been able to eliminate choice C, the Declaration of Independence (written in 1776). This passage was not part of the U.S. Constitution (choice A), and the main focus of Brutus No. 1 (choice B) was to encourage New Yorkers to reject the Constitution.

10. **B.** The concept of the Laws of Nature, as utilized by Jefferson, asserts that just as there are natural laws that govern the universe, there are also Laws of Nature that safeguard the inherent rights belonging to all humans that no government has the authority to subvert—those rights first defined by Enlightenment philosopher John Locke as life, liberty, and property. For Jefferson, author of the Declaration of Independence, the Laws of Nature elevate the people to a position that is both separate from and equal to their government. It is the heart of the social contract theory, which views ultimate sovereignty as belonging to the people. The power of the Laws of Nature allows citizens to consent to a government whose purpose is to protect the life, liberty, and property of the people. Therefore, choice B is the correct answer. The Laws of Nature in the context of the passage is a political reference unrelated to natural disasters of the earth (choice A). Although property ownership (choice C) is defined as a "natural right," it does not encompass the meaning of the Laws of Nature as written by Jefferson. The Declaration of Independence predates the Articles of Confederation, and slavery has no relationship to the Laws of Nature reference (choice D).

11. **B.** The *Letter from Birmingham Jail* was written while Dr. Martin Luther King Jr. was wrongly incarcerated for a peaceful march. King sought an explanation for the violation of statutes in U.S. founding documents, which promised "all" citizens unalienable, natural rights defined in the U.S. Constitution and the Declaration of Independence, choice B. The abuse of the imprisoned, including exposure to harsh prison conditions and maltreatment during peaceful demonstrations, was not the main reasons for Dr. King's letter, eliminating choices A and C. Minorities were not interested in forming an independent government (choice D). African Americans and other minorities simply wanted to be treated fairly by the U.S. local, state, and federal governments.

12. **C.** Conservatives often point to judicial activism as an example of "legislating from the bench" (rulings based on personal feelings rather than the interpretation of the law), choice C. For example, in *Roe v. Wade* (1973), the Supreme Court ruled that restricting abortions was unconstitutional. Conservatives believed that this ruling was judicial activism because it favored liberal views on abortion. Judicial review (choice A) is the right of the judiciary to review decisions made by the executive and legislative branches. Judicial restraint (choice B) is rooted in the idea of justices refraining from using their power to strike down laws unless the laws are expressly unconstitutional. Judicial theory (choice D) is a broad term that is not relevant to the question.

13. **A.** *Shaw v. Reno* addressed the issue of redistricting based on race, choice A. *Engel v. Vitale* (choice B) addressed the role of prayer in public schools and whether or not it violated the Establishment Clause. *Brown v. Board of Education of Topeka* (choice C) addressed the inequality of segregated facilities. *United States v. Lopez* (choice D) addressed the Commerce Clause and gun-free school zones.

14. **C.** The bicameral Congress created by the Constitution consists of the House of Representatives and the Senate. This structure and how representation would be allotted in each chamber was the center of one of the most contentious debates at the Constitutional Convention. The issue was finally resolved by the Great Compromise, and thus the bicameral Congress is a defining structural feature of the Constitution, choice C. A term in the House of Representatives is 2 years (Article I, Section 2), while a Senate term is 6 years (Article I, Section 3). The length of the terms is important to the way Congress functions, but is not a defining structural feature, eliminating choice A. Electoral votes are determined by the number of congressional seats apportioned to a state (House single-member district seats plus 2 senators), so choice B is incorrect. A unicameral, single-chamber legislature was a structural feature of the Articles of Confederation, not the Constitution, so choice D is incorrect.

15. **B.** Federalist No. 51, written by James Madison, defends the checks and balances system and advocates for a separation of powers, choice B. In Federalist No. 10 (choice A), Madison argues in favor of the large and diverse democratic republic established by the Constitution as the best means of suppressing the fractious impact of political factions and the possibility of tyranny imposed by an emerging majority faction. Federalist No. 70 (choice C), written by Alexander Hamilton, argues for a powerful executive branch. In Federalist No. 78 (choice D), Hamilton addresses the judicial review process.

16. **C.** The Voting Rights Act (1965) helped African Americans overcome statutory barriers to voting passed by states, thereby putting federal enforcement authority behind their constitutional right to vote under the Fifteenth Amendment. The Voting Rights Act *did not* enable the federal government to appropriate funds to bolster voter turnout, making choice C the correct answer. The Voting Rights Act empowered the federal government to monitor state voting registration, choice A, prohibited the imposition of literacy tests as a requirement for voter registration, choice B, and prohibited local and state authorities from imposing poll taxes on voters participating in federal elections, choice D. Note: The elimination of poll taxes in state elections was accomplished through passage of the Twenty-Fourth Amendment.

17. **A.** Shays' Rebellion was a turning point in governance and inspired the writing of the Constitution. Choice A is the *best* choice from the answers listed. The central government was intentionally weak and ineffective under the Articles of Confederation because state representatives were concerned about "absolute power" of a central government. The Articles gave the central government limited powers to govern so that local governance wouldn't be threatened, but the Articles proved too limited after Shays' Rebellion. During Shays' Rebellion, rural farmers revolted against the wealthy men who controlled the state's government. Because farmers were heavily taxed by the government, they had to borrow money from merchants. When farmers couldn't pay the rich merchants, their farms were taken away from them in the state's courts. Although the agricultural industry was declining and farmers were revolting against the unfair taxation, choice B is not the best answer among the choices listed. Choice D is also a true statement; the central government was granted little power and it was difficult to raise an army to stop the violent protests. However, choice D is not the best answer among the choices listed. The war debt was crushing local farmers who were paying the taxes, not crushing the rich merchants, eliminating choice C.

18. **B.** The Pendleton Act, also known as the Pendleton Civil Service Reform Act, was enacted in 1883 to abolish the existing civil service *patronage system* (spoils system), choice B, in favor of a merit-based system. Prior to 1883, government officials made it a practice to appoint friends and supporters for government jobs. Various constitutional amendments and Supreme Court cases worked to end state-sponsored segregation (choice A). The Pendleton Act addressed civil service reform, not gerrymandering (choice C). *Engel v. Vitale* (1962) ruled that public school prayer (choice D) was unconstitutional.

19. **B.** It is incorrect to assert that the U.S. is a *direct democracy* (also called a pure democracy). The U.S. is a *representative democracy* (also called a republic) because citizens elect representatives who make decisions on their behalf, choice B, instead of citizens directly making decisions. Individuals directly elect all congressional leaders (choice A). While some may charge that some populations still experience disenfranchisement (choice C), this choice is unrelated to the question of a direct democracy. The size of the eligible voter population (choice D) is irrelevant to the definition of a direct democracy.

20. **C.** The main goal of the McCain-Feingold Act of 2002 (known as the Bipartisan Campaign Reform Act) was to prevent "soft money" contributions to state and federal political party organizations from being funneled to federal candidates. This circumvented the limits put in place by the Federal Election Campaign Act (FECA) on "hard money" contributions made directly to candidates, choice C. The act

was designed to stem the flow of special interest money into political campaigns but did not specifically target wealthy corporations (choice A). While the McCain-Feingold Act did establish negative ad parameters, the purpose was to protect the democratic process, not necessarily to prevent negative information about a candidate from being divulged (choice B). While "soft money" and "hard money" regulations have been enacted to minimize the excessive influence of big corporations, the purpose of McCain-Feingold was not about ensuring equal access to candidates (choice D).

21. **A.** America has a complex relationship with guns, but as this poll highlights, a majority of Americans support five of the seven legislative options for regulating guns, choice A. Since five of the seven options were supported in the poll by a majority, it is not possible to conclude that no option has majority support (choice B). While there is nearly universal support (90 percent) for a ban of weapons sales to convicted felons and the mentally ill, since the majority supports rather than opposes registration of guns, choice C is also incorrect. Finally, while Americans are closely divided on a ban on high-capacity ammunition clips, with 60 percent supporting and 40 percent opposing (choice D), they are more closely divided on limiting the number of guns per individual, with 57 percent opposing and 43 percent supporting.

22. **D.** This question focuses on student knowledge about the demographics of voting behavior, elections, and the impact of public opinion polling on politicians. The politician least influenced by this polling would have to be the Republican House member from a conservative district in Missouri, choice D. For this House member, the choice to oppose gun control legislation despite the poll results is obvious. The House member was elected in a "red" state where the voters in the single-member district are conservative. Since Republicans are conservatives and conservatives tend to oppose gun control, the results of this poll would have little to no impact on the House member from a conservative district in Missouri; therefore choice D is the correct answer. While the president is formally chosen by the Electoral College, electoral votes are determined by the outcome of at-large voting on a state-by-state basis. Considering the polling data, support for reasonable regulation of guns on the part of the president would have widespread approval in statewide polling and/or would help in at-large statewide voting outcomes in a bid for re-election. Clearly, the president would likely be influenced in a decision about gun control by this poll, eliminating choice A. A Democratic House member from a marginal district in New York (choice B) would also be wise to take this polling into account when deciding whether to support gun regulation. Marginal districts have significant numbers of Republican, Democratic, and Independent voters and so can go either "red" (Republican) or "blue" (Democrat) in any given election. All things being equal, a Democratic House member elected in a marginal district is probably in the ideological center and must stay there to be re-elected. However, in this case, with the majority of Americans supporting federal action on the issue of gun regulation, the House member would have to pay attention to this polling. A vote in the House supporting gun control would very likely be met with approval in the ranks of Democratic voters as well as among a significant number of Independents. Such a vote might be worth the risk of losing the support of large numbers of conservative votes among members of the GOP. Senators, like the president, rely on statewide at-large election results. Further, battleground states, like marginal districts, can go "red" or "blue" in any given election. Therefore, the choices and political calculus would be similar for the senator described in choice C as it would be for the House member from a marginal district. How much he/she could rely on the support of a coalition of Democratic and Independent voters based on a vote on gun control legislation would have to be considered. Therefore, this poll could potentially be influential on the decision of a Senator from the battleground state of Michigan (choice C).

23. **C.** In the illustrated scenario, Senator Smith and Senator Brown are exchanging votes to achieve their own purposes, which describes logrolling, choice C. Gerrymandering (choice A) is the act of drawing

district boundaries to favor a particular group or party. Pork barrel spending (choice B) is government-sponsored projects that deliver funds to a specific constituency. Discretionary spending (choice D) is a budgetary distinction between mandatory spending and spending requiring a Congressional appropriation each year and is unrelated to this question.

24. **D.** To answer this question, you will need to know the constitutional amendments. The Twenty-Sixth Amendment lowered the voting age from 21 years old to 18 years old, choice D. The Fifteenth Amendment (choice A) addresses the right for all citizens to vote without being discriminated against based on race. The Seventeenth Amendment (choice B) was passed to allow the direct election of senators by their respective state citizens. The Twenty-Fourth Amendment (choice C) prohibits state and local polling taxes.

25. **A.** This question requires essential knowledge of concepts important to understanding civil rights and liberties and the required Supreme Court cases relevant to these concepts. Choice A correctly aligns the Free Exercise Clause with the Supreme Court case in which free exercise was the issue: *Wisconsin v. Yoder* (1972).

A.	Free Exercise Clause Important civil liberty guaranteed by the First Amendment that prevents the government from interfering with an individual's religious practices.	*Wisconsin v. Yoder* (1972) In this Supreme Court decision, Justices ruled that the government cannot compel students to attend school past the eighth grade, citing the Free Exercise Clause of the First Amendment.
B.	Due Process Clause Key provision of the Fourteenth Amendment protecting all Americans from discrimination in the required processes followed by police and judicial authorities during criminal proceedings.	*Brown v. Board of Education of Topeka* (1954) Supreme Court ruling which compelled states and school districts to address *de facto* segregation in public schools through remedies such as busing.
C.	Voting Rights Act (1965) Federal law passed to prohibit states from taking legislative action which served to deliberately suppress the voting rights of African Americans or any other racial/ethnic minority.	*Tinker v. Des Moines Independent Community School District* (1969) Freedom of speech case in which the Court endorsed the protection of symbolic speech and the free speech rights of students within a public school setting (with some limitations).
D.	Second Amendment Guarantees the right to keep and bear arms, a right the Supreme Court has ruled extends to individuals for the purpose of self-defense.	*Baker v. Carr* (1962) In this Supreme Court decision regarding freedom of speech, Justices established the "bad tendency" test for speech that poses a threat to public safety.

Section II

Free-Response Questions

Question 1

This quantitative analysis question asks you to interpret the information provided in the map. You must analyze the data in the map to determine what the map tells you about the U.S. cultural factors that influence political attitudes toward Medicaid expansion. Based on your knowledge of political socialization, you should be able to narrow down your topic considerably.

To receive full credit of 4 points, you must address all parts. A good response should:

- Identify the state Medicaid expansion decision for states in the Northeast (0–1 point).
- Compare the Medicaid expansion decision made by two states or two regions by describing a similarity or difference in the decision (0–1 point), and draw a conclusion about that similarity or difference (0–1 point).
- Explain how Medicaid spending and the expansion of Medicaid coverage under the Affordable Care Act (ACA) impacts the federal budget (0–1 point).

Note: The sample responses for parts (a), (b), and (c) in the table below are for instructional purposes only. On the actual exam, you must write ONE complete essay.

Part	Task	Explanation	Sample Response
(a) (1 point)	Identify the state Medicaid expansion decision for the states in the Northeast.	Part (a) asks you to identify the attitudes of the population in the northeastern states. Ask yourself what the popular conservative or liberal views are that contribute to political socialization?	States located in the northeastern United States, including New York, Delaware, Maryland, Massachusetts, Vermont, and New Jersey, experienced an expansion of Medicaid. States at the northernmost point of the Northeast, including Maine and New Hampshire, also experienced an expansion through the "waiver" addendum. Waivers allow individual states to customize how their respective Medicaid programs are run.
(b) (1 point) (1 point)	Compare the Medicaid expansion decision made by two states or two regions by describing a similarity or difference in the decision. Draw a conclusion about that similarity or difference.	Part (b) asks you to think about the attitudes about Medicaid expansion of the populations in specific regions (states). Draw a conclusion about political views that might disrupt or continue the process of development of political socialization (i.e., popular conservative or liberal ideological views).	Comparatively, southern states largely opted out of Medicaid expansion, which is not surprising, given the prevailing conservative Southern sentiment toward entitlement programs. Conservativism is strongest in the South, with particular holds in the southeastern U.S. Conservatives are ideological proponents of smaller government and, by extension, fewer government-run programs. It is, therefore, not surprising that the majority of southern states disapproved of the Medicaid expansion. Similarly, it is not surprising that the majority of northeastern states approved of the Medicaid expansion; liberal Democrats have large strongholds in the New England area. And, as proponents of increased government spending, it is logical that northeastern states favored the Medicaid expansion. It is important to note that while individual voters do not always decide directly on state spending issues like Medicaid, individual voters do elect representatives who presumably voice the collective opinion of the representatives' respective constituents.

Part	Task	Explanation	Sample Response
(c) (1 point)	Explain how Medicaid spending and the expansion of Medicaid coverage depicted on the map impacts the federal budget.	Part (c) can be answered by making a distinction between discretionary and mandatory spending and connecting mandatory programs like Medicaid, and the expansion of this program under the ACA, to the discretionary side of the federal budget ledger.	Medicaid is a federal entitlement program established in the 1960s as part of President Lyndon Johnson's "War on Poverty." As a federal entitlement, Medicaid is considered mandatory spending. All medical care for anyone meeting the income requirements must be paid for regardless of how many meet those qualifications. Mandatory spending accounts for a large percentage of federal government spending and as mandatory spending increases, the amount left over for discretionary spending decreases. Discretionary spending funds programs that can be cut or expanded by appropriation decisions made by Congress. Expanding Medicaid under the ACA means more low-income people qualify for medical care paid for by the government, but reduces discretionary funds to spend on other programs.

Question 2

To achieve the maximum score of 6 on this argument essay question, your response must address the scoring criteria components in the table that follows.

Scoring Criteria for a Good Argument Essay		
Question 2: Develop an argument that explains why racial segregation is incompatible with the Founders' intent to establish a constitutional government by and for a free people.		
Scoring Criteria	**Disciplinary Practice**	**Examples**
A. THESIS/CLAIM		
(1 point) Presents a historically defensible thesis that establishes a line of reasoning. (Note: The thesis must make a claim that responds to *all* parts of the question and must *not* just restate the question.)	Practice 5.a	A good response to this question has a central thesis that reveals why racial segregation throughout the course of American history has been incompatible with the Founders' intended meaning of government as a social contract between a free people and those who govern. In your opening paragraph, your thesis should set the stage for the entire essay, including a brief statement mentioning at least one or two of the documents that you will be referencing in the body of your essay and a succinct summary of the historical background that sets the contextual stage of your essay.

Continued

Scoring Criteria	Disciplinary Practice	Examples
B. EVIDENCE		
(3 points) Uses TWO pieces of specific and relevant evidence to support the argument (must be linked to the question). OR **(2 points)** Uses ONE piece of specific and relevant evidence to support the argument (must be linked to the question). OR **(1 point)** Describes one piece of evidence that is accurately linked to the topic of the question. (Note: To earn more than 1 point, the response must establish an argument and have earned the point for Thesis/Claim.)	Practice 5.b	Remember to aim for the most possible points. To accomplish this, you must address at least two pieces of relevant evidence to support your argument. First, select a founding document from the list—*Letter from Birmingham Jail,* the U.S. Constitution, the Declaration of Independence, or the Supreme Court case of *Brown v. Board of Education of Topeka.* Here is supporting evidence from each of the founding documents used in the sample response. **Declaration of Independence** ❑ Statement of natural rights ❑ Explain what natural rights are as derived from Enlightenment ideals. **Constitution** ❑ Preamble contained "We the People" as inclusive language. ❑ Fourteenth and Fifteenth Amendments ***Brown v. Board of Education of Topeka*** ❑ Ruling contrasted with the precedent set by *Plessy v. Ferguson.* ❑ Sanctioned integration as opposed to segregation.
C. REASONING		
(1 point) Uses reasoning to organize and explain how or why the evidence supports the thesis or claim. (Note: To earn this point, you must have earned a point for Evidence.)	Practice 5.c	The essay should provide reasoning for the specific evidence—how does it support the thesis? The Declaration of Independence and the Constitution contain inclusive, rather than exclusive, language. *Brown v. Board of Education of Topeka* and the constitutional amendments are evidence of supporting why segregation as a philosophy is incompatible with the Founders' original goals for America.

Scoring Criteria	Disciplinary Practice	Examples
D. ALTERNATIVE PERSPECTIVES		
(1 point) Responds to an opposing or alternative perspective using refutation, concession, or rebuttal that is consistent with the argument. (Note: To earn this point, your response must have a claim or thesis.)	Practice 5.d	After determining which foundational documents to use, tie those together in a coherent, persuasive argument that articulates a solid defense of your thesis. You must also be able to use an alternative perspective that is consistent with the argument. The counterclaim implicitly addressed in this response concerns the prevalence of racism and discrimination throughout various eras as a practical outworking of the Founders' original intent. The counterclaim is negated by pointing to the Founders' initial comments and the development of a more refined sense of justice (aligned with the Founders' intents) across time. The sample response below cites the progressive history of the U.S. alongside the development of the documents provided to provide a high-level analysis.

Sample Student Response

When the Founders gathered to draw up the nation's documents, the ideal of "freedom" was not peripheral; instead, it was central to American values. From the initial drafting of the Articles of Confederation to the dynamic Constitution of today, the resonating theme of American history has always been to preserve that which every man possesses—inalienable rights to life, liberty, and the pursuit of happiness, principal to freedom itself. Unfortunately, however, the intent to safeguard individual rights, including the ability to self-govern and to remain free from fear of absolute tyranny, was severely obscured from the outset. Regardless of the Founders' individual motives concerning racial identity, it must be asserted, based on the text of the foundational documents themselves, that is, from the drafting of the Declaration of Independence to the revisions to the U.S. Constitution, that the American ideal was, is, and will always be freedom for all its citizens.

When the Declaration of Independence speaks of the Laws of Nature and a certain endowment of rights by humankind's Creator, it does so without discrimination. Put simply, it does not exempt a particular race, tribe of people, or gender from possessing these rights. While the Constitution is more practical than theoretical or philosophical in nature, and thus an elaboration of these ideals is rather scarce, the first words of the Preamble do universally affirm the rights of all, by virtue of "We the People." Unfortunately, though, the question as to whom the "We" exactly pertained to was debated for some time, made apparent through the turbulent crises of slavery, Jim Crow, and the embarrassing "separate but equal" ruling issued by the Supreme Court in Plessy v. Ferguson. Even still, the numerous amendments to the Constitution, along with the powerful Court rulings and honored words from civil rights leaders, bring to mind the real progressive consciousness that aligns U.S. actions, laws, and institutions with the Framers' actual words and thoughts themselves, manifested by the ideal of freedom for all.

Although it arrived nearly 100 years after the Constitution itself was ratified, the Fifteenth Amendment granted African American men the right to vote. Sadly, though, this reality was more codified than actualized, with poll taxes and literacy tests imposed to ensure practical disenfranchisement. Following the passage of the Fifteenth Amendment, the legacy of Jim Crow and enforced segregation,

49

particularly in the South, prevented the American dream of freedom from reaching all U.S. citizens. Although slavery was legally abolished, it was also legally sanctioned by virtue of Supreme Court landmark rulings, most significantly that of Plessy v. Ferguson, wherein the Court's decision that "separate was, in fact, equal" reversed all of the nation's progress to that point.

By the mid-1900s, the lingering effects of Jim Crow laws reinforced the notion that African Americans were exempt from realizing the Founders' intent for establishing a free people. Clearly, this misconception was incompatible, and was scrutinized under the lens of a new Court and a new wave of civil rights heroes who called attention to such a fundamental mistreatment. In 1954, the case of Brown v. Board of Education of Topeka, which involved racially unequal access to public education facilities, reached the steps of the Supreme Court. The Warren Court, known for its invocation of judicial activism at times, delivered a crushing blow to segregationists all over the South by reversing the precedent set by Plessy v. Ferguson. Citing the Equal Protection Clause of the Fourteenth Amendment, the Court enacted integration as a national touchstone, not segregation. In doing so, Brown v. Board of Education of Topeka cast a new vision for America, although this vision was not a unique one indeed. That is to say, the Warren Court determined what the Founders themselves knew to be true: that everyone is endowed with natural, inalienable rights, deserving of equal treatment and, by extension, access, under the law.

While segregation seemed to have won in various eras of American history, the resounding truths that the Founders' espoused have ultimately reigned supreme. Although equality of treatment and access for all Americans may still be but a dream, it is a dream first articulated by the Founders themselves. To assert that the intent for forming this unparalleled democracy was ultimately driven by segregation is to ignore the inclusive language that the original documents themselves contain.

Chapter 4

Unit 1: Foundations of American Democracy

Unit 1 explores the establishment of a political system of government.

- Balance of Power
- Political Compromises
- The Preservation of Basic Freedoms
- The Division of Federal and State Powers

Overview of AP U.S. Government and Politics Unit 1

The overarching concepts for this chapter address the formation of the early republic and the important historical compromises that led to the creation of the U.S. Constitution.

The four main College Board content outlines for Unit 1 are as follows:

- **Government balance of power.** A balance between governmental power and individual rights has been a hallmark of American political development.
- **Political compromises.** The Constitution emerged from the debate about weaknesses in the Articles of Confederation as a blueprint for limited government.
- **Preservation of basic freedoms.** The Constitution created a competitive policymaking process to ensure that the people's will is represented and that freedom is preserved.
- **Division of federal and state powers.** Federalism reflects the dynamic distribution of power between federal and state governments.

AP U.S. Government and Politics Key Concepts

Success on the exam depends on your ability to make connections to the key concepts as described in the content outlines of *AP U.S. Government and Politics Course Framework*. Remember that these concepts highlight the fundamental ideas that every student should take with them into the AP GOV exam and beyond.

Use the chart that follows to guide you through the specific knowledge that is covered in Unit 1. The information contained in this chart is an abridged version of the content outlines with topic examples. Visit https://apstudent.collegeboard.org/apcourse/ap-united-states-government-and-politics for the complete updated AP GOV course curriculum framework.

AP U.S. Government and Politics Key Concepts: Unit 1	
Key Concept	Content
Big Idea 2: Liberty and Order **A balance between governmental power and individual rights has been a hallmark of American political development.**	The U.S. government is based on ideas of limited government, including natural rights, popular sovereignty, republicanism, and social contract. The Declaration of Independence, drafted by Jefferson with help from Adams and Franklin, provides a foundation for popular sovereignty, while the U.S. Constitution, drafted at the Philadelphia convention led by George Washington, with important contributions from Madison, Hamilton, and members of the Grand Committee, provides the blueprint for a unique form of political democracy in the U.S. Representative democracies can take several forms along this scale: participatory democracy, pluralist democracy, and elite democracy. Different aspects of the U.S. Constitution, as well as the debate between Federalist No. 10 and Brutus No. 1, reflect the tension between the broad participatory model and the more filtered participation of the pluralist and elite models. The three models of representative democracy continue to be reflected in contemporary institutions and political behavior.
Big Idea 1: Constitutionalism **The Constitution emerged from the debate about the weaknesses in the Articles of Confederation as a blueprint for limited government.**	Madison's arguments in Federalist No. 10 focused on the superiority of a large republic in controlling the "mischiefs of faction," delegating authority to elected representatives and dispersing power between the states and federal government. Anti-Federalist writings, including Brutus No. 1, adhered to popular democratic theory that emphasized the benefits of a small decentralized republic while warning of the dangers to personal liberty from a large, centralized government. Specific incidents and legal challenges that highlighted key weaknesses of the Articles of Confederation are represented by the lack of centralized military power to address Shays' Rebellion and of tax-law enforcement power. Compromises deemed necessary for adoption and ratification of the Constitution are represented by the Great (Connecticut) Compromise, the Electoral College, the Three-Fifths Compromise, and the Slave Trade Compromise. Debates about self-government during the drafting of the Constitution necessitated the drafting of an amendment process in Article V that entailed either a two-thirds vote in both houses or a proposal from two-thirds of the state legislatures, with final ratification determined by three-fourths of the states. The compromises necessary to secure ratification of the Constitution left some matters unresolved that continue to generate discussion and debate today. The debate over the role of the central government, the powers of state governments, and the rights of individuals remains at the heart of present-day constitutional issues about democracy and governmental power, as represented by debates about government surveillance resulting from the federal government's response to the 9/11 attacks, and the debate about the role of the federal government in public school education.

Key Concept	Content
Big Idea 4: Competing Policy-making Interests **The Constitution created a competitive policymaking process to ensure that the people's will is represented and that freedom is preserved.**	The powers allocated to Congress, the president, and the courts demonstrate the separation of powers and checks and balances features of the U.S. Constitution. Federalist No. 51 explains how constitutional provisions of separation of powers and checks and balances control abuses by majorities. Multiple access points for stakeholders and institutions to influence public policy flow from separation of powers and checks and balances. Impeachment, removal, and other legal actions taken against public officials deemed to have abused their power reflect the purpose of checks and balances.
Big Idea 1: Constitutionalism **Federalism reflects the dynamic distribution of power between federal and state governments.**	The exclusive and concurrent powers of the federal and state governments help explain the negotiations over the balance of power between the two levels. The distribution of power between federal and state governments is to meet the needs of changes in society, as reflected by grants, incentives, and aid programs, including federal revenue sharing, mandates, categorical grants, and block grants.

Heads Up: What You Need to Know

As you study the topics of Unit 1, it is important that you grasp the terms and concepts so that you can answer free-response questions that begin with one of these task verbs:

- **Compare.** What are the similarities and differences? For example, compare and contrast the representative forms of democracies: participatory democracy, pluralist democracy, and elite democracy.

- **Explain.** What are the straightforward facts, details, data, principles, processes, and outcomes? For example, can you explain how the concept of limited government is embedded in the U.S. Constitution?

- **Describe.** What is the relevant evidence or supporting examples to paint an overall picture? For example, describe the importance of the Bill of Rights.

- **Analyze.** How can you synthesize the main points to form an interpretation? For example, based on your knowledge of the Articles of Confederation, what were its strengths and weaknesses?

- **Interpret.** What logical conclusions can be drawn from the information? For example, what was the political advantage of the Three-Fifths Compromise?

Study Questions

Glance through the study questions before you start the review section. Take notes, highlight questions, and write down page number references to reinforce your learning. Refer to this list as often as necessary until you feel comfortable with your knowledge of the material.

1. How are democratic ideals reflected in the Declaration of Independence and the U.S. Constitution? (Hint: Think about the Founding Fathers' basis of the government, and the ideas of limited government, natural rights, popular sovereignty, republicanism, and the social contract.)
2. Explain the models of representative democracy. (Hint: Participatory democracy, pluralist democracy, and elite democracy. Think about how Federalist No. 10 and Brutus No. 1 are reflected in pluralist and elite models.)
3. How are Federalist and Anti-Federalist views of government different? (Hint: Think about early foundational documents. Federalists emphasized the benefits of a federal government in Federalist No. 10, whereas Anti-Federalists emphasized the benefits of state-controlled government in Brutus No. 1.)
4. What are the constitutional principles of separation of powers and checks and balances? (Hint: Think about how our Founding Fathers wanted to protect people from tyranny through the separation of branches of government—legislative, executive, and judicial.)
5. How does the development and interpretation of the Constitution influence the allocation of power between federal and state governments? (Hint: The distribution of the balance of powers at two levels is reflected in aid programs, federal revenue sharing, grants, and incentives.)
6. How have the balance of federal and state powers been interpreted differently? (Hint: The interpretation of the Tenth and Fourteenth amendments regarding the implied powers of federal and state governments has changed over time. Think about the Supreme Court cases: *McCulloch v. Maryland* (1819) and *United States v. Lopez* (1995).)

Important Terms and Concepts Checklist

This section is an overview of the terms, concepts, ideas, documents, and court cases that specifically target the AP GOV exam. Additional vocabulary is included to aid in your understanding.

As you review the material covered in this chapter, remember that the required foundational documents and required Supreme Court cases (see the Appendix) are noted among the key academic terms, concepts, and language.

Note the abbreviations in the table that follows:

RFD – Required Foundational Documents
RSCC – Required Supreme Court Cases

As you study the terms and concepts, simply place a check mark next to each and return to this list as often as necessary to check your understanding. After you finish the chapter review section, reinforce what you have learned by working through the practice questions at the end of the chapter. Answers and explanations provide further clarification into perspectives of U.S. government and politics.

Term/Concept	Big Idea	Study Page	Term/Concept	Big Idea	Study Page	Term/Concept	Big Idea	Study Page
Anti-Federalists	CON	pp. 67–68	Federalist No. 10	RFD; LOR; CON	pp. 69–70	Popular sovereignty	LOR	p. 59
Article V	RFD; CON	pp. 70–71	Federalist No. 51	RFD; PMI	p. 78	Republicanism	LOR	p. 58
Articles of Confederation	RFD; CON	pp. 55–56, 59–60	Federalists	CON	pp. 66–68	Reserved powers	CON	pp. 83–84
Bill of Rights	RFD; CON	pp. 65–66	Federalist Papers	LOR	pp. 68–70	Separation of powers	PMI	pp. 76–77
Brutus No. 1	RFD; LOR; CON	p. 70	Grand Committee	LOR	p. 62	Shays' Rebellion	CON	pp. 72–73
Checks and balances	PMI	pp. 64, 77–78	Great Compromise	CON	pp. 71–72	Slave Trade Compromise	CON	pp. 73–74
Commerce clause	CON	pp. 81, 82, 85	Impeachment	PMI	p. 79	Social contract	LOR	p. 58
Concurrent powers	CON	pp. 83–84	Limited government	PMI	pp. 60–61	Sovereignty	LOR	p. 59
Declaration of Independence	RFD; LOR	pp. 56–57	McCulloch v. Maryland	RSCC; CON	pp. 81, 84–85	Supremacy Clause	CON	p. 65
Electoral College	CON	p. 71	Natural rights	LOR	p. 58	Tenth Amendment	RFD; CON	p. 76
Elementary and Secondary Education Act	CON	p. 75	Necessary and Proper Clause	CON	p. 64	Three-Fifths Compromise	CON	p. 74
Elite democracy	LOR	p. 62	No Child Left Behind	CON	p. 75	United States v. Lopez	RSCC; CON	pp. 82, 85
Exclusive powers	CON	p. 83	Participatory democracy	LOR	p. 61	U.S. Constitution	RFD; CON	pp. 62–66
Federalism	CON	pp. 79–85	Pluralist democracy	LOR	p. 61			

Chapter Review

In the 18th century, the first effort to establish a framework of government in the newly independent American states was the Articles of Confederation, which laid the groundwork for the United States Constitution.

The setting for developing the U.S. Constitution was hot in more ways than one! During the stifling summer of 1787, 55 delegates from all states except Rhode Island arrived in Philadelphia, where, 10 years earlier, delegates had convened to form the first United States government under the Articles of Confederation. Meeting in secrecy, shutters tightly wedged in window frames, the delegates gathered daily in the airless convention hall. The task before them was to replace the existing "firm league of friendship" formed by largely sovereign states under the Articles with a model for government that bonded the 13 states in a stronger, more centralized union. This idea, however, was neither universally loved among the revolutionary generation nor endorsed by all the delegates. Fear drove many of their concerns—fear of tyranny born of centralization, of loss of state sovereignty and personal liberty, and of the majority using its power to overwhelm the minority. A series of tense meetings in the convention hall over the course of 5 months often devolved into contentious debate among all state delegates meeting as the Committee of the Whole, only to be resolved by compromises reached by groups of select delegates sitting in smaller committees. From this process emerged a thoughtful constitutional framework for the American democracy. It is within this context that the topics in this chapter should be comprehended.

> **TEST TIP:** As you acquire essential knowledge and become familiar with the required foundational documents and Supreme Court cases, think about how you would use your understanding to meet the learning objectives. For example, after studying the essential knowledge associated with Unit 1, can you compare the political philosophies of the Anti-Federalists and Federalists and explain their key differences? Can you interpret Brutus No. 1 and Federalist No. 10 to demonstrate your understanding of how the two factions differed on their views about whether small or large republics best preserved the blessings of liberty?

Balance of Power

Heads Up: What You Need to Know

The learning objectives that you must be able to accomplish are:

Explain how democratic ideals are reflected in the Declaration of Independence and the U.S. Constitution.

Explain how models of representative democracy are visible in major institutions, policies, events, or debates in the U.S.

It is important to understand the competing interests and philosophical arguments that led to our constitutional democracy. This section focuses on the balancing act at the heart of the Constitution and the ongoing political evolution of the United States.

Read through the topics below to better understand the contributions and challenges that our Founding Fathers faced.

The Foundations of the New Government

After the American Revolution, the 13 colonies gained their independence from the British Empire and formally issued a **Declaration of Independence.** In an attempt to create a new political system and centralize government, the first written constitution was established—the **Articles of Confederation.**

Declaration of Independence (1776)

The **Declaration of Independence** was drafted by Thomas Jefferson and ratified by the Second Continental Congress in 1776. The Declaration announced the intention of the 13 colonies to break away from Britain and form an independent nation. Its list of grievances also provided a justification for this act of revolution.

The Importance of the Declaration of Independence

Part poetry and part straightforward enumeration of complaints, the Declaration provided an enduring articulation of the political values embraced by the Founding Fathers as well as a global inspiration for those seeking independence built on republican principles. What links the poetic preamble with the grievances lodged against King George III of Great Britain is the affirmation of the existence of natural rights and of the aspirations of a free people to have a government formed by their consent, which closely adheres to those rights. It was the growing gap between the rights and aspirations of American colonists and British government policies, embodied in the Declaration's list of complaints, that left Americans with no rational choice but to declare themselves independent of Britain. The failed Articles of Confederation and the U.S. Constitution were the attempts made by the Founders to provide a framework of government within an ordered society that more closely adhered to and ensured the "self-evident" truth of the people's natural rights, which Jefferson highlighted in his famously lyrical preamble.

Did you know? People all over the world were inspired by the European *Enlightenment* (a philosophical movement that welcomed ideas to transform society and government through reason and knowledge). Before the Enlightenment, Europeans blindly followed the unquestionable authority of the monarchy and the Church. From politics and religion to economics and culture, the philosophers of the Enlightenment believed that reason could fix the problems of any contemporary society. Shared ideas from the Enlightenment sparked Thomas Jefferson's contributions to the Declaration of Independence.

Enlightenment Concepts That Influenced American Ideals

Enlightenment philosophical concepts contributed to the formation of the new American government and political ideals, including ideas that promoted *natural rights* (all people were entitled to God-given rights), a *social contract* (an agreement between a government and its people), *republicanism* (a government founded on the power of the people), *egalitarianism* (equality), and *liberty* (freedoms).

Jefferson wrote, "I know of no safe depositary of the ultimate powers of society, but the people themselves; and if we think them not enlightened enough to exercise their control with a wholesome discretion, the remedy is not to take it from them, but to inform their discretion by education." Jefferson expressed a commonly held belief among Enlightenment thinkers—ultimate sovereignty lies with the people and is superior to other forms of government that are based on absolutism and the "divine right of kings." A sovereign nation cannot function if the people are uneducated and uninformed!

Heads Up: What You Need to Know

On the AP GOV exam, it's important to be familiar with the following terms: **natural rights, social contract, popular sovereignty,** and **republicanism.**

Enlightenment Concepts That Helped Form Democratic Ideals	
Conceptual Ideals	Why is this conceptual ideal important?
Natural rights Enlightenment-Era thinkers believed that certain rights (life, liberty, and property, as identified by John Locke) were either God-given or part of a universal order that could not be modified by man. In recognition that man's controlling self-interest and venality might lead him to try to rob others of these rights, particularly in collusion with others, government must be instituted with powers specifically focused on protecting the natural rights of all people.	The concept of natural rights formed the foundation of *social contract theory* and Locke's writing on these subjects provided Thomas Jefferson with the blueprint for the Declaration of Independence. Natural rights also established the goal for the Founding Fathers when writing the Constitution. The overarching purpose of the Founders was to create a government framework that could best protect the natural rights of the people, an idea inextricably tied to the principle of limited government.
Social contract The social contract is a theory of government most commonly associated with John Locke, though it was endorsed by many Enlightenment political philosophers such as Jean-Jacques Rousseau and Baron de Montesquieu. Social contract theory postulates that legitimate governments are based on the consent of the governed. To ensure protection of their natural rights to life, liberty, and property against the self-interested nature of their fellow man, those who would be governed agreed to give up to a government some of the absolute freedom they enjoyed in the state of nature. In turn, the government would provide the benefits of ordered society focused on the protection of those unalienable natural rights. When governments lose sight of their purpose and become abusive to the people's rights, the governed then have a right to seek a new government. Locke's contract theory found in the "Second Treatise of Civil Government" provided the philosophical basis for the preamble of Jefferson's Declaration of Independence.	When Locke identified natural rights as life, liberty, and property, by *property* he did not simply mean land, but also ownership of oneself and one's conscience; in other words, liberty. It was this unalienable liberty that formed the foundation of the social contract—an understanding that individuals would voluntarily forfeit some of their freedoms and submit themselves to a government as long as that government remained accountable to them for the protection of their rights. The liberty to choose for themselves allows the people to protect themselves against an abusive government that fails in its core purpose by removing that government and replacing it with another.
Republicanism Republicanism is a philosophy of governing that places sovereignty in the hands of the people and the authority to govern with representatives elected by the people to serve the common good.	In Article IV, Section 4, of the Constitution, there is an unamendable provision: "The United States shall guarantee to every state in this Union a republican form of government." The term *republican* in this context, and that of the larger union of the United States, should not be confused with the Republican Party. Republicanism goes hand in hand with popular sovereignty and supports the existence of a representative democracy. In such a system, representatives are accountable to the people through periodic elections. This concept was at the core of Anti-Federalist wariness about the impulse to centralize authority in a federal government. Are the people's will and the common good served more effectively at the state level or at the federal level where the laws are granted supremacy over the states (Constitution; Article VI)? Is accountability more readily accomplished when power is exercised locally than it is at the federal level where the center of power is geographically remote from most people?

Conceptual Ideals	Why is this conceptual ideal important?
Popular sovereignty **Sovereignty** is the power and authority to govern. Popular sovereignty is an idea that asserts that the people are ultimately the source of that power and authority.	Popular sovereignty is at the heart of democracy and of social contract theory. A belief that power and authority can be granted by the people, but also can be taken away when governments abuse their power, is the founding principle of both the Declaration of Independence and the Constitution (read: Preamble to the Constitution; https://www.archives.gov/founding-docs/constitution-transcript). Popular sovereignty is most clearly expressed today when citizens vote directly for those who represent them during federal, state, and local elections. It is also on display in those states that allow citizen initiatives (voting on citizen-proposed laws), referendums (voting on existing laws passed by legislatures), and recalls (voting to remove officials from office before their term is up).

Articles of Confederation (Formulated in 1777; Ratified in 1781)

The Articles of Confederation was the first framework for government formulated in 1777 for the newly independent United States. In the aftermath of the outbreak of hostilities with Britain and declaring independence, Americans had to create a government that could act on behalf of the new nation. The Articles remained in effect after the successful conclusion to the Revolutionary War, but as the country shifted its footing to the post-war launch of a new nation, many wondered if the Articles were adequate to address all the challenges of nation building.

The dilemma for the Second Continental Congress hung on the question of how much power they should grant to a central government.

The delegates sent to the Confederation Congress were empowered only to engage in defense of the nation, to make war, negotiate treaties, mediate disputes between two or more states, and regulate weights, measures, and coinage. These constrained powers are counted among the confederation government's other salient drawbacks, which included:

- A requirement that laws could only be passed with the assent of delegates from 9 of the 13 states.
- Lack of taxing authority, which impacted its ability to undertake defense, conduct war, or implement any of its other decisions.
- No authority to regulate interstate or foreign commerce and trade.
- Disproportionate representation; every state, large or small, had only one vote in the Confederation Congress.
- Lack of an executive empowered with the authority to enforce the law.
- Unanimous consent requirement (all 13 states) for any changes to the Articles.

Consisting of 13 articles, the Confederation document created a "firm league of friendship" of sovereign states. This confederation of sovereign states would soon reveal its weaknesses, but from the outset it clearly reflected a fundamental concern among the leading revolutionary Founding Fathers—the centralized national authority. By creating a decentralized government that allocated the lion's share of power and authority to the states and creating a national government with a short list of powers, the Founders addressed this concern head on. However, once cracks in the system were revealed, there was very little flexibility to address them due to the unanimous consent provision for amending the existing Articles.

Whether or not to scrap the Articles entirely in favor of a more centralized constitutional government highlighted a fundamental cleavage in American political thought between advocates of states' rights and those in favor of the unifying authority of a strong central government, a divide that persists to the present day with the debate over small government versus big government.

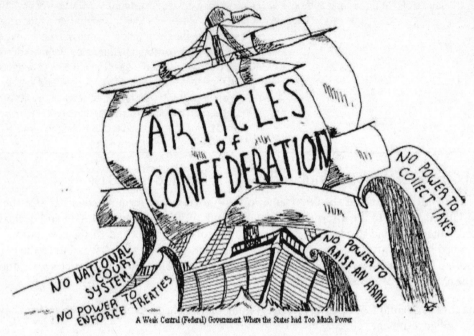

A Weak Central (Federal) Government Where the States had Too Much Power

"Rough Sailing Ahead?"

The Articles had unified the states during the American Revolution. However, as depicted in the image, they had given the government limited powers to conduct military engagements, negotiate treaties, resolve controversies among states, and settle territorial issues. Even though the Articles were ineffective, they served as an important bridge to the formation of the U.S. Constitution.

The Importance of the Articles of Confederation

Congress had fears that a strong centralized government would threaten the states, so Congress made the Articles intentionally weak and powerless. Many delegates believed that liberty was best protected within small republics where democratically elected representatives, accountable to local voters, acted in the expressed interest of their constituents. A highly centralized government, remote from the best interests and rights of its people, was, after all, exactly what the revolution had sought to overthrow. Thus, the Articles of Confederation emphasized the exercise of decentralized power by sovereign states with a highly restrained centralized government acting for the nation of the United States. The bridge it provided led to the more purely federal system of shared sovereignty provided in the Constitution.

Limited Government

Limited government is a constitutional principle dating back to Aristotle's assertion that only governments of law, not of men, could defend the people against tyranny. It forms the philosophical basis of constitutionalism, "the rule of law." This Aristotelian notion was also familiar to the Founding Fathers through their exposure to the traditions of English governance. England's *Magna Carta* dated back to 1215 and represented the first of many actions taken by Parliament to explicitly impose restrictions on the absolute authority of England's monarch. It is important to note that written constitutions are the means used to achieve limited government. The creation of a framework for government on paper with its powers clearly enumerated restrains the exercise of power by government officials. Other principles such as separation of powers, checks and balances, bicameralism, and the Bill of Rights embedded in America's Constitution strengthened limitations on government power and ensured that the people's rights to life, liberty, and property would be protected against abuse by any one person or group within the government.

Models of Representative Democracy

TEST TIP: On the AP GOV exam, you must be familiar with the perspectives of Federalists, and Anti-Federalists on the models which best ensure democratic government. Further, it is essential to understand the modern models of democracy—participatory, pluralist, elite. These models are at the center of ideological debates over what democracy really means and what it looks like at the practical policymaking level in the American government.

Participatory Democracy

Participatory democracy is a form of democracy that emphasizes broad participation and engagement in political decision making. More than simply voting, participatory democracy provides various opportunities for citizens to contribute to civil society within their communities and to affect policy outcomes in the political arena. To be truly participatory, these opportunities must be made widely available to as many people as possible. Individual efforts combine with the work of elected representatives to form a participatory system.

Democracy, after all, means "the people rule." Participation over a broad spectrum of activities by all citizens, along with the policymaking responsibilities undertaken by their representatives, more closely aligns the participatory model with the democratic ideal. It also increases faith in political institutions, promotes political efficacy among citizens, and makes the government more accountable. Participation does include voting, but extends to include community activities, political activism through petition drives and demonstrations, organizing in support of equal opportunity in the workplace, volunteering, writing and publishing critiques of the political process, attending public meetings, joining political organizations, etc.

Pluralist Democracy

Pluralist democracy emphasizes non-governmental collective activism through interest groups that organize to influence public policy. There are myriad groups operating in the political arena representing broad policy focus on economic, labor, professional, agricultural, environmental, consumer, ideological, and public-interest issues, as well as those organized to influence policy on narrowly defined single issues (e.g., the National Rifle Association's focus on gun control).

Pluralist democracy reflects a belief in freedom of association as individuals seek to use their collective power, rather than individual activism, to get their voice heard along with others who share the same interest. In theory, interest groups participate in dialogue about public policy issues and align into coalitions in support of particular policy initiatives when their interests overlap. For example, Common Cause, the Sierra Club, and the Organic Trade Association might find common cause on policies addressing the use of chemical fertilizers and pesticides. The system is still democratic, but the impact of individuals is filtered through group participation.

Elite Democracy

Elite democracy is a form of representative democracy in which policymaking is dominated by elected representatives acting as *trustees* (representatives given the authority by voters to use their best judgment on behalf of constituents regarding public policy) within a policy network that includes economic elites.

For the most part, constituents expect their elected representatives to operate as *delegates* within the government, directly acting on the expressed interests and policy expectations of the people. However, representatives at times act as trustees, which may be acceptable to constituents, even necessary, when there is no clear consensus among the constituency regarding an issue or when they are not well informed about the complexities of a given policy. In such circumstances, they trust the judgment of their representatives, and give them free rein to do what they think is best. Problems arise with the trustee model when the free agency of representatives is used to serve the narrow interests of economic elites rather than the common good. The dominance of the policymaking process by political and economic elite networks tends to filter out the voice of rank-and-file participants in civic affairs and to be impervious to traditional democratic processes, which then underscores a perception of corrupted democracy. This sense that "the system is rigged" undermines public faith in government and has a negative impact on the participatory democratic model as many in the rank-and-file view their participation as meaningless and their political efficacy as non-existent.

U.S. Constitution (1787)

The first attempts to establish an early republic were not perfect, but they laid the foundation for our political system today with checks and balances, a separation of powers, and divided executive, legislative, and judicial branches of government.

The **U.S. Constitution** was a blueprint for a new United States government designed to replace the faltering Articles of Confederation. Drafted in 1787 by delegates from every state except Rhode Island (a fiercely independent state that was distrustful of plans to invigorate the power of the central government), the Constitution was finally ratified in 1788.

Did you know? The **Grand Committee** was a group of Founding Fathers composed of one delegate from each of the 11 states who were present at the Constitutional Convention in July 1787. This included the grand old man of the convention, 84-year-old Benjamin Franklin. The Committee met to reach an agreement on one of the issues that most stubbornly resisted resolution by the Committee of the Whole (all delegates): how representation in the national Congress, specifically the Senate, would be determined.

Why is the Grand Committee important on the AP GOV exam? The issue of apportionment of representatives highlights the challenge faced by the Founding Fathers in creating a functioning government aligned with the philosophical underpinnings of the Declaration of Independence. At the core of this debate was the practicality of popular democracy based on consent of the governed, a question that extended to the apportionment of representatives in the chambers of Congress. Disagreement on this central structural issue stalled the convention. The work of the Grand Committee would eventually be reported out to the Committee of the Whole and adopted by the Convention. The solution hammered out by the Grand Committee allowed further work on the Constitution to move forward and created a unique form of political democracy in which an elite element was balanced against the forces of the popular will (see "Great Compromise," pp. 71–72).

Importance of the U.S. Constitution

The principal changes to the government under the Articles instituted by the Constitution included the creation of a central government. The fight over its ratification revealed a philosophical rift that persists to the present day. While controversial in its time, it was also revolutionary in its structure for government. Regardless of the ongoing debate over its interpretation and the application of its provisions, the expansive sovereignty granted to the three separate branches of government included checks and balances that have avoided tyranny and allowed the constitutional government to last for over 230 years.

Source: KF Wimer, "Defending the Constitution," 2007. Originally printed in *The Denver Business Journal,* March 20, 2009. The plight of American cartoonists who help to defend the Constitution.

Key Principles of the U.S. Constitution

Separation of powers. The central government consists of three branches: legislative, executive, and judicial. The legislative branch, Congress, creates the laws. The executive branch, the president, executes the laws. The judicial branch, the Supreme Court, interprets the laws.

Federalism. An expanded list of enumerated powers granted to these branches shifted the exercise of sovereignty in some areas from the states toward the central government. A basic framework for the geographic distribution of power between the central (federal) and state governments was spelled out, including a more proportional approach to state representation in the national Congress.

Checks and balances. To ensure a balanced rule, each of the branches of government is granted specific powers that enables it to check the use of power by the other branches. The system is designed specifically to avoid the tendency toward tyranny when an individual or group within the government acts in ways that go beyond its constitutional constraints. Students should be familiar with the various constitutional checks (e.g., only Congress can declare war, presidents can exercise the veto authority, the Supreme Court can declare acts of Congress and executive actions unconstitutional, etc.).

Popular government. The power to elect government officials was placed in the hands of its citizens, and a system was defined for electing government representatives.

Heads Up: What You Need to Know

In addition to the key principles of the Constitution, there are two specific provisions that you should be familiar with for the AP GOV exam—the **Necessary and Proper Clause** and the **Supremacy Clause.**

Provisions in the Constitution		
	Definition	Why is it important?
Necessary and Proper Clause	Section 8, Article I, of the Constitution, which enumerates the powers granted to Congress. The Necessary and Proper Clause is the very last power granted in this extensive list and gives Congress the authority to: "make all Laws which shall be necessary and proper for carrying into Execution the foregoing Powers, and all other Powers vested by this Constitution in the Government of the United States…"	The implicit value in enumerating the powers granted to government is placing limitations on its actions. By listing what the government can do, anything not on the list is prohibited. Powers enumerated in Section 8 include the clear and specific authority to carry out certain functions like laying and collecting taxes and regulating interstate and foreign commerce. It would be easy, therefore, to determine the boundaries of congressional authority. However, that last power, the Necessary and Proper Clause, erased those boundaries in the eyes of Anti-Federalist critics. In effect, they argued, it gave Congress the power to do anything it pleased. It prompted one Anti-Federalist writing as "An Old Whig" to ask, "Where then is the restraint?" The trade-off for keeping the Necessary and Proper Clause was the inclusion of the Bill of Rights. The clause also established the foundation for the implied powers doctrine. (See *McCulloch v. Maryland*, pp. 84–85.)

	Definition	Why is it important?
Supremacy Clause	Within Article VI of the Constitution is clause 2, which asserts that the Constitution and all laws and treaties made by the government of the United States are the "supreme law of the land," superseding any state laws, including state constitutions, in conflict with the Constitution or federal laws and treaties.	The Supremacy Clause is the foundation for the "preemption doctrine," which allows the federal courts to invalidate state laws in conflict with the Constitution, federal laws, and treaties. It is the glue that binds the nation together as a singular federal republic adhering to the rule of law. Without the Supremacy Clause, any state could legally do the reverse, that is, declare federal laws invalid or nullify them. The Supremacy Clause sounded alarm bells among Anti-Federalists during the ratification debate. Taken in conjunction with the Necessary and Proper Clause, the bells rang louder still. Since Anti-Federalists viewed state sovereignty as the key to republicanism and liberty, the fact that the federal government could override actions by the states was troubling indeed. The original version of the Constitution had no Bill of Rights, the argument among some at the convention being that it was unnecessary since all states had a Bill of Rights in their own constitutions. However, how strong a protection would such guarantees be if Congress was empowered to do anything it deemed "necessary and proper," and such decisions would then become the supreme law of the land? It was the Supremacy Clause that made the inclusion of the Bill of Rights in the Constitution so imperative and, thanks to the arguments raised by Anti-Federalists in the great newspaper debates with the Federalists, the point was conceded and the Bill of Rights was added.

Heads Up: What You Need to Know

Why is the Bill of Rights important on the AP GOV exam? The Bill of Rights became a platform for the role of the federal judiciary in interpreting the extent and/or limitations of these rights in case after case, a process that continues to the present day.

It was the lack of protections for individual liberties and due process of the law in the original draft of the Constitution that proved to be the greatest sticking point in the fight for ratification. Some delegates at the Constitutional Convention had argued that most states included a Bill of Rights in their own constitutions and that these protections were sufficient. Those delegates wary of strong national authority embodied in the Necessary and Proper and Supremacy clauses argued that state protections would almost certainly not be adequate to protect the people from abuse of power by the federal level of government. With a promise to add a Bill of Rights after the Constitution was successfully ratified, those state legislatures reluctant to approve the new government framework finally got in line, and the Constitution became the law of the land.

Bill of Rights (1791)

The **Bill of Rights** consists of the first 10 *amendments* (changes) to the Constitution added in the immediate aftermath of *ratification* (approval and adoption by the states). These amendments put in place protection for the rights and civil liberties of individuals against the authority of the central government and included assurances to the states of their continued sovereignty over state and local issues.

Political Compromises

Heads Up: What You Need to Know

The learning objectives that you must be able to accomplish are:

Explain how Federalist and Anti-Federalist views on central government and democracy are reflected in U.S. foundational documents.

Explain the relationship between key provisions of the Articles of Confederation and the debate over granting the federal government greater power formerly reserved to the states.

Explain the ongoing impact of political negotiation and compromise at the Constitutional Convention on the development of the constitutional system.

The Constitution is often referred to as a bundle of compromises. It could only be so, given the hard lines drawn between Federalist and Anti-Federalist beliefs about the nature of their republic and which of their views best adhered to social contract theory and popular sovereignty. This debate and the compromises cobbled together in Philadelphia in 1787 are key to understanding America's constitutional democracy.

Political Divisions—Federalists and Anti-Federalists

In 1787, key supporters of the Constitution wrote the *Federalist Papers* (pp. 68–70). The *Federalist Papers* sought to explain and justify that the constitutional framework for a federal republic was a superior system that would effectively address the weaknesses of the Articles of Confederation. Anti-Federalists opposed the Constitution under the federal system being proposed because they worried that the people's will expressed in their state and local communities would be overwhelmed by the tyranny of centralized power.

Source: Granger, "Congressional Pugilists, Congress Hall in Philadelphia," February 15, 1798. Political cartoon depicting the Federalists vs. Anti-Federalists in Congress.

Comparing Federalists and Anti-Federalists		
	Federalists (Federal)	**Anti-Federalists (States)**
Political position	Federalists favored a large federal republic to better organize and defend the newly created United States, arguing that centralized administration of the nation's interests with input from state representatives in Congress was the best means to protect individual freedoms. According to the Federalists, the Constitution formed a stronger central government with expansive powers needed to ensure the survival of the United States as a nation.	Anti-Federalists advocated for strong state and local governments and a weak national (federal) government. They argued that the Federalists took too much power away from the states, entities that most closely reflected the will of the people. Anti-Federalists opposed the Constitution and the redistribution of sovereignty it proposed as a replacement for the foundering Articles of Confederation.
Key supporters	Early Federalist supporters of the Constitution who opposed the ineffective Articles of Confederation included George Washington, Alexander Hamilton, John Adams, and John Jay.	Key supporters who wanted the Articles of Confederation to be amended, not discarded, included Thomas Jefferson, Samuel Adams, James Monroe, and Patrick Henry.

Continued

	Federalists (Federal)	Anti-Federalists (States)
Economic position	Federalists mainly resided in urban and industrialized areas that were dominated by big business interests. They supported centralized economic oversight of the nation's business through creation of a national bank and a program to pay off the nation's debts. Federalists believed the economic future of the nation would be ensured by an emphasis on manufacturing and industry rather than agriculture.	Anti-Federalists mainly resided in rural and farming areas. They rejected centralized economic decision making, with the national bank serving as a symbol for their opposition. Anti-Federalists believed in the republican ideal of a democratic society, which they believed could only be maintained in an agrarian economy of small farmers. A future of manufacturing and industry supported by investment and finance would lead to a corruption of "government of the people."
Impact	The influence and prestige of the leading Federalists led directly to the meeting in Philadelphia in 1787, the writing of the Constitution, and the ratification of the new plan for government via the *Federalist Papers* penned by Alexander Hamilton, James Madison, and John Jay.	The Anti-Federalists' efforts before and during the constitutional debates to guard individual liberty and the prerogatives of the states contributed to the final wording of the Constitution. Amending the final version of the Constitution to include the Bill of Rights was a direct result of Anti-Federalist opposition during the ratification debates.

Federalist Papers

Heads Up: What You Need to Know

Why is it important to learn about the Federalists and Anti-Federalists for the AP GOV exam? Influential figures of the day such as George Washington and Alexander Hamilton met in 1786 at the Annapolis Convention, along with delegates of five other states, who guided discussions toward the idea of calling for more states to attend a convention in Philadelphia in May 1787 to participate in a broad discussion of problems with the Articles of Confederation.

The Federalists proposed a shift of power away from the states toward a more centralized federal government. This fundamental change in the distribution of power raised fears among many of the revolutionary generation, who viewed the struggle for independence as grounded in a fight against tyranny and a defense of liberty. Federal centralized power threatened what states had achieved. Anti-Federalists voiced their objections during the Constitutional Convention and continued their resistance during the ratification process, writing under pseudonyms like "Cato" (likely George Clinton), "a Federal Farmer," and "Brutus" (likely Melancton Smith or Robert Yates from the New York delegation).

The *Federalist Papers* were a series of 85 essays authored by James Madison, Alexander Hamilton, and John Jay in defense of the Constitution (though Jay penned only a handful). The authors not only envisioned a large republic, but they also established a basis for judicial review and suggested that a strong federal government was the best protection for individual rights.

After the final draft of the Constitution was presented for ratification by the states in September 1787, whether it would be approved by the requisite number of nine states was in question. Anti-Federalist opponents of the Constitution had been raising their concerns throughout the drafting phase, and as the ratification process began, they published their own essays in newspapers read throughout the land. In response, the *Federalist Papers* published in 1787–1788 took on Anti-Federalist arguments, explaining the philosophical and practical underpinnings of the decisions reached at the Constitutional Convention. Their persuasive arguments helped carry the Constitution over the top during the ratification process and remain the most clear, rational defense of the federal republic of the United States.

> TEST TIP: Students do not need to know the content of all the essays, but four Federalist essays and one Anti-Federalist essay are considered required foundational documents. In this chapter, of the four required Federalist essays, Federalist No. 10 and Federalist No. 51 are highlighted.

Federalist No. 10

Federalist No. 10 was one of the *Federalist Papers* published in 1787. In Federalist No. 10, James Madison addressed the size of the constitutional republic, which many Anti-Federalists believed would collapse under the weight of rival interests; the inevitable insurrections that these competing interests would produce; and the tyrannical power that the centralized government would ultimately use to suppress any such insurrection.

The Importance of Federalist No. 10

James Madison discussed at length this issue of factions, which he identified as competing groups whose members shared a common interest. Madison argued that the formation of factions was natural in any group of people, particularly given the obvious and most prevalent driver of divergent interests, the unequal distribution of property. Trying to eliminate people's freedom to associate with like-minded individuals could not be done without oppressing liberty. Further, simply trying to eradicate factions was impossible; therefore, civil societies must attempt to control their effects. Given their more limited diversity, the smaller republican states, Madison argued, would be a much more likely venue for a tyrannical majority to emerge to oppress the minority. More effective in controlling the "mischief" of factions would be a union of the geographically, culturally, religiously, and economically diverse 13 states into a single constitutional republic in which power was geographically distributed between and among the federal government and the states.

Madison argued that the idea of a single majority faction of shared interests emerging at the federal level would simply be improbable, and in addition, governance through representatives and the dispersal of power through many levels (local, state, federal) would minimize the harmful influence of singularly powerful factions. Madison's argument tempered the more coercive argument made by Alexander Hamilton in Federalist No. 9. Like Madison, Hamilton argued for a union based on confederation in which the states retained sovereignty over local matters but were subordinate in matters of the larger union. The republican confederation of states would act to suppress factional insurrections since all states would freely combine forces against the usurpation of the authority by one state or combination of states.

> **Did you know?** It was James Madison's reasoning regarding the value of a large republic, in which a multiplicity of diverse interests and the structural character of the Constitution act "organically" rather than coercively as safeguards against factions, that became the most frequently cited support for a large federal republic.

Brutus No. 1

Brutus No. 1 was a powerful articulation of Anti-Federalist arguments against immediate ratification of the Constitution as a replacement for the Articles of Confederation. While acknowledging problems with the Articles, "Brutus" questioned whether the formation of one large republic with executive, legislative, and judicial branches exercising expansive powers over tremendously diverse populations in each of the states was a good remedy. To the contrary, the author argued that the potential for tyranny in such a design was far too great.

In Brutus No. 1, Anti-Federalist Robert Yates (or Melancton Smith; the author is rumored to have been either of them) addressed a fundamental understanding of the *social contract* (an agreement between the government and its people) that Jefferson had previously highlighted in the Declaration of Independence. There is an acknowledgment that achieving the common good with the consent of the people is ultimately the purpose of civil government. However, a government of men cannot be expected to avoid the propensity of all other men to exceed boundaries of civil behavior and succumb to the temptations of power, thus putting individual rights at risk. The natural rights of life and of conscience should never be surrendered to a government of men, "Brutus" argued, and must be explicitly protected against a government that claimed to be supreme to all state governments (Article VI; the Supremacy Clause). Anti-Federalist arguments like this defended the idea that decentralized power with sovereignty localized in the states was the best manifestation of the republican ideal and was also instrumental to extracting a promise for adding the Bill of Rights to the Constitution in exchange for ratification.

Article V

Article V provides two methods for proposing and ratifying constitutional amendments. One method allows Congress to propose amendments by a two-thirds vote in both houses; the other provides for a convention of the states to propose amendments at the request of two-thirds of the state legislatures. A ratification vote by three-fourths of the state legislatures or state conventions follows.

The Importance of Article V

Self-government was at the forefront of political discussions among the revolutionary generation. Their challenge was to create a strong government for the United States that was directly responsive to the will of the people. Initially, they believed that the Articles of Confederation achieved just that by decentralizing power and granting sovereignty to 13 small republics. However, the focus on state autonomy and the constraint of the national Congress created a fragile union held together by only "a rope of sand," as stated by George Washington in a letter to his friend Henry Knox. Amendment of the Articles illustrates this point, requiring that all 13 states ratify any attempt by Congress to change the blueprint of the government.

The near-impossibility of achieving a unanimous vote robbed the Confederation government of any flexibility to address the Articles' weaknesses. The delegates at the Constitutional Convention grappled with the amendment issue, but the initial version of Article V prompted harsh criticism from delegate George Mason for giving ultimate control of the amendment process to Congress, a proposal that violated the principle of popular sovereignty. Mason called the plan "exceptionable and dangerous," and so a new version eventually made it into the Constitution, allowing proposals for amendments to be made by Congress or by a convention of the states, and requiring ratification of any amendments by three-fourths of the states.

Electoral College

The **Electoral College** is a method for selecting the president and vice president of the United States established in Article II, Section 1, of the Constitution. Section 1 provides that electors be apportioned to each state equal in number to its senators and members of the House of Representatives. Today, the electors cast their votes in December following a November presidential election. In January, after all electoral votes have been received from the states, the votes are counted by the president of the Senate in the presence of that body. The candidate receiving the majority of electoral votes (today the magic number is 270) is declared president-elect. Originally, the second-place finisher became vice president, but this was changed via the Twelfth Amendment, which required separate nominations of presidential and vice-presidential candidates.

The Importance of the Electoral College

The process for electing the president was not an easy matter for the delegates at the Constitutional Convention. The debate highlights a distrust of popular democracy and the will of the majority as well as the critical nature of the Founding Fathers' belief in the principle of separation of powers. James Madison's Virginia Plan served as the platform for debate. Madison suggested that the Executive (president) should be elected by Congress. The Committee of Detail, which took over the drafting of the Constitution from the contentious Committee of the Whole, determined that election by Congress would not provide the president with sufficient independence from the will of the legislative branch. They also rejected the idea of a popularly elected president, as such a system would minimize the voice of smaller states in presidential elections and open the door to tyranny of the majority. The compromise was the Electoral College system, which maintained a separation of the executive and legislative branches and a more proportional voice for the states. In addition, giving to the states through their electors the power to choose the executive of the federal government, the Electoral College became an important and enduring feature of the Constitution's federal design.

Great Compromise

The **Great Compromise** was an agreement reached by the Grand Committee regarding representation in Congress, creating a democracy in which elements of the elite and popular democracy were balanced between the two chambers of Congress.

The Importance of the Great Compromise

Consent of the governed is a principle espoused in Jefferson's Declaration of Independence; it is the will of the people viewed as the ultimate sovereignty in a free democratic government. This vision bumped up against political practicality and the realities of human fallibility when the Founding Fathers sat down to create a functional government. The concept of popular sovereignty can easily be translated as "the majority rules," but should it? What about minority interests? Were minority interests and the future of the new nation to be held hostage to an unruly majority? Within the first few months of the start of the Convention, delegates had agreed in principle to James Madison's plan, which called for a bicameral Congress, but the Virginia Plan also called for representation in both houses to be apportioned proportionately based on the population of the states. This seemed only fair to the delegates of larger states since they contributed more to the defense and the treasury of the nation. Delegates from the smaller states were adamant, however, that this design would place their interests at the mercy of the majority. They refused to endorse it, insisting instead on equal representation in both chambers of Congress, a suggestion that the large states would simply not countenance.

The Grand Committee then set to work and made the following proposal to the convention: representation in the popularly elected House would remain proportional by population. In the Senate, however, each state would have an equal number (two) to be chosen by their state legislatures. Key to gaining the support of the large states for this design was Benjamin Franklin's suggestion that senators be considered free agents who would vote their conscience on matters of national importance, rather than as a bloc of votes directed by their respective legislatures to promote state interests. In addition, Franklin suggested that while most bills could originate in either the Senate or the House, all revenue (tax) bills could only originate in the House of Representatives. Thus, a unique form of democracy was created in which the will of the majority expressed in the House could be checked and/or modified by minority interests in the Senate, whose members were not directly accountable to the popular will of voters.

Heads Up: What You Need to Know

Shays' Rebellion was directly connected to the writing of the U.S. Constitution. Understanding why it happened and why it prompted a crisis of faith in the government in the Articles of Confederation is important to understanding the backstory of the Constitution and its creation of a strong federal government that limited the sovereignty of the states and empowered federal institutions (Congress, the president, the courts) to take actions that would hold the nation together under the flag of a democratic federal republic.

Shays' Rebellion

Shays' Rebellion (1786–1787) was a revolt among farmers in rural western and central Massachusetts against taxation, farm foreclosures, and lack of political voice in state politics. Rebels commandeered control of local courthouses to stop the issuance of foreclosure orders and tried to take over the federal arsenal located in Springfield. The series of uprisings is collectively referred to by the name of one of its leaders and symbol of the spirit of the revolt, Revolutionary War veteran Captain Daniel Shays. The uprising was eventually put down by a militia paid for by Massachusetts merchants.

In the aftermath of the Revolution, lingering debt issues, economic hardship, and political resentments reverberated in poor farming communities from New Hampshire to South Carolina. Uprisings were not uncommon, but it was Shays' Rebellion that was the most renowned. In response to unpaid debts, European merchants cut off further credit to merchants in affected states until their existing debts were paid in hard currency. To quickly dispatch the burden of debt, leaders in the Massachusetts statehouse turned to taxation. Struggling farmers—among them, Revolutionary War veterans who were already floundering because neither the state nor the central government had made good on promises to deliver back pay owed to them for their wartime service—ended up in legal disputes that resulted in foreclosure on their farms. Discontent among these westerners, who were underrepresented in the statehouse, erupted during the summer of 1786. When Massachusetts appealed to the Confederation government for help in putting down the rebellion, there was simply nothing the government was empowered to do in response to a local uprising.

Reasons That Shays' Rebellion Led to the U.S. Constitution	
Motivating Reasons	Consequences
States did not support the war. One of the reasons Revolutionary War soldiers had not been fairly compensated during the fighting in the first place was the inability of the Confederation Congress to compel states to support the war effort, leaving the government few options but to seek loans overseas and issue promises of future pay to soldiers slogging it out in the field. **Debt crisis.** In the years after the Revolutionary War, without any power to tax of its own accord or to develop a unified economic policy, the central government was also without the necessary tools to effectively address the debt crisis. **States' private resources.** Finally, as demonstrated during Shays' Rebellion, states would have to rely on private resources to raise the necessary militia forces to deal with uprisings since the central government had neither the access to resources nor the power to restore order and stability.	The totality of Shays' Rebellion brought problems with the Confederation into sharp focus. With local revolts bubbling to the surface in several frontier regions, George Washington, the most influential political figure of his time, followed events in Massachusetts closely. He was utterly convinced by the actions of the "Shaysites" that the Articles of Confederation must be replaced with a different form of government based on stronger centralized authority that would provide greater economic stability and the ability to protect property rights against potential uprisings.

Slave Trade Compromise

The **Slave Trade Compromise** was one of several key compromises that emerged during negotiations at the Constitutional Convention. The Slave Trade Compromise resolved differences between those at the convention who were adamantly opposed to the continued importation of slaves and those equally adamant about their desire to see the slave trade continue. Ultimately, a special committee agreed that Congress would not be empowered to ban the slave trade until 1808 (see Article I, Section 9).

The Importance of the Slave Trade Compromise

At several points during the convention, proceedings were deadlocked and members threatened to walk out and bring the whole process to an inauspicious end. It was decided early on to leave to the states the question of banning the institution and practice of slavery itself. The underlying theory among the opponents of slavery was that it was such an outmoded and inefficient means of production that bonded labor would die out on its own. The forced capture and trading of slaves was another matter; however, Georgia, South Carolina, and North Carolina continued to import slaves. These states refused to entertain the idea that Congress was empowered to end the practice and threatened to walk out if the delegates voted to do so. The issue of a centralized authority acting to intervene in state affairs once again threatened the formation of a new constitutional union. Holding the states together in a federal union ultimately outweighed the fight against the slave trade, and a compromise was reached, postponing the possibility of congressional action against slave trade for 20 years.

Three-Fifths Compromise

The **Three-Fifths Compromise** was an agreement reached at the Constitutional Convention that allowed southern states to count their slaves for the purposes of apportioning representative seats in the House of Representatives and Electoral College votes, but only at the discounted rate of three-fifths of their actual number. To induce the states to accept reducing the total number of slaves counted within their population totals, the three-fifths formula was also applied to the taxing of slaves as property.

Source: Josiah Wedgwood, "Am I Not a Man and a Brother?" 1787. American Anti-Slavery Society emblem.

The political advantage gained by southern slave-holding states via this compromise allowed them to dominate the federal government until 1861, thus giving fuel to an ongoing debate within the government about states' rights over federal authority. Again, compromise allowed the convention to continue its work to hammer out a Constitution, but the cost of that compromise was to endorse a fundamental political divide that would tear the Union asunder by acts of secession and civil war less than a hundred years after the nation's founding.

Did you know? The Constitution did not set forth voting requirements; such guidelines were left to the states. As a result, voting rights varied from state to state. However, generally speaking, at the outset of the Union, only male property owners could vote. Women, Native Americans, and African Americans were excluded from the suffrage. The democratization of the United States through the expansion of voting rights over time is an important part of the American political story.

Contemporary Connections to Political Divisions

The College Board has identified two specific issues used to represent present-day constitutional debates grounded in the tension between the role of the federal government and the powers of the states. One of these issues is public education. The Tenth Amendment in the Bill of Rights reserved to the states powers not delegated specifically to the central government. The powers delegated to the central government are clearly enumerated in Article 1, Section 8, and nowhere is there any mention of public education. Public school education policy was then left to the states, but the federal government has carved out an evolving role for itself for over 150 years. From the creation of the Office of Education (1867), later elevated to a cabinet-level position with the Department of Education (1980), to the *Brown v. Board of Education of Topeka* decision (1954), to the passage of the Elementary and Secondary Education Act (1965) that provides federal funding to support equity in education, all three branches of the federal government have weighed in on education policy. Generally, federal involvement has focused on standardization of access, teaching and learning, and academic outcomes to ensure at least a minimum quality of education for all children regardless of their state of residence. However, this expanded involvement has gone hand in hand with a federally enforced end to race-based segregation in public schools, federal mandates, oversight, and reporting, as well as standardized testing. Many have argued that education policy has contributed to the disappearance of the line drawn by the Tenth Amendment between federal and state sovereignty.

Highlighting the educational issue and the proper role of the federal government are a series of laws passed by Congress beginning in 1965. As a key element of President Johnson's "War on Poverty," the **Elementary and Secondary Education Act (ESEA)** targeted equal access to quality primary and secondary education based on high standards and accountability. The act provided funding in primary and secondary levels of public education for professional development, instructional materials, additional resources to support educational programs, and the promotion of parental involvement. The subdivisions of the ESEA are referred to as titles—for example, Title I, which provides funding to schools in economically disadvantaged areas; and Title IX of the Education Amendments Act of 1972, which bans gender discrimination in any public school program receiving federal funding. The funding appropriations were designed to be carried out over the course of 5 fiscal years, but the act has been reauthorized by every presidential administration since. Revisions and amendments have been added with each reauthorization, among the most controversial being the **No Child Left Behind (NCLB)** reauthorization under the George W. Bush administration in 2002 and the **Every Student Succeeds Act (ESSA)** signed in 2015 by President Barack Obama.

Heads Up: What You Need to Know

On the AP GOV exam, the AP Readers will expect you to emphasize recent developments. Pay close attention to the Elementary and Secondary Education Act (ESEA) reauthorizations: No Child Left Behind and the Every Student Succeeds Act.

No Child Left Behind (NCLB) is the 2002 reauthorization that created new federal mandates regarding grade-level standardized testing and accountability, teacher qualifications, placement of teachers, and the ability of students to transfer out of low-performing schools. The law was roundly criticized for its impact on teaching and learning, but for your purposes on the AP GOV exam, the criticism has focused on federal overreach into policy, which is rightly reserved to the states.

Every Student Succeeds Act (ESSA) is the 2015 reauthorization that leaves the accountability through standardized testing provisions in place but allows state and local governments to determine their own plans for achieving goals for academic growth. These goals must be submitted to the Department of Education for input and approval.

The Preservation of Basic Freedoms

The Constitution took the powers of government to legislate, execute, adjudicate, and interpret the laws that make up public policy and divided them among separate branches. Because public policy is complex and involves the different branches at various levels, the powers and responsibilities for governance were purposely designed to overlap in a competitive power grid that encouraged each branch to exert its own authority against the other two. By this means, the Founding Fathers of the Constitution, who created the framework, believed they had designed a delicately balanced structure for a government that defended and promoted the will of the people and the liberties later outlined in the Bill of Rights.

Heads Up: What You Need to Know

The learning objectives that you must be able to accomplish are:

Explain the constitutional principles of separation of powers and checks and balances.

Explain the implications of "separation of powers" and "checks and balances" for the U.S. political system.

The Tenth Amendment

The final amendment in the collective Bill of Rights delegates certain enumerated powers to the federal government and reserves to the states all powers not delegated to the national institutions or specifically denied to the states in the Constitution.

The Importance of the Tenth Amendment

The Tenth Amendment was designed to alleviate concern among the states about their loss of sovereignty under the Constitution. Many expressed concern that state sovereignty would completely disappear due to the Necessary and Proper and Supremacy clauses included in the Constitution. The Anti-Federalists who forced the issue of providing protection against tyranny exercised by an all-powerful federal government sought protection for individual liberties as well as the sovereignty of states. The Tenth Amendment explicitly addressed and defended a federal system in which power is distributed between levels of government. It established a system of "dual federalism" in which each level of government (federal, state, local) exercised sovereignty within its own sphere of interest. Much of the modern debate over states' rights versus federal authority is grounded in the Tenth Amendment guarantees.

Separation of Powers

Separation of powers is the dividing of powers that all governments wield (to write laws, to put laws into execution, and to oversee the proper implementation of the laws) into three distinct branches to avoid the tyranny that can result when all the powers are put into the hands of one person or small group of elites. A governmental system based on a separation of powers commonly consists of three branches: legislative, executive, and judicial.

The Importance of Separation of Powers

Separation of powers is a fundamental principle upon which the constitutional framework is built. It is the focus of the first three articles of the Constitution which articulate the distinctions between the three separate branches of the new government and the institutions (Congress, president, and Supreme Court) that would exercise the powers of those branches.

Checks and Balances

Checks and balances is the concept of governance that supports the avoidance of tyranny and protection of the social contract via mechanisms designed to ensure against the usurpation of power by any one person or group within a government. The "checks" used to maintain a balance among separate branches of government consist of specific powers granted to each branch to restrain the exercise of power by the others.

Did you know? In his historical study of governments across time, French Enlightenment philosopher Baron de Montesquieu argued that problems attributable to tyrannical government could be diminished by separating government's powers into distinct branches. In his *The Spirit of Laws,* Montesquieu further argued that checks and balances were indispensable to maintaining separation among the branches, for without the ability of one branch to restrain abuse of power by another, the mere act of separation was pointless. His example of such a system was Britain's constitutional monarchy, a government limited in its power because the executive authority of the monarch was separate from and checked by the powers of the legislative branch (Parliament). Montesquieu's work is considered a major influence on America's constitutional Founding Fathers.

The Importance of Checks and Balances

Checks and balances are essential to a governmental system based on a separation of the governing powers into different branches. The checks provided to each branch in the Constitution are designed to maintain the distribution of power among the three branches by setting the competing interests of executive, legislative, and judicial authority against one another through specific powers granted to each branch, allowing them to restrain actions by the others viewed as abusive of their constitutional constraints.

Heads Up: What You Need to Know

It is important for students to be familiar with the constitutional system of checks and balances. When responding in writing to any prompt on the AP GOV exam, the use of concrete examples is required. If a prompt addresses the relationship between the institutions of the federal government and their interactions, having a working knowledge of the various checks granted to each branch of government will make the writing task easier and the response more successful. A summary of the checks and balances for the three branches is given in the table that follows.

Three Branches of Government: Checks and Balances		
Executive branch President	Checks against legislative branch ❏ Can propose policy initiatives ❏ Can veto laws ❏ Can call special sessions of Congress ❏ Can appoint heads of executive agencies of the federal government ❏ Can negotiate foreign treaties	Checks against judicial branch ❏ Can appoint federal judges and justices to the Supreme Court ❏ Can grant pardons or commutation of sentences of offenders convicted in federal courts
Legislative branch Congress (House of Representatives and Senate)	Checks against executive branch ❏ Can override presidential vetoes with concurrence of a two-thirds majority in both Houses ❏ Can confirm or reject executive appointments ❏ Can ratify (approve) or reject treaties negotiated by the executive branch ❏ Can appropriate funding ❏ Has the authority to impeach and remove the president	Checks against judicial branch ❏ Has the authority to create the lower federal courts ❏ Can impeach and remove judges/justices ❏ Can propose amendments to the Constitution that override judicial rulings ❏ Has the authority to approve judicial appointments
Judicial branch Federal courts (Supreme Court)	Checks against executive branch ❏ Can declare executive actions and orders unconstitutional ❏ Has a lifetime tenure (cannot be fired or removed without cause)	Checks against legislative branch ❏ Can declare laws passed by Congress unconstitutional

Federalist No. 51

Federalist No. 51 was one of the 85 essays compiled in the *Federalist Papers*. Its author, James Madison, addressed the subject of his essay in its title, *The Structure of the Government Must Furnish the Proper Checks and Balances Between the Different Departments*. The body of the text presents Madison's arguments in favor of the constitutional structure of the government into separate branches and the importance of the checks and balances in a scheme to use the internal workings and interactions of the three branches to avoid the concentration of power in the hands of a few.

The Importance of Federalist No. 51

In his essay, Madison famously argued, "If men were angels, no government would be necessary. If angels were to govern men, neither external nor internal controls on government would be necessary." It embodies a commonly held Enlightenment-Era belief that men are driven by self-interest; self-interest, in fact, drives human impulse. The impulse to corner the market on power is human nature, so simply separating the powers of government into different branches is not enough to protect the people against tyranny. It was certainly not enough for those who feared the potential for tyranny in the new model for government in which so much power was centralized. Madison argued that not only did the constitutional federal design rely on the division of sovereignty between the federal government and the states as one form of protection against tyranny, but also a double security was provided by separating the powers of government at both the state and federal levels into three branches, with checks granted to each branch to restrain the other branches. Madison's clear and logical explanation of how the internal structure of the Constitution would secure liberty was essential in persuading those reluctant to ratify the new government framework.

Heads Up: What You Need to Know

On the AP GOV exam, you should be familiar with **impeachment**—the process provided in the Constitution that empowers Congress to investigate alleged treason, bribery, or other crimes committed by the president while in office and to remove him/her if found guilty. When presented with evidence of a crime uncovered through investigation, the House of Representatives has the sole power to impeach the president by a majority vote of its members in support of articles of impeachment (two-thirds constitutes a "super majority" requirement rather than a simple majority vote). If, by House vote, the president is brought up on articles of impeachment, he/she is tried before the Senate with the Chief Justice of the Supreme Court presiding. If found guilty by a two-thirds vote of the Senate, the president can then be removed from office.

Impeachment is one of the key checks against executive abuse of power granted to Congress. Impeachment is not a step Congress takes lightly—only three presidents have had articles of impeachment brought against them (Andrew Johnson, Richard Nixon, and Bill Clinton); the Senate failed to convict either Johnson or Clinton, and Richard Nixon resigned before an impeachment vote was taken. Charges were brought by the Judiciary Committee, but Nixon was not impeached. However, talk of possible impeachment (with the votes in Congress to back it up) or charges of impeachment that fail in the Senate have the effect of chastening a sitting president who might be too aggressive in his use of power. The power to impeach can easily be used by students to meet the learning objective of illustrating the purpose of checks and balances.

Federalism: The Division of Federal and State Powers

In addition to a framework of separated powers distributed among the three branches of the federal government, the Constitution divides power geographically between the central authority of the federal government and the states. Such a division of power underscored the foundational principle of limited government by specifically enumerating the powers of the federal government and reserving other powers to the states. The creation of a federal republic also had a practical side, as it was unlikely that state delegates to the Constitutional Convention would have agreed to give up all sovereignty over their own affairs they enjoyed under the Articles of Confederation. To give up local decision making to a remote central government was a recipe for destroying the liberty of the people. The doubts raised during the constitutional debates by Anti-Federalist critics of centralized power were not entirely alleviated by the protections for liberty embedded in the federal design of the Constitution. The tensions between advocates for states' rights versus those who support a stronger role for the federal government continue to this day and are at the heart of the dynamic and changing nature of federalism over time.

Heads Up: What You Need to Know

The learning objectives that you must be able to accomplish are:

Explain how societal needs affect the constitutional allocation of power between federal and state governments.

Explain how the appropriate balance of power between federal and state governments has been interpreted differently over time.

Explain how the distribution of powers among the three federal branches and between federal and state governments impacts policymaking.

Constitutional Division of Powers

To better understand the constitutional divisions between federal and state powers, let's begin with defining the political system of federalism.

Federalism

Federalism is a form of government in which power is geographically distributed between and among a central government and various local governing entities. It allows for unified governance over issues impacting the nation, such as defense, foreign trade, treaty making, currency standardization, and international relations, while reserving policy decisions affecting local affairs to state, regional, and/or municipal government institutions. The most explicit statement of the federal nature of the constitutional government of the United States is found in the Tenth Amendment, which delegates those powers enumerated in the Constitution to the federal government and reserving all others to the states.

Heads Up: What You Need to Know

On the AP GOV exam, you must be able to explain the historical importance of federalism and its evolution over time.

Federalism is the system adopted by the Founding Fathers as the basis for the new constitutional government. The confederation model under the Articles established a government in which 13 sovereign states were loosely united in name and by agreement under the Articles of Confederation. While power was also geographically distributed in the Confederation, the distribution weighted decision-making authority to each individual state and granted few real powers to the central government. The constitutional form of federalism that replaced the Confederation shifted the distribution to give the central or federal government expanded powers and the authority to enforce the will of the federal government, if necessary. It is the fabric of the federal design that gave the new nation its strength and resiliency; however, the redistribution of power required under the Constitution set the stage for an ongoing political debate spanning the entire history of the United States. Would a stronger Union guided by federal authority come at the expense of liberty and the people's will under a states' rights system of local sovereignty?

The decentralized and asymmetrical distribution of sovereignty that was the foundation of the Articles of Confederation undermined the creation of a truly national union. With the introduction of the constitutional federal republic, a new stronger Union was initiated, but the meaning of the federal relationship between the federal government and the states has remained fluid and dynamic throughout the course of U.S. history.

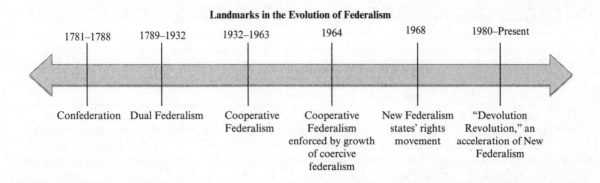

Landmarks in the Evolution of Federalism

1781–1788	1789–1932	1932–1963	1964	1968	1980–Present
Confederation	Dual Federalism	Cooperative Federalism	Cooperative Federalism enforced by growth of coercive federalism	New Federalism states' rights movement	"Devolution Revolution," an acceleration of New Federalism

The Evolution of Federalism	
1781	**Articles of Confederation** ratified. As the first government for the United States, its guiding principle was the safeguarding of liberty by ensuring state independence. This principle was ensured by a framework that created a highly decentralized federal system consisting of a federal government granted a very limited set of powers and 13 largely sovereign states.
1788	**Constitution** ratified. The revised framework of government replaced the Confederation with a federal republic of divided powers. While states retained a measure of sovereignty, ultimate authority was granted to the federal government via the Supremacy Clause (Article VI).
1791	**Bill of Rights** ratified. Included the Tenth Amendment, which underscored the federal nature of the new government by guaranteeing the exercise of constitutionally delegated powers to the national (federal) government, while reserving all others to the states. The Tenth Amendment defined a system of "dual federalism" with separate and distinct spheres of sovereignty for the federal government and the states.
1819	*McCulloch v. Maryland* decided by the Supreme Court under the leadership of Chief Justice John Marshall. In the first test case of the Supremacy Clause, the Marshall Court declared a state law to be unconstitutional, null and void, as it conflicted with a law passed by Congress under the authority of its implied powers.
1821	*Cohens v. Virginia* decided by the Marshall Court. Marshall asserted the Court's authority to review the decisions of state courts, "in all cases where a state shall prosecute an individual who claims the protection of an act of Congress." The basis of Marshall's decision, as in *McCulloch v. Maryland,* was the Supremacy Clause and was an early example of the "preemption doctrine," which allows the federal courts to intervene in state attempts to nullify federal law.
1824	*Gibbons v. Ogden* decided by the Marshall Court. Refined the definition of the Commerce Clause, drawing a clear line around the federal government's absolute authority over interstate commerce, broadening the meaning of "commerce" to include any commercial activity between two or more states, and allowing the federal government to regulate the means used to transport goods involved in interstate trade.
1833	*Barron v. Baltimore* In this case, the city of Baltimore was sued based on eminent domain and the Takings Clause of the Fifth Amendment. Barron's wharves were destroyed when the city diverted water into the harbor for construction projects in the city. The Takings Clause insists that the government can only take over private property for legitimate public use and the owner must receive compensation for the property taken. Barron argued that his property, in effect, had been taken for the benefit of public improvements and he had not been compensated for the loss of his wharves. The Supreme Court ruled against Barron since the Bill of Rights applied to the federal government only; the states (and/or municipalities like Baltimore) cannot be incorporated into its protections. This case held firm to the Tenth Amendment line between state and federal sovereignty. It was not until the Fourteenth Amendment was passed, prohibiting states from denying citizens equal protection and due process, that the states were finally incorporated into the protections provided by the Bill of Rights through the judicial process of "selective incorporation."

Continued

1933	**New Deal** initiated. In response to the Great Depression, FDR's administration launched the greatest expansion of the federal bureaucracy and its authority into the states via "grants-in-aid." The grants were designed to provide federal funds to the states, which the states, in turn, would combine with their own resources to help address the goals specified in New Deal legislation. States accepting the funds were then, and are currently, required to comply with "conditions of aid" (federal rules, regulations, and auditing requirements). Federal grants-in-aid formed the basis of "cooperative federalism" as opposed to the earlier dual system.
1958	***Cooper v. Aaron*** decided by the Warren Court. Applying the preemption doctrine, the Court rejected attempts by the state of Arkansas to defy the order to desegregate public schools with "all deliberate speed" imposed by the earlier *Brown v. Board of Education of Topeka* (1954). Demonstrated the Warren Court's determination to use the "equal protection clause" of the Fourteenth Amendment to move in defense of civil rights and racial equality against reluctant states.
1964	**Great Society,** initiated in response to President Lyndon Johnson's "War on Poverty" and the Civil Rights Movement, launched a myriad of federal programs to address equal opportunity, early childhood education, affordable housing, etc. The categorical (program-specific) grants established to address each goal of the Great Society and the federal agencies created to implement the goals and oversee the grants constituted the greatest expansion of federal authority into the states since the Great Depression and the New Deal. **Civil Rights Act** passed by Congress. Based on its interstate commerce regulatory authority as defined in *Gibbons v. Ogden,* Congress included Title II, which prohibited racial discrimination in hotels, motels, inns, restaurants, and other facilities of public accommodation. ***Heart of Atlanta Motel v. United States*** decided by the Warren Court. The decision upheld the constitutionality of Title II and a lower federal court decision imposing a permanent injunction against the Georgia motel, banning the owner's practice of racial discrimination against African American customers. These developments, taken together with use of federal **mandates** (direct orders) and **sanctions** (punitive actions against states to compel compliance with federal programs), were viewed by some critics as indicative of a new "coercive federalism" associated with the Civil Rights Movement, the environmental movement, and other forms of social engineering forced on the states by Congress using its commerce authority and by the federal courts using the preemption doctrine.
1968	**New Federalism** launched by President Richard Nixon. Nixon hoped to use "fiscal federalism" to restore clearer lines between state and federal authority exercised within the states. New Federalism introduced the idea of consolidating numerous categorical grants into a handful of **block grants** designated for broadly defined government purposes such as "community development." States could then decide which programs to fund and would administer the programs with few federal strings attached. Nixon achieved limited success with block grants, but was more successful with **revenue sharing,** a program that returned a formula-based portion of federally collected tax revenue to the states, allowing state officials to determine the best use of the money with minimal federal interference.
1981	**"Devolution revolution"** launched by President Ronald Reagan. Put renewed energy behind Nixon's New Federalism. Central to the devolution revolution was the elimination of revenue sharing and expanded use of block grants to replace categorical grants given for narrowly defined purposes. It was argued that this would return decision making to the states and reduce the size and cost of the federal bureaucracy. The devolution revolution also focused on reining back the use of the Commerce Clause by Congress and the courts as a vehicle to assert federal authority in the states.
1995	***United States v. Lopez*** decided by the Rehnquist Court. Regarded as part of the devolution revolution, the Supreme Court narrowed the definition of what constitutes interstate commerce and thereby restrained Congress' ability to regulate activities (in this case the possession of handguns) more properly reserved to the states.

The Relationship between the Federal Government and the States

Heads Up: What You Need to Know

It is important to recognize specific examples of the concepts covered on the AP GOV exam or to provide those examples in the context of your writing. Be sure you can identify exclusive, reserved, and concurrent powers when responding to questions involving the federal relationship between the federal government and the states.

Exclusive Powers

- Declare war
- Mint currency
- Maintain standards for weights and measures
- Establish a postal system
- Regulate interstate commerce
- Grant and protect patents

Concurrent Powers

- Levy and collect taxes
- Establish courts
- Regulate banks
- Borrow money
- Regulate interstate commerce
- Punish criminals

Reserved Powers

- Establish local governments
- Set up schools
- Regulate intrastate commerce
- Establish and regulate corporations
- Make laws regarding marriage and family

Exclusive Powers

Exclusive powers are powers delegated to the federal government and enumerated in the Constitution that can be exercised solely by the institutions of the federal government (Congress, the president, federal courts).

The exclusivity of powers delegated to the institutions representing the three branches of the federal government draws a clear line between federal and state sovereignty. Without this clarity, the stronger federal union the Founding Fathers hoped to achieve through the Constitution would have failed to address the problems inherent in a confederation in which the lines of authority were unclear or asymmetrical in favor of the states.

Concurrent Powers

Concurrent powers can be exercised simultaneously by both the federal and state governments. For example, Congress has the power to levy taxes on citizens of the United States, and the states (as well as counties and municipalities) also exercise this power concurrently with the federal government. This explains why citizens pay federal income taxes and often also pay state income taxes, county property taxes, and municipal sales taxes at the same time. In other words, states are just as responsible for the general welfare of their communities as the federal government is for the general welfare of the nation. Concurrent powers make this shared responsibility possible.

Concurrent powers are those that most governments exercise regardless of level. Concurrent powers provide the constitutional model of dual federalism with the flexibility to allow state and local governments to meet the needs of their communities and constituents for safety, support of the economy, and punishment of criminal behavior without interfering in the prerogatives of the federal government.

Reserved Powers

Reserved powers fall solely within the sovereignty of the states. By reserving certain powers to the states only, the Tenth Amendment preserved and guaranteed a level of sovereignty for the states to deal with their own internal affairs as the citizens of the states saw fit. Without this clarity regarding state sovereignty, in all likelihood the Constitution would not have been ratified.

Key Division of Powers Supreme Court Cases		
Supreme Court Case	Argument	Significance
McCulloch v. Maryland (1819)	Involved a lawsuit brought against the state of Maryland on behalf of the cashier of the Baltimore branch of the National Bank, James McCulloch. McCulloch refused to pay a tax imposed on the bank by the Maryland legislature and was fined $500. The lawsuit was based on the claim that Maryland's law was invalid. The Supreme Court, under the leadership of Chief Justice John Marshall, ruled in favor of McCulloch and declared Maryland's tax law unconstitutional.	This case illustrates the ongoing struggle over state vs. national sovereignty and the relationship between the states and the federal government, a debate that continued even after the Constitution was ratified. The old Anti-Federalist faction, by this time organized as the Democratic-Republican Party, had long opposed the creation of a National Bank, the brainchild of Federalist stalwart Alexander Hamilton. Centralizing economic power in a bank removed from the authority of the states was viewed as dangerous, and Federalist opponents also argued that Congress overstepped its authority by establishing a bank that the Constitution gave it no explicit power to create. Attempting to rid itself of the National Bank branch in its state, Maryland's legislature passed a law levying a tax on all banks not chartered by the state. Given that the National Bank branch was the only bank chartered outside the state, the Marshall Court viewed the law as targeting the Baltimore bank specifically, with the intent of running it out of business. As Justice Marshall famously noted, "The power to tax is the power to destroy." The Marshall decision had two significant elements: (1) The recognition of the legitimacy of implied powers as exercised under the authority of the Necessary and Proper Clause. The government was authorized to collect revenue, borrow

Supreme Court Case	Argument	Significance
		money, pay the nation's debts, and spend the revenue collected. It was certainly "necessary and proper" to establish an institution to undertake, organize, and oversee these financial responsibilities. (2) Applying authority granted by the Supremacy Clause, Marshall and his court declared Maryland's law unconstitutional, setting a precedent for the federal courts to act when state laws conflict with the objectives of federal law.
United States v. Lopez (1995)	A Supreme Court case involving the issue of gun possession on a school campus. Citing its authority under the Commerce Clause, Congress passed the federal Gun-Free Schools Zone Act in 1991. The position of the government was that violent crime in an area affects the overall economy by increasing insurance costs and limiting travel (and therefore commerce) within the affected area. It was this law that Alfonso Lopez Jr. was convicted of violating when he carried a .38 revolver onto his high school campus. Lopez appealed his conviction, with his lawyers arguing that Congress had exceeded its authority under the Commerce Clause by attempting to regulate activity on school campuses, a matter traditionally reserved for the states. The 5th Circuit Court of Appeals agreed with Lopez and reversed his conviction. The U.S. government then filed a petition for *certiorari* (a request for review by a higher court of a lower court decision). In its ruling, the Supreme Court upheld the 5th Circuit Court's ruling and imposed the first restrictions on Congress' commerce authority since the New Deal. The court identified three broad categories of activity that Congress could legitimately regulate under the Commerce Clause: ❏ The *channels* of interstate commerce (e.g., interstate highways, coastal waters, air traffic lanes) ❏ The *instrumentalities* of interstate commerce, or *persons or things* in interstate commerce ❏ Activities that substantially affect or substantially relate to interstate commerce	On the AP GOV exam, you must be able to explain how this case, as well as the McCulloch case, demonstrates the ways in which the balance of power between the federal and state governments has changed over time depending on the rulings delivered by the Supreme Court. The McCulloch ruling occurred early in the history of the republic when Federalists dominated in the government and focused their efforts on strengthening the Union through the assertion of national power. In the nearly two centuries that passed between the McCulloch ruling and the Lopez case, the federal relationship between the states and the federal government underwent a significant evolution (see "Landmarks in the Evolution of Federalism," p. 81). By the 1990s, the conservative reaction against a balance of power that they believed had tipped too much in the direction of the federal government had firmly set in. The days of the Warren Court, which endorsed a broad interpretation of federal authority used to compel states to conform to goals set at the federal level, were long gone. On the conservative-leaning Rehnquist Court sat justices, including Chief Justice William Rehnquist himself, appointed by "New Federalism" Republican presidents Nixon, Reagan, and G. H. W. Bush. The Lopez decision is viewed as an important achievement in the devolution revolution.

Chapter Review Practice Questions

The practice questions show the types of questions that may appear on the exam. Practice questions are for instructional purposes only and may not reflect the format of the actual exam. On the actual exam, some questions may be grouped into sets containing one source-based prompt (document or image) and two to five questions. The questions and explanations that follow focus on essential knowledge, the learning objectives, and political science skills.

Multiple-Choice Questions

Question 1 refers to the following excerpt.

> 2: This Constitution, and the Laws of the United States which shall be made in Pursuance thereof; and all Treaties made, or which shall be made, under the Authority of the United States, shall be the supreme Law of the Land; and the Judges in every State shall be bound thereby, any Thing in the Constitution or Laws of any State to the Contrary notwithstanding.

—Article VI, U.S. Constitution, September 17, 1787.

1. Based on the content in the excerpt and your knowledge of government and politics, which of the following political factions would have most likely supported it?

   A. Federalists
   B. Shaysites
   C. Southern elites
   D. Anti-Federalists

Question 2 refers to the following excerpt.

ACA Repeal Defeated in Senate
A vote to repeal the Affordable Care Act and replace it with a "skinny repeal" bill failed in the early morning hours of Friday, July 28.

The months of phone calls, rallies, and online advocacy, your voices were instrumental to securing this massive victory for our health care system.

How did your senators vote? Use our email tool to thank them for voting "no" or condemning their "yes" vote.

Just because the vote is over does not mean that our health care is safe.
The Trump Administration still has the ability to sabotage the Affordable Care Act in multiple ways and Medicaid cuts are still possible in states. Sign up to get the latest updates in the weeks and months ahead.

—*Families USA*, "The Voice for Healthcare Consumers," October 2017.

2. Which of the following models of democracy most accurately corresponds with the excerpt?

   A. Representative
   B. Participatory
   C. Elite
   D. Pluralist

Questions 3 and 4 refer to the following two excerpts.

Articles of Confederation and perpetual Union between the states of New Hampshire, Massachusetts-bay, Rhode Island and Providence Plantations, Connecticut, New York, New Jersey, Pennsylvania, Delaware, Maryland, Virginia, North Carolina, South Carolina, and Georgia.
I.: The Stile of this Confederacy shall be "The United States of America."
II.: Each state retains its sovereignty, freedom, and independence, and every Power, Jurisdiction, and right, which is not by this confederation expressly delegated to the United States, in Congress assembled.

—Articles of Confederation, March 1, 1781.

2: This Constitution, and the Laws of the United States which shall be made in Pursuance thereof; and all Treaties made, or which shall be made, under the Authority of the United States, shall be the supreme Law of the Land; and the Judges in every State shall be bound thereby, any Thing in the Constitution or Laws of any State to the Contrary notwithstanding.

—Article VI, U.S. Constitution, September 17, 1787.

3. According to the excerpts, which of the following highlights a clear distinction between the framework of government provided by the Articles of Confederation and that established by the Constitution?

   A. The existence of a federal judiciary branch under the Constitution did not exist under the Articles of Confederation.
   B. State laws not conforming to federal law can be preempted under the Constitution, while under the Articles, state sovereignty preempted federal authority.
   C. Federal Constitution granted all sovereignty to Congress rather than to the states in contrast to the Confederation government.
   D. The states were granted more sovereignty in the Constitution via nullification than under the Articles.

4. In which of the following Supreme Court cases did Article VI play a key role in defining the relationship between the federal government and the states?

   A. *Marbury v. Madison*
   B. *Gibbons v. Ogden*
   C. *McCulloch v. Maryland*
   D. *United States v. Lopez*

Question 5 refers to the following excerpt.

Tuesday, Aug. 21

Mr. RUTLEDGE, of South Carolina, did not see how the importation of slaves could be encouraged by this section. He was not apprehensive of insurrection, and would readily exempt the other States from the obligation to protect the Southern against them. Religion and humanity had nothing to do with this question. Interest alone is the governing principle with nations. The true question at present is, whether the Southern States shall or shall not be parties to the Union. If the Northern States consult their interest, they will not oppose the increase of slaves, which will increase the commodities of which they will become the carriers.

Mr. ELLSWORTH, of Connecticut, was for leaving the clause as it stands. Let every State import what it pleases. The morality or wisdom of Slavery are considerations belonging to the States themselves. What enriches a part enriches the whole, and the States are the best judges of their particular interest. The old Confederation had not meddled with this point, and he did not see any greater necessity for bringing it within the policy of the new one.

—*Madison Papers,* Vol. III, p. 1,388.
Recorded notes regarding debates at the Constitutional Convention, 1787; published in 1860.

5. Which of the following was NOT a point raised at the Constitutional Convention regarding the question of whether the Constitution should include provisions abolishing the slave trade?

   A. States' rights
   B. Unity
   C. The economic benefits of slavery
   D. The values of the revolutionary cause

Questions 6 and 7 refer to the following excerpt.

The picture which you have exhibited, and the accounts which are published of the commotions, and temper of numerous bodies in the Eastern States, are equally to be lamented and deprecated. They exhibit a melancholy proof of what our trans-Atlantic foe has predicted; and of another thing perhaps, which is still more to be regretted, and is yet more unaccountable, that mankind when left to themselves are unfit for their own Government.... You talk, my good Sir, of employing influence to appease the present tumults in Massachusetts. I know not where that influence is to be found; and if attainable, that it would be a proper remedy for the disorders. Influence is no Government. Let us have one by which our lives, liberties and properties will be secured,...

—Letter to Henry Lee from George Washington. Mount Vernon, October 31, 1786.

6. Based on your knowledge of U.S. government and politics, Washington's reference in his letter to Henry Lee is

   A. America's peace negotiations with the British after the Revolutionary War
   B. The Whiskey Rebellion
   C. Shays' Rebellion
   D. The Regulator Movement

7. According to Washington, what was required to effectively deal with the "commotions" and "tumults" referenced in his letter to Henry Lee?

   A. A stronger response from state governments
   B. A government empowered to enforce the law against internal rebellions and uprisings
   C. The influence of high-profile and respected leaders
   D. A greater role for Congress in protecting the general welfare

Question 8 refers to the following excerpt.

> The U.S. Capitol far in the background like an afterthought, Marjory Stoneman Douglas junior Cameron Kasky stood on a stage overlooking Pennsylvania Avenue and told a crowd stretching farther than he could see that the power to change America's gun laws lay before him, not behind. "Don't worry. *We* got this," he told the hundreds of thousands who joined the Washington March For Our Lives. "Welcome to the revolution."
>
> Students who just five weeks ago were cowering in classroom closets took command of the nation's capital Saturday, relegating members of Congress to bystanders in an event that felt like a coming-out party for the country's youngest generation. Propelled out of Parkland by the mass killing of 17 students and faculty, they promised to enlist an army of young voters to throw out lawmakers they see as unsympathetic, like Florida Sen. Marco Rubio, whom they repeatedly torched.
>
> And they brought reinforcements, sharing a massive stage with black and brown students from around the U.S. who've watched guns tear apart families and communities from Chicago to Los Angeles. Together, in a sign of the broadening scope of America's student-led gun-control movement, they came to the U.S. Capitol not to seek permission from lawmakers for an assault-weapons ban but to demand it.
>
> —David Smiley and Alex Roarty, "Washington," McClatchy News Service, *Miami Herald,*
> March 24, 2018.

8. The passage best illustrates which of the following in relation to policymaking?

   A. The relationship between government structure and the political process
   B. The effectiveness of grassroots activism in comparison to lobbying
   C. The importance of public demonstrations in achieving policy goals
   D. Federal authority over gun laws

Question 9 refers to the following image.

Source: Nate Beeler, "Obamacare Angling," *The Columbus Dispatch,* February 24, 2017.

9. Which of the following best describes what the cartoon references?

A. The ideological differences between Republicans and Democrats
B. Republican support of the devolution revolution
C. The importance of the federal government stepping in to solve a national policy crisis
D. The failure of the checks and balances system in the era of polarization

Question 10 refers to the following excerpt.

When in the Course of human events it becomes necessary for one people to dissolve the political bands which have connected them with another and to assume among the powers of the earth, the separate and equal station to which the Laws of Nature and of Nature's God entitle them, a decent respect to the opinions of mankind requires that they should declare the causes which impel them to the separation.

We hold these truths to be self-evident, that all men are created equal, that they are endowed by their Creator with certain unalienable Rights that among these are Life, Liberty and the pursuit of Happiness. — That to secure these rights, Governments are instituted among Men, deriving their just powers from the consent of the governed.

—Declaration of Independence, 1776.

10. Which of the following democratic ideals is represented in this excerpt?

    A. Popular sovereignty
    B. Pluralism
    C. Limited government
    D. Constitutionalism

Free-Response Question

1 question

20 minutes (suggested)

Directions: Write your response on lined paper. The question will not require that you develop and support a thesis statement. Use complete sentences—bullet points or outlines are unacceptable. Answer **all** parts of the question to receive full credit.

Question: Use the scenario below to answer all parts of the question that follows.

It appears from these articles that there is no need of any intervention of the state governments, between the Congress and the people, to execute any one power vested in the general government, and that the constitution and laws of every state are nullified and declared void, so far as they are or shall be inconsistent with this constitution, or the laws made in pursuance of it, or with treaties made under the authority of the United States. — The government then, so far as it extends, is a complete one, and not a confederation. It is as much one complete government as that of New-York or Massachusetts, has as absolute and perfect powers to make and execute all laws, to appoint officers, institute courts, declare offences, and annex penalties, with respect to every object to which it extends, as any other in the world. So far therefore as its powers reach, all ideas of confederation are given up and lost.

—Brutus No. 1, October 1787.

1. After reading the scenario, respond to (a), (b), and (c) below.

    (a) Describe one of the articles of the Constitution referenced in the scenario.
    (b) Explain the response in part (a) in relation to the concerns outlined in the scenario.
    (c) Explain how the Bill of Rights addressed the concerns outlined in the scenario, referencing parts (a) and (b).

Answers and Explanations

Multiple-Choice Questions

1. **A.** To answer this question, you must be familiar with the aspects of the debate between Federalists and Anti-Federalists regarding democratic participation, and you must be able to compare how models of representative democracy are visible in major debates in the United States. You must also interpret the excerpt in light of the Federalist/Anti-Federalist debates. When interpreting the excerpted text, you should recognize the faction that would have supported a strong assertion of central government (federal) authority, choice A. By making a clear claim to the supremacy of the Constitution, laws passed by Congress, and treaties negotiated and ratified at the federal level, the federal government was greatly strengthened, while the sovereignty of the states was diminished. This binding of the country together under the authority of a singular central government is what Federalists like Washington, Hamilton, and Madison viewed as essential to the survival of the United States government beyond its infancy, while Anti-Federalists (choice D) viewed it as the pathway to tyranny. The Shaysites (choice B) is a reference to those who participated in Shays' Rebellion, the 1786 Massachusetts backcountry revolt against the state government. They were not a defined political faction with an ideological message extending beyond their local dispute over taxation and farm foreclosures. Southern elites (choice C) is a socioeconomic classification rather than a political faction. Members of this group were prominent among the Anti-Federalists opposing the Constitution, so if the answer choices focused on socioeconomic classifications (e.g., New England merchants, Mid-Atlantic farmers, urban manufacturers, and Southern elites), then Southern elites would have been the correct choice.

2. **D.** This question requires that you know the different models of democracy found in representative systems like the United States and how those models are reflected in contemporary institutions and political behaviors. The answer choices require you to compare how models of representative democracy are visible in government institutions, policies, events, or debates. The correct answer describes the model that is highlighted by the content of the excerpt. While the mention of contacting senators in the excerpt might lead you to conclude that the excerpt highlights a representative model (choice A), the excerpt actually focuses on the efforts of consumers acting collectively under the banner of Families USA to influence a vote in the Senate on the Affordable Care Act. In a pluralist democracy, choice D, non-governmental groups of individuals sharing a common interest, such as Families USA, compete for access and influence to affect policy. Due to the references in the excerpt to making phone calls and attendance at rallies, one might select participatory democracy (choice B) as the correct model, but participatory democracy is defined by individual activism rather than collective activism. Choice C is incorrect because elite democracies derive their power from a limited group of individuals (usually wealthy and more educated) who influence policymaking. In the scenario, it is clear that a wider group of constituents is being implored without regard to a specific demographic (such as an elite democracy). Because Families USA is acting to organize collective activism on behalf of the ACA, pluralist democracy is the more appropriate choice.

3. **B.** This question requires you to compare the two excerpts and identify the answer choice that best explains an ideal enshrined in the Constitution—in this case, federalism. In the Articles of Confederation, Article II consists of an explicit statement claiming the "sovereignty, freedom, and independence" of the states in every "Power, Jurisdiction, and right" not delegated to the federal government. Those delegated powers were few, generalized, and vague, granting the states wide latitude to walk their own path, given the sovereignty asserted in Article II. Article VI of the Constitution

(the Supremacy Clause), on the other hand, takes on that assertion of sovereignty, directly citing "This Constitution, and the Laws of the United States…; and all Treaties made" as "the supreme Law of the Land" and binding state judicial branches to federal law regardless of laws passed by the states; therefore, choice B is the correct answer. The Articles of Confederation did not establish a judiciary branch; it was established in Article III of the Constitution. Therefore, neither of the excerpts makes reference to the judiciary (choice A). The Supremacy Clause asserts that the Constitution binds the nation together under one supreme authority so that any state law in conflict with the Constitution is null and void. It does not grant all sovereignty to Congress (choice C), allowing states to freely institute their own laws as long as those statutes remain consistent with the Constitution. The Supremacy Clause includes no provision or possibility for state nullification of federal law (choice D).

4. **C.** This question requires you to know your required Supreme Court cases and to which concepts of government and politics they apply. All the cases listed are important, precedent-setting cases and three of them are required Supreme Court cases for the AP GOV exam. However, Article VI, cited as a source document for this question, is the Supremacy Clause, which directly relates to the federal relationship between the federal government and the states. Only in *McCulloch v. Maryland*, choice C, was a state law challenging federal authority in question. In a ruling based on the federal authority granted under the supremacy clause, the Marshall Court declared a Maryland law unconstitutional. *Marbury v. Madison* (choice A) involved a ruling on the constitutionality of a law passed by Congress; it did not involve the Supremacy Clause. *Gibbons v. Ogden* (choice B) was a case in which the Commerce Clause, rather than the Supremacy Clause, was center stage. *United States v. Lopez* (choice D) involved a ruling on the federal Gun-Free Schools Zone Act and the limits of Congressional authority under the Commerce Clause and, as such, did not involve the Supremacy Clause.

5. **D.** This question requires you to recall essential knowledge about the compromises reached at the Constitutional Convention and how they were necessary for the adoption and ratification of the Constitution. John Rutledge and Oliver Ellsworth are clearly addressing the compromise on the slave trade. One a Northerner, and the other a Southerner, raised three points in their advocacy against placing any provision in the Constitution imposing an outright ban on the slave trade. Rutledge of South Carolina pointedly raised the issue of unity (choice B) and the threat of a walkout by delegates from slave-trading states by stating, "The true question at present is, whether the Southern States shall or shall not be parties to the Union." He also inserts a comment about the mutual economic benefits gained by the North and South from the institution and practice of slavery (choice C). Additionally, Ellsworth of Connecticut declared, "The morality or wisdom of Slavery are considerations belonging to the States themselves," a clear argument for retaining a level of state sovereignty within the constitutional system to assuage the concerns among Southern delegates about the slavery issue (choice A). What was not discussed at all here were the values explicitly stated in the Declaration of Independence and fought for in the revolution; therefore, choice D is correct.

6. **C.** This question requires you to know about incidents and issues leading to the Constitutional Convention and to interpret the meaning of text to explain the relationship between the framework of the Articles of Confederation and the debates about centralized federal power versus state sovereignty. Washington's reference to "commotions" in the Eastern states (from his vantage point in Virginia, Massachusetts was an Eastern state) and the "tumults in Massachusetts" are clearly references to the tax revolts in western Massachusetts led by Daniel Shays; therefore, choice C is correct. The peace negotiations with the British ending the Revolutionary War were concluded in 1783, 3 years before Washington wrote this letter to Henry Lee, eliminating choice A. The Whiskey Rebellion (choice B) began in 1791 after the Constitution was written and Washington had been elevated to the presidency. The Regulator Movement (choice D), or War of Regulation, took place in the Carolina colonies from 1765–1771 when America was still under British rule.

7. **B.** Again, this question requires you to know about incidents and issues leading to the Constitutional Convention and interpret the meaning of text to explain the relationship between the framework of the Articles of Confederation and the debates about centralized federal power versus state sovereignty. Knowing the background of Shays' Rebellion and that this uprising was one of the key incidents prompting leaders like Washington and Alexander Hamilton to call for a Constitutional Convention makes this an easy question to answer. Washington dismissed action by state governments as an exercise in futility as they, in Washington's reasoning, had already demonstrated that people are "unfit for their own Government…" (choice A). He also rejected the notion of influential leaders to affect the situation (choice C), noting the difficulty of finding those who could exert influence over Shays rebels and by stating, "Influence is no Government" (choice C). The Congress (choice D) he did not even mention as under the Articles, Congress had no power whatsoever to intervene in state affairs. He closes his argument with the assertion that the only remedy to the instability of revolts such as Shays' Rebellion was a government granted the power and authority to secure "our lives, liberties and properties"; therefore, choice B is correct.

8. **A.** This question requires you to know about the multiple access points to policymakers made possible by separating power into different branches. The excerpt highlights the grassroots activism of students and young people across the nation in an effort to shine a spotlight on the gun-control issue. Grassroots interest groups are a form of linkage institutions that use demonstrations and protests to gain media attention for their policy demands. The target of the "March for Our Lives" media-driven pressure is clearly Congress. Demonstrators are focused on voting against any sitting member of Congress who does not act to impose reasonable regulation on guns; therefore, the role of the students in the political process (e.g., elections and policymaking) and the structure of separated powers focuses their attention on the branch of government responsible for legislation, making choice A correct. While the excerpt addresses grassroots activism (choice B), it does not address its effectiveness as an alternative to lobbying. The excerpt focuses on the activism and the goals of the demonstrators but does not address tangible legislative policy outcomes (choice C). The excerpt focuses on student activism, not the level of federal authority over gun ownership (choice D).

9. **B.** This question requires you to know about the evolution of federalism over time and the grounding of ideological differences in the old Federalist/Anti-Federalist fight over "big government" or "small government" (states' rights). By the 20th century, the Democratic Party was the driving force behind the two greatest expansions of federal power and bureaucracy in U.S. history—the New Deal and the Great Society. The Republican Party, in contrast, led the charge against "big government" with Nixon's New Federalism and Reagan's devolution revolution. When Barack Obama, a Democrat, became president of the United States, his signature legislative achievement was the Affordable Care Act, or ACA ("Obamacare"), a federal program designed to ensure affordable healthcare to all Americans. The repeal of Obamacare became the centerpiece of GOP attacks against "big government" in line with the devolution revolution, choice B. The shark in the image representing Obamacare is huge and aggressive—another step in the unwanted expansion of federal authority into the states and, as such, an encroachment on the liberty of the people, according to Republicans. The elephant, the symbol of the Republican Party, is seen trying to reel in the ACA and "big government." While the big government/small government divide between the Democrats and Republicans is ideological (choice A), this statement is too broad to capture the very specific meaning of the giant ACA shark vs. the elephant in his very small boat. The cartoon does not communicate a value judgment about the

importance of the federal government tackling a national crisis such as healthcare (choice C). There is a nominal reference to checks and balances with its focus on Congressional Republicans trying to repeal the signature policy of the executive branch under Barack Obama, but that is not the central message of the cartoon (choice D).

10. **A.** This question requires you to explain the significance of foundational documents (e.g., the Declaration of Independence and the Constitution). In this case, the preamble to Jefferson's Declaration of Independence speaks of the social contract between the people and their government. He states that governments are instituted by men with their consent. This is a clear articulation of popular sovereignty, choice A, stating that, ultimately, power resides in the people. Pluralism (choice B) is a modern model of democracy, which is not addressed by Jefferson, nor was the form of democratic rule discussed. There is no explicit reference to limited government (choice C) or constitutionalism (choice D).

Free-Response Question

This concept application question asks you to interpret the information in the scenario. You must analyze the scenario to determine its meaning relative to constitutionalism.

To receive full credit of 3 points, you must address all three parts. A good response should:

- Provide a description of one of the articles of the Constitution referenced in the scenario (0–1 point).
- Explain how the response in part (a) affects the political the concerns outlined in the scenario (0–1 point).
- Explain how the Bill of Rights addressed the political concerns outlined in the scenario, referencing parts (a) and (b) (0–1 point).

Sample Student Response

Brutus No. 1, written by an anonymous Anti-Federalist in opposition to the Constitution, referenced certain parts of the Constitution. One of the articles the author talked about was Article 6, or the Supremacy Clause. The Supremacy Clause made the Constitution the ultimate law of the land within the federal system. This meant that states could not pass laws that conflicted with the Constitution. The Supremacy Clause became the basis of the preemption doctrine, which allowed the federal courts to stop states from carrying out laws declared unconstitutional because they conflict with a law passed by Congress or with a Supreme Court ruling. For example, in McCulloch v. Maryland, the Court pre-empted a Maryland law placing a tax on the Bank of the United States because the law was passed with the intent of destroying the bank, which was established under the authority of Congress.

Brutus No. 1 expressed concern about the Supremacy Clause because the author feared it gave the federal government so much power that it would be hard for states to act in defense of their people against the federal government. The author was also worried that the Supremacy Clause undermined the idea of the states organized as a confederation. The Articles of Confederation actually was federal in its design because power was geographically distributed between a central government and the states, but power was overwhelmingly weighted in favor of the states. Used to government under the Articles of Confederation, the author expressed his concern that the Supremacy Clause would give the federal government complete power to declare state laws null and void and, therefore, destroy the confederation entirely.

The only remedy most Anti-Federalists believed could fix the problem created by the Supremacy Clause and the Necessary and Proper Clause (the other clause Brutus No. 1 addressed) was to include a Bill of Rights in the Constitution. The Founding Fathers agreed to add a Bill of Rights once the states agreed to ratify the Constitution, and they kept their promise. The first eight amendments included in the Bill of Rights provide protections for the rights and liberties of the people against the abuse of power by the federal government. For example, the government cannot abridge freedom of speech, religion, or press (First Amendment) or search a person's home or personal papers without a warrant (Fourth Amendment). The Bill of Rights also included the Ninth Amendment, which said the government cannot deny any rights of the people just because they weren't listed among the enumerated amendments. In this way, the Bill of Rights addressed Brutus No. 1's concern that the states wouldn't be able to protect the people from the government. The Bill of Rights also addressed the concern that the concept of confederation would be completely destroyed by the Constitution. The Tenth Amendment acknowledged the delegated powers of the federal government to exercise authority over national affairs and at the same time established the reserved powers doctrine. Under the Tenth Amendment, the states retained sovereignty to govern in matters affecting their own citizens.

Chapter 5

Unit 2: Interactions among Branches of Government

Unit 2 explores how power among the branches is distributed and how checks prevent one branch from usurping all governmental power.

- The Legislative Branch
- The Executive Branch
- The Judicial Branch
- The Federal Bureaucracy

Overview of AP U.S. Government and Politics Unit 2

The main concepts for this chapter address the three distinct branches of the United States government and the institutions—Congress, the president, and the federal courts—that exercise the powers delegated to them in the Constitution. While separate, the branches are interconnected by a fabric of checks and balances to ensure that power and public policy are not monopolized by any one branch.

The four main College Board content outlines for Unit 2 are as follows:

- **The legislative branch.** The republican ideal in the U.S. is manifested in the structure and operation of the legislative branch.
- **The executive branch.** The presidency has been enhanced beyond its expressed constitutional powers.
- **The judicial branch.** The design of the judicial branch protects the Supreme Court's independence as a branch of government, and the emergence and use of judicial review remains a powerful judicial practice.
- **The federal bureaucracy.** The federal bureaucracy is a powerful institution implementing federal policies with sometimes questionable accountability.

AP U.S. Government and Politics Key Concepts

Success on the exam depends on your ability to make connections to the key concepts as described in the content outlines of *AP U.S. Government and Politics Course Framework*. Remember that these concepts highlight the fundamental ideas that every student should take with them into the AP GOV exam and beyond.

Use the chart that follows to guide you through what is covered in Unit 2. The information contained in this chart is an abridged version of the content outlines with topic examples. Visit https://apstudent.collegeboard.org/apcourse/ap-united-states-government-and-politics for the complete updated AP GOV course curriculum framework.

AP U.S. Government and Politics Key Concepts (Unit 2)	
Key Concept	**Content**
Big Idea 1: Constitutionalism **The republican ideal in the U.S. is manifested in the structure and operation of the legislative branch.**	The Senate is designed to represent states equally, while the House is designed to represent the population. Different chamber sizes and constituencies influence formality of debate. Coalitions in Congress are affected by term-length differences. The enumerated and implied powers in the Constitution allow the creation of public policy by Congress (passing the federal budget, declaring war, and enacting legislation). By design, different powers and responsibilities of the Senate and House affect policymaking. Chamber procedures, rules, and roles impact policymaking (chamber and debate rules, roles of the Speaker of the House or president of the Senate, filibuster, cloture, holds and unanimous consent in the Senate, roles of the Rules Committee and Committee of the Whole, and treaty ratification). Congress must generate a budget that addresses both discretionary and mandatory spending. Pork barrel legislation and logrolling affect lawmaking. Congressional behavior and governing are influenced by ideological divisions, gerrymandering, redistricting, elections that have led to a divided government, and role conceptions of "trustee," "delegate," and "politico."
Big Idea 1: Constitutionalism **The presidency has been enhanced beyond its expressed constitutional powers.**	Presidents use powers and perform functions of the office to accomplish a policy agenda. Formal and informal powers of the president include vetoes, foreign policy, bargaining/persuasion, executive orders, and signing statements. The potential for conflict with the Senate depends on the type of executive branch appointments (cabinet, ambassadors, or White House staff). Justifications for a single executive are set forth in Federalist No. 70. Term of office, constitutional-power restrictions, and the passage of the Twenty-Second Amendment demonstrate changing presidential roles. Perspectives on the presidential role continue to be debated. The communication impact of the presidency can be demonstrated through modern technology, social media, nationally broadcast State of the Union messages, and the president's bully pulpit.

Key Concept	Content
Big Idea 1: Constitutionalism **The design of the judicial branch protects the Supreme Court's independence as a branch of government, and the emergence and use of judicial review remains a powerful judicial practice.**	The foundation for powers of the judicial branch and how its independence checks the power of other institutions and state governments are set forth in Article III, Federalist No. 78, and *Marbury v. Madison* (1803). Precedents and *stare decisis* play important roles in judicial decision making, and ideological changes in the Supreme Court due to presidential appointments have led to establishing new or rejecting existing precedents. Controversial or unpopular Court decisions can lead to challenges of the Court's legitimacy. Political discussion about the Court's power has caused an ongoing debate over judicial activism versus judicial restraint. Restrictions on the Supreme Court are represented by congressional legislation, constitutional amendments, judicial appointments, the president and states evading (or ignoring) Court decisions, and legislation impacting jurisdiction.
Big Idea 4: Competing Policymaking Interests **The federal bureaucracy is a powerful institution implementing federal policies with sometimes questionable accountability.**	Tasks performed by departments, agencies, commissions, and government corporations are represented by writing/enforcing regulations, issuing fines, testifying before Congress, and issue networks and iron triangles. Political patronage, civil service, and merit system reforms all impact the effectiveness of the bureaucracy by promoting professionalism, specialization, and neutrality. Discretionary and rule-making authorities to implement policy are given to bureaucratic departments, agencies, and commissions. Oversight and methods used by Congress to ensure that legislation is implemented as intended are represented by committee hearings and the power of the purse. As a means to curtail the use of presidential power, congressional oversight serves as a check on executive authorization and appropriation. Presidential ideology, authority, and influence affect how executive branch agencies carry out goals of the administration. Compliance monitoring can pose a challenge to policy implementation. Formal and informal powers of Congress, the president, and the courts over the bureaucracy are used to maintain its accountability.

Study Questions

Glance through the study questions before you start the review section. Take notes, highlight questions, and write down page number references to reinforce your learning. Refer to this list as often as necessary until you feel comfortable with your knowledge of the material.

1. How does the Senate represent states equally, while the House represents the total population? (Hint: The number of senators and House representatives differ.)

2. What is the practical difference between enumerated power and implied powers in the Constitution in regard to public policy creation by Congress? (Hint: Passing a federal budget vs. declaring war and maintaining the armed forces.)

3. How do the structure, powers, and functions of both houses of Congress affect the policymaking process? (Hint: Chamber reliance on committees, chamber-specific rule making, pork barrel legislation, and logrolling.)

4. How is congressional behavior influenced by the election processes, partisanship, and a divided government? (Hint: Congressional ideological divisions, gerrymandering, lame-duck presidents, and differing conceptions of constituent accountability.)

5. How does the president implement a policy agenda? (Hint: Use of informal and formal powers, including vetoes and pocket vetoes, bargaining, and issuing executive orders.)

6. How can the president's agenda create tension and frequent confrontations with Congress? (Hint: Executive branch appointments, Senate confirmation hearings, and policy initiatives.)

7. What is judicial review and how does it check on other institutions and state governments? (Hint: Article III of the Constitution, Federalist No. 78, and *Marbury v. Madison*.)

8. How can other branches of government limit the Supreme Court? (Hint: Congressional legislation, amendments, appointments and confirmations, and the president evading Court decisions.)

9. How does bureaucracy carry out the responsibilities of the federal government? (Hint: Writing and enforcing regulations, testifying before Congress, issue networks, and iron triangles.)

10. How does the president ensure that executive branch agencies carry out their responsibilities? (Hint: Presidential ideology and compliance monitoring.)

Important Terms and Concepts Checklist

This section is an overview of the terms, concepts, ideas, documents, and court cases that specifically target the AP GOV exam. Additional vocabulary is also included to aid in your understanding.

As you review the material covered in this chapter, remember that the required foundational documents and required Supreme Court cases (see the Appendix) are noted among the key academic terms, concepts, and language.

Note the abbreviations in the table that follows:

RFD – Required Foundational Documents
RSCC – Required Supreme Court Cases

As you study the terms and concepts, simply place a check mark next to each and return to this list as often as necessary to check your understanding. After you finish the chapter review section, reinforce what you have learned by working through the practice questions at the end of the chapter. Answers and explanations provide further clarification into perspectives of U.S. government and politics.

Term/Concept	Big Idea	Study Page	Term/Concept	Big Idea	Study Page	Term/Concept	Big Idea	Study Page
Appointment Power	CON	p. 124	House of Representatives	CON	p. 104	Patronage	PMI	p. 148
Article III	RFD; CON	pp. 133–134	Iron triangle	PMI	pp. 147–148	Political party leadership	CON, PMI	p. 105
Baker v. Carr	RSCC; CON	p. 120	Issue networks	PMI	p. 148	Politico	PMI	p. 106
Bicameral Congress	CON	p. 103	Judicial activism	CON	p. 140	Pork barrel spending	CON	p. 110
Civil service	PMI	p. 148	Judicial decision making	CON	pp. 139–140	Precedent	CON	p. 139
Cloture	CON	p. 109	Judicial restraint	CON	p. 140	President of the Senate	CON	p. 105
Committee of the Whole	CON	p. 116	Judicial review	CON	p. 138	Rules Committee	CON	p. 116
Discharge petitions	CON	pp. 116–117	Lame-duck president	CON	p. 124	*Shaw v. Reno*	RSCC; CON	p. 121
Discretionary spending	PMI	p. 115	Logrolling	CON	p. 110	Speaker of the House	CON	p. 105
Disproportionate representation	CON	pp. 103–104	Mandatory spending	PMI	p. 115	*Stare decisis*	CON	p. 139
Federalist No. 78	RFD; CON	p. 133	*Marbury v. Madison*	RSCC; CON	pp. 138–139	Trustee	CON	p. 106
Filibuster	CON	p. 109	Merit system	PMI	p. 149	Twenty-Second Amendment	RFD; CON	p. 123
Gerrymandering	CON	p. 119	Necessary and Proper Clause	CON	p. 107	Unanimous consent	CON	p. 110

Chapter Review

The information discussed in this chapter covers the constitutional system of checks and balances, the three U.S. branches of government and their relevance to political ideologies and party lines, and the federal bureaucracy. While the judiciary must remain decidedly neutral in political opinion, party lines and ideologies strongly guide both the legislature and the president. Over time, a variety of factors have led government branches to hold both great strengths and considerable weaknesses.

Overview of the U.S. Branches of Government

The Founders who attended the Constitutional Convention to draft a new plan of government (also referred to as the Framers) had to structure a system that would prevent any one branch of government from holding absolute power and control. The Constitution was designed with three branches to separate power: legislative (Congress), executive (president), and judicial (courts). Each branch checks the other to retain a balance of power as set forth by the three constitutional articles. Specific powers are granted to each branch, with congressional powers described in Article I, expressed powers of the president described in Article II, and the federal judiciary powers described in Article III. The diagram that follows illustrates the separation of each of these government powers.

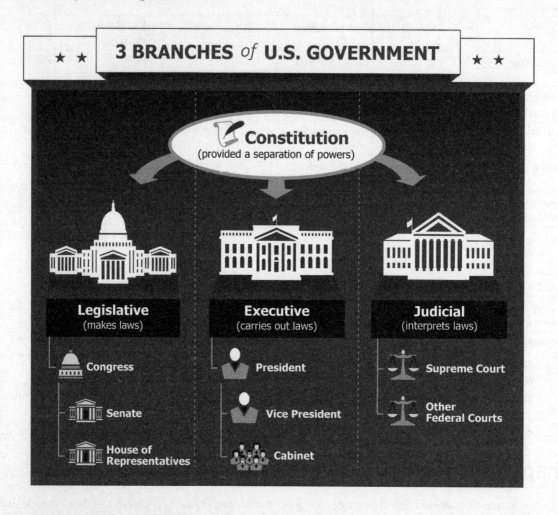

3 BRANCHES *of* U.S. GOVERNMENT

Constitution
(provided a separation of powers)

Legislative (makes laws)	Executive (carries out laws)	Judicial (interprets laws)
Congress	President	Supreme Court
Senate	Vice President	Other Federal Courts
House of Representatives	Cabinet	

TEST TIP: When considering any viewpoint of American government, remember to think like our Founding Fathers. Politics never occurs in a vacuum and is intended to guide our political leaders and branches of government. Although each branch of government has its own responsibilities through separation of powers, look for connections that are relevant through checks and balances. For example, the president can veto a bill passed by Congress, but Congress can override the veto with a two-thirds vote of both houses of Congress. In addition, Congress can pass a law (with the president's approval), but the Supreme Court can declare the law unconstitutional.

The learning objectives that you must be able to accomplish are:

Describe the different structures, powers, and functions of each house of Congress.

Explain how the structure, powers, and functions of both houses of Congress affect the policymaking process.

Explain how congressional behavior is influenced by election processes, partisanship, and divided government.

The Legislative Branch

Congress

The U.S. Congress as established by the Constitution describes a legislative branch of government that is composed of a *bicameral* (two houses) legislative body. The two chambers or houses are designated as the **House of Representatives** and the **Senate.**

The History of Congress

Why didn't the Framers of the Constitution decide on a single-chambered Congress instead of creating the House and Senate as separate entities? While the colonists rebelled against the sovereignty of the British government, they did not totally reject the British legislative model. The Founding Fathers modeled the U.S. government after the British government. The British Parliament had the House of Commons and House of Lords, one representing the interests of the common people and the other representing the interests of the aristocracy. It is important to note that the legislative **bicameral Congress,** like the other two branches of government, engenders the foundational principle of checks and balances. The Framers understood that by not vesting absolute power in either the House or the Senate, the legislature would resist the lure of tyranny. The appointed Senate of elites, akin to the aristocracy in the House of Lords, would act as a check on the majoritarian impulses of the popularly elected House and vice versa.

Why was the creation of a bicameral Congress important? The Framers wanted to establish a bicameral Congress that would adequately address the concerns of a wide range of people across varying states. In fact, the Great Compromise, a resolution introduced at the heated debates of the Constitutional Convention in 1787, was a decision based on ensuring adequate state representation.

The Articles of Confederation (ratified in 1781) called for a Congress of the Confederation, which was a *unicameral* body (one legislative chamber) that granted each state equal representation. Although this sounded great in theory, such a scheme made for **disproportionate representation;** that is, some states like Massachusetts had a much larger population than Georgia, for example. Further, each state also reserved a veto over each state's action. Should a small state be able to overturn the will of a much larger population residing elsewhere in the nation? Thus, a bicameral Congress was created with one chamber in which representation was proportionate to the population in each state (the House of Representatives) and one in which the voting power of each state was equal (the Senate) and capable of acting as a check on the will of the majority as expressed in the House. Again, balancing power was the key to the constitutional design. Thus, a bicameral Congress, while maintaining the republican principle of representative democracy, also balanced state power and provided a check against a tyranny of the majority.

The Organization of Congress

Before we discuss the function and powers of Congress, let's take a look at the organization, leadership, member roles, and committee system.

Organization of Congress		
	House of Representatives	**Senate**
Size	**435 members (based on district populations).** The apportionment of representatives is allotted to each state based on its population, as determined by the official U.S. Census, conducted every 10 years. House members are directly elected by their constituencies and have been since 1789. Although the size of the House has grown to meet population demands, the Reapportionment Act of 1929 fixed the number of total House members at 435. In 1964 the Supreme Court ruled in *Wesberry v. Sanders* that these districts follow the *one-man, one-vote principle;* consequently, each of the single-member districts apportioned to the states must be substantially equal in the size of their population.	**100 senators (2 from each state).** Originally, members of the Senate were appointed by their respective state legislatures. This method of selecting senators lasted until 1913. During the great wave of Progressive reform in the early 19th century, the Seventeenth Amendment (1913) was passed requiring direct election of senators by voters in their home states.
Elected term	Representatives serve **2-year terms** with no imposed term limits. <u>All</u> House seats are up for election every 2 years.	Senators serve **6-year terms** with no imposed term limits. The terms are staggered; that is, every 2 years, roughly one-third of the total 100 seats are up for grabs. Elections for Senate seats for each state occur in different cycles to ensure continuity of representation in the chamber; i.e., every state always has at least one senator who is veteran to the chamber and is current on ongoing policy debates and the legislative agenda. If a vacancy in a Senate seat occurs, that state's governor appoints a replacement to fulfill the 6-year term, thus maintaining the staggering of election cycles and continuity of representation.
Qualifications	Prospective members of the House of Representatives must meet three criteria: (1) must be at least 25 years old, (2) must be a U.S. citizen for at least 7 years, and (3) must be a resident of the representative state at election time.	Similar to the number of qualifications outlined by the Constitution for the House, senators must meet three qualifications: (1) must be at least 30 years old, (2) must be a U.S. citizen for at least 9 years, and (3) must be a resident of the representative state at election time.

TEST TIP: Be aware of the wording of test questions regarding the Constitution. Look out for the use of "in the original Constitution," which means <u>before</u> any of the amendments were passed. If a question using this wording addresses Congress, remember that senators were appointed rather than being popularly elected, reflecting the Framers' distrust of the popular will. The Progressive Era of the early 20th century emphasized extending democratic participation in the political arena, resulting in the Seventeenth Amendment establishing popular election of senators and the Nineteenth Amendment extending the vote to women.

The Leadership of Congress

Leadership of Congress		
Role	House of Representatives	Senate
Leadership	❏ **Speaker of the House** presides over the House, acting as the administrative head of the chamber and leader of the majority party. ❏ The Speaker is nominated by the House majority party. ❏ The Speaker establishes and maintains order within the chamber and recognizes speakers. ❏ The Speaker appoints special committees and can remove committee chairs. ❏ The Speaker determines the agenda and confers with legislative leaders and negotiates with members of the executive branch.	❏ The vice president of the executive branch is the **president of the Senate.** ❏ The vice president does not vote (except to break a tie) to maintain the principle of separation of powers. ❏ The vice president presides over joint sessions of Congress. ❏ The vice president has historically presided over regular proceedings, but in recent history is often absent while addressing additional duties as assigned by the president. ❏ In the event of the vice president's absence, the **president pro tempore** presides. This role is traditionally granted to the longest-sitting member of the Senate in the majority party.
Political party leadership	❏ Party leadership roles are represented by **floor leaders** who are elected by secret ballot within their own party caucus. ❏ The majority party retains the Speaker of the House role. ❏ The minority party retains the minority leader role. ❏ The minority leader provides campaign assistance, presents the party agenda, and develops strategies to advance party initiatives and interests. ❏ Party **whips** serve as lieutenants to the floor leaders, keeping track of voting on legislation currently before the chamber, stepping in to "whip up" support for legislation that the party supports when the necessary votes are lacking.	❏ The **senate majority leader** in a legislative body is from the political group with the most voting members. ❏ The senate majority leader is the main spokesperson for the Senate. ❏ The senate minority leader in a legislative body is from the political group with the least number of voting members. ❏ Both party representatives manage legislative and executive business. ❏ Party **whips** serve identical roles to whips in the House of Representatives.

Note: The only constitutionally mandated leadership positions are Speaker of the House and the president pro tempore of the Senate, and neither is designated as a party leader. Remember, political parties are not mentioned in the Constitution as a mandated part of the government structure. The designation of these two positions as party leaders and the additional leadership apparatus were imposed by the parties in Congress to organize and advocate for their party agendas.

The Roles of Congressional Representatives

Members of Congress have two primary responsibilities: to legislate (make laws) and perform oversight of the executive branch and its agencies to ensure that laws are being implemented and administered as intended. Through the course of their terms, members also respond to constituent concerns and educate the public through various forms of media, town hall meetings, and other communications with constituents. The degree to which congressional members take on certain roles, activities, appointments, and committees may depend on their personal style of representation—trustee, delegate, partisan, or politico.

Key Terms about the Style of Congressional Representatives

Trustee. Trustees are legislators who base their vote on personal judgments and ideological alignments. Trustees rely on facts and political-philosophical tenets to guide their voting; they are not easily swayed by public opinion or their respective constituencies unless there is a strong political consensus on an issue within their district. (Representatives cannot completely ignore the will of those who elect them!)

Delegate. Delegates are legislators who base their vote on how they think people in their district (or state) would want them to vote. Instead of being guided by personal or ideological beliefs, delegates literally advocate for the "will of the people." Delegates take seriously the fact that they have been elected for a specific purpose and set out to accomplish that purpose based on constituents' concerns.

Partisan. Partisans believe they must always vote along political party lines. Loyalty to the political party is of the utmost importance.

Politico. Politicos are a combination of a trustee, delegate, and partisan. Politicos are inclusive and always consider constituent concerns, political party lines, and personal opinions, ideologies, and philosophies. In this way, politicos act as true politicians. They vote in ways that are politically expedient and, ultimately, personally beneficial.

> TEST TIP: On the AP GOV exam, the term *oversight* commonly appears in questions. In government, the term refers to "congressional oversight." Oversight is one of the functions of Congress to review, monitor, and investigate the activities and policies of federal agencies, including the executive branch of government. Though the Constitution does not specifically mention oversight, it was implied: "Legislators are not only legislators, but they possess inquisitorial powers" (George Mason, August 7, 1787).

The Powers of Congress (Article 1, Section 8)

The scope of congressional powers is enumerated in the Constitution: Article I, Section 8. On the AP GOV exam, you should be familiar with two important terms—*explicit* (stated in the Constitution) and *implicit* (not directly stated in the Constitution). Explicit powers define the limitations placed on powers to be exercised by the institutions of the national government. Implicit powers exist because the Framers included the Necessary and Proper Clause in Article I, Section 8, in anticipation of the ever-changing circumstances and needs surrounding public policy. Clearly, no one could anticipate every action that might have to be undertaken by Congress in either the immediate or far-distant future to "raise and maintain an army and navy," "promote science," or "regulate foreign and interstate commerce." That implicit powers do indeed exist, and that Congress has the authority to use them, was endorsed emphatically in 1819 by the Supreme Court in *McCulloch v. Maryland*. Think of explicit powers as the "broad" powers enumerated in Article I, Section 8, and implied powers as "specific" powers that make it possible for Congress to carry out its constitutional responsibilities.

Explicit Powers	Implied Powers
Enumerated in the Constitution	Necessary and Proper Clause

Explicit powers (also called *expressed powers*) are the 27 enumerated powers written in the Constitution. Some examples include:

- The power to establish and collect taxes and tariffs
- The power to coin money and regulate its value
- The power to borrow money
- The power to regulate foreign and interstate commerce
- The power to create naturalization laws and bankruptcy laws
- The power to create post offices and federal courts lower than the Supreme Court
- The power to raise an army and navy
- The power to promote science and the arts (copyrights and patents)

Implied powers are implicit powers that are not directly stated in the Constitution, but are suggested by those powers stated in the Constitution and endorsed by the Necessary and Proper Clause. Under the implied powers doctrine, Congress has the power to make reasonable deductions about specific actions needed to carry out its expressed powers.

Heads Up: What You Need to Know

On the AP GOV exam, you should be familiar with the **Necessary and Proper Clause** (elastic clause).

The clause was problematic for the Framers of the Constitution, especially for the Anti-Federalists, who contended that this clause essentially granted the government limitless power. Alexander Hamilton and James Madison argued against the Anti-Federalists and claimed that without the Necessary and Proper Clause, Congress would be helpless to resolve issues beyond those that were immediately clear during the Constitution's drafting.

The Necessary and Proper Clause has helped to enact legislation that addresses a wide range of economic, environmental, and social issues, but it is unsurprising that a number of Supreme Court cases have arisen over the years regarding this contentious congressional right. Notable examples of Supreme Court cases for the AP GOV exam are *McCulloch v. Maryland,* and *Lambert v. Yellowley.*

Examples of the Powers of Congress

This section provides selected examples of the powers of Congress to use on your AP GOV free-response essays.

The congressional process of raising revenue. Under Article I, Section 7, sometimes referred to the **origination clause,** the House retains the right to begin the revenue-raising process. Much like other powers that the House reserves, this does not mean that the Senate is uninvolved with the process. In fact, the Senate oftentimes sends revisions to the proposed amendments set forth by the House until a compromise is reached. Once that compromise is reached, though, the bill is sent off to the president to sign.

The congressional process of coining money. Under the Articles of Confederation, both the states and the Confederation Congress had the power to coin money. Practically unsustainable, the Constitution determined that Congress must reserve the sole right to coin money. Unique from the Articles, Congress was also given the right to regulate both the value of coins issued domestically and the value of coins distributed internationally. Understandably, the vagueness of the right to coin money has caused controversy about the types of coinage Congress can authorize. Questions about the utilization of paper or metal have often been debated.

> **Did you know?** Prior to the Civil War, Congress did not "coin" paper money. Paper notes were used as a type of verification of money owed or a bill. It was not until the passage of the **Legal Tender Act** (1862) that *greenbacks* (dollar bills) were considered a form of money. Throughout the 19th century, the Supreme Court heard a number of cases about the paper money controversy. With growing inflation, however, it is almost impossible to imagine a world in which literal coins are the only form of monetary exchange within the U.S.

The congressional process of declaring war and maintaining armed forces. The Constitution divides war powers between the legislative and executive branches. Under Article I, Section 8, Congress has the sole power to declare war. However, according to Article II, Section 2, the president is the armed forces commander in chief. The waging of war, once declared by Congress, falls firmly under the purview of the president. Congress has ceded its power to declare war to a succession of presidents since the end of World War II. U.S. troops have engaged in military operations throughout the world at the direction of the executive branch, most notably in Korea, Vietnam, and, more recently, Afghanistan and Iraq.

It was the Vietnam War that brought the issue of expanded executive control over military operations to a head by the 1970s. Starting with President Kennedy's commitment of Special Forces to act as advisers in Vietnam, escalating to the use of ground troops by President Johnson under the authority of the **Gulf of Tonkin Resolution,** Congress finally took action to restrain executive war-making after President Nixon expanded the war beyond the borders of Vietnam. The Gulf of Tonkin Resolution granted the president unlimited authority to take military action in Southeast Asia against the threat of Communism. With increasing public protest against a war that had no conceivable end in sight, Congress passed the **War Powers Act** in 1973. Passed to restore a role for Congress regarding the assertion of American military power across the globe, it grants to the president, as commander in chief of the military, the power to commit troops anywhere in the world for 60 days with a requirement to inform Congress of the action within 48 hours of its commencement. Thereafter, Congress can vote to extend the military action for an additional 60 days, or it can refuse to extend the troop commitment and within 30 days troops must return home.

The Act has proven to be ineffective, as a succession of presidents have ignored it, arguing that congressional interference in war-making collides with the executive's authority as commander in chief. The nature of modern warfare, including the nuclear threat and terrorist actions, which require rapid response and secrecy, has tended to support executive war-making without the cumbersome processes of Congress being involved. The **Authorization to Use Military Force** granted to President George W. Bush in the wake of the 9/11 terrorist attacks in 2001 once again gave the president unlimited authority to wage war, this time against terrorism anywhere in the world.

The remaining check on the president's war-making power is through Congress' constitutional control over military funding. However, once troops are in the field, Congress is usually reluctant to pull funding that might undermine the military's efforts and put troops in the field at risk; hence, this power has also been ineffective in curbing executive authority over war-making.

Concerning Congress's maintenance of the armed forces, states are allowed to maintain their own respective militias (National Guard units), but this ability to self-maintain is done as a secondary power endowment. Congress' right to engage and "federalize" the National Guard to suppress disorderly circumstances supersedes the states' right to governance of their own armed forces.

> **TEST TIP:** The issue of war powers appears frequently on the AP GOV exam, so make the effort to understand how those powers have evolved over time, shifting the balance of power toward the executive branch.

The Legislative Process

Now that we have discussed the legislative power of Congress, let's cover the topics related to the legislative and non-legislative process of policymaking.

- Legislative key terms
- Legislative policymaking: "How a bill becomes a law"
- Legislative House and Senate rules
- The federal budget
- The legislative committee system
- Legislative divisions
- Reapportionment
- Non-legislative function of Congress

Key Legislative Terms

Before we discuss the process of how a bill becomes a law, let's cover some important Senate and House key terms.

Senate Legislative Key Terms	
Term	**Definition**
Filibuster	A filibuster is a strategy that senators use to prevent action on a bill or nomination. Originally, during a filibuster, senators made long speeches on the *Senate floor* (Senate meeting room in the U.S. Capitol) in order to block or postpone an action on a proposed bill. Today, the act of making extended speeches is rare. Senators can merely call for a filibuster and all action stops unless a cloture vote successfully brings the filibuster to a close (see below). The filibuster was designed with the deliberative nature of the Senate in mind, allowing minority interests to slow down the legislative process and encourage more consideration of a proposed bill. Today, in practice, Senate majority leadership uses the filibuster in a partisan manner to stop the opposition's legislation from moving forward, hoping their majority will allow them to survive a cloture vote.
Cloture	Cloture is an action that allows the Senate to break a filibuster, given a three-fifths majority vote. The cloture rule (Rule 22) was adopted in 1917 as a way to stop endless opposition to a bill moving forward for a vote. In 1975, the Senate voted to alter the required two-thirds majority to three-fifths majority. Even still, cloture has not always been effective, as it can be difficult to attain a majority vote.

Continued

Term	Definition
Hold	A hold is the practice of allowing one or more senators to block a motion on the Senate floor. Although holds are informally communicated to the Senate's floor leader, the floor leader is not obligated to adhere to the senator's wishes. Still, holds can be very effective and often signal in advance that a senator may call for a filibuster.
Unanimous consent	Unanimous consent is also called *general consent*. On the Senate floor, a senator may request a unanimous consent to expedite the legislative process by passing the need for formal votes if no opposition to a proposed motion or resolution exists. Requests that seek to disrupt the Senate floor's schedule or infringe upon the rights of another senator are not usually vocalized.

Source: Dave Granlund. "Senate Filibuster Rules Change." November 22, 2013.

House Legislative Key Terms	
Term	**Definition**
Pork barrel spending	Pork barrel spending is often associated with another legislative term, **earmarks.** During the process of finalizing bills before they go to the floor for a vote, legislators "earmark" funds for projects in their home districts. Pork barrel spending has become controversial in recent years, blamed for rising deficits in the federal budget. However, this type of spending has been an integral part of the legislative process for decades, not only returning benefits from Washington back to home districts, giving the people tangible evidence of Washington working for them, but also in winning support for a given piece of legislation through logrolling.
Logrolling	Logrolling is an understanding among two or more Congress members who make an advance agreement to vote for one another's bills. These legislators trade votes to pass bills that often include earmarks that benefit their districts. This usually means the Congress member exchanges an unimportant legislative vote for one that is meaningful to him or her.

Did you know? *Pork barrel*, *earmarks*, and *logrolling* have their origins in America's rural past. Before refrigeration, pork was often stored in barrels with layers of fat and salt preserving the meat. The fat represented the richest ingredient in the barrel and, thus, became a metaphor for giving away the riches of the government in the form of funding for pet projects back home. As for earmarks, these were notches cut into the ears of livestock, including hogs (in keeping with the pork metaphor), to indicate ownership, date of birth, or other information. Earmarks on congressional legislation note an amount of money, where it is going, and for what project. Logrolling references a practice among neighbors of agreeing to help each other clear land to build their homes by rolling logs.

Legislative Policymaking

The primary purpose of Congress is to enact proposed **legislation** (bills). For a proposed bill to be passed, the House and Senate must confer, debate, and enact legislation. Only one version of a bill can be forwarded to the president for signature; a bill debated, amended, and passed by each chamber must be identical. Because House members are elected every 2 years and senators are elected every 6 years, House members are more likely to consider the most pressing issues of their respective constituencies and are more heavily influenced by public opinion. While the Senate is also concerned with public opinion when considering policy, it often contemplates the long-term effects, ramifications, and outcomes of legislation.

Although the two congressional chambers have varying responsibilities and scopes of power, for a bill to pass, the House and Senate must act in a cooperative, collaborative manner rather than as independent legislating bodies. If a bill does get through the intensive negotiation process, it makes its way to the office of the president, who can either officially sign the bill into law, or veto it, sending it back to Congress for revision. The president does not reserve absolute power to veto a law. A two-thirds majority in Congress can advance a previously vetoed bill, at which point it becomes the law of the land.

The simplified illustration that follows shows the steps that must be taken before a bill becomes law. Notice that legislative action begins with an initial idea that anyone can present for approval, but for a bill to be signed into law, both congressional chambers must approve the exact wording—there is no deviation. While theoretically anyone can come up with an idea for a bill, it is important to note that the majority of legislative initiatives begin in the White House with members of the president's party in Congress translating these initiatives into legislation, which is then placed in the "hopper" for consideration by the House or introduced directly to members on the floor in the Senate.

HOW DOES A BILL BECOME A LAW?

1 EVERY LAW STARTS WITH AN IDEA

That idea can come from anyone, even you! Contact your elected officials to share your idea. If they want to try to make it a law, they will write a bill.

2 THE BILL IS INTRODUCED

A bill can start in either house of Congress when it's introduced by its primary sponsor, a Senator or a Representative. In the House of Representatives, bills are placed in a wooden box called "the hopper."

3 THE BILL GOES TO COMMITTEE

Representatives or Senators meet in a small group to research, talk about, and make changes to the bill. They vote to accept or reject the bill and its changes before sending it to:

the House or Senate floor for debate or to a subcommittee for further research.

Here, the bill is assigned a legislative number before the Speaker of the House sends it to a committee.

4 CONGRESS DEBATES AND VOTES

Members of the House or Senate can now debate the bill and propose changes or amendments before voting. If the majority vote for and pass the bill, it moves to the other house to go through a similar process of committees, debate, and voting. Both houses have to agree on the same version of the final bill before it goes to the President.

DID YOU KNOW?

The House uses an electronic voting system while the Senate typically votes by voice, saying "yay" or "nay."

HOUSE MAJORITY SENATE MAJORITY

5 PRESIDENTIAL ACTION

When the bill reaches the President, he or she can:

✓ **APPROVE and PASS**
The President signs and approves the bill. The bill is law.

THE BILL IS LAW

The President can also:

Veto
The President rejects the bill and returns it to Congress with the reasons for the veto. Congress can override the veto with 2/3 vote of those present in both the House and the Senate and the bill will become law.

Choose no action
The President can decide to do nothing. If Congress is in session, after 10 days of no answer from the President, the bill then automatically becomes law.

Pocket veto
If Congress adjourns (goes out of session) within the 10 day period after giving the President the bill, the President can choose not to sign it and the bill will not become law.

Legislative House and Senate Rules

On a day-to-day basis, the House and the Senate convene to discuss policy and bills that may become laws. Since the Constitution forbids either house to meet outside of the U.S. Capitol building, its members convene in separate chambers. During the House and Senate legislative sessions, the general rules and procedures for considering bills may be different.

Compare and Contrast House and Senate General Rules	
House of Representatives	**Senate**
The Rules Committee determines special rules, which then determine whether a bill is introduced to the floor and under what conditions it may be debated. For example, a closed rule sends a bill to the floor for a vote but does not allow for any debate.	A unanimous consent dictates legislation considerations.
Does not invoke holds.	Individual senators can hold a measure, preventing it from being raised.
Debate time is limited.	The Senate debate time is unlimited; defined as a "deliberative body," the Senate is supposed to discuss and debate a bill at length.
Committee control over the content of a bill is nearly absolute. The initial **mark-up** of a bill consisting of amendments and language changes occurs in committee.	Senate committee consideration of a bill is not mandatory. Bills are often introduced directly to the floor for debate and amendment. Once initiated, committee consideration of a bill can be more easily stopped.
Speaker of the House determines order of consideration for bills on the floor.	Rulings from leadership can be opposed.
Speaker of the House recognizes which members of the House can speak.	The Senate presiding officer wields far less power in allowing senators to speak.
Debates can be ended by a majority vote.	Debate can be held up by a **filibuster,** an attempt to "talk a bill to death." Unique to the Senate, filibusters support the role of the Senate as a deliberative body. Filibusters slow down the debate process and invite further consideration on a bill. Filibusters can only be ended by a **cloture** vote (Rule 22), allowing a bill to move forward to the floor for final consideration.
Concludes at end of day.	The Senate recesses, instead of "ending" or "adjourning." The legislative days on the calendar can be ongoing.

The Federal Budget

The federal budget is central to congressional policymaking. The fiscal decisions and funds generated by the federal budget influence many legislative actions. Congress has gradually refined its procedures for developing the federal budget over the years. In the 20th century, laws were passed to create federal agencies like the **Office of Management and Budget** and the **Congressional Budget Office**, which were established to oversee and regulate the federal budget.

Key Facts about the Federal Budget

To understand congressional politics and the federal budget, let's discuss the president's role in the federal budget and a few of the key 21st-century budget-related challenges.

The president's role in the federal budget. The executive branch of government does not have a constitutionally defined role in the budgeting process, but the president does work with Congress to initially provide budget requests. The president works with the Office of Management and Budget (OMB) to identify and report on his budget priorities. After forwarding White House budget requests to Congress, the House and Senate committees on the budget develop concurrent resolutions that reflect their own budget priorities for 20 broadly defined functions such as national defense, agriculture, transportation, veterans services, and net interest. Budget resolutions are not legislation and therefore are not given to the president for his signature; they are passed on to the House and Senate Appropriations committees to make decisions about where funds should be allocated. In reality, no single budget bill is passed by Congress; instead, individual appropriations bills for the various functions, once agreed to by both houses of Congress, are sent on to the president for signature.

The challenges of passing the federal budget in the 21st century. In the 21st century, passing the federal budget has become a politically charged debate among members of Congress. The budget proposes the government's expenses for each year, but if Congress does not agree on the budget, it can lead to a *government shutdown* (non-essential federal government services are frozen). The reason for congressional debates about spending is the ballooning federal **debt.** The federal budget is mostly financed by tax revenue, but the shortfall between revenue and proposed government spending—the **deficit**—is paid for by government borrowing. Year after year, the annual budget deficit adds to the accumulated debt.

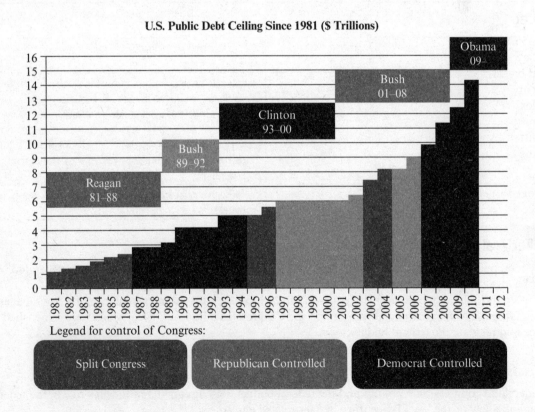

U.S. Public Debt Ceiling Since 1981 ($ Trillions)

Heads Up: What You Need to Know

On the AP GOV exam, you should be familiar with two types of government spending: mandatory spending and discretionary spending.

Mandatory spending. This type of spending refers to budgeted funds that must be put aside for certain programs, such as Social Security, Medicare, and Medicaid, established by law and that provide services to those who meet the eligibility requirements. No appropriations are required since spending on these programs is dictated by the number of citizens who meet the eligibility standards rather than congressional discretion. Net interest paid on the national debt is also mandatory.

Discretionary spending. To understand discretionary spending, it is first important to understand discretionary revenue. Discretionary revenue is the amount of income that remains after all mandatory spending is funded. Hence, discretionary spending is considered non-essential spending. As expenditures increase, the government has three options: cut programs, increase taxes, or borrow. Budget resolutions and appropriations bills address discretionary spending, the largest proportion of which goes to the military and defense.

The Legislative Committee System

The 435 members of the House and 100 members of the Senate must make decisions covering a broad range of policy areas such as agriculture, the environment, national security and foreign intelligence, energy, the federal budget, science and technology, the armed services, and more. Over 10,000 bills addressing the various policy areas are introduced in Congress every session. Because of the high volume of bills to consider and complexity of legislative issues they address, the committee system has become essential to the work of Congress. By breaking legislative consideration up by subject matter, bills can be assigned to the appropriate committee, thereby making the legislative process more efficient. Every member of Congress serves on standing committees (usually two) and on subcommittees within their larger standing committee assignments.

On the AP GOV exam, you should be familiar with the three main types of congressional committees that carry out the legislative, investigative, oversight, and internal administrative responsibilities of Congress. Note: Most committees assign subcommittees to accomplish specific tasks, draft reports and bills, and hold hearings.

The Legislative Committee System		
	House of Representatives	**Examples**
Standing committees	Permanent legislative committees often referred to as "subject matter committees." These committees consider bills and make recommendations.	Agriculture, Appropriations, Energy and Commerce, Armed Services, Education and the Workforce, Ethics, Homeland Security, Housing, Transportation and Infrastructure, Veterans Affairs, Banking and Finance, Housing and Urban Affairs
Joint committees	Permanent legislative joint-task committees consisting of members from both the House and the Senate. Joint committees often perform housekeeping tasks and conduct studies, rather than consider legislative bills. A *conference committee* is a temporary joint committee that drafts compromises to help resolve differences between versions of House and Senate bills when they arise.	Economics, Taxation, Solvency of Multiemployer Pension Plans, Library, and Budget and Appropriations Process Reform

Continued

	House of Representatives	Examples
Select committees	Temporary legislative committees that address a specific investigation or study outside the scope of the standing or joint committees. The Senate sometimes uses the term *special committee* instead of select committee.	Aging, Ethics, Indian Affairs, and Intelligence Note: Former investigative committees include the Watergate Committee and the Iran-Contra Committee.

Key Facts about the Legislative Committee System

The House. At present, there are 21 congressional committees, 20 standing committees, 1 select committee, and 95 subcommittees. The Budget, Ethics, and House Administration committees are not subdivided into smaller committees. The Speaker of the House can create ad hoc select committees; this is usually reserved for times when an issue is so fragmented or overlapping that no one standing committee has purview. Committees have more impact on final legislation than floor debates.

The Senate. At present, there are 16 permanent Senate committees, known as *standing committees,* and 4 joint committees. Temporary committees can be formed if needed. Committees oversee the confirmation or rejection of presidential nominees, but most legislation is introduced directly to the floor, where it is debated and amended. Consequently, committees do not have the same legislative importance that they do in the House.

The House Rules Committee. The **Rules Committee** is one of the oldest-standing committees, dating back to 1789. The Rules Committee determines debate rules, establishes floor order, oversees special rules, and manages original matters of jurisdiction. It is sometimes called the Speaker's Committee because it is through the Rules Committee (dominated by majority party members at a ratio of 2 to 1) that the Speaker controls activity on the floor. There are two types of jurisdiction matters: **original jurisdiction** and **special orders.** Original jurisdiction matters are administrative in nature, involving proposed changes to the rules that guide the processes and procedures under which House membership operates. By far, most of the Rules Committee's time is spent on special orders that address the consideration of legislation. Under this jurisdiction, the committee issues **special rules** that set the terms and conditions under which legislation can be debated. Special rules include *open rules,* which allow 5 minutes for debate and are permitted during any amendment; modified open rules, which have minor restrictions on otherwise open rules; structured rules, which entail parameters that allow strict consideration of certain amendments and debate restraints; and closed rules, which disallow consideration of any amendments. The committee can also refuse to grant a rule, at which point the legislation in question is considered dead.

The Committee of the Whole (House). Quite literally a committee of the Whole House or all 435 members, but a quorum of only 100 members is required to proceed. The Committee of the Whole was originally designed to take under its consideration bills on the Union Calendar; that is, any bills that raised revenue (taxes) or appropriated money. Over time, so many bills involved expenditures that the majority of bills ended up on the Union Calendar in the modern Congress. The decision to resolve into the Committee of the Whole is usually made when members want to work out problems or discuss issues involved in a bill without the constraints of procedural rules. Once the committee reports its conclusions (an amended bill or a report of no progress) to the Speaker of the House, the Committee of the Whole is dissolved and normal order is resumed.

Discharge petitions (House). Used after a bill has been referred to a committee and 30 days have passed without the bill being reported out to the floor for consideration. Committee chairs, at the request of House leadership, can refuse to put a bill on their committee's agenda, thereby killing it. Under these conditions a House member can file a motion to have a bill released (discharged) from consideration by the committee.

For a discharge petition to pass, the member must convince a majority of the House, or a total of 218 members, to sign. Should the petition acquire the minimum 218 signatures, the House reviews and debates the motion to discharge before a vote. Should the vote support the discharge, the bill will be removed from committee consideration. While discharge petitions have been invoked successfully in the past, they are rare, as members do not want to be a target of retribution by the leadership. When a discharge vote is threatened, the leadership often moves the legislation in question forward to avoid the embarrassment of public rebuke.

Legislative Divisions—a Divided Government

Political party unification is ultimately required to achieve common legislative goals, but it has become increasingly difficult for opposing political parties to come to an agreement to pass legislation. This section will discuss the legislative political party and executive branch divisions that make it difficult for bills to become laws.

Legislative Political Party Divisions

Political party divisions have played a principal role in preventing bills from becoming laws, resulting in **legislative gridlock.** In accordance with the Constitution, either chamber can initiate a bill, but once passed, the bill must go on to the other chamber, where it can be accepted as is, rejected, or the second chamber can pass its own version of the bill, at which point a conference committee consisting of members from both chambers convenes to work on a compromise bill. The drawing of a hard party line casts the different political and ideological priorities of the opposition on the other side of that line, thus hampering the ability of members to resolve their conflicts and find a compromise. Compromise is difficult and time-consuming in the best of circumstances, but it becomes particularly problematic in the current era of polarization and hyper-partisanship. When the major parties are polarized and a situation exists in which one party holds the majority in one chamber of Congress while the opposition party controls the other chamber, it often becomes difficult to pass a bill into law in one house let alone two.

Congressional Productivity

Laws enacted by each Congress through September 22 of final year of its 2-year term, by type. Congress still on track to be among the least productive in recent history.

	Ceremonial	Substantive
113th 2013–2014	41	124
112th 2011–2012	49	125
111th 2009–2010	80	157
110th 2007–2008	133	190
109th 2005–2006	91	190
108th 2003–2004	93	210
107th 2001–2002	61	163
106th 1999–2000	68	206
105th 1997–1998	36	201
104th 1995–1996	33	167

Legislative and Executive Divisions

The executive branch can also be divided along party lines from the legislative branch; that is, when one political party (either Republican or Democratic) controls the executive branch (president) and the other political party controls Congress (the House and/or the Senate). Historically, the government has been united with the same political party controlling both the executive and legislative branches of government. However, in the late 20th century, a **divided government** became the norm, not the exception, frustrating presidents during this era in their pursuit to achieve policy goals and priorities. While it is impossible to pinpoint whether shifting ideologies impact election outcomes or vice versa, political scientists do agree that larger numbers of independent voters and split-ticket voters are contributing factors, leading to a politically divided government. On the positive side, divided government can force a president to compromise with the opposition in Congress to get legislation passed. However, divided government can also mean bitter fights over legislation, leading to an increase in presidential vetoes and congressional attempts to override those vetoes. Further, in a hyper-partisan political era like the current one, presidents can be plagued with congressional investigations launched by the opposition. While these investigations can focus on legitimate wrongdoing (e.g., the Watergate and Iran-Contra hearings), they are often nuisance investigations that do not lead to evidence of improper conduct by the president or executive branch officials, take up a tremendous amount of time in Congress, and divert the chief executive's time and attention away from achieving his policy goals.

Key Examples of Executive and Legislative Branch Divisions

The Nixon administration (1969–1974). The investigation of wrongdoing by Republican President Richard Nixon's reelection committee in 1968 and the subsequent cover-up by White House officials, including the president, became known as the Watergate Scandal. The investigation of the burglary of the Democratic National Committee headquarters located in the Watergate Hotel set the events of the scandal in motion. Congress was controlled by the Democratic Party, and the party leadership took the opportunity to convene the Senate Watergate Committee in 1973, with Sam Ervin (Dem., North Carolina) serving as chair. Eventually, under considerable pressure and the threat of impeachment, Nixon resigned. Vice President Gerald Ford succeeded to the presidency, and the Democrats maintained control of Congress. President Ford found himself opposing much of the Democratic congressional agenda, vetoing 48 bills, 12 of which the Democrats were successful in overriding.

The Reagan administration (1981–1989). President Ronald Reagan's Supreme Court nominee, Robert Bork, was rejected by the Democratic majority in the Senate, despite being considered by many within the legal and judicial community to be a capable candidate. Reagan pooled support for his nominee among Republicans and conservative Southern Democrats, but could not overcome the Democratic majority, and Bork failed to win confirmation.

The Clinton administration (1993–2001). During the 8 years that President Bill Clinton was in office, Congress was divided. This caused a government shutdown in 1995 and 1996 over the federal budget and funding for Medicare, education, the environment, and public health. In 1998, a highly partisan Senate investigation of Clinton and his wife, Hillary, over a failed land deal in Arkansas led to over 50 hearings over the course of a year and the taking of depositions from over 250 witnesses. The investigation yielded no evidence of wrongdoing. At the same time, a special prosecutor was appointed to continue investigating the Clintons, which eventually led to another scandal involving the president's relationship with a young White House intern. The Republican-controlled House voted to impeach Clinton for lying under oath to a federal grand jury about his relationship with the young woman, but he was later acquitted.

Reapportionment

The AP GOV exam will ask you to be familiar with important concepts related to congressional reapportionment, redistricting, and gerrymandering.

Reapportionment involves the constitutionally mandated redistribution of House seats to account for population changes determined by the decennial census (Article I, Section 2). Every state's population is viewed relative to that of the others. Those experiencing an overall population increase gain seats, while states with declining numbers lose seats. Beyond consideration of the makeup of the House, this has important implications for the Electoral College, as each state is granted electoral votes equal to the number of their House seats, plus their two senators.

Redistricting involves the drawing of congressional district boundaries within a state after reapportionment is completed. Boundaries should account for shifts in the population so that districts are relatively equal in size. Although this responsibility was not mandated to the states in the Constitution, the process was turned over to the states in 1929.

Gerrymandering is an intentional process whereby congressional district boundary lines are redrawn to ultimately benefit one political party or one voting bloc in an election. If one group or party dominates a state legislature, it has the advantage of drawing district boundaries to benefit itself. The purpose of gerrymandering is to create **safe seats** that suppress voter turnout among the opposition and discourage potential qualified opponents from entering the race, factors that amplify the imbalance in electoral outcomes. It is accomplished by one of two methods or a combination of both. **Packing** is the drawing of boundaries so that voters within a given bloc are concentrated into as few districts as possible to ensure that surrounding districts are "safe." **Cracking** refers to the drawing of district boundaries so that given voting blocs are broken up and distributed throughout several districts in which their votes are too few to have an impact. Is it possible for voters in one group or party to be in the majority in a state overall but end up with a minority of representatives in a legislative body? By using packing and cracking, it certainly is! Critics often argue that a ban on gerrymandering would (1) make every House election more competitive and create a higher level of voter interest and turnout, and (2) provide fair representation in the one-man, one-vote tradition.

> **TEST TIP:** Students should be able to discuss the details of reapportionment and why it is controversial more than 200 years after the process was first initiated. Much of the controversy stems from the Reapportionment Act of 1929, which fixed the number of House seats at 435. The problem with holding the number of House seats constant at 435 is that population growth has substantially exceeded the Framers' expectations that each representative would act on behalf of 30,000 to 60,000 constituents. Today, the district population represented by House members in some states can exceed 900,000, while the people in other states may have anywhere from 500,000 to more than 800,000 residing in their districts. This *malapportionment* results in a proportionally larger voice in the House for some states than for others and has the same effect on the Electoral College. It is a fundamental challenge to the notion of equal representation and the principle of one man, one vote. The problems associated with gerrymandering also stem from the Reapportionment Act of 1929, which left the drawing of state congressional district boundaries to politically motivated state legislatures.

Source: Phil Hands, "How Gerrymandering Would Work in Sports."
Wisconsin State Journal, Tribune Content Agency, 2017.

Key Reapportionment Supreme Court Cases		
Supreme Court Case	**Argument**	**Outcome**
***Baker v. Carr* (1962)**	**Question.** Can the Supreme Court decide questions of legislative districting? **Argument.** Baker was a resident of Shelby County, Tennessee, who challenged Secretary of State Carr because the state's General Assembly districts were required to be substantially equal in population, and yet the state had not redrawn its boundaries since 1901, despite significant demographic changes within the state. Tennessee's refusal to redraw these districts resulted in disproportionate representation in the General Assembly for sparsely populated white rural districts. Baker argued that urban Shelby County, with 10 times more residents than rural districts, was underrepresented. The Supreme Court had long adhered to the political questions doctrine, which allows the Court to deny a hearing in cases involving purely political matters rather than an issue requiring interpretation of the law. The Court injecting itself in political questions that are more appropriately resolved legislatively violates the separation of powers. Was the fairness of the redistricting process a purely legislative matter or was there a legal issue at stake?	**Court ruling.** Yes, the Fourteenth Amendment's Equal Protection Clause guarantees equal representation to all citizens. Baker raised legitimate questions on this basis, and therefore the Court viewed the case as *justiciable* (qualified for a judicial hearing). **Significance.** In ruling that the questions Baker raised in his lawsuit were not at all political, the Court reformulated the political questions doctrine and in addition, created the *one-man, one-vote* standard for legislative redistricting; that is, each individual must be weighted equally in matters of redistricting. *Baker v. Carr* became the *stare decisis* case for all questions of redistricting and opened the floodgates for lawsuits challenging both state and federal legislative redistricting plans in nearly every state of the Union.

Supreme Court Case	Argument	Outcome
Shaw v. Reno (1993)	**Question.** A U.S. District Court ruled that a challenge to racially gerrymandered districts in North Carolina contained no constitutional claim. An appeal was filed to the Supreme Court, which was asked to decide if the lawsuit in question had a legitimate constitutional claim under the Fourteenth Amendment's Equal Protection Clause. **Argument.** Five white North Carolina residents argued that their state's redistricting plan violated the Fourteenth Amendment right to equal protection (see *Baker v. Carr*) by creating a **majority-minority district** in which African Americans were the majority. The initial redistricting plan had included only one majority-minority district, but this plan was rejected by Attorney General Janet Reno as an inadequate attempt to comply with provisions of the Voting Rights Act. (It is important to note that while North Carolina had a significant population of African Americans, it had not had a single African American elected to the House of Representatives since the 1890s.) The appellants argued that by amending the original plan to include a second majority-minority district in which African Americans were the majority, the General Assembly created a new district that failed to adhere to the contiguous and compact standards for drawing legislative districts; therefore, it constituted an illegal gerrymander to segregate voters based on race.	**Court ruling.** Yes, North Carolina violated the Fourteenth Amendment's Equal Protection Clause by creating a racially gerrymandered district. **Significance.** In noting the "bizarre" boundaries of North Carolina's second majority-minority district, the Court ruled that redistricting based on race must be held to a standard of strict scrutiny under the Equal Protection Clause, while at the same time ensuring, per the Voting Rights Act, that legislative bodies (or special commissions) doing redistricting are conscious of race to avoid the historical diluting of voting strength and representation for minority groups through the practices of cracking and packing. In other words, gerrymandering to ensure fairness and equality for minorities whose voting rights had been historically violated is constitutional as long as such racially gerrymandered districts pass a strict scrutiny test (i.e., the creation of such districts meets a compelling governmental interest such as compliance with the Voting Rights Act).

The Non-Legislative Function of Congress

Beyond Congress' fundamental legislative function is the non-legislative constitutionally mandated functions of oversight and investigation. Congress reserves the right to monitor and investigate the executive branch of government. To accomplish this weighty task, congressional committees oversee the work and activities of the president and of the entire executive branch, which includes the massive federal bureaucracy consisting of executive departments and agencies. Oversight is a vital element in the system of checks and balances, allowing Congress to ensure that actions to implement public policy and legislative actions that are taken by the president or the executive departments and agencies remain legal, are in line with legislative policy goals, and conform to constitutional limitations placed on executive authority. Oversight can include the investigation of the president preliminary to possible charges of impeachment if alleged presidential wrongdoing qualifies as a high crime, a misdemeanor, treason, or bribery. The House and Senate can also use their oversight authority to remove federal judges and other individuals serving in a federal capacity, if necessary.

In addition to their constitutionally mandated functions (legislating and oversight), members of Congress represent their *constituents* (the people who elected them to office). Congress' bicameral structure is designed to ensure adequate representation of each state to guard against any one state having absolute, functional power over another state. Because every congressional member represents a unique constituency, the elected representative is charged with the responsibility of defending the concerns of the district or state. Topics of concern can range from healthcare, education, energy, economy, employment, environment, transportation, affordable housing, immigration, gun safety, taxes, or small and large business regulations.

Did you know? Under the Constitution, House members can have other members expelled with a two-thirds vote. While this is an uncommon practice, it has occurred five times since the House's inception.

The Executive Branch

The executive branch of government consists not only of the presidency, but also the executive departments represented in the cabinet (e.g., the Department of Agriculture, the Department of Defense, the Department of Energy) and all the agencies that implement public policy under the auspices of those departments. The role of the United States president is the head of the vast federal apparatus of government, the chief executive, and the commander in chief of the armed forces who issues directives for federal policies, federal budgets, and federal laws.

Heads Up: What You Need to Know

The learning objectives that you must be able to accomplish are:

Explain how the president can implement a policy agenda.

Explain how the president's agenda can create tension and frequent confrontations with Congress.

Explain how presidents have interpreted and justified their use of formal and informal powers.

Explain how communication technology has changed the president's relationship with the national constituency and the other branches.

History of the Executive Office of President

The size, scope, and influence of the presidential administration has significantly changed over the course of U.S. history. The role of the president today is very different from the role of a president in the 18th century. For example, our first president, George Washington (1789–1797), did not even belong to a political party, but over time, political party affiliations have become commonplace.

In its earliest days, the presidency only exerted influence over national emergencies, but in recent years the role of the president has expanded to meet the increased complexities of social, economic, and foreign affairs; for example, modern-day economic crises like the Great Depression of the 1930s and the economic collapse of 2008, the world wars of the 20th century, and the 9/11 terrorist attacks. Such events have served to solidify the presidential authority as a powerful institution, rather than as just a representative head of the government.

Source: The official seal of the office of the president.

President's Term of Office

In between the 2-year terms for elected members of the House of Representatives and the 6-year Senate terms lies the presidency, which has a 4-year term of office. Although there were originally no constitutional limits placed on the number of terms a president could serve, George Washington served two terms (8 years) and then retired from public life. Presidents thereafter followed Washington's precedent and left office after two terms. To every rule there are exceptions, and this proved to be true of the two-term tradition. Theodore Roosevelt ran for a third term and lost in the election of 1912, and his distant cousin Franklin D. Roosevelt not only ran successfully for a third term, but also extended his election winning streak to capture a fourth term.

Source: Clifford K. Berryman, "Anti-Third Term Principle," October 1, 1912. *U.S. Senate Collection Center for Legislative Archives.*

Given the tumultuous nature of the Great Depression, FDR lifted the morale of a badly shaken nation. The collective support of the president, who truly seemed to care about the welfare of the people, easily led to his reelection in 1936. The people's support did not waiver as the president faced the looming threat of Nazism in Europe and Japanese militarist expansion in the Pacific, leading to his election to a third term in 1940. By 1941, the U.S. entered World War II, and unwilling to abandon the leader who brought the country through so much, the Democratic Party turned to FDR once again, nominating him for a fourth term. Though FDR won the election of 1944, suffering from congestive heart failure, he succumbed within days of embarking on his 13th year as president.

Although FDR was a widely beloved figure who enacted tremendously positive societal change and led the country through some of its darkest hours, Republicans moved quickly upon the heels of his death to introduce the **Twenty-Second Amendment,** limiting the presidency to two terms. The amendment was officially ratified and adopted into the Constitution in 1951. To make provision for the possibility of a vice president succeeding to the presidency after the midway point of his predecessor's term, the amendment allows for a full two terms, and places a limit of a combined 10 years on holding the office of the presidency.

TEST TIP: On the AP GOV exam, it's important to be familiar with the term "lame duck." After a November election and a new president-elect is chosen, the sitting president is considered a *lame duck*; that is, he loses his political clout and ability to persuade as all the focus and media attention is on the incoming president. Lame-duck status applies both to presidents who are at the end of their second term and particularly to those who fail to win reelection to a second term, a signal of vanishing political support even among former followers—e.g., presidents Jimmy Carter and George H. W. Bush.

Executive Powers

The office of the president has always retained certain powers under the Constitution, including formal or enumerated powers, implied powers, and informal powers.

Presidential Powers Informal and Formal Authority		
Power	Type	Detail
Removal power	Formal	The president can remove appointees without conferring with Congress.
Appointment power	Formal	The president has a broad range of appointment power allowing for selection of key officials subject to the confirmation of the Senate. The presidential appointment power includes nominating cabinet secretaries, the heads of executive agencies, judges on the federal bench, and justices to the Supreme Court.
Veto	Formal	According to Article I of the Constitution, the president has the constitutional power to *veto* (reject) legislative proposals. As discussed in the previous section, for a bill to become law, the president must sign it. If the president does not sign a bill, it will become law without a signature after a 10-day period. George Washington and other presidents in the early years of the republic deferred to the principle of legislative supremacy and rarely if ever lifted their veto pens. Over time, as they exerted more executive power, presidents like Grover Cleveland (414 vetoes), Franklin Roosevelt (635 vetoes), and Harry Truman (250 vetoes) vetoed considerably more legislation. **Regular veto.** The president can veto any bill before it becomes law, sending it back to Congress within 10 days of receiving the bill. After receiving the rejected bill, Congress can override the president's veto with a two-thirds vote from each chamber. **Pocket veto.** A pocket veto cannot be overridden. If the president receives a bill and is unable to return the bill to Congress during the 10-day period because Congress is adjourned, the bill cannot become law because it lacks the president's signature and Congress' formal objections. Pocket vetoes are part of an ongoing congressional debate about what qualifies as "adjournment."

Power	Type	Detail
Foreign policy	Formal and informal	**Formal.** The president is the commander in chief who presides over the armed forces and can ratify treaties given Senate approval. **Informal.** The president can freely negotiate with international officials leading to treaties between the United States and foreign countries or, in some cases, executive agreements between the president and another head of state. In this role, the president acts as the nation's chief diplomat.
Bargaining and persuasion	Informal	The president has the power to persuade and the power to bargain. Informal powers include the president's power to leverage status of office and influence public opinion through what is referred to as the **bully pulpit.** The bully pulpit is most effectively utilized by presidents who are likeable, trusted, and charismatic. FDR, for example, often resorted to the public airwaves in his famous "fireside chats" to rally the people behind his programs.
Executive orders	Implied formal	The president can modify major policy measures by issuing orders that impact implementation. They do not carry the force of law because only Congress can legislate; therefore, executive orders are only binding during a president's term in office. A newly elected president can allow executive orders issued by previous administrations to stand or can rescind them. Congress can attempt to pass laws contravening an executive order, but the president would likely veto such a law. Executive orders are also subject to judicial review. There is no remedy for the president if his executive orders are ruled by the Court to be unconstitutional.
Signing statements	Formal	Form of communication from the president on the occasion of signing a bill into law. Signing statements are essentially the president's commentary on a bill, often raising objections to certain provisions of a law or raising constitutional issues regarding some of the content of a bill. They are viewed as a guide to executive agencies regarding how the president wants the law to be implemented. The frequency of signing statements and their extensive length in recent years has raised objections about the extent to which signing statements seek to modify the meaning of a statute, and therefore violate the principle of separation of powers.
Pardoning	Formal	According to Article II of the Constitution, the president has the power to grant pardons and reprieves for federal (not state) offenses made against the United States.

Heads Up: What You Need to Know

On the AP GOV exam, it's important to be familiar with the term **executive privilege.** It means that the president (and other executive branch officials) can resist subpoenas demanding confidential communications and information issued by either the legislative or the judicial branch. Despite no explicit mention of executive privilege in the Constitution, the Supreme Court ruled that in principle the privilege is implied by the separation of powers doctrine. In other words, in order for the executive branch and members of the administration to do their job, free from interference by either of the two other branches, sensitive communications must be kept confidential.

However, executive privilege is not absolute. As a result of a special prosecutor's investigation into the Watergate scandal, seven of Nixon's closest aides were indicted. When Nixon defied a subpoena from the special prosecutor demanding tapes of conversations held in the Oval Office involving these aides, he claimed the tapes were protected by executive privilege. In the *United States v. Nixon* (1974), the Court again endorsed the constitutionality of executive privilege, but ruled that neither separation of powers nor confidentiality were undermined by keeping conversations among administration officials involving conspiracy and underlying crimes privileged. Preference must be given to "the fundamental demands of due process of law in the fair administration of justice." Similarly, when Clinton aides were called to testify during the Monica Lewinsky scandal, Clinton claimed executive privilege to block their testimony, but a federal judge rejected the president's argument and the aides were ordered to testify.

Organization of the Executive Branch

Article II of the Constitution establishes presidential powers but does not provide directions for the day-to-day tasks of the executive branch of government. The Opinion Clause of the Constitution, however, does refer to the "principal officers in each of the executive departments," suggesting that the president may appoint executives so that important decisions are not made alone.

The following departments and agencies help the president perform a wide range of advisory tasks, including policymaking formation, acting as legislative liaisons, supervising the budget, hiring personnel, and overseeing press relations. Executive heads and their staff work tirelessly to form working partnerships with various government agencies, Congress, interest groups, and the press.

- The White House staff
- The executive office of the president (EOP)
- The president's cabinet
- U.S. ambassadors
- Federal judges, Supreme Court justices, federal attorneys, and federal marshals

The White House Staff

The White House staff has grown in size and scope since its early formation in the 1700s. Before World War II, in the late 1930s, an executive management committee recommended sweeping changes to the White House, stating, "The president needs help." At the time, there were only about 30 staff members, and now there are about 600 White House staff members.

The role of the White House staff is to advise, inform, and implement decisions that demonstrate the president's views about major policies and issues. In general, staff members meet with and confer with the president every day, but the president's chief of staff is responsible for the overall functioning of White House operations. The chief of staff also serves as the administration's spokesperson and legislative negotiator. A few presidents have elected to not select a chief of staff, including Franklin Roosevelt, Harry Truman, and Jimmy Carter in the first years of his presidency.

Unlike cabinet members, the White House staff does not go through a Senate nomination or confirmation process. Staff members are personally appointed by the president and reflect the president's tone and style. Many are selected based on personal loyalty to the president. Some have played important roles in the election campaign and some have had long-time prior relationships with the president. Most staff members are not accountable to Congress, and it is common for the White House staff members to come into conflict with congressional members who pride themselves on being elected to serve based on merits rather than on their presumed loyalty.

Heads Up: What You Need to Know

Students should be familiar with the two models for organizing a White House staff: the hierarchical model (known as pyramid) and the circular model (known as hub and spokes).

The **hierarchical model** functions with a chief of staff in place. Access to the president is controlled by the chief of staff. This model, favored by Ronald Reagan, makes for greater efficiency, as the demands on a president's time and attention on any given day are innumerable. To prioritize for the president and maintain focus on critical issues, the chief of staff decides who gets into the Oval Office to speak directly to the president and acts as a filter for information that reaches the president's desk. The downside of this model is that an unelected official unaccountable to the people is given tremendous power over what the president hears or does not hear, reads or does not read, and sees or does not see, potentially blocking out important facts or points of view that the president should consider.

The **circular model** favored by Franklin Roosevelt, Harry Truman, and Jimmy Carter functions without a chief of staff, allowing everyone on the White House staff access to the president. This avoids excessive filtering of information reaching the president and allows for a free-flow of ideas for the president to consider regarding specific issues. Ultimately, the person elected by the people prioritizes who has access to the Oval Office. This model, too, has its problems; at times it lends itself to a chaotic approach to policymaking and, unless the president has a strong sense of his responsibilities, to getting weighed down with the day-to-day minutiae of White House activities. Another important drawback is that the circular model encourages "group think." Access to the president means power, and to avoid being shut out of access, staffers around the president will tend to agree with him instead of raising important questions that he should consider.

The Executive Office of the President

Established by Franklin D. Roosevelt in 1939, the executive office of the president comprises a variety of federal administrative agencies that work directly with the White House. The three most important agencies are

- The Office of Management and Budget
- The National Security Council
- The Council of Economic Advisers

The President's Cabinet

Cabinet members are part of an advisory group selected by the president. Members serve as personal advisors and consultants who answer to the president. The cabinet includes 15 executive department heads, including:

Attorney general	Secretary of housing and urban development
Secretary of state	Secretary of agriculture
Secretary of education	Secretary of labor
Secretary of defense	Secretary of energy
Secretary of health and human services	Secretary of transportation
Secretary of the treasury	Secretary of veterans affairs
Secretary of homeland security	Secretary of commerce
Secretary of the interior	

In recent years, the vice president has been included in meetings of the cabinet.

The U.S. president is elected from one of the two major political parties (Democratic or Republican) and appoints the executive cabinet and the heads of agencies that make up the federal bureaucracy based on the party's established agenda. Thus, it is not surprising when cabinet officials carry out policies that align with the president's goals. It is important to note that this is not always the case, however. The executive departments are made up of lifelong civil servants who will continue in their positions long after a president is out of office. Bureaucratic resistance to dramatic changes in personnel, policies, and procedures can hamper a president's agenda if the officials he or she places in charge of the executive departments and their agencies act without regard for the experience, expertise, and advice of career bureaucrats. Members of the cabinet often have to walk a fine line between loyal service to a president's agenda and their own loyalty to the people who work for them and help the executive departments function.

While the president personally selects cabinet members, appointees must be confirmed by the Senate. Following a vote to recommend confirmation from the appropriate committee (e.g., the president's nominee for secretary of the treasury must be questioned by the Senate Banking and Finance Committee), a vote is taken on the floor. If the majority of senators agree to confirm the nominee, then that nominee is sworn in and installed in the president's cabinet. The only two positions within the cabinet exempt from the confirmation process are the vice president and the chief of staff.

Did you know? In 1989, President George H. W. Bush nominated U.S. Senator John Tower to assume the role of secretary of defense. Tower, who was notable for having opposed the Civil Rights Act and Voting Rights Act of the 1960s, also gained a reputation for excessively indulging in alcohol and engaging in other nefarious activities. During Tower's confirmation hearings, many Republicans and Democrats questioned the senator's personal integrity, citing that the FBI was formally investigating his suspicious activities. Although the FBI did not find Tower guilty, the Senate's investigation revealed that Tower had accepted more than $1 million over 2 years for having advised several defense contractors. Senators were rightly concerned that his formal dealings presented a conflict of interest. With a final tally of 53 to 46 against Tower, Tower's appointment was rejected by the Senate. The president, however, did not allow the Senate to influence his opinion of Tower, and Bush decided to appoint him as the chairman of the Foreign Intelligence Advisory Board, which did not require a confirmation vote from the Senate.

U.S. Ambassadors

Ambassadors serve "at the pleasure of the president," indicating that they can be discharged at any time. Like other officials in the executive branch, ambassadors are appointed by the president but must be confirmed by the Senate. Ambassadors can serve as foreign service officers or political appointees. Political appointees are frequently selected for their political influence rather than their foreign or domestic policy experience. Some estimates show that roughly 30 percent of a president's selections for ambassadorships have a political motivation, rather than a regard for the nominee's knowledge of foreign policy. President Richard Nixon was quoted as saying, "Anybody who wants to be an ambassador must at least give (in campaign dollars) $250,000." Naturally, Nixon's sentiment caused great rifts between the Senate and the nomination process, especially because it was a divided government at the time. Even today, political appointees may not always be the most qualified for the role in which they have been nominated.

Federal Judges and Supreme Court Justices

Judicial appointments are of perhaps the greatest importance to securing a president's legacy because federal judges and Supreme Court justices serve for life. When a judicial seat becomes vacant, whether at the district court, circuit court of appeals, or Supreme Court level, the president confers with a variety of sources to determine who may serve best in the open seat in a process known as **vetting.** Relying on the expertise and knowledge provided by members of the Department of Justice, Congress, and the FBI, the president is handed a **short list** of those jurists from which the president should draw his nominee. After listening to pros and cons and reviewing documents that include judicial decisions written by the candidates, the president arrives at an appointment. In general, the four criteria on which the judicial selection process is based include experience, political persuasion (ideology), political party alignment, and ethnicity and/or gender.

Did you know? *Vetting* is a term associated with horse racing. Before a race, veterinarians must certify that a horse meets the qualifying criteria to run in the contest. So too, the White House "vets" candidates for the Supreme Court to assess their ideological and judicial fitness to sit on the high court.

Source: Bruce Russell, "The Hands of Dictatorship!" *The Los Angeles Times*, February 6, 1937. FDR Library. Copyright © 1937. Los Angeles Times. Used with permission.

TEST TIP: On the AP GOV exam, it's important to be familiar with the term *political litmus test*. A political litmus test is commonly used in the selection of Supreme Court justices to determine the nominee's political and ideological attitudes. The phrase *litmus test* is taken from chemistry. A chemistry litmus test is a test to determine the general acidity of a substance. A political litmus test is simply a series of questions that an appointee is asked to determine political values, attitudes, and ideological beliefs regarding certain hot-button issues, like abortion, same-sex marriage, or race and gender issues. Although many politicians explicitly oppose the notion of a litmus test, it is almost impossible for the president and other congressional leaders to avoid the issue of ideological slants or records of voting if they hope to stack the courts with judges and justices who will likely rule on ideological and political matters in line with the president's views, upholding his legacy in cases in which his signature legislative or policy achievements are challenged.

Policy Initiatives of the Executive Branch

The success of a president is often dependent on the president's legislative power and policy initiatives. The Constitution gives the president considerable legislative authority, but it is often difficult to move policies through Congress when the president and Congress disagree regarding political and ideological issues. When a government is divided, it is especially hard for the two branches to interact in a way that mutually benefits the nation.

One way that the president can circumvent the influence of Congress is by advancing his or her own policy initiatives, and if necessary, vetoing bills and issuing executive orders. As previously mentioned in this chapter, the scope and influence of the presidency has expanded markedly over the last century, and sometimes this expansion has been at the expense of congressional power. While the checks on the president by the legislative branch are available when constitutionally prescribed, implied powers enable the president to exercise executive discretion. In addition, new legislation can give the president more power. For example, legislation like the International Economic Powers Act of 1977 authorizes the president to impose international economic sanctions. Executive orders, which enable the president to almost unilaterally guide implementation of policies passed into legislation by Congress, have also soared since the 20th century; FDR, for example, signed 3,522 executive orders.

Did you know? Many presidents have used their executive powers to promote agendas, circumvent policymaking competitors, announce foreign policy initiatives, and handle a crisis. President Theodore Roosevelt, a Progressive-Era president, was the first to use the bully pulpit strategy to advance policy changes. The bully pulpit has been successful by providing the president a platform to speak out about important policy objectives that can sway public opinion.

Federalist No. 70

In 1788, Alexander Hamilton published Federalist No. 70 as part of the *Federalist Papers*. In Federalist No. 70, Hamilton argued that a strong **unitary executive** is necessary as a source of energy in quickly addressing the nation's policy needs and as a protection against the self-interest of factions.

Federalist No. 70 Features for a Successful Executive: Argument and Reason	
Argument	**Reason**
Accountability	Because one person is forced to shoulder blame for misdeeds, a single executive is more likely to be inclined to exhibit good behavior while in office.
Expediency	Checked by an institutionally slower Congress characterized by debate and negotiation, a single executive head can act decisively and quickly. Unity of the executive authority in a single figure rather than a plural executive enables "decision, activity, secrecy, and dispatch," all of which are necessary to ensure that the president can adequately respond to constituents. Pointing to ancient models of government that relied on shared executive power, Hamilton saw no advantage and only mischief arising from rivalry.

Continued

Argument	Reason
Duration	Length of presidential term contributes to governmental stability. More thoroughly reviewed in Federalist No. 73.
Financial support	While public service is a noble endeavor, it must be supplemented with reasonable financial incentive to attract the most qualified individuals.
Competent powers (veto)	Veto protects against redundant, excessive, and burdensome lawmaking. More fully reviewed in Federalist No. 51.

The Impact of Technology on the Presidency

The evolution of technology has changed the role of the president in American history at an unprecedented rate. Modern-day developments in technology (radio, television, the Internet, and social media) have changed the president's relationship with other branches of government, the media, and the general public.

Key Facts about the Impact of Technology on the Presidency

History of technology impacting the presidency. Almost 60 years ago, the first televised presidential debate between John F. Kennedy and Richard Nixon significantly impacted the election results and ushered in a new understanding of the importance of technology and media exposure on public opinion. The Kennedy-Nixon debate is one of the most popularly cited examples when discussing the influence of media. Analysis of the 1960 presidential debates showed that Nixon appeared to have more knowledge about important issues than his opponent. In fact, people who only listened to the debate on radio scored Nixon as the winner. The problem for Nixon was that over 65 million television viewers witnessed an on-camera image of him looking "shifty-eyed," sweaty, and disheveled, the dark "five-o'clock shadow" of his facial hair showing through his thick stage makeup—a sharp contrast to the healthy, relaxed, confident, and charismatic appearance of Kennedy. In the end, unlike radio listeners, viewers of the debate overwhelmingly saw Kennedy as the victor. The debates damaged Nixon's chance of winning the election. He became known as "tricky Dick" and Chicago's mayor reportedly said, "My God, they've embalmed him before he even died." Thus began the era of presidential candidates as media stars and the presidential election as a popularity contest.

Radio and television. Radio and television have served as powerful vehicles for delivering presidential speeches, including the annual State of the Union address. The first public address, via radio, was delivered by Calvin Coolidge in 1923. Two and a half decades later, Harry S. Truman spoke to the nation through a live, televised network broadcast. Televised speeches and public addresses became possible throughout the nation (and the world), including the presence of continuous news coverage networks like CNN, Fox, and MSNBC, making the State of the Union and presidential news conferences into media events.

Internet. By the late 1990s, many homes had computers that were connected to the Internet. The landscape for mass communication from the White House changed once again. With an unlimited number of websites reporting uncensored political articles, news clips, news stories, and political interviews, many Americans began relying on the Internet as the primary outlet for acquiring information about American politics. It was easy for users to filter out information that did not align with their own thinking and political views and instead access only the information that validated what they already believed to be true. Then came social media.

Social media. The evolution of social media has created a unique challenge in the 21st century. Today, social media platforms are easily accessible through mobile devices (smartphones), and have created another forum through which politicians can directly communicate with voters, weigh in on issues of public interest at lightning speed, and advertise without payment. Most recently, the election of President Donald J. Trump has ignited a series of ethical questions about the use of social media as a political platform. The president, along with other political leaders, is now able to directly release communications to the general public. President Trump communicates regularly with the American people through his personal Twitter (social media website) account. This revolutionary form of unfiltered discourse circumvents official communications from the White House and has caused political scientists to question the future of American politics.

Did you know? John F. Kennedy was called the "first television president," while Barack Obama has been called the "first social media president."

The Judicial Branch

Heads Up: What You Need to Know

The learning objectives that you must be able to accomplish include:

Explain the principle of judicial review and how it checks the power of other institutions and state governments.

Explain how the exercise of judicial review in conjunction with life tenure can lead to debate about the legitimacy of the Supreme Court's power.

Explain how other branches in the government can limit the Supreme Court's power.

Overview of the Judicial Branch

The judicial branch of government establishes the meaning and application of the laws set forth by the Constitution and has the authority to interpret laws and declare executive and congressional actions unconstitutional.

The History of the Judicial Branch

Under the Articles of Confederation, there was no provision for a centralized, national judicial system. Even more interesting, while the judicial branch comprised one-third of the U.S. government's power, it was the branch least debated during the Constitutional Convention in 1787. The lack of attention to the third branch of government is noted by Alexander Hamilton in **Federalist No. 78** in his statement that the judicial branch was without question the weakest of the three. Granted "no influence over either the sword or the purse," Hamilton argued it was left only with judgment and no power to rob the people of their liberty by force.

Judicial power in the United States was established by our nation's Founders in the Constitution under **Article III,** which states that "the judicial power of the United States shall be vested in one Supreme Court, and in such inferior courts as the Congress may establish."

Article III of the U.S. Constitution	
Section	**Description**
Section 1	Article III, Section I, requires one Supreme Court and the establishment of inferior (lower) courts. The judges shall have the power to interpret the law and shall remain in office during "good behavior." Given that the Constitution does not state a specific time limit, this was interpreted to mean lifetime tenure. According to Alexander Hamilton in Federalist No. 78, it is this tenure that ensured the ability of the judicial branch to defend itself against the other two branches, despite its status as the weakest of the three.
Section II	Article III, Section II, describes the jurisdiction of federal courts. This section introduced the ideas of original and appellate jurisdiction.
Section III	Article III, Section III, focuses on the definition of treason and the punishment for committing acts of treason. Treason, under Section III, is described as levying war against the U.S. or giving aid to our enemies.

Heads Up: What You Need to Know

Our nation's Founders understood the importance of enforcing the rule of law by creating a fair and unbiased judicial system. On the AP GOV exam, you should be able to provide examples of how Article III of the Constitution protected the independence of the judicial branch from undue influence by public opinion or the political and ideological interests of the other branches.

For this reason, our nation's Founders created the following judicial rights to help judges apply laws freely and fairly.

1. Federal judges are appointed, not elected. Elections imply accountability to the popular will; consequently, removing that accountability by making judicial seats appointed gives members of the federal bench the freedom to be impartial.
2. Federal judges serve a lifetime tenure. Judges do not have to fear that they will be fired or removed for their judicial decisions.
3. Federal judges cannot have their salaries reduced. Judges cannot be manipulated, coerced, or punished by affecting their compensation.

The Selection of Justices

The Constitution has broad boundaries for the judicial nomination process. When a seat becomes vacant in the federal judicial system, the president must nominate someone to fill the position. The selection of a judge for federal district courts, the circuit court of appeals, and Supreme Court justices can impact the nation and the course of political history for many generations. Justices on the Supreme Court have delivered landmark rulings on voting rights, abortion, immigration, and due process that have long outlasted their tenure. Recent rulings regarding the financing of political campaigns and LGBT rights have the same potential for fundamental and long-term impact. For this reason, the nomination process is frequently a highly political undertaking. Many historians believe that the appointment of a Supreme Court justice is often the most important decision a sitting president makes. Republican presidents tend to nominate judges who align with Republican Party ideals and Democratic presidents tend to nominate judges who align ideologically with their party.

While the president has the important task of determining nominees for judicial vacancies, the Senate Judiciary Committee is required to thoroughly investigate the proposed nominee. If approved, the nominee goes before the Senate for confirmation. Under conditions of a divided government, confirmation may not be an easy task. A hardline conservative judge nominated by a Republican president would have a very difficult time winning confirmation from a Democratic majority in the Senate. The reverse would be true if a liberal judge was nominated by a Democratic president dealing with a Republican majority. This often results in a president seeking out judges for the inferior federal courts and justices for the Supreme Court who have centrist reputations; that is, their views are not highly ideological or extreme, but are more moderate in tone and outcomes. By selecting a centrist candidate, the president can increase the chances of gaining a coalition of support from both Republican and Democratic senators. Once a nominee is confirmed by a majority vote, he or she is formally appointed to a federal court. The confirmation process is another constitutional check on the president by the Senate to prevent the president from having absolute power.

The Organization of the Judicial Court System

The judicial branch oversees the local, state, and federal court systems. The federal government and each state government have their own court systems. The federal court system is divided into three main categories, starting with district courts (trial courts with original jurisdiction only), circuit courts of appeal (appellate courts with no original jurisdiction), and the Supreme Court (the highest appellate court with limited original jurisdiction as defined in Article III).

Let's take a look at the three main tiers of the federal judicial court system—district, circuit, and Supreme courts. The lower district courts hold original jurisdiction. It is in these courts that federal cases get their first hearing; they are considered trial courts. If a party involved in a district court case believes the district court improperly decided the case, appellate relief is sought at the next tier up, the circuit court of appeals. The parties involved in a case before the circuit court can once again seek appellate relief against the decision rendered by filing a *writ of certiorari,* requesting review by the Supreme Court. If at least four of nine justices agree, the Supreme Court will call for review of the case (the *rule of four*).

The Judicial Court System

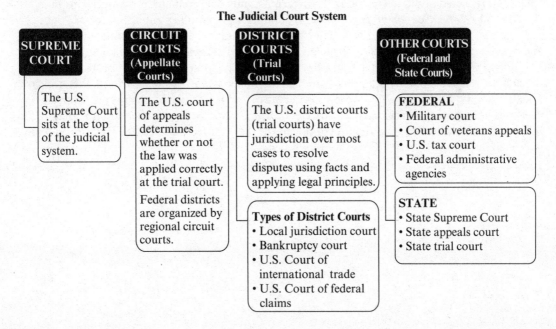

SUPREME COURT	CIRCUIT COURTS (Appellate Courts)	DISTRICT COURTS (Trial Courts)	OTHER COURTS (Federal and State Courts)
The U.S. Supreme Court sits at the top of the judicial system.	The U.S. court of appeals determines whether or not the law was applied correctly at the trial court. Federal districts are organized by regional circuit courts.	The U.S. district courts (trial courts) have jurisdiction over most cases to resolve disputes using facts and applying legal principles.	**FEDERAL** • Military court • Court of veterans appeals • U.S. tax court • Federal administrative agencies
		Types of District Courts • Local jurisdiction court • Bankruptcy court • U.S. Court of international trade • U.S. Court of federal claims	**STATE** • State Supreme Court • State appeals court • State trial court

TEST TIP: The main difference between the court systems is *jurisdiction* (how judicial authority is legally divided between courts)—each court is responsible for reviewing disputes within a defined geographic and/or government authority. All courts have a limited jurisdiction. The two types of jurisdiction that you should be familiar with on the AP GOV exam are *original jurisdiction* (the court has the right to hear a case the first time), and *appellate jurisdiction* (the higher court has the right to hear a case that comes from a lower court).

The Supreme Court

The Supreme Court of the United States (SCOTUS) is the final arbiter and the highest court in the United States. The role of the Supreme Court is to evaluate and interpret the constitutionality of laws. If a case makes its way to the Supreme Court, the Court is under no obligation to hear the case (only 4 percent of all cases get heard in the Supreme Court). The Court consists of nine Supreme Court justices whose goal is to provide "equal justice under law."

Heads Up: What You Need to Know

On the AP GOV exam, it is important to provide evidence and case examples in your free-response questions. One of the best examples of how the course of American history was transformed over time can be found in the landmark decisions delivered by Supreme Courts headed by prominent chief justices. For example, questions involving decisions handed down by Supreme Courts associated with the tenures of Chief Justices John Marshall, Earl Warren, and Warren Burger appear frequently on the exam. Under the guidance of Justice Marshall, the Court declared the Supreme Court can invalidate an act of Congress if the act is inconsistent with the Constitution, *Marbury v. Madison* (1803). The ruling in *Marbury v. Madison* (1803) changed the relationship between the judiciary and the legislative branches by firmly asserting the power of **judicial review** and is still reflected in the Court today. The Warren Court delivered landmark decisions in *Brown v. Board of Education of Topeka* (1954) banning segregation in public schools, *Baker v. Carr* (1962) establishing the one-man, one-vote standard for redistricting, and in several due process cases such as *Gideon v. Wainwright* (1963) and *Miranda v. Arizona* (1966). The Burger Court made its own mark in cases involving the First Amendment protections for freedom of religion, speech, and press as well as the *Roe v. Wade* (1973) abortion rights decision. Today's Roberts Court is decidedly more conservative and has rendered highly controversial decisions in high-profile cases such as *Citizens United v. FEC* (2010) and *Obergefell v. Hodges* (2015). Being able to cite these cases and, more importantly, the required Supreme Court cases, will make your goal of passing the AP GOV exam that much easier!

How the Supreme Court Works

HOW THE SUPREME COURT WORKS

The U.S. Supreme Court is:

- The highest court in the country
- Located in Washington, DC
- The head of the judicial branch of the federal government
- Responsible for deciding whether laws violate the Constitution
- In session from early October until late June or early July

How a Case Gets to the Supreme Court

Most cases reach the Court on appeal. An appeal is a request for a higher court to reverse the decision of a lower court.

Most appeals come from federal courts. They can come from state courts if a case deals with federal law.

Rarely, the Court hears a new case, such as one between states.

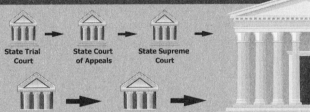

State Trial Court → **State Court of Appeals** → **State Supreme Court** →

Federal Trial Court → **U.S. Court of Appeals** →

1. Dissatisfied parties petition the Court for review

Parties may appeal their case to the Supreme Court, petitioning the Court to review the decision of the lower court.

2. Justices study documents

The Justices examine the petition and supporting materials.

3. Justices vote

Four Justices must vote in favor for a case to be granted review.

What Happens Once a Case is Selected for Review?

1. Parties make arguments

The Justices review the briefs (written arguments) and hear oral arguments.

In oral arguments, each side usually has 30 minutes to present its case. The Justices typically ask many questions during this time.

2. Justices write opinions

The Justices vote on the case and write their opinions.

- The majority opinion shared by more than half of the Justices becomes the Court's decision.
- Justices who disagree with the majority opinion write dissenting or minority opinions.

3. The Court issues its decision

Justices may change their vote after reading first drafts of the opinions. Once the opinions are completed and all of the Justices have cast a final vote, the Court "hands down" its decision.

All cases are heard and decided before summer recess. It can take up to nine months to announce a decision.

Every year:

The Court receives 7,000-8,000 requests for review and grants 70-80 for oral argument. Other requests are granted and decided without argument.

About the Justices

There are nine Justices:

- A Chief Justice, who sits in the middle and is the head of the judicial branch.
- Eight Associate Justices

When a new Justice is needed:

- The President nominates a candidate, usually a federal judge.
- The Senate votes to confirm the nominee.
- The Court can continue deciding cases with less than nine Justices, but if there is a tie, the lower court's decision stands.

Justices are appointed for life, though they may resign or retire.

- They serve an average of 16 years.

Judicial Review

The judicial branch requires insight, precision, and loyalty to the Constitution in rendering its legal decisions. The complexity of political, economic, and social interactions has required the judicial branch to review cases and interpret the meaning of the Constitution many times over.

One of the most salient powers exercised by the judiciary is **judicial review,** a process for challenging the constitutionality of legislative and executive actions.

Heads Up: What You Need to Know

The AP GOV exam will expect you to be familiar with select *Federalist Papers* written by Alexander Hamilton. Federalist No. 78 discusses the power of the judicial review process. Hamilton's foundational essay argues that the judicial branch determines the lawfulness of proposed statutes. Instead of vesting sole power in the legislature to decide what is legal, the judicial branch is charged with the task of defending the rights of the people and, in effect, protecting them from any potential abuse from the hands of unconstitutional legislation.

Marbury v. Madison (1803)

Marbury v. Madison is a landmark Supreme Court case decided by the Marshall Court regarding judicial review. It strengthened constitutional checks and balances and has served as the foundation of U.S. constitutional law for more than 200 years. The decision asserted the authority of the federal judiciary to rule an act of Congress unconstitutional when it conflicts with the Constitution. Such a ruling renders the statute null and void, of no force or effect.

The case began with President John Adams' appointment of staunch Federalist William Marbury as Justice of the Peace. After being defeated by Democratic-Republican Thomas Jefferson during the 1800 election, Adams wanted to retain a Federalist-controlled judiciary as a check against what he feared would be the revolutionary impact of a Democratic-Republican presidency and Congress. Just days before leaving office, Adams initiated the "midnight" appointments of 16 Federalist circuit justices and 42 Federalist justices authorized by the **Judiciary Act** (1801). Marbury was one of those judges. The lame-duck Federalist majority in the Senate quickly confirmed the appointments. It was then up to Adams' secretary of state (ironically, John Marshall himself) to deliver the judicial commissions to the newly confirmed judges. However, John Marshall was on his way to the Supreme Court as the newly appointed chief justice and he failed to ensure that all the commissions were delivered. As luck would have it, one of those commissions had William Marbury's name on it.

When Jefferson assumed the presidency, Marbury petitioned the new secretary of state, James Madison, to have his commission delivered, but Madison refused. In addition, when the new Democratic-Republican 7th Congress began meeting, the first order of business was to reverse the Judiciary Act of 1801 and replace it with the Judiciary Act of 1802, reinstating the Judiciary Act of 1789 and effectively eliminating William Marbury's appointment.

Marbury, who was furious with Madison's refusal to comply with his duty to deliver the commission, went directly to the Supreme Court and Chief Justice Marshall seeking a *writ of mandamus* (an order from the Court instructing a public official to do their job). While Marshall agreed that Marbury was legally entitled to his commission, he also ruled that the Judiciary Act of 1789 was unconstitutional. The law had extended the Supreme Court's constitutionally mandated original jurisdiction, but changing the wording of the Constitution can only be accomplished through the amendment process, not by a legislative act of Congress—hence, Marshall's ruling. In other words, Marbury won Marshall's support on the merits of his case, but lost because, given Marshall's invalidation of the Judiciary Act of 1789, Marbury's assumption that the Supreme Court had original jurisdiction in his case was also invalid. While the fate of Marbury's judicial commission was long forgotten by history, it was Marshall's act of striking down the Judiciary Act of 1789 that has been remembered and that continues to reverberate within the checks and balances system of the U.S. government.

> TEST TIP: The *Marbury v. Madison* Supreme Court case frequently appears on the AP GOV exam. This precedent-setting case affirmed that the Court was granted the right to review legislation or executive actions and decide on their constitutionality—the power of judicial review. The Supreme Court is the primary interpreter of constitutional law when legislative and executive actions are subject to review using the following judicial process: (1) citizen(s) contest federal or state laws through lawsuits, (2) the decision of federal or state courts is appealed, (3) the Supreme Court reviews the case and interprets how the U.S. Constitution applies to the law, and (4) the Supreme Court applies the Constitution to make a decision.

Judicial Decision Making

This section will cover how judges reach their decisions. The dominant model of judicial **decision making** comes from the idea that a judge reasons from facts, logic, experience, legal *precedents* (previous decisions), statutes, and the Constitution.

Key Facts about Judicial Decision Making

Stare decisis. A key principle related to judicial decision making is *stare decisis,* which literally translates "to stand by things decided." If a lower court renders a decision, it is likely that a higher court will defer to its ruling. This does not mean that a higher court will always agree with a lower court, but unless an obvious judicial error has been made, the higher court will always consider the legal deliberations and reasoning of the lower court. In terms of the legal system in its totality, *stare decisis* supports interpretive consistency from one court to the next and continuity from the lower to the higher courts. It fosters faith in the judicial system as well as a reliance on the integrity of its judges and justices. Further, it avoids re-litigation of the same issue multiple times, which promotes expediency, efficiency, and cost savings. It is the foundation for the rule of precedent.

Precedent. A decision in a case that establishes a legal principle or rule that is binding on judges and courts in all cases in which similar circumstances or facts are under adjudication. The legal reasoning and rulings in the precedent-setting case are often referenced by federal judges and justices of the Supreme Court in similar cases that follow. For example, in federal cases involving the Commerce Clause, *Gibbons v. Ogden* is often cited in the written opinions issued from the bench. Likewise, *Baker v. Carr* is the precedent for all cases involving redistricting. Precedents provide the foundation for future legal decisions and promote judicial consistency.

Reversing a ruling. Different time periods present unique legal challenges. As a matter of policy, prior precedents do not prevent new evidence from being admitted in a case to reverse the previous ruling. Although precedents are likely considered in court decisions, justices have been known to reverse a ruling if it is constitutionally justifiable. For example, in *Plessy v. Ferguson* (1896), the Supreme Court ruled in favor of "separate but equal," but in the subsequent case, *Brown v. Board of Education of Topeka* (1954), the Supreme Court overturned the previous ruling, determining that "separate but equal" was unconstitutional.

This was mainly due to the changing ideological makeup of the Court. The 1896 case ruling was 7–1 in favor of Plessy, while the 1954 case was a 9–0 unanimous decision in favor of Brown. Clearly these decisions reveal the ideological dichotomy of each era (see Chapter 6).

> TEST TIP: For the AP GOV exam, think about this critical thinking question: "How much power do you think judges should have?" To help you reflect on the answer, you should be familiar with two important terms that describe how judges interpret laws in order to secure a decision—*judicial activism* and *judicial restraint*.

Judicial Philosophies

Few Supreme Court decisions are universally popular. Many court decisions are controversial, and the uproar around them often comes down to differences over judicial philosophy. Should justices be able to "legislate from the bench," interpreting and applying the Constitution in ways that change its meaning (**judicial activism**)? Or should justices restrain themselves from applying contemporary standards and the need to promote social progress and stick to the original meaning of the wording, applying only their understanding of the Framers' intent and the literal text of the Constitution (**judicial restraint**)?

Judicial activism and judicial restraint represent the two primary philosophical approaches to interpreting the Constitution. In essence, one is the opposite of the other, as the case of *Gideon v. Wainwright* (1963) illustrates:

Gideon, an indigent man in Florida, was charged with a felony in state court. Unable to afford an attorney, he requested one from the court, a request that was denied. Ultimately convicted, Gideon appealed his case to the Supreme Court, raising the question, does the Sixth Amendment right to counsel in criminal cases extend to felony defendants in state courts, and if the defendant cannot afford an attorney, should the state be required to provide one?

The "activist" Warren Court ruled in Gideon's favor in a 9–0 decision. What protection does the Sixth Amendment provide if states are allowed to prosecute those accused of crimes even when they do not have adequate counsel to represent them? Further, Justice Tom C. Clark stated that there was no constitutionally valid reason to apply the protections of due process to some cases and not to others.

Justice Antonin Scalia, who came to the high court over 50 years after the Gideon decision, disagreed with the Warren Court's decision in the case. Scalia viewed himself as an originalist advocating for restraint. He believed that justices had to rely on the meaning of the text at the time it was written. He argued that the right to counsel guaranteed only that the government could not deny to a person accused of a crime the assistance of an attorney for his defense if he chose to have one. It did not, Scalia argued, demand that the government take an affirmative action to provide counsel to those without the means to afford one. The wording of the Sixth Amendment simply did not assert such a guarantee, according to Scalia.

Conservatives on the federal bench are often viewed as supporters of restraint, while liberal justices and judges are tied to activism. In fact, both liberal and conservative members of the Court demonstrate activism and restraint depending on the issue at hand. Although justices are charged with the task of impartially interpreting the Constitution, their political, ideological, and even religious views cannot be entirely filtered out of their deliberative processes. The two approaches turn out to be very elastic and their application to deliberation and rulings quite fluid, depending more on circumstances and issues than on a hard-and-fast adherence to one philosophy or the other.

Judicial Activism vs. Judicial Restraint		
Judicial Term	**Description**	**Examples**
Judicial activism	Judicial activism occurs when judges take an active role in resolving legal issues through an interpretation of the Constitution that emphasizes present-day values and contemporary standards and leads to a greater willingness to invalidate laws and executive actions as well as setting aside legal precedent. Activism supports the idea of a "living Constitution" that evolves to address the complexities of the modern world not present or relevant at the time the Constitution was ratified.	❑ States are mandated to provide access to public education to illegal immigrants (*Plyler v. Doe*, 1982). ❑ The death penalty does not apply to those who are mentally disabled (*Atkins v. Virginia*, 2002). ❑ The right to privacy is implied in the Fourth and Fifth amendments to the Constitution, and as a constitutional right, privacy applies to a woman's decision to have an abortion (*Roe v. Wade*, 1973).
Judicial restraint	Judicial restraint is a philosophy that argues for limiting judicial decisions and interpretation to the "original intent" of the wording in the Constitution, allowing Congress or the states to resolve contemporary issues legislatively. When justices advocate for restraint, they are often referred to as "originalists" or "textualists."	❑ In a case pitting a monopoly granted by the state of New York to a steamboat ferry business operating between New Jersey and New York (Aaron Ogden) against a federally licensed ferry business (Thomas Gibbons), the Court ruled that states cannot interfere with the power of Congress to regulate commerce; thus, they reversed a New York judicial decision imposing an injunction to stop Gibbons from operating his steamship business. (*Gibbons v. Ogden*, 1824). ❑ The Court upheld the constitutionality of FDR's Executive Order 9066, which authorized the move of people of Japanese ancestry, regardless of citizenship, into internment camps during World War II. Justices argued that such an action was not about the race of the individuals involved but was instead justified by the war powers granted to the president and Congress to do what was required to wage war successfully (*Korematsu v. United States*, 1944).

Source: Jesse Springer, "Bout." November 3, 2005.

Supreme Court Limitations by Other Branches of Government

Congressional Legislation

Although most prevailing conceptions of the Supreme Court consider its judgments absolute within the system of checks and balances, Congress can act to modify the impact of a decision rendered by the federal courts. One means at Congress' disposal is the passage of legislation. For example, in more than five Supreme Court cases in 1989, the Court made rulings restricting workers' rights to sue employers for racial discrimination. In 1991, Congress effectively overrode the series of 1989 decisions by enacting the Civil Rights Act of 1991 that granted workers supplementary rights to overcome discrimination in the workplace. In *Oregon v. Smith* (1990), the high court ruled that it was permissible for a division of Oregon's Human Resources Department to deny unemployment benefits to Native American employees fired for violating a state law against the use of peyote even though peyote is an important sacrament in the religious rituals of the Native American Church. Public uproar over the rights of Native Americans prompted Congress to pass the Religious Freedom Restoration Act in 1993 and to amend the American Indian Religious Freedom Act in 1994 to provide protection for religious practices of the Native American Church.

Constitutional Amendments

Just as Congress can reduce the influence of the Court's decision by passing legislation, Congress can also pass constitutional amendments to override the Court's decisions. Once an amendment is proposed, it must pass by a two-thirds majority in both congressional chambers. If a two-thirds vote is achieved, the proposed amendment must then be ratified by the states. Ratification requires approval by the legislatures of three-fourths (75 percent) of the states.

The Federal Bureaucracy

Heads Up: What You Need to Know

The learning objectives that you must be able to accomplish are:

Explain how the bureaucracy carries out the responsibilities of the federal government.

Explain how the federal bureaucracy uses delegated discretionary authority for rule making and implementation.

Explain how Congress uses its oversight power in its relationship with the executive branch.

Explain how the president ensures that executive branch agencies and departments carry out the responsibilities in concert with the goals of the administration.

Explain the extent to which governmental branches can hold the bureaucracy accountable given the competing interests of Congress, the president, and the federal courts.

Overview of Federal Bureaucracy

The federal bureaucracy is organized into government agencies, departments, corporations, and commissions that perform tasks for the government. It employs several million government officials who are responsible for creating and implementing the rules, regulations, and processes to bring federal policies to fruition. It is often viewed as the fourth institution of the federal government, alongside the president, Congress, and the courts. While the executive branch is the functional manager of the federal bureaucracy, Congress oversees some departments, and the judicial branch may intervene in cases where a government agency violates the bounds of its jurisdiction.

Federal bureaucracies are organized hierarchically and follow a chain of command. The rules and regulations implemented by bureaucracies are based on the requirements of the law, what is allowable under the Constitution, and the interests of the other three branches, the public, and of interest groups.

Organization of the Federal Bureaucracy

Federal bureaucracy started with the presidential cabinet consisting initially of only the Departments of State, Treasury, and War (now Defense). The Department of Justice under the attorney general was added in 1870, and in the intervening years more departments were added to meet the needs of a growing nation. Currently, there are 15 executive departments. Although some efforts have been made to decrease the size of the federal bureaucracy over the past 25 years, it currently consists of over 500 subunits, each with an area of specialization.

With the exception of the heads of executive departments and federal agencies, the bureaucracy is staffed with individuals selected based on qualifications, area of specialization, and years of experience. The work of these civil servants is *nonpartisan* in nature; that is, the party affiliation of individuals within the bureaucracy is not a consideration in hiring and is irrelevant to their work responsibilities.

TEST TIP: On the AP GOV exam, you should be familiar with the term *nonpartisan*. Federal government departments do not have allegiances to one particular political party. Why is this important? The federal government plays a key role in dealing with homeland security, public safety, emergency services, natural disasters, taxation, education, food, medicine, infrastructure, transportation, etc. To effectively perform tasks and carry out public policies, government officials must directly and indirectly refrain from political biases. The federal bureaucracy represents *all* American citizens, not just a select few. In fact, our Founding Fathers considered nonpartisanship vital to the well-being of our nation. Historians have interpreted Federalist No. 10 to imply that our Founding Fathers intended the government to be nonpartisan.

The four broad categories of the federal government are cabinet departments, government agencies, regulatory commissions, and government corporations.

Cabinet Departments

Cabinet departments manage specific policies that are the responsibility of the executive branch to implement and enforce (see "The President's Cabinet," p. 128). The 15 cabinet departments include department heads (called *secretaries*) who are appointed by the president, and staff members consisting of undersecretaries, deputies, and assistants.

Cabinet Departments	
Department	**Description**
State	Apprises the president on foreign policy matters. Oversees negotiations abroad.
Treasury	Manages coin and paper bill production, tax collection, and borrowing money.
Defense	Ensures national security and retains standing military forces.
Justice	Represents the U.S. in courts, enforces laws, maintains federal prisons, and pursues federal law violations.
Interior	Oversees national parks and public lands.
Agriculture	Manages forests, provides assistance to farmers and other agricultural workers, and provides oversight for nutrition assistance and school lunch programs.
Commerce	Promotes national interests in terms of commerce and economic growth.
Labor	Determines minimum wages, sets maximum work hours, and ensures safe conditions for workers; manages unemployment and workers' compensation.
Health and Human Services	Prevents and controls disease, advises Medicare and Medicaid programs, and funds healthcare research.
Housing and Urban Development	Administers the Federal Housing Administration (FHA) mortgage lending and housing construction standards; supports community development and access to affordable housing.
Transportation	Oversees public highway operation and transportation, including mass transit, railroads, and air travel.
Energy	Advocates for renewable energy interests and manages nuclear weapon programs.
Education	Provides federal aid to education programs and conducts research.
Veterans Affairs	Assists military veterans with benefits and medical programs.
Homeland Security	Maintains border and transportation security and oversees all emergency preparedness situations, including responses to chemical and biological warfare threats.

Government Agencies and Regulatory Commissions

The myriad executive branch agencies that make up a significant part of the federal bureaucracy are organized by "parent agency" (executive departments). For example, the parent agency for both the Administration for Children and Families and the Centers for Disease Control is the U.S. Department of Health and Human Services. Executive branch agencies each have an appointed administrator or director with any number of assistants or deputies working under his or her direction. Independent agencies such as the Federal Election Commission (FEC), the Federal Reserve Board (FRB), and the Environmental Protection Agency (EPA) operate outside of the direct control of the executive branch and are often run, in the case of the FEC and the FRB, by a small group or committee.

Independent regulatory agencies are considered part of the executive branch but are meant to implement and enforce regulations free from political pressure. One such independent regulatory agency is the Consumer Product Safety Commission. While the heads of executive branch agencies "serve at the pleasure of the president" and can be removed on the president's say-so, the heads of independent regulatory agencies can only be removed for cause.

Together, agencies and commissions are charged with managing day-to-day government operations and the implementation of public policy. They are organized for a variety of reasons—overseeing government functions, ensuring that government activities follow the law, and ensuring that policies are implemented. You may already be familiar with some of the following selected agencies and commissions that play important roles in our U.S. government.

Federal Bureau of Investigation (FBI)

Central Intelligence Agency (CIA)

Federal Trade Commission (FTC)

Consumer Product Safety Commission (CPSC)

Federal Communications Commission (FCC)

Federal Aviation Administration (FAA)

Occupational Safety and Health Administration (OSHA)

Securities and Exchange Commission (SEC)

Small Business Administration (SBA)

Social Security Administration (SSA)

United States Postal Service (USPS)

Government Corporations

Government corporations operate like private businesses and are chartered by the federal government to provide public services. They enjoy the highest degree of independence of any entities within the federal bureaucracy. One of the first government corporations was the Panama Railroad Company (1903), chartered under the Theodore Roosevelt administration to oversee the construction of the Panama Canal and a transcontinental railroad, making it possible to cross from the Atlantic to the Pacific Ocean and transport goods from Central America. In the 1930s, the Tennessee Valley Authority (TVA) and the Reconstruction Finance Corporation were established during the Great Depression to boost economic development. The TVA continues to exist today, providing electricity throughout portions of the southern United States. Additional current examples of government corporations include the Neighborhood Reinvestment Corporation, the National Park Foundation, and the Federal Crop Insurance Corporation.

Tasks of the Federal Bureaucracy

The federal bureaucracy is responsible for carrying out tasks for the federal government using *standard operating procedures* (SOPs). SOPs are step-by-step instructions that aid government workers to carry out complex tasks. The goal is organizational efficiency, but sometimes "bureaucratic **red tape**" can cause bureaucrats to lose sight of their purpose, causing a negative impact. For example, have you ever had to stand in a long line at the Department of Motor Vehicles or the U.S. Post Office because government employees have to systematically follow SOPs when completing each transaction? These formal rules cause excessive paperwork, time, and frustration.

Key Facts about the Tasks of the Federal Bureaucracy

Writing and enforcing regulations. Government agencies handle the important task of writing and enforcing legislation. In doing so, government agencies, commissions, and departments create rules and regulations, but it is a complex process (see "Rule-Making Authority" and "Discretionary Authority" on the next page).

Issuing fines. Because various bureaucratic organizations are endowed with considerable power to enforce legislation, infractions committed can total billions of dollars each year. Sometimes fines benefit the public (for example, cases that include consumer product defects). Other fines are funneled back to Congress and subject to the legislature's discretion (for example, sensitive data compromises).

Testifying before Congress. Congressional oversight is a check on the executive branch's power. Although oversight is not an enumerated power of the Constitution, congressional review is an implied power. While the Supreme Court has heard a substantial number of cases that have challenged congressional oversight, the majority of the Court's opinions have landed in favor of empowering the legislature to conduct the necessary reviews or investigations. The process of oversight often requires officials and agencies and/or departments within the federal bureaucracy to provide information and answer questions during congressional oversight hearings.

Forming relationships. The federal bureaucracy forms mutually supportive relationships between networks and within Congress, interest groups, and individuals who are united by the formation and implementation of public policy (see descriptions on pp. 148–149 and pp. 267–270).

Rule-Making Authority

The rule-making authority of the federal bureaucracy is covered under the Administrative Procedures Act (1946). Under the rule-making authority, federal agencies must (1) draft comments about the nature of the regulations and make them available for public notice or formal hearings, (2) provide the public 30–180 days to review a draft after its publication, and (3) pending modifications, publish the final rules on the Federal Register website. You can search official government documents at www.federalregister.gov. The process for creating general and permanent federal regulations is similar to rule making found in the Code of Federal Regulations.

Discretionary Authority

Discretionary authority allows bureaucratic agencies to apply their expertise and knowledge to the adoption of initiatives, rules, and regulations for the implementation of legislation adopted by Congress. For example, Congress passed the Clean Air Act in 1963 and additional amendments in the 1970s. The provisions of this law and its amendments required states to take a number of affirmative steps to combat air pollution. It was then up to the Environmental Protection Agency (EPA) to provide data regarding emissions standards to the states, outline the steps states were required to take in developing a plan of action for reaching emission goals, oversee state compliance, and set the rules qualifying businesses for permits to operate. Unless challenged and overturned by the federal courts, policies adopted through decisions made by federal agencies carry the force of law. A list of departments with discretionary authority are listed in the table that follows.

Department/Agency	Rule-Making Authority
Department of Homeland Security (DHS)	❑ Enforces and administers immigration laws. ❑ Averts terrorism and enhances U.S. security. ❑ Ensures digital security, including safeguarding cyberspace. ❑ Manages U.S. borders.
Department of Transportation (DOT)	❑ Plans and supports the infrastructure of land, air, and sea-based travel. ❑ Develops and implements policies concerning the usage of roads, highways, airports, and seaports. ❑ Oversees billion-dollar federal grants provided to local authorities to improve transportation around the country.

Department/Agency	Rule-Making Authority
Department of Veterans Affairs (VA)	❏ Provides healthcare services to veterans and their respective dependents. ❏ Manages benefits programs, medical centers, and nursing homes. ❏ Veterans Benefits Administration provides education and housing benefits.
Department of Education (ED)	❏ Establishes education policy and coordinates funding. ❏ Enforces federal education laws ensuring privacy and civil riches.
Environmental Protection Agency (EPA)	❏ Oversees national efforts to reduce negative environmental risks. ❏ Ensures and enforces federal laws regarding human health. ❏ Reviews marketplace chemicals.
Federal Election Commission (FEC)	❏ Enforces campaign finance law. ❏ Discloses campaign finance information. ❏ Oversees the transmission of funds between individuals, candidates, and political parties.
Securities and Exchange Commission (SEC)	❏ Maintains fair and efficient markets. ❏ Facilitates capital formation. ❏ Sets laws and regulations that govern the securities industry.

TEST TIP: On the AP GOV exam, you should be familiar with four key terms that are related to the federal bureaucracy forming relationships: (1) the iron triangle, (2) issue networks, (3) the spoils system, and (4) the merit system.

The Iron Triangle

The **iron triangle** describes an alliance between a department or agency of the federal bureaucracy, a congressional subject matter committee or subcommittee, and specific interest groups. In iron triangles, relationships are formed to advance policies that directly benefit all groups in the triangle and may result in policies that serve the public interest. The diagram illustrates the mutually beneficial relationship between the constituent parts of the triangle. Collective policy goals ranging from seeking stricter environmental regulations to advocating against abortion drive the relationship. Iron triangles are not necessarily defined by ideology, but a dominant ideology often emerges.

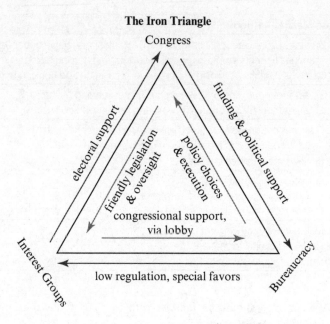

The Iron Triangle

Congress

electoral support

funding & political support

friendly legislation & oversight

policy choices & execution

congressional support, via lobby

Interest Groups

Bureaucracy

low regulation, special favors

Issue Networks

Issue networks bring together people from interest groups, congressional staffs, the federal bureaucracy, universities, and the media to focus on a particular public policy issue. They regularly share information and debate their shared issue, inviting what can often be contentious arguments drawn along ideological, partisan, or socioeconomic lines. Presidents often look to issue networks when searching for people to head government agencies.

The Spoils System

The **spoils system** (also known as **patronage**) is a term coined during the administration of President Andrew Jackson. It entitles a newly elected president to fill certain jobs within the government bureaucracy with political supporters, cronies, and party loyalists. Qualification, experience, and expertise are not the primary criteria used to choose government officials in a patronage system. The system was modified for the vast majority of **civil service** jobs with the passage of the Pendleton Civil Service Reform Act in 1883. Selection of government employees was to be based on competitive examination focusing on merit rather than patronage to ensure both nonpartisanship in the carrying out of civil service duties and a minimum level of competency for the job. The spoils system continues to be in play for appointed positions such as cabinet secretaries, White House staff, heads of executive agencies, and ambassadorships.

The image at left depicts President Andrew Jackson riding a pig that is eating "fraud," "bribery," and "spoils." Jackson was known for employing the spoils system. One of his first acts as president was to fire dozens of federal workers and replace them with his supporters.

After the passage of the Pendleton Act in 1883, the federal government officially ended the spoils system. The civil service reform movement, which gave rise to the Pendleton Act, called for elected officials to appoint leaders based on nonpartisanship, rather than on the basis of party alignment.

Source: Thomas Nast, In Memoriam—Our Civil Service as It Was, "To the Victors Belong the Spoils." *Harper's Weekly,* April 28, 1877.

The Merit System

The **merit system,** as its name implies, is the process of filling job positions within the government bureaucracy based on experience, qualification, and demonstrated ability to perform the position's duties. In contrast to the spoils system, the merit system is a comprehensive process that facilitates the most competent leaders to be selected for government positions. The merit system is designed to preclude favoritism as an evaluative factor in recruitment.

Chapter Review Practice Questions

The practice questions show the types of questions that may appear on the exam. Practice questions are for instructional purposes only and may not reflect the format of the actual exam. On the actual exam, some questions may be grouped into sets containing one source-based prompt (document or image) and two to five questions. The questions and explanations that follow focus on essential knowledge, the learning objectives, and political science skills.

Multiple-Choice Questions

Questions 1–2 refer to the following political cartoon.

Source: Mike Keefe, "Supreme Court Location," *The Denver Post*, October 7, 2004. caglecartoons.com.

1. Which of the following statements best describes the interpretation of the political cartoon?

    A. Supreme Court justices are influenced in their opinions by whoever is sitting in the White House.
    B. The choice of Supreme Court justices has become increasingly ideological.
    C. The congressional role in the judicial nominating process would be diminished after the 2004 election.
    D. The Supreme Court tries to hold itself above partisanship.

2. Which of the following is NOT a contributing factor to the point of view depicted in the image?

    A. The use of litmus tests in vetting judicial nominees
    B. The connection between presidential elections and the political nature of the high court
    C. Partisan control of the Senate
    D. Judicial activism

Question 3 refers to the following two graphs.

Divisions of Congressional Districts

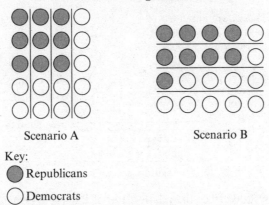

Scenario A   Scenario B

Key:
● Republicans
○ Democrats

3. Based on the results shown in the two scenarios, which of the following best explains why Scenario A is an example of gerrymandering?

    A. Republicans outnumber Democrats.
    B. Democrats outnumber Republicans.
    C. Voters have been divided to give a clear advantage to Republicans.
    D. Voters have been divided to give a clear advantage to Democrats.

Questions 4–5 refer to the following passage.

> It is emphatically the province and duty of the judicial department to say what the law is…
>
> It is also not entirely unworthy of observation that in declaring what shall be the supreme law of the land, the constitution itself is first mentioned; and not the laws of the United States generally, but those only which shall be made in pursuance of the constitution, have that rank.
>
> Thus, the particular phraseology of the constitution of the United States confirms and strengthens the principle, supposed to be essential to all written constitutions that a law repugnant to the constitution is void; and that courts, as well as other departments, are bound by that instrument.
>
> —Source: Court decision delivered by John Marshall, *Marbury v. Madison*, 1803.

4. Which of the following is the constitutional basis for Marshall's reasoning?

    A. Necessary and Proper Clause
    B. Supremacy Clause
    C. Advice and Consent Clause
    D. Faithfully Executed Clause

5. Which of the following was established based on Marshall's argument on behalf of the Court?

    A. Judicial review
    B. Legislative supremacy
    C. Appellate jurisdiction of the Supreme Court
    D. Original jurisdiction of the Supreme Court

Question 6 refers to the following image.

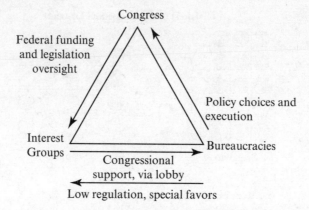

6. Which of the following best describes the relationship of federal agencies, businesses, and congressional committees illustrated in the diagram above?

   A. Issue network
   B. Iron triangle
   C. Legislative cycle
   D. Collective interest

7. Which of the following best describes the power exercised by the office of the presidency over the last century?

   A. Diminished
   B. Expanded
   C. Stagnated
   D. Weakened

8. The *filibuster* is best defined as

   A. A vote conducted by the Senate to end debate
   B. A mandate issued by the Senate to check the president's power
   C. A committee established by the Senate to learn more about a proposed law
   D. A tactic employed by senators to disrupt the legislative process

9. Which of the following branches of government is addressed in Federalist No. 70?

   A. Executive branch
   B. Legislative branch
   C. Judicial branch
   D. Executive cabinet

Question 10 refers to the following graph.

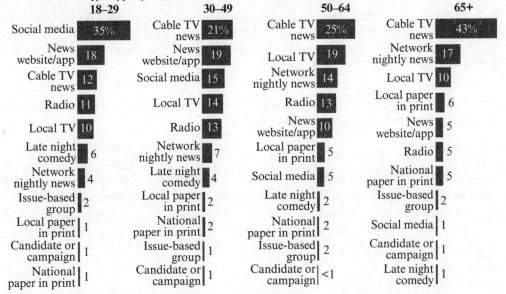

Social Media and the 2016 Presidential Election
Among those who learned about the 2016 presidential election in the past week, % who say the most helpful type of source is...

Source: "Social Media as a Learning Source for the 2016 Election." Pew Research Center, January 12–27, 2016.

10. Based on the data presented in the graph, which of the following best describes the media trends during the presidential election of 2016?

   A. Cable news is becoming an increasingly popular source of political news among all demographics.
   B. Social media was the main source of information for those in the youngest age demographic.
   C. Website application use is declining among voters in the younger demographics.
   D. Print news use is declining among older demographics.

Free-Response Question

1 question
40 minutes (suggested)

Directions: It is suggested that you take a few minutes to plan and outline your essay. Write your response on lined paper. You must demonstrate your understanding of course content, disciplinary practices, and reasoning processes. Your essay is considered a first draft and may contain some grammatical errors that will not be counted against you. However, to receive full credit, your essay must demonstrate defensible content knowledge with substantive examples where appropriate.

Question: Develop an argument that defends the Fourteenth Amendment as the most important protection that Americans have for safeguarding their fundamental liberties.

In your essay, you must:

1. Articulate a defensible claim or thesis that responds to the prompt and establishes a line of reasoning.
2. Support your claim with at least TWO pieces of accurate and relevant information.
   (a) At least ONE piece of evidence must be from one of the following foundational documents and/or required Supreme Court cases:
   - The Constitution
   - Federalist No. 10
   - *McDonald v. Chicago* (2010)

   (b) Use a second piece of evidence from the list above or from your study of the judicial review.
3. Use reasoning to explain why your evidence supports your claim/thesis.
4. Respond to an opposing or alternative perspective using refutation, concession, or rebuttal.

Answers and Explanations

Multiple-Choice Questions

1. **B.** The cartoon in the image was published in October 2004, as stated in the source note. This was one month before the next presidential election. Cranes stand ready to move the Supreme Court to the "right" or the "left," which are ideological terms associated with conservative (right) and liberal (left). Since the president nominates Supreme Court justices, one can infer from the cartoon that an incoming Democratic president would be expected to fill any vacant seats with liberal judges, while a Republican president would fill vacancies with conservative nominees, pointing to the appointment of justices as increasingly ideological, choice B. Supreme Court justices enjoy lifetime tenure in order to ensure their independence from the other two branches, so choice A is incorrect. The congressional role in the confirmation process, choice C, is not a subject of this cartoon, and clearly, by depicting the shifting ideological tilt of the Court, the cartoonist does not view the justices as being immune from partisanship, choice D.

2. **B.** With specific references in the cartoon to the upcoming presidential election and the left/right shift of the Court, the connection between elections and how this can impact the Court politically is the correct answer, choice B. The vetting process for judicial nominees (choice A), partisanship in the Senate (choice C), and judicial activism (choice D) are not the subjects of this cartoon.

3. **C.** The question requires you to be familiar with the term *gerrymandering* (the intentional process of redrawing congressional district boundaries to benefit one group over another). The figure uses lines to represent the boundaries of four congressional districts. The figure also depicts *partisan gerrymandering,* given that Republican voters and Democratic voters are the two groups involved. With this information, you can eliminate choices A and B because the figure gives no indication of how many voters there are in each party, but instead addresses how those party supporters are distributed throughout the four districts. Scenario B (choice D), indicates that district lines have been drawn in a manner which would likely result in an even split of the four congressional districts, two for each party. In Scenario A (choice C), however, Democratic voters have been "packed" into one district and the remainder have been "cracked" to distribute a small number of them in each of the remaining Republican-dominated districts, thus diluting their collective voting strength. In all likelihood, Republicans would emerge from a congressional election with three seats to the Democrats' one seat. Therefore, Scenario A, choice C, is clearly the gerrymandered district plan.

4. **B.** Marshall noted that the Constitution is considered the supreme law of the land and that any law in conflict with the Constitution ("repugnant to the constitution," in Marshall's words) is to be considered void. Thus, the Supremacy Clause, choice B, is the correct answer. The Necessary and Proper Clause (choice A), the Advice and Consent Clause (choice C), and the Faithfully Executed Clause (choice D) are not cited in Marshall's opinion.

5. **A.** By stating that the Supremacy Clause makes any law not in line with the Constitution void and that "it is emphatically the province and duty of the judicial department to say what the law is...," Marshall asserted the right of the Supreme Court to review laws passed by Congress to assess them for their constitutionality, choice A. Marshall clearly argued that the Constitution is supreme, not the voice of the legislative branch (choice B). While appellate jurisdiction (choice C) and original jurisdiction (choice D) were issues in this case, neither is directly addressed by Marshall in the excerpt.

6. **B.** This relationship illustrates an iron triangle, choice B. Iron triangles consist of a congressional committee or subcommittee, an agency or department of the federal government, and a special interest group with a particular policy focus in common. Collaborating in crafting legislation and oversight of implementation, the three sides of the triangle serve their own interests in a mutually beneficial relationship, as illustrated in the graphic. Issue networks (choice A) involve many groups representing non-government agencies, universities, congressional staffs, and public interest groups which debate rather than make public policy. Choices C and D are unrelated. The legislative cycle (choice C) would emphasize the steps a bill takes to become law. Collective interest (choice D) might also be translated as the public interest, but the graphic assigns no role to collective interest of the public.

7. **B.** Through expanded use of executive orders, signing statements, executive agreements, and war powers during the modern presidency, power associated with the office of the presidency has grown considerably in size and scope, choice B. It has not diminished in size (choice A), stagnated (choice C), or weakened (choice D).

8. **D.** A *filibuster* is a tactic employed by senators to prevent legislation from coming to the floor for a vote, thus hampering the legislative process, choice D. A vote conducted by the Senate to end a debate (choice A) is a called a cloture. The Senate does not check the president's power by issuing a mandate (choice B), and a filibuster is not a committee (choice C).

9. **A.** Federalist No. 70 originated from a series of essays written by Alexander Hamilton regarding the power of the executive branch, choice A. Hamilton's essay addresses the benefits of having a unitary rather than a plural executive. All of the other choices are not associated with Federalist No. 70.

10. **B.** Social media is growing as a platform for sharing political information, but was clearly dominant during the 2016 election for the youngest voting demographic, choice B. The data in the graphic represent only activity relevant to the 2016 election; it does not compare one election to another. Whether cable news (choice A), websites (choice C), or print media (choice D) have increased or decreased in use or popularity cannot be measured for any of the demographic groups represented.

Free-Response Question

Scoring Guide

This is an Argument Essay question. To achieve the maximum score of 6, your response must address the scoring criteria components in the table that follows.

Scoring Criteria for a Good Argument Essay		
Question: Develop an argument that defends the Fourteenth Amendment as the most important protection that Americans have for safeguarding their fundamental liberties.		
Scoring Criteria	**Disciplinary Practice**	**Examples**
A. THESIS/CLAIM		
(1 point) Presents a historically defensible thesis that establishes a line of reasoning. (Note: The thesis must make a claim that responds to *all* parts of the question and must *not* just restate the question.)	Practice 5.a	A strong thesis establishes the centrality of the Fourteenth Amendment to the development and protection of basic liberties via its explicit prohibition against actions taken by states that deny due process to any citizen. In addition, the thesis incorporates and highlights the relevance of the foundational documents or Supreme Court case selected to the overall argument.
		In this case, the selected documents, which include Federalist No. 10 and the Supreme Court decision in *McDonald v. Chicago*, should be woven into an introductory paragraph that contextually (that is, from a historic perspective) progresses. It is important, therefore, that no matter which document is selected, its incorporation into your essay is woven into a cohesive, coherent thesis structure.
B. EVIDENCE		
(3 points) Uses TWO pieces of specific and relevant evidence to support the argument (must be linked to the question). OR **(2 points)** Uses ONE piece of specific and relevant evidence to support the argument (must be linked to the question).	Practice 5.b	To receive the maximum number of points in this scoring domain, a minimum of two specific pieces of relevant information must be selected. In this case, Federalist No. 10 and *McDonald v. Chicago* were selected.
		For this category, it is important to relate the documents to your thesis. As such, your essay must demonstrate an evidence-based approach to ensure viable thesis support.
		Federalist No. 10:
		❏ Authorial intent and relevance to your thesis are vital to convey here. Relevant information to include: Madison's concern regarding factions and the tyranny of the majority. Madison went on to use the state of Rhode Island as an example of a small

Scoring Criteria	Disciplinary Practice	Examples
OR **(1 point)** Describes one piece of evidence that is accurately linked to the topic of the question. (Note: To earn more than 1 point, the response must establish an argument and have earned the point for Thesis/Claim.)		republic in which the dangers of the will of a majority overwhelming minority rights was greater than in a large diverse republic like the United States. ❑ Why does the document matter? Madison's own argument contradicts the original intent of the Bill of Rights as a protection against the central government's abuse of its power against its citizens. If states are more likely to abuse their authority than the government of the United States, why were the states not included in the Constitution? How did the Fourteenth Amendment rectify this oversight? ***McDonald v. Chicago*** **(2010):** ❑ Background on the court case? Legal context? ❑ How does this case illustrate the doctrine of selective incorporation, a doctrine only made possible because of the Fourteenth Amendment? ❑ Why is this relevant to your thesis? Answering these basic questions will help ensure that your essay meets the evidence-based format that the scoring criteria requires in order to receive the maximum score. This essay addresses the preceding questions in the following way: ❑ Identifies Madison's affiliation as a Federalist defender of the Constitution. ❑ Addresses the content of Federalist No. 10 by unveiling Madison's intent in highlighting the "mischief" caused by factions, not the least of which is the collaboration among the members of a majority faction to subvert the rights of the minority. ❑ While defending a large and diverse republic like the United States as the best defense of one majority faction emerging, Madison argues that the smaller sovereign state republics that existed under the Articles of Confederation actually posed a greater threat to minority rights. ❑ Background on *McDonald v. Chicago* includes a rundown of the case's essential facts and their relevance to Second Amendment protections under the Fourteenth Amendment. ❑ Both documents are relevant to the thesis because they provide the underpinnings for an argument that is was only the inclusion of the Fourteenth Amendment in the Constitution that prohibited states from denying individual liberties.

Continued

Scoring Criteria	Disciplinary Practice	Examples
C. REASONING		
(1 point) Uses reasoning to organize and explain how or why the evidence supports the thesis or claim. (Note: To earn this point, you must have earned a point for Evidence.)	Practice 5.c	Answering this category effectively comes from sufficiently satisfying the previous domain. After selecting appropriate evidence and providing the sufficient background, supplied reasoning will only serve to further bolster an already high score. For example, the provided sample response carefully details how and why arguments made in Federalist No. 10 and the outcome of *McDonald v. Chicago* point to the critical nature of the Fourteenth Amendment in defending the rights of the people against state authority.
D. ALTERNATIVE PERSPECTIVES		
(1 point) Responds to an opposing or alternative perspective using refutation, concession, or rebuttal that is consistent with the argument. (Note: To earn this point, your response must have a claim or thesis.)	Practice 5.d	Although a good essay can technically provide a refuting analysis at any stage of the essay's development, it is often the best approach to bring up any alternative perspectives or counterarguments in your concluding paragraph. Counterarguments or opposing perspectives do not have to be exhaustively detailed, but they should be explicitly stated so that the AP Reader is not forced to make implicit connections (which may, as relevant to your particular essay, be incorrect). One could argue that the Bill of Rights itself is more critical to the protections of basic liberties than the Fourteenth Amendment. The Anti-Federalists argued that the state constitutions each included their own protections for citizens, so it was the federal government that needed the firm parameters set down in the Bill of Rights. This alternative perspective could be demonstrated by quoting the First Amendment and its prohibition against acts of Congress that deny freedom of speech, press, religion, etc.—the states are never mentioned. It can also be argued that state adoption of a list of rights guaranteed to citizens predated the constitutional Bill of Rights, making the Fourteenth Amendment superfluous. These possible refutations are countered, however, by the statement beginning with "While it may be posited that…" Of course, a one-sentence rebuttal may not always be sufficient, but insofar as your essay can progressively support your central thesis, you will naturally anticipate (rhetorical) objections and can successfully meet them in the process of writing.

Sample Student Response

At the Constitutional Convention, one of the most salient debates arose regarding the protection of the rights and liberties of the people. Fear of tyranny exercised by the new constitutional government led to the addition of the Bill of Rights. While the Bill of Rights was an important step forward in the protection of civil liberties, a major loophole existed for decades, leaving citizens unprotected from the abuse of government authority exercised by state governments. The Fourteenth Amendment changed everything, explicitly prohibiting states from denying due process and equal protection to its citizens. A clear argument for the need to protect citizens from state authority was made, perhaps inadvertently, by James Madison in Federalist No. 10 before the Constitution was even ratified. By enacting the Fourteenth Amendment, Congress bridged the gap left by the Constitution between the guarantees made to citizens to protect them against federal authority and the extension of those same protections to the states. In doing so, Congress gave citizens a platform to assert their rights in the courts in lawsuits lodged against their state and local governments. McDonald v. Chicago is one such case. It is through the threat to civil liberties posed by the states, first highlighted by Madison in Federalist No. 10, and the ability of citizens to pursue selective incorporation of their states into the protections of their civil liberties based on the due process clause that make the Fourteenth Amendment the most important development in the safeguarding of the basic liberties enjoyed by American citizens.

Perhaps the greatest argument for incorporating the states into the protections of civil liberties was made by James Madison in Federalist No. 10. The premise of his argument in defense of the Constitution was that the inevitable human tendency toward dividing into factions put the minority at risk of tyranny exercised by the majority. An important element of his argument was that the demographic uniformity of the mini-republics represented by the states lent itself to the formation of a majority faction which would oppress the minority. A large, diverse republic like the United States, however, would protect against the emergence of a singular majority. Though Madison did not make the argument explicitly, he certainly implied that states posed the real threat to liberty. When the Founders added the Bill of Rights to the Constitution, explicitly addressing only prohibitions against federal government abuse of individual rights, they created a loophole big enough for every state to drive a truck through.

The loophole remained open until the passage of the Fourteenth Amendment, whose due process, equal protection, and privileges and immunities clauses specifically prohibit states from denying rights and liberties to citizens. By utilizing the due process clause, citizens brought lawsuits against state governments throughout the 20th and 21st centuries, allowing the federal courts to selectively incorporate the states into the protections guaranteed in the Bill of Rights. In case after case, all but a few provisions of the first ten amendments have been selectively incorporated. For example, in McDonald v. Chicago, the Second Amendment was incorporated. In an attempt to curb handgun violence, a series of ordinances were put in place to restrict handguns in the city of Chicago. Otis McDonald, a longtime resident, tried to register a handgun for his protection in a neighborhood that had experienced economic decline and a rise in crime. Due to the ordinances, Otis could not register his handgun and non-registered handguns were prohibited. His lawsuit incorporated the states into an interpretation of the Second Amendment that recognizes an individual's right to own handguns for self-defense. Without the platform of the Fourteenth Amendment to stand on, Otis had no case. The same can be said of every other important incorporation case from Gideon v. Wainwright to Roe v. Wade.

While it is true that most Americans venerate the Bill of Rights and would argue that its freedoms and due process rights are the most important protections citizens possess, the truth is, that without the Fourteenth Amendment and the protections it provides against state abuse of its authority, those protections are frail indeed.

Chapter 6

Unit 3: Civil Liberties and Civil Rights

Unit 3 explores how the U.S. Constitution, particularly the Bill of Rights and the Fourteenth Amendment, is invoked by individuals and groups to prevent national and state governments from restricting civil liberties.

- Interpretations of the Bill of Rights
- Limitations of the Bill of Rights
- Protections of the Bill of Rights
  - Selective Incorporation
  - Due Process Clause
  - Miranda Rule
  - Exclusionary Rule
  - The Right to Privacy
- Equal Protection
- Civil Rights

Overview of AP U.S. Government and Politics Unit 3

The overarching concepts for this chapter address the provisions for protecting civil liberties and rights, as engendered in the Bill of Rights and the Due Process and Equal Protection clauses of the Fourteenth Amendment.

The five main College Board content outlines for Unit 3 are as follows:

- **Interpretations of the Bill of Rights.** Provisions of the U.S. Constitution's Bill of Rights are continually being interpreted to balance the power of government and the civil liberties of individuals.

- **Protections of the Bill of Rights.** Protections of the Bill of Rights have been selectively incorporated by way of the Fourteenth Amendment's Due Process Clause to prevent state infringement of basic liberties.

- **Equal protection.** The Fourteenth Amendment's Equal Protection Clause as well as other constitutional provisions have often been used to support the advancement of equality.

- **Civil rights.** Public policy promoting civil rights is influenced by citizen-state interactions and constitutional interpretation over time.

- **The Supreme Court's interpretations of civil rights.** The Supreme Court's interpretation of the U.S. Constitution is influenced by the composition of the Court and citizen-state interactions. At times, it has restricted minority rights and, at others, protected them.

AP U.S. Government and Politics Key Concepts

Success on the exam depends on your ability to make connections to the key concepts as described in the content outlines of *AP U.S. Government and Politics Course Framework*. Remember that these concepts highlight the fundamental ideas that every student should take with them into the AP GOV exam and beyond.

Use the chart below to guide you through what is covered in Unit 3. The information contained in this chart is an abridged version of the content outlines with topic examples. Visit https://apstudent.collegeboard.org/apcourse/ap-united-states-government-and-politics for the complete updated AP GOV course curriculum framework.

AP U.S. Government and Politics Key Concepts (Unit 3)	
Key Concept	**Content**
Big Idea 2: Liberty and Order **Provisions of the U.S. Constitution's Bill of Rights are continually being interpreted to balance the power of government and the civil liberties of individuals.**	The U.S. Constitution includes a Bill of Rights, consisting of the first 10 amendments, which are specifically designed to protect individual liberties and rights. Civil liberties are constitutionally established to guarantee the freedoms that protect citizens, opinions, and property against arbitrary government interference. The application of the Bill of Rights is continuously interpreted by the courts. **First Amendment** ❑ **Religion.** The First Amendment establishment and free exercise clauses reflect an ongoing debate over balancing religions—*Engel v. Vitale* (1962) and *Wisconsin v. Yoder* (1972). ❑ **Speech.** The Supreme Court has held that symbolic speech is protected by the First Amendment—*Tinker v. Des Moines Independent Community School District* (1969). ❑ **Speech.** Efforts to balance social order and individual freedom are reflected in interpretations of the First Amendment that limit speech (i.e., time, place, and manner; defamatory, offensive, and obscene statements and gestures; that which creates a "clear and present danger" based on ruling in *Schenck v. United States* [1919]). ❑ **Press.** The Supreme Court bolstered the freedom of the press, establishing a "heavy presumption against prior restraint," even in cases involving national security—*New York Times Co. v. United States* (1971). **Second Amendment.** The Supreme Court's decisions on the Second Amendment rest on its constitutional interpretation of individual liberty. **Eighth Amendment.** Court decisions defining cruel and unusual punishment involve interpretation of the Eighth Amendment and its application to state death penalty statutes over time. **Second and Fourth amendments.** The debate about the Second and Fourth amendments involves concerns about public safety and whether or not the government regulation of firearms or collection of digital metadata promotes or interferes with public safety and individual rights.

Continued

Key Concept	Content
Big Idea 2: Liberty and Order **Protections of the Bill of Rights have been selectively incorporated by way of the Fourteenth Amendment's Due Process Clause to prevent state infringement of basic liberties.**	The doctrine of selective incorporation has imposed on state regulation of civil rights and liberties (see *McDonald v. Chicago*, 2010). The Supreme Court has on occasion ruled in favor of states' power to restrict individual liberty (i.e., speech can increase danger of public safety). The Miranda rule involves the interpretation and application of accused persons' due process rights as protected by the Fifth and Sixth amendments, yet the Supreme Court has sanctioned a public safety exception that allows unwarned interrogation to stand as evidence in court. Pretrial rights of the accused and the prohibition of unreasonable searches and seizures are intended to ensure that citizen liberties are not eclipsed by the need for social order and security. The Due Process Clause guarantees the right to an attorney and protection from unreasonable searches (e.g., *Gideon v. Wainwright*, 1963, and the exclusionary rule). While a right to privacy is not explicitly named in the Constitution, the Court has interpreted due process to protect the right of privacy from state infringement (e.g., *Roe v. Wade*, 1973).
Big Idea 3: Civic participation in a Representative Democracy **The Fourteenth Amendment's Equal Protection Clause as well as other constitutional provisions have often been used to support the advancement of equality.**	Civil rights protect individuals from discrimination based on race, national origin, religion, and sex under Due Process and Equal Protection clauses. The leadership and events associated with civil, women's, and LGBT rights are evidence of how the Equal Protection Clause can support and motivate social movements (e.g., Dr. King's *Letter from Birmingham Jail,* the Civil Rights Movement in the 1960s, the National Organization for Women, and the pro-life [anti-abortion] movement).
Big Idea 4: Competing Policymaking Interests **Public policy promoting civil rights is influenced by citizen-state interactions and constitutional interpretation over time.**	The government can respond to social movements through court rulings and/or policies. ❑ *Brown v. Board of Education of Topeka* (1954) ❑ The Civil Rights Act of 1964 ❑ Title IX of the Education Amendments Act of 1972 ❑ The Voting Rights Act of 1965
Big Idea 1: Constitutionalism **The Supreme Court's interpretation of the U.S. Constitution is influenced by the composition of the Court and citizen-state interactions. At times, it has restricted minority rights and, at others, protected them.**	Court decisions demonstrating that minority rights have been restricted at times and protected at other times. For example, ❑ State laws and Supreme Court holdings restricting African American public access (separate but equal doctrine) ❑ *Brown v. Board of Education of Topeka* (1954) ❑ The Supreme Court upholding the rights of the majority in cases that limit and prohibit majority-minority districting ❑ The debate on affirmative action includes justices who insist that the Constitution is colorblind and those who maintain that it forbids only racial classifications designed to harm minorities, not help them.

Study Questions

Glance through the study questions before you start the review section. Take notes, highlight questions, and write down page number references to reinforce your learning. Refer to this list as often as necessary until you feel comfortable with your knowledge of the material.

1. How do the U.S. Constitution and the Bill of Rights protect against government infringement on civil liberties and civil rights? (Hint: The first 10 amendments [Bill of Rights] and the Fourteenth Amendment [Due Process and Equal Protection clauses] specifically protect individual liberties and rights.)

2. How is the Bill of Rights interpreted in the context of different historical times? (Hint: Civil rights and social justice movements influence interpretations of the Bill of Rights.)

3. How are civil liberties and civil rights defined by U.S. Supreme Court decisions? (Hint: Civil liberties are basic rights that protect people against the actions of the government, while civil rights protect individuals from unfair and discriminatory treatment.)

4. What is the connection between U.S. Supreme Court decisions and attempts to balance individual liberties with public safety and national security? (Hint: Rights guaranteed under the Constitution are not absolute in that the government can limit individual practices or liberties if said rights conflict with public safety or national security.)

5. What is the importance of the Due Process Clause? (Hint: Due process promises rights to the accused.)

6. What is the importance of selective incorporation? (Hint: Selective incorporation prevents states from enacting laws that infringe on the rights of individuals.)

7. How have social movements influenced policy outcomes? (Hint: Civil rights, women's rights, and LGBT rights are evidence of how the Equal Protection Clause can support and motivate social movements.)

Important Terms and Concepts Checklist

This section is an overview of the terms, concepts, ideas, documents, and court cases that specifically target the AP GOV exam. Additional vocabulary is also included to aid in your understanding.

As you review the material covered in this chapter, remember that the required foundational documents and required Supreme Court cases (see the Appendix) are noted among the key academic terms, concepts, and language.

Note the abbreviations in the table that follows:

> **RFD** – Required Foundational Documents
> **RSCC** – Required Supreme Court Cases

As you study the terms and concepts, simply place a check mark next to each and return to this list as often as necessary to check your understanding. After you finish the chapter review section, reinforce what you have learned by working through the practice questions at the end of the chapter. Answers and explanations provide further clarification into perspectives of U.S. government and politics.

Term/ Concept	Big Idea	Study Page	Term/Concept	Big Idea	Study Page	Term/Concept	Big Idea	Study Page
Abortion	LOR	p. 195	Fifth Amendment	RFD; LOR	pp. 182–183	*New York Times Co. v. United States*	RSCC	pp. 175–176
Bill of Rights	RFD; LOR	pp. 166–167	Firearm restrictions/ regulations	LOR	p. 180	Obscene speech and offensive speech	LOR	p. 172
Brown v. Board of Education of Topeka (Brown I)	RSCC; PMI; CON	p. 198	First Amendment	RFD; LOR	pp. 167–177	*Plessy v. Ferguson*	PMI	p. 197
Brown v. Board of Education II (Brown II)	PMI	p. 198	Fourteenth Amendment	RFD; LOR	p. 190	Pro-life movement	LOR	p. 195
Civil liberties	LOR	p. 165	Fourth Amendment	RFD; LOR	p. 185	Public safety exception	LOR	p. 183
Civil Rights Act	PMI	p. 191	Freedom of religion	RFD; LOR	pp. 167–170	*Roe v. Wade*	RSCC; LOR	p. 186
Clear and present danger	LOR	pp. 173–174	Freedom of the press	RFD; LOR	pp. 175–177	*Schenck v. United States*	RSCC; LOR	pp. 173–174
Death penalty	LOR	pp. 178–179	Free Exercise Clause	RFD; LOR	p. 167	Second Amendment	RFD; LOR	pp. 179–180
Defamatory speech	LOR	p. 172	*Gideon v. Wainwright*	RSCC; LOR	p. 184	Selective incorporation	LOR	p. 181
Digital metadata collection	LOR	pp. 186–188	*Gitlow v. New York*	LOR	pp. 174–175	Sixth Amendment	RFD; LOR	pp. 183–184
Due process	LOR	pp. 181–182	Libel	LOR	p. 175	*Tinker v. Des Moines Independent Community School District*	RSCC; LOR	p. 173
Eighth Amendment	RFD; LOR	pp. 177–179	*McDonald v. Chicago*	RSCC; LOR	p. 180	Title IX	PMI	p. 191
Engel v. Vitale	RSCC; LOR	p. 169	Miranda rule	LOR	pp. 182–183	Voting Rights Act	PMI	pp. 191–193
Exclusionary rule	RFD; LOR	pp. 184–185	National Organization for Women	PMI	pp. 194–195	*Wisconsin v. Yoder*	RSCC; LOR	pp. 169–170

Chapter Review

The struggle to balance individual liberties and civil rights with national and state interests is an ongoing and challenging process. Over the course of American history, the Supreme Court has heard a variety of cases. Some decisions have landed on the side of the individual, and others on the side of the state or federal government. The Bill of Rights and other relevant amendments have been thoroughly scrutinized, assessed, and employed to set precedents by the highest court in the land. However, changing times have also led the Court to readdress previous rulings and, in many instances, reverse established precedents and ultimately deem previous rulings unconstitutional. Civil rights and social justice movements have also influenced the legal interpretation of formerly sanctioned illegalities and, by extension, public policy, including the long-standing history of racial segregation.

Let's begin by discussing the differences between the terms *civil liberties* and *civil rights*. Although these terms are often used interchangeably, there is a distinction between the two.

Civil Liberties vs. Civil Rights		
Term	Definition	Examples
Civil liberties	**Civil liberties** are the basic freedoms guaranteed in the Bill of Rights to protect individuals against actions by the government.	Examples include freedom of religion, freedom of speech, freedom of the press, freedom of assembly, and a variety of due process guarantees such as the right to counsel and the right to a speedy and public trial.
Civil rights	**Civil rights** guarantee basic rights to protect people against discriminatory and unfair treatment—to be free from unequal treatment. Civil rights are based on the Fourteenth Amendment's Equal Protection Clause.	Examples include laws that protect people against age, gender, race, or disability discrimination in employment, housing, and education.

TEST TIP: As you work through this chapter, keep this fundamental principle in mind: Civil liberties enshrined in the Constitution are not absolute rights and are subject to legislative restriction and judicial interpretation, depending on the circumstances in which liberties are being exercised. For example, public demonstrations are protected by the First Amendment guarantees of freedom of speech and of assembly. However, in the interest of public safety, the *time, place, and manner* of demonstrations can be regulated by local authorities. While personal liberties cannot be abridged arbitrarily, rights are relative rather than absolute, and there are select instances in which a more compelling government interest (e.g., public safety) outweighs individual liberty.

Interpretations of the Bill of Rights

Heads Up: What You Need to Know

On the AP GOV exam, you should understand how the interpretation and application of the First Amendment's Establishment Clause and Free Exercise Clause reflect an ongoing debate over balancing majoritarian religious practices and the free exercise of religion.

It is also important to understand *how* and *why* the Supreme Court attempted to balance individual freedom while preserving public order and safety. First, we'll focus on the federal government's response to cases involving civil liberties as protected in the Bill of Rights.

The learning objectives that you must be able to accomplish are:

Explain how the U.S. Constitution protects individual liberties and rights.

Describe the rights protected in the Bill of Rights.

Explain the extent to which the Supreme Court's interpretation of the First and Second amendments reflects a commitment to individual liberty.

Explain how the Supreme Court has attempted to balance claims of individual freedom with laws and enforcement procedures that promote public order and safety.

Limitations of the Bill of Rights

The **Bill of Rights** was passed in 1791 as a response to Anti-Federalist fears that the Necessary and Proper Clause, in combination with the Supremacy Clause, did not provide the people with adequate protections against abuse of their liberty by the government of the United States. While the Bill of Rights, or the first 10 amendments of the Constitution, protects all Americans from excessive power exerted by the central government, it does not grant absolute rights to everyone. Given certain conditions, civil liberties can be limited.

The first eight amendments pertain to specific individual rights guaranteed to the people, while the Ninth and Tenth amendments provide broad protections for rights not specifically enumerated in the Constitution or listed in the Bill of Rights, which were to be reserved to the states and retained by the people. What exactly those rights entailed has been a question largely determined by the federal courts, particularly the Supreme Court. The Bill of Rights is a dynamic document whose meaning has been interpreted and reinterpreted in different historical and social contexts. It is also important to remember that Court rulings over the course of American history have been rendered by justices with different philosophical leanings and biases as to constitutional interpretation. In some instances, the Court has upheld the cause of the state and in others, the cause of the individual. Although any number of Court rulings have imposed restrictions on civil liberties, such restrictions are not arbitrarily imposed but instead are adopted when a persuasive case can be made that the restrictive intent is constitutionally justifiable.

Heads Up: What You Need to Know

Certain individual liberties and rights are specifically highlighted in the College Board Course Framework for your attention. To do well on the AP GOV exam, focus your attention on them.

- First Amendment: Freedom of religion, emphasizing the Free Exercise Clause and the Establishment Clause, freedom of speech (in all its forms), and freedom of the press.
- Second Amendment: The right to keep and bear arms.
- Fourth Amendment: Protections against unwarranted intrusions (right to privacy implied).
- Fifth Amendment: Guarantee of due process and the protection against self-incrimination.
- Sixth Amendment: The assistance of counsel.
- Eighth Amendment: Ban on cruel and unusual punishment and the application of this prohibition to the death penalty.
- Fourteenth Amendment: Protection from discrimination via the Equal Protection Clause and the Due Process Clause. Prohibits states from denying equal protection and/or due process of the law to any citizen. It is the basis of key civil rights Court decisions (e.g., *Brown v. Board of Education of Topeka,* 1954) as well as important legislation passed by Congress (e.g., the Civil Rights Act of 1964).

Remember, the first 10 amendments were only intended as protections for the people against abuse of power by the central government, not the states. The Fourteenth Amendment opened the door for the courts to incorporate the states into the meaning and application of those protections and for Congress to provide enforcement through legislation.

The First Amendment

The **First Amendment** includes a list of fundamental American liberties. This section will cover the Free Exercise Clause and the Establishment Clause, which form the foundation of the freedom of religion guarantee and the Required Supreme Court Cases (RSCC) that have impacted the meaning and practice of freedom of religion, freedom of speech, and freedom of the press.

First Amendment: Freedom of Religion

Two First Amendment clauses concerning **freedom of religion** that you should be familiar with for the AP GOV exam are the Establishment Clause and the Free Exercise Clause.

The **Establishment Clause** forms what Thomas Jefferson referred to as "the wall of separation" between church and state. It states, "Congress shall make no law respecting an establishment of religion." In other words, the government cannot impose a religion on the people. The government is to take no role in advancing one religion or prohibiting another. This guarantee is designed to protect all people professing faith from the coercive power of the government, regardless of their religion. It also protects those who choose not to profess a faith in the tenets of any religion. In other words, it promotes freedom of conscience for all. The protection cuts both ways; that is, government should not play a role in endorsing or inhibiting any religion, and religion should play no role in government decision making.

The **Free Exercise Clause** prevents the government from prohibiting religious practices.

Source: Dave Granlund, "Celebrating the First Amendment Freedoms," December 13, 2010.

Heads Up: What You Need to Know

On the AP GOV exam, you should know that through precedent the Supreme Court has established that religious liberty is the greatest protection among all the rights enshrined in the First Amendment. However, religious freedom is not without limits. The government can limit religious practices that violate public safety or disregard laws. A 19th-century ruling by the Court in *Reynolds v. United States* (1878) reflected the tone of the Court regarding religious practice and the law. The Court upheld the prosecution of a Mormon man in Utah, George Reynolds, for violating a federal law against bigamy (simultaneously being married to multiple spouses), something Reynolds argued was a requirement of his religion. The Court ruled that Congress couldn't outlaw the belief in polygamy but could outlaw its practice. People can *believe* what they choose, but *actions* based on those beliefs cannot ignore the law. The Court stood firmly on this line between religious belief and illegal acts for decades until the 1960s, when things began to shift. The Warren Court signaled a willingness to consider whether existing laws placed "a considerable burden" on a person's religious practices. The legal question surrounding the proper balance between majoritarian religious beliefs (*majoritarianism* refers to a level of primacy enjoyed by those in society who are part of the dominant majority) and the First Amendment continues to be modified and refined in case after case placed on the Supreme Court docket. The rulings in *Engel v. Vitale* and *Wisconsin v. Yoder* illustrate this point.

Freedom of Religion Required Supreme Court Cases		
Court Case	Argument	Outcome
Engel v. Vitale (1962)	**Question:** Is the endorsement of prayer by government officials for use in public schools a violation of the First Amendment? YES **Arguments:** The New York State Board of Regents crafted a nondenominational prayer that was incorporated into the daily classroom routine of each public-school classroom. Students recited the prayer, along with the Pledge of Allegiance. In 1959, Hyde Park, New York, parents gathered to sue the school board president, William Vitale, on behalf of the students. The parents argued that the prayer violated the First Amendment's Establishment Clause, and by extension, the Fourteenth Amendment. Because the prayer was voluntary, Vitale reasoned, no violation existed under the First Amendment. Initially, the state courts ruled in favor of Vitale, claiming that there was no reinforcement of a particular religion by employing the nondenominational prayer. This ruling was further upheld by the state appellate court.	**Court ruling:** The Supreme Court ruled that school-sponsored prayer in public schools is unconstitutional. In an overwhelming majority (6–1) decision, the Court overturned the previous rulings. Justices reasoned that prayer is by definition a religious activity. When government officials write and distribute a prayer for recitation in public schools, whether nondenominational and voluntary or not, they are promoting religion. Moreover, simply making the wording vague does not avoid conflict with the Establishment Clause, particularly, in this case, since the use of "Almighty God" promotes a family of religions that acknowledge the presence of a singular God. **Significance:** Despite the Court's ruling, the matter of school prayer remains decidedly controversial within large religious constituencies; the controversy was further magnified as this case set the stage for other religious activities traditionally incorporated into public events and ceremonies to be challenged as violations of the Establishment Clause.
Wisconsin v. Yoder (1972)	**Question:** Did a Wisconsin statute requiring that all parents send their children to school at least until the age of 16, thereby criminalizing the actions of parents who refused to comply with the law for religious reasons, violate the First Amendment's Free Exercise Clause? YES **Arguments:** Three Amish parents, members of the Conservative Amish Mennonite Church, were convicted of violating Wisconsin's compulsory school attendance law by refusing to enroll their children in either public or private school after the children had completed the eighth grade. The parents won their appeal in the State Supreme Court of Wisconsin, arguing that (1) Amish children continued their education after the eighth grade through vocational training at home in keeping with the rural lifestyle dictated by three centuries of Amish belief and practice, and (2) high school attendance was	**Court ruling:** While the state has legitimate social concerns in enforcing compulsory education, its power to do so is not absolute when it infringes on other fundamental rights. In this case, such enforcement violated the religious freedom of the respondents. By affirming the State Supreme Court of Wisconsin's decision, the U.S. Supreme Court ruled in its 7–0 decision that compulsory education is not mandatory and enforceable when such education violates sincerely held religious beliefs. The Court's decision highlighted not only the consistency of Amish religious beliefs of rejecting materialism and embracing simplicity held for over three centuries, but also the success of the Amish community in providing vocational education for their children at home after their years in public education were completed. Their beliefs and approach to education for their children kept their communities economically and socially viable.

Continued

Court Case	Argument	Outcome
	contrary to their religion and way of life; thus, forcing them to enroll their children in high school endangered their salvation. The state of Wisconsin appealed the decision to the U.S. Supreme Court, arguing that the state was empowered as *parens patriae* (protector of citizens) to ensure the secondary education of all children regardless of the parents' wishes.	**Significance:** The Court did not take its decision lightly, noting that a claim of religious freedom as a reason for taking children out of school should not be frivolous or unsupported by evidence of sincere religious belief. This case is often cited as support for the home school movement initiated by evangelical Christian leaders in the 1990s.

TEST TIP: The AP GOV exam requires not only knowledge of the Supreme Court cases, but also how they demonstrate why a certain ruling is either upheld in accordance with a lower court's determination or why a ruling is struck down in accordance with a lower court's determination. Understanding this relationship is important because you may be asked to explain how school sponsorship of religious activities violates the Establishment Clause (i.e., *Engel v. Vitale*) and why disregarding religious convictions may legally infringe on an individual's right to free exercise (i.e., *Wisconsin v. Yoder*).

First Amendment: Freedom of Speech

Freedom of speech is the civil liberty that is arguably the definitive touchstone of the United States as a constitutional democracy. It is intended to protect expressions of thought both *symbolic* (demonstrated through actions) and *direct* (expressed in spoken or written words) to ensure that ideas representing the widest possible spectrum of debate on public policy issues is shared by and among the people. There is no other means to a functioning constitutional democracy but through limits placed on the government's ability to censure speech, and, most particularly, speech that expresses either a minority or an unpopular view. The Framers shared a belief in the fundamental principle that citizens should not be subject to a government that controls the transmission of speech or regulates rhetorical exchanges. Individuals must be allowed to determine for themselves what speech they deem meaningful.

Keeping in mind not only that all rights are relative rather than absolute, but also the critical nature of the free speech guarantee, it should not be surprising that the Supreme Court has had to examine numerous cases over the course of the nation's history in which freedom of speech has been challenged.

- **Symbolic speech.** Freedom of speech can involve the right to express oneself through actions rather than literal speech. Such actions that the Court has endorsed as constitutionally protected speech include the right to burn the national flag (*Texas v. Johnson*, 1989), to wear clothing in solidarity with a cause or movement (*Tinker v. Des Moines Independent Community School District*, 1969), and refusal to salute the flag or recite the Pledge of Allegiance (*West Virginia State Board of Education v. Barnette*, 1943).
- **Spoken or written speech.** Generally speaking, freedom of speech means that the government cannot impose a legal burden on individuals or organizations in the expression of their views in spoken or written form.

Limits on Free Speech

As stated, the civil liberty protections asserted in the Bill of Rights do not confer an absolute prohibition against government intervention in the exercise of those rights. In regard to free speech, the government reserves the right to restrict the *time, place, and manner (TPM)* of speech in the public arena if there is a compelling government interest in doing so that is content-neutral. For example, a public demonstration planned for a given street at noon, during which demonstrators will lie down in the street blocking access, would pose a risk to public safety; therefore, a local government can deny a permit. They cannot deny the permit because they do not approve of the reason for the demonstration or of the scheduled speakers. In other words, context and the responsibility of public officials to maintain social order matter, according to the Supreme Court. Can the passing out of leaflets be banned because they cause litter? No. In a veiled attempt to prohibit Jehovah's Witnesses from passing out their "Watchtower" magazine, can municipalities require permits for door-to-door soliciting in the interest of fraud protection and privacy rights? No. These and many other questions have come before the Court and demonstrate the many facets involved in the First Amendment's free speech protections.

Heads Up: What You Need to Know

On the AP GOV exam, you must keep in mind that balancing social order and freedom is an effort reflected in interpretations of the First Amendment that limit speech.

1. Time, place, and manner restrictions
2. Defamatory, offensive, and obscene statements and gestures
3. Clear and present danger speech

Key Facts about Time, Place, and Manner (TPM) Restrictions

The following list describes the essential framework of the TPM restrictions:

Time. While the government does not typically regulate political expression, the government is compelled to intervene if such expression is cause for legitimate societal concern. The right to assemble as a means of political expression is protected by the Constitution; however, if an assembly disrupts the flow of traffic, its crowd becomes uncontrollable, or there is another problematic situation, the government is authorized to become involved.

Place. The place in which individuals opt to express their opinions or beliefs is categorized as follows: traditional public forums, limited public forums, and nonpublic forums.

- Traditional public forums are defined as easily accessible areas, like parks and streets, which are particularly important for individuals who are unable to utilize other, more exclusive kinds of mediums (print media, television, etc.). It is in these areas that the government tends to impose lighter restrictions.

- Limited public forums are those that are designed for the main purpose of fostering civic discourse. These platforms include public universities and state capitol buildings, to name a few. The government is authorized to exercise more graduated regulations on limited public forum expressions.

- Nonpublic forums are areas restricted to only a limited number of individuals, personal residences, military bases, and other properties that are not primarily or secondarily designed to accommodate free speech expressions. The government is most likely to intervene to protect the primary purpose of nonpublic forums, as compared to traditional public and limited public forums.

Manner. Restrictions placed on the manner of free speech are most likely to fall into the category of symbolic speech. Symbolic speech is that which is not necessarily written or spoken, but can include gestures, flag burning, or even sleeping in public parks or facilities. The mode, or manner, of speech is scrutinized more heavily if a group or individual is attempting to suppress the rights of others to symbolically express themselves.

Key Facts about Defamatory, Offensive, or Obscenity Restrictions

Although freedom of speech is vast in scope, courts have recognized that there are some instances of free speech that are not protected by the First Amendment. Beyond TPM restrictions, the Court must also assess the content of controversial speeches and gestures by determining if they fall under the criteria of a **defamatory, offensive,** or **obscene** speech. If a direct or symbolic speech falls in one of these three categories, then the Court is obligated to place restrictions on the expression.

Speech not protected by the First Amendment includes:

Defamatory speech. Defamatory speech includes libelous (written) and slanderous (spoken) words that express false statements of fact to misrepresent an individual, business, or organization in a way that unduly disparages or wrongly undermines their credibility.

Offensive speech. Offensive speech is gauged by the rule of "fighting words." According to the Court, "fighting words" qualify as that which seeks to incite riots for the purpose of disrupting the peace or issuing an abusive statement to an individual that might cause the harmed individual to retaliate with violence. For example, to incite actions that might harm others, like falsely shouting "fire" in a crowded theater, or to make false threats of terrorism that might cause a public outcry.

Obscene speech. Obscene speech is interpreted in accordance with applying the *Miller test* (its name is derived from *Miller v. California* [1973]; also called the three-prong obscenity test). The Miller test sets the basic guidelines for obscene speech. According to the three-part Miller test, speech is "unprotected" by the First Amendment when it (1) defies community decency standards; (2) exhibits sexual conduct condemned by state law; and (3) is void of any legitimate literary, artistic, political, or scientific value.

TEST TIP: On the AP GOV exam, you should know that symbolic speech is protected by the First Amendment, as demonstrated in *Tinker v. Des Moines Independent Community School District* (1969). However, all forms of speech must comply with the "clear and present danger" rule established in *Schenck v. United States* (1919).

Freedom of Speech		
Required Supreme Court Cases		
Court Case	**Argument**	**Outcome**
Tinker v. Des Moines Independent Community School District (1969)	**Question:** Does a prohibition on wearing armbands in a public school as a form of protest violate the students' right to free speech? YES **Arguments:** Free speech protections guaranteed by the First Amendment were violated when Mary Beth Tinker (13 years old) and a group of her peers were suspended from school and denied readmittance until they removed the black armbands they wore in school to demonstrate their solidarity with protestors marching against the Vietnam War in 1965. On their behalf, their parents sought damages and an injunction to keep the school district from enforcing their rule against wearing armbands. The school board argued that the rule imposed against armbands was necessary to its efforts to enforce school discipline. The District Court agreed, ruling that the school district's actions were reasonable in support of their efforts to uphold school discipline. The Court of Appeals for the Eighth Circuit affirmed.	**Court ruling:** The Court reversed the lower court rulings. In the Court's majority opinion (7–2), it was argued that the armbands, as an expression of the students' opinion, were a form of "pure speech" unrelated to traditional areas of school discipline such as aggressive acts by students or violations of the dress code. Further, First Amendment protections are extended to students and teachers, protections they do not forfeit simply by walking onto school property. Without evidence that the speech would result in a substantial disruption of school discipline or would interfere with the rights of others to pursue academic learning, the ban on armbands was deemed unconstitutional. **Significance:** Not only did the Court recognize symbolic acts used to express an opinion as a form of speech protected by the First Amendment, but it also endorsed First Amendment rights for students with the assertion that students do not "shed their constitutional rights to freedom of speech or expression at the schoolhouse gate."
Schenck v. United States (1919)	**Question:** Is the First Amendment violated when Congress passes a law that punishes dissent during a time of war? NO **Argument:** Socialist Party member Charles Schenck argued that his conviction for distributing leaflets urging citizens to resist the draft as a violation of the Thirteenth Amendment's prohibition against involuntary servitude was unconstitutional. His argument was based on his claim that the Espionage Act of 1917 (during World War I) violated the First Amendment guarantee that "Congress shall make no law…abridging the freedom of speech." Schenck was convicted of violating Section 3 of the law, which prohibited the willful interference in recruiting or enlistment service in the U.S. military.	**Court ruling:** The Court ruled unanimously in favor of the government. While conceding that in "many places and in ordinary times" Schenck would have the right to distribute his pamphlets, Justice Oliver Wendell Holmes asserted that how far free speech protections go depends on the circumstances. In times of war Congress has the right to restrict speech that hinders the nation's war efforts. Holmes famously continued, "The question in every case is whether the words are used in such circumstances and are of such a nature as to create a **clear and present danger** that they will bring about the substantive evils that Congress has a right to prevent."

Continued

Court Case	Argument	Outcome
	The government argued that Schenck's pamphlets were intended to weaken the loyalty of soldiers and to obstruct military recruiting, thus giving aid and comfort to the enemy during a time of war.	**Significance:** The **clear and present danger test** has been applied in many other free speech cases. It remains controversial and has been criticized by legal scholars and Supreme Court justices as well. Renowned justice the late Hugo Black was emphatic and unflinching in his denunciation of the clear and present danger test, arguing that in balancing free speech against some other government goal, the protection is destroyed entirely.
Gitlow v. New York (1925)	**Questions:** Could the Supreme Court extend its authority over limitations set forth in the First Amendment in cases involving statutes passed by state governments? YES Did New York's Criminal Anarchy Law prohibiting speech that encouraged violence against the government deprive Gitlow of his right to free speech? NO **Arguments:** In its first major First Amendment case argued before the Supreme Court, the American Civil Liberties Union (ACLU) argued that Benjamin Gitlow's "The Left Wing Manifesto" presented a Marxist-based historical analysis rather than an incitement to overthrow the government, as charged in his conviction by the state of New York for violating the Criminal Anarchy Law. New York argued for its authority to criminalize political advocacy involving the overthrow of the government "by force, violence, or assassination" to minimize the threat of political violence and harm to public safety.	**Court ruling:** As to the first question, the Court found that the authority to intervene in First Amendment cases involving state laws was granted by the Due Process Clause of the Fourteenth Amendment; therefore, the state cannot use its authority to act in the public interest to impose statutes restricting speech that are arbitrary or unreasonable. As to the second question, the Court ruled that governments have reasonable interest in preventing speech that threatens their existence. Finding in favor of New York, the Court applied the **bad tendency test,** which permits restrictions on speech by government if, in its view, the sole tendency of the speech is to incite or cause illegal activity. States can adopt preventative measures to restrict the expression of ideas that may be sufficient to lead to an imminent danger that violent acts against the government will follow. **Significance:** The lasting impact of this case has been (1) the continued Court endorsement of government censorship of political dissent speech through application of the **bad tendency test,** and (2) the Court's assertion of what has become known as the **incorporation doctrine**—that is, the use of the Court's authority under the Fourteenth Amendment's Due Process Clause to incorporate the states into the meaning and application of civil liberties under the Bill of Rights. This incorporation is considered "selective" in that the *Gitlow* decision did not

Court Case	Argument	Outcome
		incorporate the entire Bill of Rights, only the First Amendment protections for free speech. All other rights had to be incorporated by the Court on a case-by-case basis. By this process almost all of the protections of the Bill of Rights have subsequently been incorporated.

First Amendment: Freedom of the Press

Freedom of the press enables the use of multiple forms of media (broadcast, print, and Internet-based) to publish, circulate, and disseminate opinions without fear of censorship by the government. However, as with freedom of speech, freedom of the press does not come without limitations.

Heads Up: What You Need to Know

On the AP GOV exam, you should know the limitations on freedom of the press.

Limits on Freedom of the Press

What justifies government restrictions on **freedom of the press?** The Supreme Court has recognized a set of specific circumstances that authorize the government to place the following limits on free press:

- Prohibiting **libel** (defamation of character and reputation in print) against private citizens and organizations
- Punishment for publication of defamatory material targeting public figures if the injured party can prove *actual malice* (the knowing and reckless publication of false information)
- Restricting publication of obscene materials
- Restricting publication of material designed to incite immediate violence or other unlawful activity
- Authorizing the government to compel reporters via subpoena to identify the source for a published story if the source violated federal law by leaking confidential information (e.g., the name of a covert CIA operative; transcripts of closed grand jury testimony)

Freedom of the Press Required Supreme Court Case		
Court Case	Argument	Outcome
New York Times Co. v. United States (1971)	**Question:** Was the effort by the Nixon administration to exercise prior restraint* to prevent the publication of "classified information" a violation of the First Amendment and therefore unconstitutional? YES	**Court ruling:** The Supreme Court ruled that the government did not prove that further publication would infringe on national security, so it failed to overcome a "heavy presumption against" prior restraint of the press. In addition, the use of the word "security" was too broad in nature to justify the

Continued

Court Case	Argument	Outcome
	Arguments: In 1971, after an initial publication by *The New York Times* of parts of a comprehensive and confidential 7,000-page report on the history of U.S. involvement in Vietnam by military analyst Daniel Ellsberg, the Nixon administration secured a restraining order preventing both *The New York Times* and *The Washington Post* from publishing any further parts of the report. Ellsberg's massive study was based on information gleaned from classified Pentagon documents (the "Pentagon Papers"). The president argued that "prior restraint" was necessary to protect national security. He was exercising his executive authority, claiming the First Amendment was subordinate to the need of the executive branch to protect the secrecy of the information in question. Nixon's attorney general also argued that the publication violated the Espionage Act. The Court combined the *New York Times* and *Washington Post* cases, allowing attorneys for the newspapers to collaborate on the arguments presented to the Court: (1) The government provided no basis for a "reason to believe" the publication would cause injury to the United States or provide an advantage to any foreign nation; further, (2) it was irrelevant to cite a criminal statute (the Espionage Act) in a civil proceeding; and (3) the First Amendment exists to protect the very type of publication represented by the Pentagon Papers, which expose government misjudgments and outright misconduct. **Prior restraint* is an extreme form of print censorship involving a prohibition against dissemination of information <u>before</u> publication.	violation of fundamental rights guaranteed in the First Amendment. Finally, the publication would not cause any inevitable or immediate reaction imperiling American military forces. Given the justices' reasoning, prior restraint was unjustified. **Significance:** Invoking the Founders' hopes and dreams, the Court proclaimed that "only a free and unrestrained press can effectively expose deception in government…the newspapers nobly did that which the Founders hoped and trusted they would do." The Court's decision placed clear limits on an executive's broad application of the term "national security" to prevent publication of materials that expose official misdeeds, misrepresentations, and/or mistakes in judgment.

Source: Mike Dater "Truth About Vietnam," 2001. The Pentagon Papers were significant because before the press became involved, Americans were lied to by the government about the U.S. motives to fight in Vietnam.

Did you know? Prior restraint was found to be unconstitutional in *Near v. Minnesota* (1931), a judicial standard subsequently applied to free speech generally. The actions taken by the Nixon administration in 1971 to stop publication of the Pentagon Papers was the first time that officials in the government successfully secured a prior restraint by arguing that "national security" superseded the prior restraint standard established 40 years earlier. *Near v. Minnesota* was cited as precedent in the Court's ruling in *New York Times Co. v. United States* that the prohibition against prior restraint cannot simply be set aside through a broad application of "national security." An Oscar-nominated movie, *The Post* (2017), recounts the legal battle enjoined by *The Washington Post* and *The New York Times* against the president of the United States in defense of freedom of the press.

The Eighth Amendment

The **Eighth Amendment** prohibits the government from imposing excessive bail, excessive fines, or cruel and unusual punishment, including torture. It raises the concern of to what extent the government can enforce punishment on convicted criminals (see also the section "Due Process Clause," pp. 181–182).

TEST TIP: On the AP GOV exam, questions focusing on the Eighth Amendment highlight the controversial use of capital punishment (the "death penalty") and whether government-sanctioned executions violate the prohibition against "cruel and unusual punishment."

Key Facts about the Eighth Amendment

Punishment must fit the crime. The Eighth Amendment prohibition against "excessive fines" and/or "cruel and unusual punishment" infers that punishment for a crime must be "proportional" to the crime committed, meaning the punishment must mirror the gravity of the offense. When a jury or a court is asked to impose a sentence, the individual circumstances surrounding the crime must be examined and the final sentence must adhere to sentencing guidelines to ensure the appropriateness of the sentence in keeping with Eighth Amendment protections.

Cruel and unusual punishment. "Cruel and unusual" refers to objectionable punishment inflicted intentionally to cause pain, humiliation, or suffering on a person. The Eighth Amendment declares that individuals should not be subjected to punishments classified as "cruel and unusual."

The death penalty. The Eighth Amendment has been used as the legal foundation for challenging the constitutionality of the **death penalty** based on an assertion that as a form of punishment, it is "cruel and unusual." The death penalty is perhaps one of the most controversial 20th-century subjects shaping American political discourse focused on crime and punishment.

Under the U.S. federal system, the power to define crime and determine punishment is concurrent; that is, while decisions defining federal crimes and assigning punishments for such crimes are legislated by Congress, the states determine what constitutes a crime within their territory and how those crimes should be punished. Consequently, state laws regarding the death penalty differ, with a number of states banning its use as a punishment altogether.

What constitutes "cruel and unusual" in legal terms? In the case of *Furman v. Georgia* (1972), the high court found all state schemes for imposing the death penalty were "cruel and unusual" and, therefore, unconstitutional. The 5–4 decision indicated that the justices were as divided as the rest of the nation. However, the majority expressed their concern about the arbitrariness in imposing the death penalty under existing laws and what appeared to be a racial bias against black defendants in imposing a death sentence. Justice William Brennan went on to outline four principles that determine what qualifies a punishment as "cruel and unusual."

1. If the punishment is degrading to human dignity, especially via torture.
2. If the punishment is severe and arbitrarily inflicted.
3. If the punishment is rejected by society as a whole (national consensus).
4. If the punishment is otherwise unnecessary.

At the time of the *Furman* decision, 35 states immediately took steps to draft new death penalty legislation that would avoid the pitfalls highlighted by Justice Brennan. To date, 19 states and the District of Columbia have banned use of the death penalty, while 31 states continue to recognize its legitimacy.

Did you know? The death penalty is reserved for the most heinous acts of murder and felony murder (an act of murder committed while perpetrating another felony act). Yet, some states have attempted to impose the death penalty for crimes other than murder. In these instances, the Supreme Court applies the **national consensus test.** The consensus test was highlighted in *Kennedy v. Louisiana* (2008). The Louisiana legislature made it legal to execute defendants found guilty of the rape of a child under the age of 12. When that law was challenged in court, Louisiana officials argued that six other states had similar laws. The Court ruled that six states did not constitute a national consensus, and thus, Louisiana's law was an unconstitutional violation of the "cruel and unusual" standard established by the Eighth Amendment and given the specific guidelines set forth by Justice Brennan in *Furman v. Georgia.*

The Second Amendment

The **Second Amendment** guarantees the following: "A well-regulated militia, being necessary to the security of a free state, the right of the people to keep and bear arms, shall not be infringed." What the Framers intended by the wording of the Second Amendment is at the heart of the contentious national debate over gun ownership and attempts by states to regulate the ownership and possession of guns. Did the Framers' recognition for states to call on a citizen militia for their defense in times of emergency guarantee an individual's right to own and possess firearms? What about those who suffer from mental illness or have a violent criminal history—does their liberty to possess firearms outweigh public safety? What is meant by "well regulated"? Having written the Second Amendment at a time when no standing army existed and the deadliest weapon people owned was likely a musket, does the protection in the modern era extend to deadlier, more technologically advanced, military-grade fire power? These are among the key questions that continue to drive the national debate over gun control. As with all issues at this level and intensity of attention, the Supreme Court has weighed in.

Source: Paul Tuma, "Dueling Axes—Bipartisan Erosion of the Bill of Rights," 2009.

Did you know? The regulation of gun ownership falls under the purview of the states. Registration of firearms, background checks, permits to carry concealed weapons, and prohibitions against carrying guns on school campuses are variations on gun regulation statutes that vary widely from state to state. In its review of cases involving gun regulation, which in effect prohibits the possession of firearms, the Supreme Court has come down on the side of individual liberty. In *District of Columbia v. Heller* (2008), a 5–4 majority ruled that handguns are considered "arms" under the Second Amendment and individuals have the right to possess handguns for self-defense in the home irrespective of service in the militia, a right that cannot be denied.

It is important to note that the District of Columbia is a federal district under the jurisdiction of Congress; consequently, the *Heller* decision applied only to any action taken by Congress to ban possession of handguns. It was not until 2 years later under the Court's ruling in *McDonald v. Chicago* (2010) that the states were incorporated into the Second Amendment protection of the right of individuals to own and possess firearms.

The Right to Keep and Bear Arms
Required Supreme Court Case

Court Case	Argument	Outcome
McDonald v. Chicago (2010)	**Question:** Does the Due Process Clause of the Fourteenth Amendment incorporate the Second Amendment, thus making the individual right to own a firearm for self-defense applicable to the states? YES **Arguments:** Otis McDonald, a resident of Chicago concerned about gang violence in his neighborhood and denied the right to possess a handgun for self-defense, filed suit against the city. His argument hinged on a Chicago ordinance requiring that all handguns be registered but denying registration for any guns not previously registered before 1982. This, in effect, banned gun ownership to anyone like McDonald who attempted to buy and register a handgun after 1982 and denied him the right of self-defense. Under the Fourteenth Amendment's Due Process Clause, the constitutional standard decided in *District of Columbia v. Heller* (2008), a similar Court case involving gun restrictions, should also apply to the states. Lawyers for the city of Chicago argued that states should be able to develop **firearms restrictions** that are based on local conditions. To overturn Chicago's firearms statute would have a future effect on the ability of states to regulate the possession of handguns, thus fundamentally impacting the ideal of federalism.	**Court ruling:** Justice Samuel Alito, writing for the majority, referred to the *Heller* decision in which the majority of the Court had ruled that the liberty to arm and defend oneself is both "fundamental "and "deeply rooted" in the nation's history and traditions. As such, the right of self-defense must be protected. The Due Process Clause included in the Fourteenth Amendment prohibits states from depriving individuals of their liberty, thus incorporating the states into the Second Amendment protection of an individual's right to own and possess a firearm for self-defense, as highlighted in the *Heller* case. **Significance:** Strong dissenting opinions were issued by four justices. The justices claimed that the majority's reasoning in the *Heller* case was flawed. The four justices reasoned that the historical analysis lacked evidence of private armed defense as a fundamental right or that belief in such a right motivated the Framers in crafting the Second Amendment. The *Heller* and the *McDonald* decisions remain controversial, both among gun control advocates and those defending the reserved powers of the states.

Protections of the Bill of Rights

On the AP GOV exam, you must be able to identify the doctrine of **selective incorporation** and explain how it has imposed limitations on state violations of civil liberties. It is important to understand how the **Due Process Clause** is applied, including how the Court has interpreted the Due Process Clause in the Fourteenth Amendment to protect the state from infringing upon individual liberties and privacy.

Heads Up: What You Need to Know

The learning objectives that you must be able to accomplish are:

Explain the implications of the doctrine of selective incorporation.

Explain the extent to which states are limited by the Due Process Clause from infringing upon individual rights.

Selective Incorporation

Selective incorporation is the term used to describe judicial decisions by the federal courts that incorporate the states into the body of protections guaranteed by the Bill of Rights. Before passage of the Fourteenth Amendment in 1868, this was not possible, as the Bill of Rights was intended to protect citizens and the states from abuse of power by the federal government. This fact was underscored in the case of *Barron v. Baltimore* (1833) involving a lawsuit in which John Barron sought compensation under the Takings Clause of the Fifth Amendment for property lost during street construction undertaken by the city of Baltimore, Maryland. The ruling in this case by the Marshall Court made it clear that the Bill of Rights placed restrictions on the federal government only. The wording of the Fourteenth Amendment changed everything. It specifically enjoins <u>states</u> from enacting laws that violate a person's right to due process. Incorporation is "selective" because the decision to incorporate a specific protection or guarantee is done on a case-by-case basis. Presently, only four protections remain unincorporated:

- Third Amendment – quartering troops
- Fifth Amendment – indictment by a grand jury
- Seventh Amendment – jury trial in civil cases
- Eighth Amendment – excessive bails and fines

Due Process Clause

In the U.S., civil liberties are granted to all citizens, including, and most especially, those accused of crimes. It is only through due process guarantees that citizens can be assured that the government will act fairly and not use its immense power and authority to target dissenters, those in the minority, or those otherwise out of favor through abuse of the system of justice.

Due process consists of the assurance that the government will abide by requirements that it operate within the boundaries of the law to ensure fair procedures in the administration of justice. The Due Process Clause enshrined in the Fifth and Fourteenth amendments establishes due process as an entitlement that cannot be denied to any person by the government of the United States (Fifth Amendment) or by the government of their state (Fourteenth Amendment). Some of the legal boundaries imposed on agencies of the government are articulated in the Fourth, Fifth, and Sixth amendments (e.g., protection against warrantless searches, protection against self-incrimination, the right to counsel, and the right to a trial by jury). It is, however, the Due Process Clause that provides the broadest sweep of protection and promise for fairness and legality, reserving to the people rights and expectations for fair treatment, which may not be expressly stated elsewhere in the Constitution.

"No person shall be deprived of life, liberty, or property, without due process of law."

> TEST TIP: The due process guarantees included in the Constitution were designed to ensure that individual liberty is not eclipsed by the government's legitimate need to provide for social order and public safety. Is society made safer, is social order achieved, by government unrestrained in its use of police power and the judicial system? Clearly, in the minds of the Framers, the answer to that question was "no." Understanding why these protections exist and how the courts act to weigh liberty against government responsibility for order and security is important to students taking the AP GOV exam. The exam focuses on three elements of due process to illustrate this enduring understanding: the protection against warrantless searches, the protection against self-incrimination, and the right to counsel.

The Miranda Rule

The **Miranda rule** refers to rights granted to the accused—protection from self-incrimination and the right to counsel. According to the **Fifth Amendment,** no individual can be "compelled in any criminal case to be a witness against himself"; that is, the state cannot force a person to confess to actions to which criminal liability is attached, nor can a person be forced at trial to take the witness stand in his or her own defense, opening the individual to cross-examination by the prosecution. This protection is grounded in two fundamental legal principles: All people are innocent until proven guilty and the burden to prove guilt is on the state. Accused individuals have no responsibility to help the state build a case of guilt and are in fact, by the words of the Fifth Amendment, protected against any attempt by the state to compel a confession or force accused individuals to provide any information that would tend to incriminate them. The right to counsel is linked to the protections against self-incrimination. Trained and competent legal counsel guide an accused person through the legal process, ensuring along the way that their client's constitutional rights are not violated. When an accused person engages the assistance of counsel, among the attorney's first acts is to tell the accused to remain silent.

Today, the public has been exposed to years of police and courtroom dramas on television, in movie theaters, and via online streaming of entertainment content. The Miranda warnings are well known and may be the only constitutional rights most citizens know! But what if it is 1963 and you are an eighth-grade dropout working as a laborer in Phoenix, Arizona, standing accused of the rape of an 18-year-old girl? Do you know that you can remain silent and refuse to talk to police? Are you aware that it is your right to call an attorney as soon as you are arrested? If you are Ernesto Miranda, possibly not, and so after 2 hours of police interrogation with no attorney representing him in the room, Miranda confessed to the rape. Miranda was subsequently convicted, a finding upheld by the Arizona Supreme Court. In its ruling on Miranda's appeal in *Miranda v. Arizona* (1966), the U.S. Supreme Court reversed the state court ruling based on an unconstitutional violation of due process. The majority on the Court reasoned if you don't know you have certain constitutional rights, how can you possibly exercise them? Not informing someone under arrest of their constitutional rights is tantamount to violating those rights. Thus, the Miranda rule was born.

When a person is arrested or questioned by law enforcement officers, the person must be *Mirandized*— informed of their legal rights under the Fifth and Sixth amendments:

- The right to remain silent.
- The right to have an attorney present during questioning.
- Statements made by the suspect can be used as evidence against them.
- An attorney will be appointed by the court if the suspect cannot afford one.

Remember, to every rule there is an exception! The reading of the Miranda warning is not required if a suspect poses an immediate or imminent threat to public safety. This exception was established in *New York v. Quarles* (1984), a case involving an assailant (Quarles) and the actions of an arresting officer, who in frisking the suspect found he was wearing an empty gun holster. The officer asked the suspect where the gun was, the suspect informed him, and the officer then *Mirandized* him and placed him under arrest. Quarles appealed his conviction, arguing that his Fifth Amendment rights were violated when the police officer asked about the gun before reading the Miranda warning. The Court upheld Quarles' conviction and established the **public safety exception** to the Miranda rule.

Did you know? The Sixth Amendment does not explicitly state that a suspect has the right to have an attorney present during police questioning, nor does it demand that the government provide an attorney, *pro bono* (at no cost), to anyone standing accused of a crime but unable to afford a lawyer. The **Sixth Amendment** explicitly guarantees the right to counsel during a "criminal prosecution," not during police questioning. It was through a ruling in *Escobedo v. Illinois* (1964) that the Court asserted once the police are no longer conducting a general investigation but have singled out and are focused on a suspect being held in police custody, denying the suspect the right to consult with an attorney at that point violates the Sixth Amendment. This new understanding of the Sixth Amendment right to have assistance of counsel immediately upon being taken into police custody explains why it is included in the Miranda warning—"you have the right to have an attorney present during questioning." Informing a suspect that "an attorney will be appointed for you if you cannot afford one" was an extension of the meaning of the right to counsel first established by the Supreme Court in its 1963 ruling in *Gideon v. Wainwright* (1963).

Due Process Clause Required Supreme Court Case		
Court Case	Argument	Outcome
Gideon v. Wainwright (1963)	**Question:** Does the Sixth Amendment compel the government to provide counsel to indigent defendants who cannot afford a lawyer? YES **Argument:** On June 3, 1961, Clarence Earl Gideon broke into a pool room of a private individual and stole several items, including $50 in change and several bottles of beverages. After Gideon was arrested and entered trial, he petitioned the judge for counsel since he was too poor to afford one himself. The trial judge rejected Gideon's request for legal aid and he was therefore forced to represent himself in court. Having only an eighth-grade education, but with no other choice, Gideon delivered an opening statement, cross-examined and presented witnesses, and argued for his innocence. The jury concluded that he was guilty, and he was then sentenced to 5 years in prison.	**Court ruling:** Citing the Sixth Amendment, the Court ruled unanimously (9–0) that states are required to provide an attorney to defendants who are unable to afford their own attorney. **Significance:** This case and the Court's ruling (9–0) highlighted a distinction in the protection of due process. *Procedural due process* involves the rules that guide the actions of police and other legal authorities; e.g., denying a defendant the assistance of counsel violates procedural due process. However, another type of due process exists—*substantive due process,* which is akin to the spirit of the law. That is, the actions of the government must ensure that the spirt of the protection is not lost merely due to a literal interpretation of the wording; e.g., if someone cannot afford the assistance of counsel and ends up with no assistance because the Sixth Amendment doesn't specifically say the government must provide counsel when indigent defendants come before the bench, then the spirit or substance of the protection is violated. This distinction is not without controversy and many conservative jurists and legal scholars insist that the concept of substantive due process has no legal foundation. However, the case is considered a victory to those who believe rights are not granted on the basis of financial status; due process must be provided to all.

The Exclusionary Rule

How does the guarantee to due process affect criminal prosecutions in the event police authorities violate the warrant process outlined in the Fourth Amendment? To answer that question, you should be familiar with the terms *exclusionary rule* and *fruit of the poisoned tree.*

Exclusionary rule. This rule refers to the rights granted to the accused—the search warrant requirement. "The right of the people to be secure in their persons, houses, papers, and effects against unreasonable searches and seizures shall not be violated, and no warrants shall issue, but upon probable cause, supported by oath or affirmation, describing the place to be searched, and the persons or things to be seized" (Fourth Amendment).

Under the **Fourth Amendment,** a search of a person and/or their property must be *reasonable*. A reasonable search entails providing a judge with some compelling evidence that a person of interest is involved in an illegal act; in other words, *probable cause* must be established in order for the judge to sign a warrant. If probable cause is established to the judge's satisfaction, a warrant is issued specifying who and what is to be searched, the location of the search, and when the search is to be conducted. This is the *due process* that must be followed for a legal search to proceed. If this process is not followed and an illegal search is conducted, the exclusionary rule prohibits any evidence found during the tainted search from being admitted into trial proceedings.

Did you know? The exclusionary rule was incorporated in the landmark Supreme Court case *Mapp v. Ohio* (1961). As a result, the introduction of evidence obtained during an illegal search is also prohibited in state criminal prosecutions.

Fruit of the poisoned tree doctrine. This doctrine established a corollary to the exclusionary rule that prevents the admission of any evidence gathered in a secondary search prompted by evidence found in an initial illegal search. For example, police authorities find the key to a storage locker during an illegal warrantless search of a home belonging to an individual suspected of running an illegal gambling operation. Later, the police use the key to open the locker and find significant amounts of cash along with betting slips. Since the key was found during the initial illegal search, the cash and betting slips are "fruit of the poisoned tree" and would thus be excluded from court proceedings.

Due Process and the Right to Privacy

Questions regarding the right to privacy frequently appear on the AP GOV exam. The Court has found that while no explicit right to privacy is mentioned in the Constitution, it is implied in the First, Fourth, and Ninth amendments. It is a basic right promised to all Americans. Court cases concerning the right to privacy, with the Court ruling on the side of individual liberty, have often been both controversial and precedent-setting. This includes the ability to view pornographic materials in one's own home (*Stanley v. Georgia*), the ability to obtain contraception (*Griswold v. Connecticut*), and perhaps the most polarizing privacy issue to date, a woman's right to privacy in her choice to terminate a pregnancy. This right, according to the *Roe v. Wade* decision, supersedes attempts by the state to ban access to pregnancy termination services, but it is not unqualified.

Due Process Clause		
Required Supreme Court Case		
Court Case	**Argument**	**Outcome**
Roe v. Wade (1973)	**Question:** Do women have a constitutional right to procure an abortion? YES **Arguments:** In 1969, "Jane Roe" (Norma McCorvey) was not permitted to seek an abortion in Texas, her state of residence. Texas law prohibited abortion with a few exceptions (the life of the mother was at risk; the pregnancy was the result of rape or incest). When the case came before the Supreme Court, attorneys for Roe argued that it was improper and unconstitutional for a state to deny any individuals the right to personal, marital, familial, or sexual right to privacy. Further, no Court had ever asserted that a developing fetus was legally a person with the "right to life," which superseded a mother's right to privacy. Arguing for the state of Texas, Jay Floyd insisted that the state has the duty to protect life and that life begins at conception. An unborn fetus is a person and is therefore entitled to the protections of the Constitution.	**Court ruling:** The First, Fourth, and Ninth amendments protect an individual's "zones of privacy." Citing earlier cases such as *Griswold v. Connecticut* (1965), the Court identified contraception, marriage, and child rearing as "zones of privacy." The majority viewed these definitions as broad enough to encompass a woman's decision to terminate a pregnancy. In addition, the Court underscored a ruling in *Griswold* that the right to privacy is an integral part of the Bill of Rights, and as such, is incorporated via the Due Process Clause of the Fourteenth Amendment. In consequence, privacy limits cannot be circumvented by the state unless the state has an overwhelmingly compelling interest. One such compelling interest recognized by the Court was the interest of the state in protecting the "potentiality of human life"; therefore, a woman's right to privacy must be weighed against the *viability* of a fetus. At the point a fetus becomes viable (able to thrive outside the womb), the state may act to regulate access to abortion. **Significance:** Although McCorvey's child was born and given up for adoption prior to the Supreme Court's decision, the highly controversial *Roe* decision set a precedent affecting privacy rights and interpretation of the Fourteenth Amendment's Due Process Clause. Its impact went well beyond the courtroom, sparking a fiery "culture war" and polarizing American politics. It impacted the Court itself as the issue of abortion and the *Roe v. Wade* decision have become litmus tests during the vetting process for potential Supreme Court nominees.

The Right to Privacy in the 21st Century

Civil liberties and protections have changed in the 21st century, raising important questions about the Fourth Amendment. Central to this debate is the government's access to digital *metadata* (information about information) for the purpose of ensuring public safety.

Key Facts about the USA PATRIOT Act—Bulk Collection of Metadata after September 11, 2001

The **USA PATRIOT Act (2001),** passed by Congress in response to the World Trade Center and Pentagon attacks, was designed to preemptively identify potential terror attacks.

History of the USA PATRIOT Act. As a result of the September 11, 2001, attacks, over 3,000 Americans died and another 6,000 were injured. Most of the 19 terrorists were from Saudi Arabia, but included one from Egypt, one from Lebanon, and two from the United Arab Emirates. Americans learned that these terrorists had entered the country without setting off any alarms, took up residence (some living in the country for a year or more), enrolled in flying lessons at commercial flight schools, tested security at airports, and then used what they had learned during these test runs to smuggle box cutters onto the planes.

Terrorist attacks launched against the United States highlighted a new type of threat from independently organized groups receiving funds from various shadowy sources and direction from leaders located in a number of places throughout the world using cell phones and the Internet. Subsequent events involving sophisticated schemes launched by foreign adversaries to hack into government computer systems have increased risks to national security. One response has been to fight technology with technology through the collection of metadata authorized by the USA PATRIOT Act and amended by the USA FREEDOM Act.

The original USA PATRIOT Act. Congress passed the USA PATRIOT Act in a rush after the attacks. The acronym stands for "Uniting and Strengthening America by Providing Appropriate Tools Required to Intercept and Obstruct Terrorism." The act details the government's ability to legally intercept any mode of telecommunication transmission deemed to be essential in protecting national security interests. In its first form, the act authorized indefinite detentions of immigrants, and the search of homes or businesses by law enforcement without the owner's consent or even knowledge of the search. The act was then used by the FBI to search telephone, e-mail, and financial records without a court order, and greater access was granted to other law enforcement agencies to obtain citizens' library and financial records.

The expanded USA PATRIOT Act. The National Security Agency (NSA) was subsequently authorized to run a bulk collection operation with the cooperation of phone companies to capture metadata from the phone records of private citizens (USA PATRIOT Act, **Section 215**). In the case of phone records, the collection of metadata meant who is being called, where they are located, how many times any given phone number is called, the duration of the calls, etc. According to the NSA, the metadata was used only to focus on the activities of suspected terrorists using "three-hop" analysis—looking at the records of the suspect to identify contacts, then looking at the records of those contacts, and finally the records of the contacts' contacts.

Source: Marshall Ramsey, "Can you hear me now?"
Creators Syndicate, June 6, 2013. By permission of
Marshall Ramsey and Creators Syndicate, Inc.

The violations of the USA PATRIOT Act. The enhanced ability of the government to access private information without the due process warrant requirements outlined in the Fourth Amendment sounded alarm bells among civil libertarians and raised a critical question: In pursuit of public safety and national security, how much erosion of the right to privacy is too much? The issue arising from passage of the USA PATRIOT Act was that it violated several rights, most starkly protections against illegal searches. These are the individual liberties that Anti-Federalist critics of centralizing power under the Constitution had fought so hard to defend by insisting on adding the Bill of Rights. In the fearful aftermath of 9/11, the long-standing concern about government overreach into the lives and freedom of its citizens came hard up against a very real threat to their personal safety. How valuable now were their liberties when faced with an external threat? How far would citizens let the government go in pursuit of security? Benjamin Franklin's words once again resonated with civil libertarians: "Those who would give up essential Liberty, to purchase a little temporary Safety, deserve neither Liberty nor Safety."

The debates about the USA PATRIOT Act. The USA PATRIOT Act has ignited polarizing debates, particularly amongst organizations dedicated to protecting the individual privacy rights of Americans against the unreasonable collection of personal communication. The bulk collection of phone data raised a red flag for the American Civil Liberties Union (ACLU). Why would a program designed to focus on the phone records of suspected terrorists require bulk collection of phone data resulting in literally billions of pieces of phone data being collected from every American using a phone? The government has argued that phone data is information that customers are aware is collected by their phone companies, and therefore every time a person uses their phone, the information is freely given. In the opinion of the district court, with these facts in mind, phone users have no reasonable expectation of privacy under the Fourth Amendment (*ACLU v. Clapper*, 2013). In 2015, arguing before the circuit court of appeals, the ACLU conceded that the government has a legitimate interest in tracking the associations of suspected terrorists, but three-hop analysis of phone records involving terror suspects could be accomplished without setting up permanent surveillance on every private citizen in America. The court of appeals agreed, ruling the bulk collection program exceeded what was authorized in Section 215 and returned the case to the district court for further consideration.

The USA FREEDOM Act (2015). Even though many of the provisions of the original law had sunset clauses that would allow them to expire in 2005, the USA PATRIOT Act has been renewed several times by Congress, and even after fear faded, parts of the act that Congress had allowed to expire were restored with the passage of the **USA FREEDOM Act** in 2015 (the acronym stands for "Uniting and Strengthening America by Fulfilling Rights and Ending Eavesdropping, Dragnet-collection and Online Monitoring"). The necessity of collecting data must be demonstrable enough to preclude limiting rights on private citizens. While the issue of homeland security is certainly a timely one, bulk collection of data is not ultimately legally justifiable. However, Congress used the bill to also address objections to Section 215. To restore public trust in the activities of the NSA and the Department of Homeland Security, the bill ended the bulk collection program and instead authorized the government to collect up to "two hops" of call records related to a suspect, if the government can prove a "reasonable" suspicion that the suspect is linked to a terrorist organization.

Heads Up: What You Need to Know

On the AP GOV exam, you may be asked to make historical connections across time periods and provide reasoning for your explanations regarding constitutional rights.

When the Constitution was drafted in 1787, the Framers had no conception of "telecommunications," but according to many legal scholars, the constitutional framework they created was a "living document" that was adaptable as society, culture, and the world evolved in incalculable ways. There is certainly another argument that has currency in political and judicial thought. If the Constitution is not a rock-solid foundation immutable over time, and if it is so flexible that its meaning can be manipulated simply because times change, then why have it at all? It is the debate as old as the split between the Federalists and Anti-Federalists, "loose constructionists" and "strict constructionists"— if the meaning of the Constitution can be changed for the expediency of the moment, to quote the anonymous author of Anti-Federalist No. 46, "where then, is the restraint?"

The fact is, through the formal amendment process and informal processes of congressional legislation, executive actions, and Supreme Court decisions, the institutions of government seek to establish a delicate balance between the need for broad-based adaptability and adherence to a set of core constitutional principles. Privacy is one of those core principles. This fact is made clear by its echoes throughout the Bill of Rights—the protection of an individual's right to express their private thoughts and beliefs (First Amendment); their right "to be secure in their persons" and to have that security extended to their homes, their personal papers, and other effects (Fourth Amendment); and the guarantee granted to all the people that they retain rights that ensure liberty beyond just those specifically enumerated in the Constitution (Ninth Amendment).

Equal Protection

Heads Up: What You Need to Know

The learning objectives that you must be able to accomplish include:

Explain how constitutional provisions have supported and motivated social movements and policy responses.

Explain how the government has responded to social movements.

Explain how the Supreme Court has at times allowed the restriction of the civil rights of minority groups and at other times has protected those rights.

Although the Bill of Rights guarantees certain rights, equal protection under the law was not specifically addressed until the Civil War and its aftermath. The three primary amendments related to equal protection include:

- **Thirteenth Amendment (1865).** Abolished slavery and involuntary servitude (except for punishment of a crime) in the United States.

- **Fourteenth Amendment (1868).** Established birthright citizenship (anyone born on U.S. soil is a citizen of the United States) regardless of former condition of servitude, thus conferring citizenship status on all former slaves. The **Fourteenth Amendment** then made provision to prohibit any state from denying to any citizen equal protection under the law and from depriving them of life, liberty, or property without due process of the law.

- **Fifteenth Amendment (1870).** Prohibited federal and state governments from denying a citizen the right to vote based on race, color, or previous condition of servitude.

These amendments were intended to legally endow every person with the civil liberties enshrined in the Bill of Rights. Unfortunately, the rhetoric and theory of these amendments require enforcement. Without the consistent diligence of the executive and legislative branches in efforts to ensure that the guarantees within the Fourteenth and Fifteenth amendments were fully realized, they were ineffectual and unenforced until the Supreme Court began to take action in the 1950s and 1960s. Thereafter, in the wake of the highly public Civil Rights Movement, the political consequences of silence began to push the other branches to follow the Supreme Court's lead, finally codifying into law the promises made 100 years before.

> **Did you know?** *Dred Scott v. Sanford* was a landmark and controversial case in which Dred Scott, a slave, petitioned for his freedom in 1857 based on his residence for a period of time in a "free" territory. The U.S. Supreme Court denied Scott's petition, ruling that African Americans, whether free or slaves, were not American citizens and therefore could not bring suit in a court of law. The lack of citizenship and the rights that go with it denied to African Americans in the Dred Scott case were not specifically redressed until passage of the Fourteenth Amendment.

Landmarks in Equal Protection and Civil Rights

1776	1861–1865	1865	1868	1870	1896	1920	1954	1964	1965	2005
Declaration of Independence Thomas Jefferson declares "All men are created equal."	**Civil War** War between the states sparked by slavery issue.	**Thirteenth Amendment** Abolishes slavery.	**Fourteenth Amendment** Requires equal protection under the law for all citizens.	**Fifteenth Amendment** Bans racial discrimination in voting.	***Plessy v. Ferguson*** The Supreme Court approves "separate but equal" doctrine endorsing segregation based on race.	**Nineteenth Amendment** Grants women the right to vote.	***Brown v. Board of Education of Topeka*** The Supreme Court rules state laws imposing racial segregation in public schools unconstitutional.	**Civil Rights Act** Bans discrimination in education and public facilities on the basis of race, color, origin, religion, and sex.	**Voting Rights Act** Makes it illegal to require voters to pass a literacy test.	***Obergefell v. Hodges*** The Supreme Court rules state laws denying same-sex couples the right to marry are unconstitutional.

Civil Rights

Civil rights protect individuals from discriminatory practices by organizations, the government, and private individuals. Protections are established on the basis of race, gender, age, disability, sexual orientation, ethnicity, political affiliation, or religious affiliation.

The Civil Rights Act (1964)

The Civil Rights Act was initially a bill introduced by President John F. Kennedy in June 1963. As protests associated with the Civil Rights Movement intensified during the last months of his presidency, Kennedy defined the civil rights crisis not only as a constitutional and legal issue, but also as a moral issue. Kennedy supported legislation that would afford all Americans equal rights. Kennedy's vision was actively opposed by legislative segregationists who sought to keep the nation divided along racial lines.

Following Kennedy's assassination on November 22, 1963, Lyndon Johnson, Kennedy's vice president, became president. Johnson took up the cause of civil rights, and in his first address to a joint session of Congress, he called on lawmakers to pass the Civil Rights Act of 1964 in honor of Kennedy's fight for equality.

Title IX of the Civil Rights Act Amendments (1972)

The **Civil Rights Act of 1964** ensured equal employment and prohibited discrimination in places of public accommodation based on race, religion, or nationality. In addition, the Civil Rights Act officially codified the illegality of discriminating on the basis of sex in the workplace. However, the act did not explicitly address disparity of sex representation in educational contexts, particularly with regard to institutional support for athletic departments.

Title IX, part of a larger body of legislation enacted by the Education Amendments of 1972, is considered an addendum to the Civil Rights Act of 1964. While most of the attention on the impact of Title IX has focused on creating equal opportunity for both males and females to participate in team and individual sports programs, the law's effect is much broader. It prohibits sex discrimination in any federally funded educational programs involving elementary and secondary schools, colleges, universities, or training programs. Non-compliance with the guidelines for fair and equal treatment results in termination of the grants that provide federal funding.

The Voting Rights Act (1965)

The Framers left the determination of voter qualifications and voter registration procedures to the states. While the Fifteenth Amendment (1870) granted African Americans the right to vote, many states, mostly in the South, used their authority to circumvent this guarantee by manipulating voter qualification and registration requirements. Some states, for example, required potential voters to pass a literacy test, knowing that the mostly rural, poor members of the African American community were illiterate. Others imposed *poll taxes* (mandatory fees for voting), a difficult hurdle for impoverished farm laborers and sharecroppers. These discriminatory practices persisted well into the 20th century, aided and abetted by violent intimidation practiced by groups like the Ku Klux Klan.

This flagrant violation of the Fourteenth Amendment's Equal Protection Clause and the principles of democracy finally prompted the federal government to act nearly 100 years after the ratification of the Fifteenth Amendment. In 1964, the **Twenty-Fourth Amendment** was ratified, outlawing the levying of poll taxes in federal elections. Congress passed the more sweeping **Voting Rights Act of 1965** the following year:

- Prohibited state and local governments from imposing any voting law that discriminated against racial or language minorities.
- Banned the use of literacy tests.

Source: *Harper's Weekly.* Editorial cartoon criticizes the use of literacy tests published January 18, 1879. "Eddikashun qualifukashun. The Blak man orter be eddikated afore he kin vote with us Wites, signed Mr. Solid South." (Education qualification. The Black man ought to be educated before he can vote with Whites.)

- Provided for federal oversight by the Justice Department of voter registration in areas where less than 50 percent of the non-white population were registered to vote.
- Authorized the attorney general of the U.S. to investigate the use of poll taxes in state and local elections.

Did you know? Poll taxes in state and local elections were finally prohibited in 1966 as the result of a Supreme Court decision. In *Harper v. Virginia State Board of Elections,* the Court ruled poll taxes in any state election to be an unconstitutional violation of the Equal Protection Clause of the Fourteenth Amendment.

Dr. Martin Luther King Jr.

Dr. Martin Luther King Jr. was a leader of the Civil Rights Movement who used nonviolent protest to shine a national media spotlight on racial injustice and to prod leading politicians toward realization of equal protection under the law as promised in the Fourteenth Amendment. His activism lasted from 1955 until his assassination in 1968.

Until he was assassinated, Dr. King devoted his life to promoting the cause of equality under the law while raising public consciousness about publicly and privately sanctioned racism reinforced by social, cultural, and economic stereotypes.

Source: President Lyndon B. Johnson meets with Martin Luther King Jr., December 3, 1963.

Key Facts about Dr. Martin Luther King Jr.'s Achievements

- **Montgomery Bus Boycott (1955–1956).** Four days after Rosa Parks was arrested for refusing to give up her seat on a bus to a white person, the first large-scale public protest focused on racial segregation was launched. Lasting from December 5, 1955, to December 20, 1956, it was during this protest that a young pastor from Atlanta, Georgia, emerged as a leading light in the Civil Rights Movement.

- **Birmingham protests (1963).** Birmingham, Alabama, was perhaps the most segregated city in America, a condition enforced by routine humiliating acts of discrimination and violence. Several civil rights organizations, including King's Southern Christian Leadership Conference, coordinated a plan to march and sit-in. A judge acted first, issuing an injunction against any "parading, demonstrating, boycotting." The marchers went ahead as planned and King was arrested. While in custody he wrote his iconic *Letter from Birmingham Jail* in response to published criticism by eight white Alabama clergymen who labeled him an outside agitator. King responded in his open letter to the clergymen that he was "here because I was invited here. I am here because I have organizational ties here. But more basically, I am in Birmingham because injustice is here."

- **March on Washington for jobs and freedom (1963).** The "Big Six" of the Civil Rights Movement brought together a coalition of civil rights activists, African American union members, and white leaders, which included King, having gained greater renown with his *Letter from Birmingham Jail*, who supported their cause. Over 200,000 people listened while King delivered his "I Have a Dream Speech" from the steps of the Lincoln Memorial. The political pressure the march put on leaders in Washington is considered instrumental to the passing of the Civil Rights Act of 1964.

- **Nobel Peace Prize (1964).** King won the Nobel Peace Prize for fighting racial inequality through nonviolence (he was the youngest recipient to date).

- **Selma Voting Rights Movement (1965).** King led the second of three marches which began in Selma, Alabama, with the intent of reaching the statehouse in Montgomery. The focus of the marches was the lack of voting rights for African Americans despite the passage of the Civil Rights Act of 1964. King delivered his famous "How Long, Not Long" speech on the steps of the statehouse. The violence endured by the peaceful, unarmed marchers beaten bloody by Alabama state troopers and "possemen" wielding clubs prompted a shaken President Lyndon Johnson to call for passage of the Voting Rights Act before a joint session of Congress.

- **Memphis Sanitation Workers Strike (1968).** Having broadened his focus to issues of poverty, King led a 64-day strike for workers protesting discrimination, low wages, and unsafe work conditions. It was here on April 4, on the balcony outside of his hotel room, that King was assassinated.

The National Organization for Women (NOW)

The **National Organization for Women,** or NOW, was founded in 1966. As a feminist organization, its roots date back to the late-19th-century women's rights activism of Susan B. Anthony, founder of the National Woman Suffrage Association. Her tireless organizing, publishing, and public advocacy work was instrumental in getting the Nineteenth Amendment passed. The formal organizing conference for NOW did not occur until October 1966. Betty Friedan, author of *The Feminine Mystique* (1963), an exposé on traditional gender roles, was named NOW's first president.

The organizers were fired up by the realization that laws like Title VII of the Civil Rights Act are only as good and as effective as their enforcement. Enforcement ignored makes for laws that are useless to those they intended to benefit. Title VII was written to prohibit unequal treatment in the workplace, but discrimination against women in hiring, promotion, and wages paid not on par with those paid to men doing the same work continued to be endemic and persistent in the workplace. With the Equal Employment Opportunity Commission, established to enforce the employment provisions of the Civil Rights Act, taking little interest in or action on women's issues, NOW stated its purpose: to push forward on various battle fronts, including the courts, to achieve full equality for women.

Key Facts about the National Organization for Women

NOW is politically liberal in its philosophy and generally supports more progressive American politicians. Over the years, NOW's core issues have expanded to include a wide variety of concerns:

- Constitutional equality
- Economic justice
- LGBT rights
- Violence against women
- Visibility in social justice cases
- Ensuring reproductive services benefits, including abortion

The Pro-Life Movement

Known for its vehement anti-abortion activism, the **pro-life movement** was formed by the National Right to Life Committee in 1968. As anti-abortion groups began to grow in response to the Supreme Court's decision in *Roe v. Wade,* the movement deemed itself "pro-life," to oppose **abortion** on both moral and sectarian grounds. The movement emphasizes caring for the unborn child as opposed to the reproductive rights of women. Pro-life groups gained traction predominantly among conservative evangelical Christians, including Protestants and Catholics alike.

The pro-life movement has two main factions. One advocates for chipping away at the *Roe v. Wade* decision by imposing state laws, regulations, and requirements that reduce access to abortions incrementally—for example, prohibiting the use of any state funds to pay for abortion services for Medicaid enrollees (32 states) or placing restrictions on private insurance coverage for abortion services (11 states). The long-term remedy it works toward is getting *Roe v. Wade* reversed by affecting the selection of conservative judges to the Supreme Court. The second faction is taking a different path, advocating for a "personhood" amendment to the Constitution, asserting that life begins at conception. If an unborn fetus is defined constitutionally as a person, then the legal groundwork is in place to challenge any access to abortion as a violation of the Equal Protection Clause.

Affirmative Action

While the public understanding of affirmative action is murky and politically polarizing, the purpose of affirmative action programs was more than the deconstruction of meritocracy, where only the most qualified rise to the top, as its critics charge. It was built on a recognition that systemic discrimination and inequalities in government, education, and the workplace have negatively impacted racial minorities and women for centuries, while tilting the balance of advantage and opportunity toward white males. The call for affirmative action simply meant that rather than allow the status quo to continue with the hope it would self-correct, the government and other cooperating organizations would take affirmative (positive) steps toward correcting the balance. While commonly associated with the Civil Rights Movement, the roots of affirmative action date back to the Civil War. Note in the following timeline, however, that the greatest impetus for affirmation action occurred during the Civil Rights Era:

Timeline of American Civil Rights

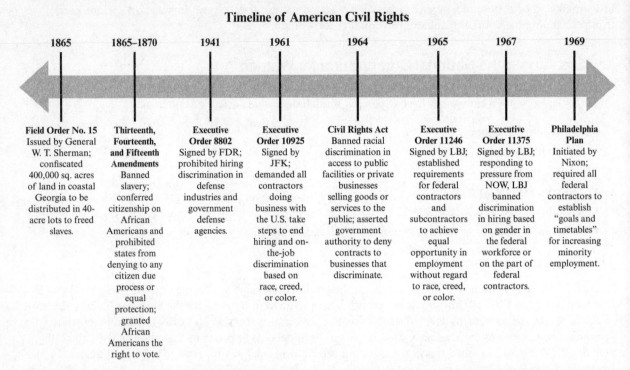

1865	1865–1870	1941	1961	1964	1965	1967	1969
Field Order No. 15 Issued by General W. T. Sherman; confiscated 400,000 sq. acres of land in coastal Georgia to be distributed in 40-acre lots to freed slaves.	**Thirteenth, Fourteenth, and Fifteenth Amendments** Banned slavery; conferred citizenship on African Americans and prohibited states from denying to any citizen due process or equal protection; granted African Americans the right to vote.	**Executive Order 8802** Signed by FDR; prohibited hiring discrimination in defense industries and government defense agencies.	**Executive Order 10925** Signed by JFK; demanded all contractors doing business with the U.S. take steps to end hiring and on-the-job discrimination based on race, creed, or color.	**Civil Rights Act** Banned racial discrimination in access to public facilities or private businesses selling goods or services to the public; asserted government authority to deny contracts to businesses that discriminate.	**Executive Order 11246** Signed by LBJ; established requirements for federal contractors and subcontractors to achieve equal opportunity in employment without regard to race, creed, or color.	**Executive Order 11375** Signed by LBJ; responding to pressure from NOW, LBJ banned discrimination in hiring based on gender in the federal workforce or on the part of federal contractors.	**Philadelphia Plan** Initiated by Nixon; required all federal contractors to establish "goals and timetables" for increasing minority employment.

The purpose of these corrective polices was to bring an end to institutional racial and/or gender discrimination and to reverse its negative effects. In the 20th century, most affirmative action programs, whether government-mandated or those embraced voluntarily by privately operated businesses and programs, tended to target access to education and employment. The affirmative action goals also included making institutions like colleges and universities, and public agencies such as police departments and fire departments, more reflective of the diverse communities they serve. Contrary to popular belief, the core affirmative action goal was not to enforce racial or gender quotas. In fact, the Nixon administration stated that the "goals and timetables" integral to the *Philadelphia Plan* (a federal program established to increase hiring in non-white construction workers) were not mandated quotas.

After the Philadelphia Plan became the federal government's official policy on affirmative action, the conservative backlash gained steam, charging that racial and gender quotas were forcing companies and public service agencies to hire unqualified women and racial minorities. Further, despite Richard Nixon's contribution to affirmative action, conservatives decried the liberals' attempt to impose "reverse discrimination." The Philadelphia Plan was the last major affirmative action policy initiative in the wake of the backlash. The anti-affirmative action momentum reached full fruition during the presidency of Ronald Reagan. Funding was cut for the Equal Employment Opportunity Commission established by Johnson, resulting in a 60 percent reduction in the number of discrimination lawsuits filed by the EEOC during Reagan's presidency. He and his allies in Congress also reduced funding for the civil rights division of the Justice Department. Reagan advocated for a relaxation of federal government efforts to achieve employment equality, believing in the "reverse discrimination' argument, and especially wanted to see the timetables and numerical goals of the Philadelphia Plan eliminated.

Did you know? The Supreme Court was asked to weigh in on affirmative action in 1978. Their ruling in *Regents of University of California v. Bakke* was applauded by the opponents of affirmative action. Alan Bakke, a white male, was twice rejected for admittance to UC Davis Medical School although his college GPA and test scores exceeded those of some minority students admitted for the 16 spots reserved for minority applicants. Bakke argued that his application was rejected based on his race. In an 8–1 decision, the Court ruled that any quota-based plan of affirmative action violates the Equal Protection Clause, and Davis was ordered to admit Bakke to its medical school. The Court, however, did not reject affirmative action itself and ruled that race remained a criterion that colleges and universities could consider in the process of admitting students to college.

TEST TIP: On the AP GOV exam, think about how you would answer a free-response question asking you to compare or contrast opposing viewpoints on affirmative action. You will want to cite specific examples of "affirmative actions" taken (see timeline on p. 196), but you do not have to commit all of them to memory. Get a general sense of how presidents used executive orders to get the ball rolling and how the momentum increased during the Civil Rights Era, citing specifically the Civil Rights Act, including Title VII and Title IX. Include in any discussion what goals these actions were designed to achieve. Discuss how opponents focused on "reverse discrimination" and the Equal Protection Clause, as well as resentments harbored over hiring preferences. The response of the Reagan administration and the *Bakke* case can serve to illustrate the backlash.

Civil Rights		
Required Supreme Court Cases		
Court Case	**Argument**	**Outcome**
Plessy v. Ferguson (1896)	**Question:** Is it constitutional to have separate accommodations for whites and African Americans on railroad cars? YES **Arguments:** At the behest of the Committee of Citizens, Homer Plessy, a man of mixed race who was classified as "black" in Louisiana, challenged Louisiana's Separate Car Act in 1890. After purchasing a train ticket, Plessy insisted on taking a seat in the "whites only" car and was subsequently arrested and fined by Judge John Howard Ferguson. Plessy's legal challenge was based on a violation of the Thirteenth and Fourteenth amendments. The state of Louisiana won its initial court cases against Plessy based on its reserved right to regulate transportation within the boundaries of the state.	**Court ruling:** While the Fourteenth Amendment was established to achieve equality of the races, separate facilities did not necessarily undermine that goal with any implication that African Americans were inferior to whites. Without any significant difference between white and black railcars, segregation was not equivalent to illegal discrimination. **Significance:** By upholding the rulings in the Louisiana courts, the Supreme Court established the "separate but equal doctrine," which gave constitutional sanction to segregation through "Jim Crow laws" for nearly 60 years.

Continued

Court Case	Argument	Outcome
Brown v. Board of Education of Topeka (1954) *(Brown I)*	**Question:** Is the segregation of public education with the sole basis for the separation being race a constitutional violation of the Fourteenth Amendment's Equal Protection Clause? YES **Argument:** This case consolidated several cases arising in Topeka, Kansas, Washington, D.C., Virginia, Delaware, and North Carolina, forming a class-action lawsuit filed by lawyers for the NAACP. The 8-year-old daughter of the named plaintiff, Oliver Brown, was forced to ride a bus to a black school over a mile from her home after being denied entrance to the neighborhood school only seven blocks away. The lower courts denied legal relief to the parents based on the *Plessy v. Ferguson* decision. The case was appealed to the Supreme Court, where NAACP lawyers, including future Supreme Court Justice Thurgood Marshall, argued that the separate but equal doctrine was but a flimsy façade behind which state government perpetuated inferior facilities and educational services, and unequal treatment.	**Court ruling:** Public education based on segregated schools is inherently unequal. The Court cited scientific studies that indicated a deleterious effect on the mental well-being and feelings of self-worth that segregation imposed on black children as the basis of its unanimous decision that racial segregation in public schools violated the Equal Protection Clause of the Fourteenth Amendment. **Significance:** The Court's ruling reversed *Plessy v. Ferguson* and put an end to the "separate but equal doctrine" as it was applied to *de jure segregation* (segregation by legal statute) in public schools. It would take the Civil Rights Movement to end segregation in all phases of American public life, but *Brown I* opened the door and provided a model for class-action lawsuits used to achieve civil rights victories.
Brown v. Board of Education of Topeka (1955) *(Brown II)*	**Question:** How should the decision reached in *Brown I* be implemented? WITH ALL DELIBERATE SPEED **Arguments:** Cases from all over the country challenged segregation in schools as states and localities did little to address the new principle of educational equality through integration established by the Court's decision in *Brown I*. The fault was not entirely theirs, as the Court did not provide any direction or timetables to the states in the original case. The NAACP argued that desegregation must begin immediately. States argued that the process would be complicated and expensive, requiring more time for them to come up with solutions.	**Court ruling:** In yet another unanimous decision, the Court ruled that states could not ignore the new principle that racial segregation in public schools is unconstitutional—thus the "all deliberate speed" ruling. The Court placed the burden of coming up with an integration plan on the states, with the goal in mind of creating a non-discriminatory admissions policy as soon as was practical. **Significance:** While still acknowledging state interest in educational policy, the Court re-emphasized the need to move immediately toward racial integration in public schools. While the Court failed again to provide a specific timetable, it gave the federal district courts the power to supervise schools and review problems faced by school districts that might delay integration plans. However, failure to yield to the Court's order would not be tolerated.

Did you know? *Brown v. Board of Education of Topeka I* and *II* dealt with ***de jure segregation***, segregation imposed by law. By 1970, as school districts continued to fail to meet integration goals set out in these two landmark cases, the Court had to deal with ***de facto segregation*** resulting from societal circumstances rather than legislation. If the plan to remedy segregation ordered by *Brown II* relied on simply assigning children to the appropriate neighborhood school, what if their neighborhoods were segregated? This was an issue the Court addressed in *Swann v. Charlotte-Mecklenburg Board of Education*, 1971. Not only did the Court assert its equity power to intervene if schools still failed to integrate, but it introduced the remedy of school busing to achieve integration in areas where de facto segregation existed. The issue of court-ordered busing was highly controversial and resulted in an explosion of violent resistance in cities throughout the United States. In a follow-up case, *Milliken v. Bradley* (1974), a district court–ordered busing plan was challenged. The plan encompassed 85 school districts in the Detroit area transporting students from the predominantly white suburbs to the predominantly black Detroit city schools and vice versa. The court ruled that school desegregation is not meant to *proactively ensure* equal demographic distributions, but rather to *prevent* schools from enacting discriminatory policies.

Unit 3: Summary of Important Supreme Court Cases		
Case	Description	Ruling
Plessy v. Ferguson (1896)	Upheld "separate but equal" racial segregation by the states.	State
Schenck v. United States (1919)	Speech creating a "clear and present danger" is not protected by the First Amendment.	State
Gitlow v. New York (1925)	States may prohibit speech having a tendency to cause danger to public safety.	State
Brown v. Board of Education of Topeka (Brown I) (1954)	Race-based school segregation violates the Equal Protection Clause.	Individual
Brown v. Board of Education of Topeka II (Brown II) (1955)	School districts and federal courts must implement the Court's decision in *Brown I* (1954) "with all deliberate speed."	Individual
Engel v. Vitale (1962)	School sponsorship of religious activities violates the Establishment Clause.	Individual
Gideon v. Wainwright (1963)	Guaranteed the right to an attorney for the poor or indigent.	Individual
Tinker v. Des Moines Independent Community School District (1969)	Public school students could wear armbands in school to protest the Vietnam War.	Individual
New York Times Co. v. United States (1971)	Bolstered the freedom of the press, establishing a "heavy presumption against prior restraint," even in cases of national security.	Individual
Wisconsin v. Yoder (1972)	Compelling Amish students to attend school past the eighth grade violates the Free Exercise Clause.	Individual
Roe v. Wade (1973)	Extended the right to privacy to a woman's decision to have an abortion.	Individual
McDonald v. Chicago (2010)	The Second Amendment right to keep and bear arms for self-defense is applicable to the states.	Individual

Chapter Review Practice Questions

Practice questions are for instructional purposes only and may not reflect the format of the actual exam. On the actual exam, some questions may be grouped into sets containing one source-based prompt (document or image) and two to five questions. The questions and explanations that follow focus on essential knowledge, the learning objectives, and political science skills.

Multiple-Choice Questions

Question 1 refers to the following passage.

> ...In the absence of a specific showing of constitutionally valid reasons to regulate their speech, [persons] are entitled to freedom of expression of their views.
>
> —Source: Justice Fortas, speaking for the majority, 1969.

1. Which of the following Supreme Court cases protects the rights of students to engage in freedom of expression that does not disrupt the learning process?

   A. *Brown v. Board of Education of Topeka*
   B. *Engel v. Vitale*
   C. *Tinker v. Des Moines Independent Community School District*
   D. *Wisconsin v. Yoder*

2. Which of the following reasons underpinned the Supreme Court's freedom of the press ruling in *New York Times Co. v. United States*?

   A. The Pentagon Papers served a public interest.
   B. *The New York Times* was printing correct information.
   C. The justification for prior restraint was unconvincing.
   D. The level of censorship was not admissible based on the time, place, and manner restrictions.

3. Based on your knowledge of U.S. government, which of the following describes the "clear and present danger" rule established by the U.S. Supreme Court as a restriction on free speech?

   A. It endorsed an unequivocal abridgment of the rights of dangerous individuals to speak freely.
   B. It prohibits speech that may incite substantive evils.
   C. It allows restriction on speech that undermines the common good.
   D. It enables law enforcement to shield government officials from criticism during times of national emergency.

4. Which of the following statements best describes the concept of *selective incorporation*?

   A. The concentrated curtailing of state intervention in the exercise of civil liberties
   B. The extension of federal protections for individual liberties to the states via the Fourteenth Amendment
   C. The absolute protection against civil liberty infringement at the state level
   D. The doctrine that selectively restrains free speech

5. Based on the Supreme Court case *Wisconsin v. Yoder,* which of the following best identifies the basis of the Supreme Court's decision upholding the rights of Amish parents to refuse to send their children to school past eighth grade?

   A. Free Exercise Clause
   B. Exclusionary rule
   C. Right to privacy
   D. Selective incorporation

Question 6 refers to the following passage.

> The Court holds that the imposition and carrying out of the death penalty in these cases constitute cruel and unusual punishment in violation of the Eighth and Fourteenth amendments. The judgment in each case is therefore reversed insofar as it leaves undisturbed the death sentence imposed, and the cases are remanded for further proceedings…

> —Source: Supreme Court case, *Furman v. Georgia*, June 29, 1972.

6. Which of the following was NOT expressly named by Justice Brennan in *Furman v. Georgia* as a test to define what constitutes cruel and unusual punishment?

   A. Punishment that debased human dignity
   B. Punishment that inflicted severity without reason
   C. Punishment that displaced religious convictions
   D. Punishment that was otherwise unnecessary

7. Which of the following Supreme Court cases incorporated the guarantee to defendants in a criminal prosecution the right to seek assistance of counsel regardless of their financial status or mental competence?

   A. *Gitlow v. New York*
   B. *Gideon v. Wainwright*
   C. *Schenck v. United States*
   D. *McDonald v. Chicago*

Question 8 refers to the following passage.

> The object of the [Fourteenth] Amendment was undoubtedly to enforce the absolute equality of the two races before the law, but in the nature of things it could not have been intended to abolish distinctions based upon color, or to enforce social, as distinguished from political, equality, or a commingling of the two races upon terms unsatisfactory to either.

> —Source: Justice Henry Billings Brown, speaking for the majority in *Plessy v. Ferguson* (1896).

8. Which of the following precedents did *Brown v. Board of Education of Topeka* (1954) strike down that was first set in the case of *Plessy v. Ferguson*?

   A. Evolving standards of decency
   B. Separate but equal
   C. Clear and present danger
   D. Reverse discrimination

9. Which of the following issues was fundamental to the founding of the National Organization for Women (NOW)?

   A. LGBT rights
   B. Gender discrimination in the workplace
   C. Reproductive rights and services
   D. Passage of the Equal Rights Amendment

10. Which of the following is the most specific constitutional principle violated by the bulk collection of telecommunications data?

    A. Unreasonable search and seizure
    B. Prior restraint
    C. Free speech
    D. Right to privacy

Free-Response Question

1 question

20 minutes (suggested)

Directions: It is suggested that you take a few minutes to plan and outline your essay. Write your response on lined paper. You must demonstrate your understanding of course content, disciplinary practices, and reasoning processes. Your essay is considered a first draft and may contain some grammatical errors that will not be counted against you. However, to receive full credit, your essay must demonstrate defensible content knowledge with substantive examples where appropriate.

Passage 1

The First Amendment was added to the Constitution to stand as a guarantee that neither the power nor the prestige of the Federal Government would be used to control, support or influence the kinds of prayer the American people can say—that the people's religions must not be subjected to the pressures of government for change each time a new political administration is elected to office. Under that Amendment's prohibition against governmental establishment of religion, as reinforced by the provisions of the Fourteenth Amendment, government in this country, be it state or federal, is without power to prescribe by law any particular form of prayer which is to be used as an official prayer in carrying on any program of governmentally sponsored religious activity.

Passage 2

Wisconsin concedes that, under the Religion Clauses, religious beliefs are absolutely free from the State's control, but it argues that "actions," even though religiously grounded, are outside the protection of the First Amendment. But our decisions have rejected the idea that religiously grounded conduct is always outside the protection of the Free Exercise Clause. It is true that activities of individuals, even when religiously based, are often subject to regulation by the States in the exercise of their undoubted power to promote the health, safety, and general welfare, or the Federal Government in the exercise of its delegated powers.

Question

(a) Identify the two First Amendment clauses that are common to both *Engel v. Vitale* (1962) and *Wisconsin v. Yoder* (1972).

(b) Based on the First Amendment principle identified in part (a), provide factual information from the Supreme Court cases and explain why the circumstances surrounding *Engel v. Vitale* led to a similar holding in *Wisconsin v. Yoder* or another non-required Supreme Court case.

(c) Explain how modern-day conservatives and liberals would most likely agree or disagree with the holding in *Engel v. Vitale*.

Answers and Explanations

Multiple-Choice Questions

1. **C.** The question is about the First Amendment and how to determine what constitutes symbolic free speech. Each of the Supreme Court cases listed includes decisions that directly apply to the general notion of education. However, *Tinker v. Des Moines Independent Community School District,* choice C, specifically addresses the Supreme Court's upholding of the symbolic speech that students demonstrated by wearing armbands as protest.

2. **C.** The Court ruled in favor of the *New York Times Co.* by striking down a restraining order issued against the paper (and *The Washington Post*), which constituted *prior restraint.* The Court found that a broad claim of "national security" was not a compelling reason to erode freedom of the press by ignoring prohibitions against prior restraint, so choice C is the correct answer. The question addresses the various ways in which the press is constitutionally empowered to freely disseminate information. While the Pentagon Papers did serve a public interest (choice A), it was not the primary reason for the *New York Times Co. v. United States* decision. Similarly, while *The New York Times* was printing accurate information (choice B), the question of information accuracy was not at issue in this case. The regulation of time, place, and manner (choice D) is not relevant to the facts or the issue in this case.

3. **B.** The case referenced in this question is *Schenk v. United States.* Schenck had encouraged men to resist the draft during World War I, putting him in violation of the Espionage Act. The Court ruled that restrictions on speech that may create a "clear and present danger" that will bring about the substantive evils that Congress has a right to prevent are constitutionally allowed, making choice B correct. A broad prohibition of the free speech rights of individuals deemed to be dangerous (choice A) is clearly unconstitutional. As with choice A, restriction on speech that undermines the common good (choice C) is too subjective and broad to be constitutional. While Congress in the past has passed sedition laws that prohibit criticism of government officials during times of war and national emergency (choice D), the case referenced in this question is *Schenck v. United States,* which involved a violation of the Espionage Act, not sedition.

4. **B.** Selective incorporation is a legal doctrine that empowers the Supreme Court to apply the liberties protected in the Bill of Rights to the states via the Due Process Clause of the Fourteenth Amendment. It is "selective" because the incorporation of a liberty or right is established on a case-by-case basis. For example, protection against warrantless unreasonable searches (Fourth Amendment) was incorporated by the decision in *Mapp v. Ohio,* while the protection against self-incrimination (Fifth Amendment) was incorporated by the Court's ruling in *Miranda v. Arizona.*

The only response that addresses both the extension of civil liberties protections to the states and the Fourteenth Amendment is choice B.

5. **A.** This question requires that you recall the Supreme Court case of *Wisconsin v. Yoder* and its precedent-setting determination. The Court ruled that punishing the parents of Amish students for objecting to compulsory attendance in school after eighth grade by refusing to enroll their children undermines and places an undue burden on their sincerely held religious beliefs, and thus violates the Free Exercise Clause of the First Amendment, choice A. The exclusionary rule (choice B) involves evidence obtained illegally during the process of a criminal case. The right to privacy (choice C) is not applicable. Selective incorporation (choice D) is also unrelated.

6. **C.** This question requires essential knowledge about what the Supreme Court has established as the standards for what constitutes cruel and unusual punishment. Since the Eighth Amendment provides protections for those having sentences imposed after conviction for crimes, the focus is on "cruel and unusual" and the forms of punishment that violate the ban on such sentences. Religious freedom, choice C, is clearly irrelevant to these issues.

7. **B.** The correct choice is the landmark criminal case *Gideon v. Wainwright*, choice B. The other three choices, *Gitlow v. New York* (choice A), *Schenck v. United States* (choice C), and *McDonald v. Chicago* (choice D), involved landmark decisions by the Supreme Court but did not involve Sixth Amendment protections.

8. **B.** To answer this question, you will need to have essential knowledge of landmark Supreme Court decisions regarding civil rights and the "rule of precedent" in which a Court decision in one case establishes the constitutional standard that all future cases addressing similar legal questions must follow. *Plessy v. Ferguson* was a 19th-century Supreme Court case in which the Court ruled that racial segregation was not unconstitutional as long as the separate facilities in question were equal. In *Brown v. Board of Education of Topeka* (1954), Plessy's "separate but equal doctrine," choice B, was reversed, setting the stage for school integration. Choice A, evolving standards of decency, is related to the Court's deliberations and rulings on free speech and obscenity. *Schenck v. United States* established the "clear and present danger" rule (choice C). *Regents of the University of California v. Bakke* involved the issue of racial quotas for university admissions and whether they were tantamount to reverse discrimination (choice D).

9. **B.** While LGBT rights (choice A) and reproductive rights and services (choice C) are currently considered among the public policy interests of NOW, its founding was sparked by the failure of the EEOC to properly enforce Title VII of the Civil Rights Act, which prohibited discrimination in hiring and employment based on gender, choice B. Passage of the Equal Rights Amendment (choice D) was part of NOW's agenda, but was not the reason it was founded.

10. **A.** Modern-day challenges to constitutional rights, made particularly salient in the advanced age of technology, are at the forefront of civil liberties litigation. To answer this question, you will need to prioritize the constitutional right most likely challenged by the bulk collection of telecommunications data. The constitutional right most at risk in bulk collection of metadata is the Fourth Amendment right of people to be secure in their person, their home, their papers, and effects against unreasonable search and seizure, choice A. Prior restraint (choice B) is an unconstitutional form of censorship that violates both freedom of speech and freedom of the press. Metadata is simply "information about information," which is not a form of free speech (choice C). While the question of privacy (choice D) is at the center of the public's objections to bulk collection of metadata, the specific protection of that privacy is the issue in this case.

Free-Response Question

This SCOTUS comparison essay question asks you to compare two First Amendment cases, *Engel v. Vitale* (1962) and *Wisconsin v. Yoder* (1972). What are the similarities and what are the differences? Based on your knowledge of government, what are these connections in contemporary America?

Scoring Guide

Part	Task	Explanation	Examples
(a) (1 point)	Identify the two First Amendment clauses that are common to both *Engel v. Vitale* (1962) and *Wisconsin v. Yoder* (1972).	Part (a) requires that you identify the two First Amendment clauses in *Engel v. Vitale* and *Wisconsin v. Yoder*.	The first item on your checklist should be identifying that both *Engel v. Vitale* and *Wisconsin v. Yoder* concern First Amendment rights, specifically regarding the freedom of religion. On SCOTUS comparison questions, look for the binding thread that connects both of the Supreme Court cases provided in the prompt. The supplemental excerpts (stimuli) provided in the prompt will aid in providing context, so be sure to read those carefully. In this instance, the first excerpt, from the *Engel v. Vitale* decision, clearly states "prohibition against governmental establishment of religion," which indicates that the case concerns the Establishment Clause. Similarly, the excerpt from the *Wisconsin v. Yoder* ruling warns against violating the Free Exercise Clause, which directly answers the question about the relevant clause.
(b) (1 point) (1 point)	Based on the First Amendment principle identified in part (a). Explain why the circumstances surrounding *Engel v. Vitale* led to a similar holding in *Wisconsin v. Yoder*.	Part (b) requires that you provide factual information from the Supreme Court cases and explain how the constitutional ramifications of *Engel v. Vitale* led to the ruling in *Wisconsin v. Yoder* or another non-required Supreme Court case.	Part (b) requires both summary and analysis. Even if you don't remember much about the Supreme Court cases asked about in the question, use context clues from the supplied passages to piece together the main idea of each case. While the supplemental information is not exhaustive, hopefully it helps to jog your memory. In this domain, it is helpful to draw on other (similar) cases to support the precedent-setting nature of the case provided. For this response, the *Santa Fe Independent School District* case involving the usage of a PA system to say a voluntary prayer was invoked to explain the precedent-setting impact of *Engel v. Vitale*.
(c) (1 point)	Explain how modern-day conservatives and liberals would most likely agree or disagree to the holding in *Engel v. Vitale*.	Part (c) can be answered by connecting modern-day conservative and liberal perspectives to the Court's decision in this landmark case.	Part (c) requires a combination of recall and analysis. First, identify the relevant political institution, behavior, or process. In this question, your knowledge of modern-day liberalism and conservatism (as ideologies) is relevant. After establishing the nature of those ideologies, try to connect them to the case. This is where the analysis comes in. After identifying the relevant institution (ideology in this case), think about how the holding in *Engel v. Vitale* would resonate with liberals and conservatives. Then, apply that reasoning to contrast their respective responses to the holding.

Sample Student Response

The issue of religious freedom is one that has been, and always will be, central to the discussion of civil liberties in the United States. Although all rights and privileges granted to Americans under the Bill of Rights are of equal importance, there has been perhaps no greater controversy than the Court's interpretation of religious liberty, as afforded by the Constitution, over the course of the nation's history.

The Court's lengthy, progressive, and shifting definitions of "religious beliefs" and the "Separation of Church and State" clearly demonstrate the interpretive significance of "freedom of religion."

Engel v. Vitale and Wisconsin v. Yoder are two landmark cases regarding the First Amendment inclusion of religious liberties. Engel v. Vitale is a Supreme Court case involving the violation of the Establishment Clause. In New York during the late 1950s, the state public school board instituted a nondenominational prayer to be recited alongside the Pledge of Allegiance. Stephen Engel, the parent of one of the students asked to recite the prayer, contested it, and brought a suit against the president of the board, William Vitale. Engel argued that enforcing a prayer, regardless of its nondenominational affiliation, violated the Establishment Clause of the First Amendment. Vitale claimed that because the prayer was to be repeated on a voluntary basis, the students' First Amendment rights were not violated. Initially, the suit was brought before the New York State Supreme Court and then the Appellate Division of the New York Supreme Court, with both courts finding no fault with including the prayer, focusing on its inherent "voluntary" nature. Engel, along with the other parents, petitioned the U.S. Supreme Court in April 1962. In a landmark decision, the Court reversed the previous rulings, stating that the prayer, no matter its voluntary nature, advocated and implemented by the state, violated the Establishment Clause of the First Amendment. This set a precedent for many forthcoming cases that the Court heard, including the 2000 case involving the Santa Fe Independent School District. A group of students in Texas decided to select a fellow student to state a prayer over the PA system prior to football games. The Court, drawing on the ruling from Engel v. Vitale, concluded that the usage of the public school's PA system for reciting a religious prayer violated the Establishment Clause.

Similar to Engel v. Vitale in terms of its First Amendment freedom of religion questions, Wisconsin v. Yoder is another Supreme Court case involving the First Amendment. Unlike Engel v. Vitale, however, Wisconsin v. Yoder concerns the Free Exercise Clause, not the Establishment Clause. The facts surrounding Wisconsin v. Yoder begin with the state of Wisconsin's requirement of compulsory school attendance until the age of 16. When three Amish parents failed to enroll their teenagers, aged 14 and 15, in public or private school, they were found by a local county court to have violated the law and were charged $5 each for noncompliance. When the Wisconsin Supreme Court sided with the parents, the state of Wisconsin appealed the case to the Supreme Court. In its 1972 ruling, the Court stated that the law requiring absolute compulsory school attendance criminalized the actions of parents who refused to enroll their children in school beyond the eighth grade for sincerely held religious beliefs violated the right to free exercise.

Both of the aforementioned cases apply broadly to the concept of protecting personal liberties, as afforded by the First Amendment. Further, while each of the cases pertains to two different principles engendered in the Bill of Rights, both are relevant to the discussion of preserving the right to practice religion freely without infringement from the state. To that end, the holding in Engel v. Vitale restrained the state from sanctioning a religious prayer in order to preserve the students' individual rights to be free from religious burdens. Similarly, the holding in Wisconsin v. Yoder restrained the state from imposing an educational requirement in order to preserve the students' individual rights to freely practice their religion.

Modern-day conservatives and liberals maintain strong opinions regarding the state's interference in religious liberties. While conservatives typically favor minimal government intervention, such is not the case with primarily social or moral issues. Conservatives forcefully advocate for the state's reinforcement of religion as a means of preserving the moral and civic good. On the other hand, liberals oppose the state's sanctioning of religion, calling for a strict interpretation of the Establishment Clause. As such, liberals would find the ruling in Engel v. Vitale consistent with their interpretation of maintaining a separation between church and state. Alternatively, conservatives are likely to oppose the ruling in Engel v. Vitale, stressing both the voluntary and nondenominational nature of the prayer.

Chapter 7

Unit 4: American Political Ideologies and Beliefs

Unit 4 explores how American political ideologies and beliefs, including public opinion, are formed.

- Political Beliefs
- Public Opinion
  - Measuring Public Opinion
- Political Ideologies
  - Democratic and Republican Ideological Differences
  - Political Ideological Roles in Market Regulations
  - Political Ideological Roles in Economic Policies
  - Economic Theories

Overview of AP U.S. Government and Politics Unit 4

The overarching concepts for this chapter address citizen beliefs about government, public opinion formation and measurement, and how policymaking is influenced by ideology and other competing interests.

The three main College Board content outlines for Unit 4 are as follows:

- **Political beliefs.** Citizen beliefs about government are shaped by the intersection of demographics, political culture, and dynamic social change.
- **Public opinion.** Public opinion is measured through scientific polling, and the results of public opinion polls influence public policies and institutions.
- **Political ideologies.** Widely held political ideologies shape policy debates and choices in American policies.

AP U.S. Government and Politics Key Concepts

Success on the exam depends on your ability to make connections to the essential knowledge of the key concepts as described in the content outlines of *AP U.S. Government and Politics Course Framework*. Remember that these concepts highlight the fundamental ideas that every student should take with them into the AP GOV exam and beyond.

Use the chart that follows to guide you through the specific knowledge that is covered in this unit. The information contained in this chart is an abridged version of the content outlines with topic examples. Visit https://apstudent.collegeboard.org/apcourse/ap-united-states-government-and-politics for the complete updated AP GOV course curriculum framework.

AP U.S. Government and Politics Key Concepts (Unit 4)	
Key Concept	**Content**
Big Idea 5: Methods of Political Analysis **Citizen beliefs about government are shaped by the intersection of demographics, political culture, and dynamic social change.**	Different interpretations of core values, including individualism, equality of opportunity, free enterprise, rule of law, and limited government, affect the relationship between citizens and the federal government and the relationships citizens have with one another. Family, schools, peers, media, and social environments contribute to the development of an individual's political attitudes and values through the process of political socialization. As a result of globalization, U.S. political culture has both influenced and been influenced by the values of other countries. Generational and lifecycle effects also contribute to the political socialization that influences an individual's political attitude. The relative importance of major political events to the development of individual political attitudes is an example of political socialization.
Big Idea 5: Methods of Political Analysis **Public opinion is measured through scientific polling, and the results of public opinion polls influence public policies and institutions.**	Public opinion data that can impact elections and policy debates are affected by scientific polling types and methods (e.g., type of poll, sampling techniques, identification of respondents, mass survey or focus group, sampling error, and the type and format of questions). The relationship between scientific polling and elections and policy debates is affected by the importance of public opinion as a source of political influence and the reliability and veracity of public opinion data.
Big Idea 4: Competing Policymaking Interests **Widely held political ideologies shape policy debates and choices in American policies.**	The Democratic Party platforms generally align more closely to liberal ideological positions, and the Republican Party platforms generally align more closely to conservative ideological positions. Because the U.S. is a democracy with a diverse society, public policies generated at any given time reflect the attitudes and beliefs of citizens who choose to participate in politics at that time. The balancing dynamic of individual liberty and government efforts to promote stability and order has been reflected in policy debates and their outcomes over time. Liberal ideologies favor more governmental regulation of the marketplace, conservative ideologies favor fewer regulations, and libertarian ideologies favor little or no regulation of the marketplace beyond the protection of property rights and voluntary trade. Ideological differences on marketplace regulation are based on different theoretical support, including Keynesian and supply-side positions on monetary and fiscal policies promoted by the president, Congress, and the Federal Reserve. Liberal ideologies tend to think that personal privacy extends further than conservative ideologies (except in arenas involving religious and educational freedom). Conservative ideologies favor less government involvement to ensure social and economic equality. Libertarian ideologies disfavor any governmental intervention beyond the protection of private property and individual liberty. Policy trends concerning the level of government involvement in social issues reflect the success of conservative or liberal perspectives in political parties.

Heads Up: What You Need to Know

As you study the topics related to Unit 4, it is important that you grasp the terms and concepts so that you can answer free-response questions that begin with one of these task verbs:

- **Explain**. What are the straightforward facts, details, data, principles, processes, and outcomes? For example, can you explain how cultural factors influence political attitudes and socialization?
- **Describe**. What is the relevant evidence or supporting examples to paint an overall picture? For example, describe the elements of a scientific poll.

Study Questions

Glance through the study questions before you start the review section. Take notes, highlight questions, and write down page number references to reinforce your learning. Refer to this list as often as necessary until you feel comfortable with your knowledge of the material.

1. How are American political beliefs formed and how do they evolve over time? (Hint: Political beliefs are formed by way of political culture and the agents of socialization.)

2. How do political ideology and core values influence government policymaking? (Hint: Policymakers are aligned with political parties representing political ideologies and certain core values.)

3. What is the practical difference between enumerated powers and implied powers in the Constitution, with regard to public policy creation by Congress? (Hint: Passing a federal budget vs. declaring war and maintaining the armed forces.)

4. How do the structure, powers, and functions of both houses of Congress affect the policymaking process? (Hint: Chamber reliance on committees, chamber-specific rulemaking, pork barrel legislation, and logrolling.)

5. How is congressional behavior influenced by the election processes, partisanship, and a divided government? (Hint: Congressional ideological divisions, gerrymandering, lame-duck presidents, and differing conceptions of constituent accountability.)

6. How does the president implement a policy agenda? (Hint: Use of informal and formal powers, including vetoes and pocket vetoes, bargaining, and issuing executive orders.)

7. How can the president's agenda create tension and frequent confrontations with Congress? (Hint: Executive branch appointments, Senate confirmation hearings, and policy initiatives.)

8. What is judicial review and how does it check on other institutions and state governments? (Hint: Article III of the Constitution, Federalist No. 78, and *Marbury v. Madison*.)

9. How can other branches in government limit the Supreme Court? (Hint: Congressional legislation, amendments, appointments and confirmations, and the president evading Court decisions.)

10. How does bureaucracy carry out the responsibilities of the federal government? (Hint: Writing and enforcing regulations, testifying before Congress, issue networks, and iron triangles.)

11. How does the president ensure that executive branch agencies carry out their responsibilities? (Hint: Presidential ideology and compliance monitoring.)

Important Terms and Concepts Checklist

This section is an overview of the terms, concepts, ideas, documents, and court cases that specifically target the AP GOV exam. Additional vocabulary is also included to aid in your understanding.

As you review the material covered in this chapter, remember that the required foundational documents and required Supreme Court cases (see the Appendix) are noted among the key academic terms, concepts, and language.

As you study the terms and concepts, simply place a check mark next to each and return to this list as often as necessary to check your understanding. After you finish the chapter review section, reinforce what you have learned by working through the practice questions at the end of the chapter. Answers and explanations provide further clarification into perspectives of U.S. government and politics.

Term/Concept	Big Idea	Study Page	Term/Concept	Big Idea	Study Page	Term/Concept	Big Idea	Study Page
Benchmark poll	MPA	p. 222	Focus group	MPA	p. 221	Opinion poll	MPA	p. 222
Bias	MPA	p. 220	Free enterprise	MPA; PMI	p. 229	Political culture	MPA; PMI	pp. 211–215
Capitalism	PMI	p. 229	Gallup poll	MPA	p. 222	Political ideology	MPA	pp. 211, 213
Closed-ended question	MPA	p. 221	Globalization	MPA	pp. 217–218	Political socialization	MPA	pp. 211, 215–217
Collectivism	MPA	pp. 214–215	Individualism	MPA	pp. 214–215	Probability sampling	MPA	p. 219
Conservative	PMI	p. 225	Keynesian economics theory	PMI	pp. 230–231	Public opinion	MPA; PMI	pp. 218–224
Demand-side economics	PMI	pp. 230–231	Liberal	PMI	p. 225	Random digit dialing (RDD)	MPA	p. 219
Demographic	MPA	p. 221	Libertarian Party	PMI	pp. 226–227	Random sampling	MPA	p. 219
Entrance poll	MPA2	p. 222	Limited government	MPA; PMI	pp. 60–61, 214	Respondent identification	MPA	p. 221
Equality of opportunity	MPA	p. 217	Mass survey	MPA	p. 221	Rule of law	MPA	pp. 213–214
Exit poll	MPA	p. 222	Monetary policy	PMI	p. 232	Sampling technique	MPA	p. 218
Federal Reserve System	PMI	p. 232	Non-probability sampling	MPA	p. 220	Supply-side economics	PMI	p. 231
Fiscal policy	PMI	p. 230	Open-ended question	MPA	p. 221			

Chapter Review

Political culture is defined as the set of attitudes, beliefs, and values that motivate and drive the political processes and behaviors within a political system (see "American Political Culture" that follows). Political culture develops over time through generational changes, cultural shifts, and societal influences. The foundational values of America's political culture were first articulated in the Declaration of Independence and the Constitution. Our collective political behavior over time, the decisions and actions taken to translate values into a working political framework, the impact of historical context on public attitudes, and political outcomes have all had an evolutionary impact on our constitutional democracy, but a core belief in the value of ideas such as liberty, equality of opportunity, tolerance, and civic engagement remain.

The transmission of political culture from one generation to the next is a process referred to as **political socialization**. From birth, individuals begin this process influenced primarily by family. As children enter school, interact with peers, attend religious services, join clubs and service organizations, and are exposed to different forms of media, their political socialization into America's political culture develops.

One of the outcomes of the socialization process is the formation of an individual's **ideology**. Every person internalizes what they learn, see, hear, and see modeled around them, developing social, cultural, and political beliefs that form the lens through which they view and perceive the world. The basic classifications for political ideology include conservative, liberal, libertarian, and authoritarian perspectives.

Within the American political culture, ideologies have traditionally translated into citizen identification with a defined **political party**. While political parties can't account for all the nuanced perspectives in an individual's worldview, the Republican and Democratic parties offer an interpretive framework for public policy. People then align themselves with the party that is most reflective of their broad ideological perspective. Traditionally, the direction of public policy is dictated by the party in the majority, working with a coalition of support within the opposition, and influenced by the prevailing public sentiment.

Political Beliefs

This section will cover the importance of public opinion in American politics and government. As political scientists continue to study how people think about and understand government and politics, measuring group and individual attitudes has become increasingly important to major political events.

Heads Up: What You Need to Know

The learning objectives that you must be able to accomplish are:

Explain the relationship between core beliefs of U.S. citizens and attitudes about the role of government.

Explain how cultural factors influence political attitudes and socialization.

American Political Culture

Political culture is described as the nation's political personality, which is formed through long-standing political characteristics that have shaped the nation. Political culture encompasses both formal and informal customs, traditions, and norms. Formally, the bedrock of political culture in the United States is the Constitution, and the "consent of the governed" political culture is defined by the agreed-upon "formal consent" to live under the rule of law of the Constitution, along with the "informal consent" to obey civic laws. Although political culture is fairly static, stable, and predictable, domestic and global events that prompt crises can cause shifts in culture.

Why is political culture important? The political culture of democracy is broadly dictated by the majority of voices in America that do not violate the basic liberties of others or supersede common laws established by the Constitution. The political culture of America has shaped the direction of public policy. Legislative and executive branches are compelled to govern based on the prevailing voices of public opinion within the American culture.

Generally, public policy reflects the core values and beliefs of the political culture, as it must be responsive to issues of the moment. In other words, while the culture is relatively stable, public policy shifts, changes, and adapts, depending on factors such as issue salience. *Salience* means there is a high degree of public interest in the issue; as a result, the issue draws media attention and greater interest on the part of government officials to act. For example, during World War II the eligible age for the military draft was lowered to 18 years old. The issue of whether the voting age should also be lowered quickly followed but failed to gain serious national attention until the Vietnam War. As the anti-war protests and youth movement of the 1960s converged, the calls for lowering the voting age to 18 years old became more urgent, and highly visible protests were covered daily in national media outlets.

The question was frequently and consistently raised: If 18-year-olds were old enough to be drafted to fight in far-off wars, why were they not considered old enough and responsible enough to exercise the right to vote? Finally, in 1970 an amendment was added to the Civil Rights Act granting 18-year-olds the right to vote in federal, state, and local elections. President Nixon subsequently signed the amendment package into law. After the Supreme Court overruled the mandated change in voting age in the states as an unconstitutional violation of the Tenth Amendment (*Oregon v. Mitchell*), the Twenty-Sixth Amendment was passed in the following year to establish 18 years old as the minimum voting age for all elections, federal and state. It was the immediacy and political urgency of the issue at the time that made it *salient* and prompted the change in policy.

Interpretations of American Political Culture

Before we discuss how political opinion is measured, let's cover some important interpretations of American political culture that will appear on the AP GOV exam. These elements will help you understand the dynamics of social and political decisions of citizens.

Use these concepts in your free-response essays when referencing public opinion.

Interpretations of American Political Culture		
Term	**Description**	**Examples**
Political culture	As discussed above, political culture is a general term used to describe the widely shared attitudes and beliefs held by a group of citizens about the assumptions and rules that govern behavior in a political system. Not all Americans share the same political ideology, core beliefs, or opinions on public policy issues, but most Americans share the same political culture of democratic ideals established by our Founding Fathers.	Democratic ideals established by our Founding Fathers— e.g., liberty, equality, rule of law, limited government, natural rights, and consent of the governed.

Term	Description	Examples
Political ideology	Political ideological views form perceptions, doctrines, and principles about how the government, laws, and authority should function. The perceptions influence underlying core beliefs about the roles of government, society, and politics.	Liberalism, conservatism, capitalism, and socialism.
Core beliefs	Core beliefs help to explain the historically deep-rooted views that citizens hold about public policies, political candidates, political parties, and public officials. These beliefs form a way of looking at the issues that shape and influence ideas, attitudes, and values of the political culture. For the AP GOV exam, keep in mind that not all Americans share the same perspective about core beliefs (e.g., economic equality).	Individualism, liberty, equality, patriotism, rule of law, limited government, free enterprise, pragmatism, and the American Dream.

As you study American ideologies, beliefs, and values, keep in mind that as society evolves, distinctive American values and beliefs change over time. And remember that American values and beliefs are different from American constitutional principles that guide our underlying system of government (e.g., popular sovereignty, limited government, separation of powers, checks and balances, republicanism, federalism, and judicial review).

Heads Up: What You Need to Know

For the AP GOV exam, you should be familiar with concepts related to American political culture and beliefs: rule of law, limited government, individualism, and collectivism.

Rule of Law

Rule of law is a standardization of rules that every person is required to follow. It is the foundation of constitutional government. In any constitutional system, the boundaries of a limited government are established, forming a government of laws, not of men. Government of men is arbitrary and unrestrained by any expectation of limits to power and authority. Government of law adheres to a framework with boundaries placed on the exercise of power and includes mechanisms that check tendencies to cross those boundaries. The constitutional framework of law also includes consequences for the illegal or improper use of power. The expectations of legality and principled action within the framework—expectations held for every person, organization, and public official up to and including the executive—are what elevate a nation based on the rule of law above one mired in tyranny and dictatorial capriciousness. The rule of law and the

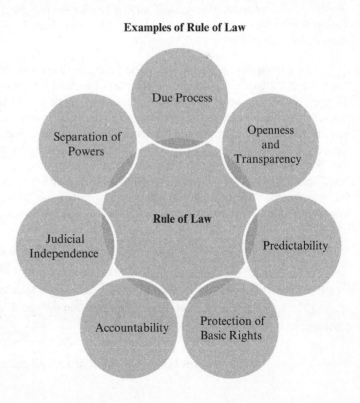

Examples of Rule of Law

Due Process

Openness and Transparency

Separation of Powers

Rule of Law

Predictability

Judicial Independence

Accountability

Protection of Basic Rights

formalized legal framework of the United States Constitution are fundamental to the American political culture. While the American framework necessarily allows a level of flexibility regarding legal interpretation of the Constitution, the principle of rule of law itself demands equal accountability for every person and, by extension, every organization within the country (see "Limited Government" in Chapter 4, p. 60).

Limited Government

Limited government is the idea that a government's power and authority over its people has limitations. It is constrained by law embodied in a constitution. Separating the powers to govern into different branches, granting to each powers to act as a check on the others, are forms of constraint and limitation. In addition, the simple act of enumerating the powers that the institutions of the government can exercise further constrains them. Of course, the specific guarantees of civil liberties contained in the Bill of Rights add a layer of protection against unlimited use of power.

Individualism vs. Collectivism

To understand the psychology of American culture, it is important to introduce two contrasting worldviews—individualism and collectivism. **Individualism** is a belief that every person has the unalienable right to live their life as they see fit. Its core value is **liberty,** the freedom of individuals to be the sovereign judge of their own actions, their own "pursuit of happiness." Individualism lies at the heart of American political culture. Many westernized countries such as Britain, France, Canada, Germany, and Australia are grounded to one degree or another in a worldview that embraces individualism.

Collectivism views society as the primary unit of concern. Individuals are important only as part of a larger society in which liberty over oneself must give way to the "greater good" of all. Countries such as China, Colombia, Indonesia, Pakistan, and Costa Rica were founded on principles of collectivism that emphasize this shared responsibility.

Both worldviews have pros and cons, and no country is either entirely one or the other. For example, while the United States was founded on principles of individual liberty, in times of crisis (e.g., the Great Depression) or increased attention on issues such as generational poverty, social programs were adopted to provide a minimal level of economic security for citizens requiring assistance. All social programs assert a communal responsibility for the "general welfare" of the community at large. The same is true of public agencies (e.g., police and fire departments) and public schools, which provide services for all citizens, paid for by all citizens through taxation, whether they avail themselves of these services or not. On the other hand, particularly in the economic realm, countries with a more collectivist outlook embrace a certain level of individualism through free enterprise to promote innovation, creativity, initiative, and global competitiveness in order to ensure national economic growth.

TEST TIP: When studying individualism and collectivism, it is important to understand why these concepts are relevant on the AP GOV exam. In the U.S. political system, individualism is a core belief, and the degree to which people embrace individualism is a contributing factor to political, economic, and social schisms that divide Americans along ideological and party lines. The tension between the two worldviews has been central to political conflict in the American body of politics for many years.

Now, let's recap the differences between individualism and collectivism in the table that follows.

Term	Description	Examples
Individualism	Individualism is a central theme in American history and has shaped the character of our nation. It emphasizes a unique notion for the preservation of personal freedoms and individual rights. Individualism is at the heart of the philosophies that guided many of our Founding Fathers, especially Thomas Jefferson, who was guided by the ideals of the Enlightenment Era. As you may recall from Chapter 4, the Enlightenment philosophical concepts contributed to the formation of the new American government and political ideals, including ideas that promoted *natural rights* (all people were entitled to God-given rights). Jefferson understood that democracy could only exist as a viable, legitimate form of government if the government itself protected and respected the rights of the individual. Circumventing individual rights would be the equivalent of invalidating the capacity to think independently and critically, an ideal upon which the nation was founded.	Self-interest, self-reliance, independence, and natural rights. Values individual liberty over security.
Collectivism	Collectivism is a broad system of thought that values the needs of the group over the needs of the individual. Rather than individual citizens as the source and agents of moral good, collectivism derives its definition of "moral good" from the needs of the group, hence the term *collective*. Typically, Communism and Socialism have the philosophical underpinnings of collectivism to guide their ideological views.	Self-sacrificing, generous, and valuing social institutions. Values security over individual liberty.

Heads Up: What You Need to Know

The AP GOV exam frequently has a question about **political socialization** and how it influences a person's political beliefs, ideology, culture, and reasons for choosing a particular political party. Political beliefs are shaped by the various agents of political socialization (family, friends, the media, education, religious organizations, and geography).

It is important to note that political socialization is an ongoing process impacted by social, economic, and demographic changes in the rapidly evolving modern world—changes magnified by globalization. Consequently, neither ideological perspective nor political party alignment is a static feature of political behavior within America's body of politics.

Political Socialization

Political socialization refers to the process by which people learn and assimilate political beliefs, attitudes, and behaviors from a variety of primary and secondary sources. Studies show that political learning is passed down from generation to generation. It is a lifelong internal process that begins during the earliest stages of development and leads to the formation of an individual's personal political ideas, values, and opinions—the realization of their own "political self."

Political socialization is why we believe what we believe about politics and the government—through environmental influences (family, peers, media, school, religion, and other social influences such as gender, race, age, and geography). The outcome of these influences affects political behavior, political opinion, and voting preferences.

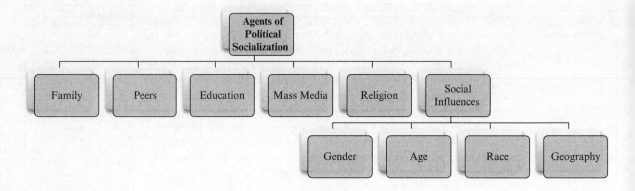

Key Facts about Agents of Political Socialization

Studies show that the five most important agents influencing political socialization are family, friends/peers, education, mass media, and religion.

Family. According to political scientists, "the family is the foremost among agencies of socialization into politics," and as the first, it is also the agent of "primary socialization." From infancy onward, children wittingly and unwittingly receive and process information at home through interactions with their immediate family. During this earliest stage of development, children begin to develop their own understanding of the world in which they live. As children witness their parents and other family members having political conversations and responding to various political phenomena, they develop similar core political belief systems (e.g., political opinions and voting preferences). While primary socialization is the product of exposure to interactions among any number of extended family members, parents remain the most important influence on a child's political development.

Friends/peers. People who are linked to a person by common interests, age, or social position serve as a source of political socialization in accordance with life stages: children, youth, and young adults. Children and youth are often influenced by friends and peers, especially in middle school, high school, and college. These relationships expose children and youth to political knowledge and perspectives that may be unique in their experience. New ideas and expressed feelings about politics and government, consciously or unconsciously, contribute to the formation of social and political beliefs.

Education. Although the family is the primary agent of socialization, schools quickly become a contributing environmental factor to the development of political attitudes in children. Education places impressionable students in a setting of concentrated learning. Students become knowledgeable about American history, government, founding documents, voting, and the political processes. For example, young children are taught patriotic values and respect for one's nation by learning the Pledge of Allegiance and singing "The Star-Spangled Banner." As students transition through upper grades, they are exposed to even more complex political information.

Mass media. The media has taken an increased role as an agent of political socialization. Millions of people can be reached through media-rich sources. Political socialization is shaped by television, radio, the Internet, social media (blogging, Twitter, Facebook, etc.), newspapers, and magazines. Teens, young adults, and adults spend much of their time using a computer, cell phone, or watching television.

Religion. Religious affiliations can play a key role in the formation of political socialization. People can be swayed by the theological and/or moral perspectives on politics, governance, and public policy, thus shaping political decision making. Religion has become one of the main predictors of a person's voting preferences. In the 1980 presidential election, the Christian Coalition and the Moral Majority played key roles in Ronald Reagan's victory.

Did you know? Generational, social, and economic influences can greatly impact political socialization. For example, during the Great Depression, economic changes impacted people on multiple levels. As unemployment and inflation skyrocketed, basic lifestyle choices changed, including living standards and the way in which people thought about government intervention. Even those who traditionally opposed government intervention understood that social programs were needed to regain a robust economy.

Political events can influence ideological persuasions and the trajectory of political socialization. For example, during the Vietnam War, 9/11, or the passage of *Roe v. Wade,* like-minded Americans joined similar ideological organizations and political coalitions. Political events can also disrupt the traditional trajectory of political opinion formation because controversy is often an impetus for contemplating personal opinions. Such controversy can lead people to take on different political views that they may not have held had unrest not been present.

Equality of Opportunity

Equality is one of the core beliefs in American political culture. It is not a belief that embraces equality of condition, but instead, **equality of opportunity**. In other words, we are not all equally wealthy, intelligent, skilled, or well-positioned within the social hierarchy, nor is it possible for society to create such equity, but no one, regardless of condition, should be denied the opportunity to access education, employment, housing, or places of public accommodation where goods or services are provided. Equality of opportunity embraces a political ideal that proposes that every person within a society should be able to compete on equal terms to ensure that anyone who seeks a fair chance can strive toward "the American Dream." Of course, equality of opportunity does not guarantee equal success, and, given the emphasis on individualism in the American political culture, success or failure is viewed as self-determined.

Although equality of opportunity is often a prerequisite in establishing a just society, many argue that access is merely a formality and that government should ensure outcomes to correct imbalances of wealth, inadequate demographic representations in schools and workplaces, and community structures that indirectly reinforce inequalities.

Globalization

Globalization is the increasing interconnectedness among various nations worldwide that is primarily fostered through advances in technology and openness to trade. Free trade between nations, unencumbered by restrictive protectionist tariffs, was a major contributing factor to rapid globalization in the late 20th century and continues to impact global economic balance. Decisions regarding trade involve policy (what governments choose to do or not do regarding issues), and policymaking is a fundamentally political act. To that end, trade agreements are developed through successful political discourse among nations.

> **Did you know?** The term *digital divide* is used to explain the economic disparity in terms of total access to information technology or, more plainly, computers. While some developing nations still experience a massive digital divide, this divide is closing. As it closes, nations are becoming more interconnected than ever before and globalization is accelerating. Not only is general information exchange occurring through international communication via technology, but cultural, political, and economic ideas are also being disseminated.

Public Opinion

Heads Up: What You Need to Know

The learning objectives that you must be able to accomplish are:

Describe the elements of a scientific poll.

Explain the quality and credibility of claims based on public opinion data.

Public opinion describes the beliefs, attitudes, and values that citizens express about government policies, issues, and candidates. The themes covered in this section explain the importance of public opinion in shaping political and government decision making. This section will cover the methods for measuring public opinion, types of scientific polls, and the credibility of claims based on public opinion. On the AP GOV exam, you should be able to identify the relationship between public opinion, scientific polling, election results, and policy debates.

Measuring Public Opinion

Individual and shared views about politics, political campaigns, election outcomes, and public policies have become an important part of the framework of government and politics. The views of everyday citizens are measured through scientific public opinion polls. In public opinion polls, a small group of people, randomly sampled, answer questions about social issues and political candidates from which generalized assumptions about the American public are extrapolated.

Heads Up: What You Need to Know

Because it is practically impossible to poll an entire population of voters, **sampling techniques** are vital to the process of collecting public opinion data. In terms of survey methodology, sampling is simply the selection of a certain statistical population to draw conclusions and assumptions about the entire population at large. Sampling is useful because it is low cost, data can be aggregated more quickly, and errors regarding the data can be corrected with greater ease.

Public opinion is important because the voice of the people is the backbone of American democracy. Scientific polls are the most common method to learn about what the public is thinking. Public opinion polls determine how people think about policies and social issues, provide predictions for election results, and determine where candidates should focus their attention during a campaign. The majority of questions asked are closed-ended, requiring only yes or no answers. Topics include voter preferences, issue priorities, political ideologies, policy choices, and office holder favorability. Researchers analyze the statistical results and publish interpretations based on the findings.

To help you better understand the process of measuring public opinion, let's examine some of the frequently asked questions.

Key Facts about Public Opinion Poll Frequently Asked Questions

What are public opinion polls? Polls can be scientific or unscientific in application.

- **Scientific polls** use **probability sampling** (a smaller group of selected people) that reflects the larger population of study. Since it is impossible to survey millions of Americans, a **random sampling** of the population can reproduce the results of the larger population. A random sample is one in which everyone has an equal chance of participating in the poll. The sampling must be random to ensure that the results of the polling are not skewed, but rather, allow poll analysts to make reasonably accurate extrapolations about the general population from the data. For example, polling conducted outside of a senior center focused on the future of Social Security is not random or scientific. Clearly, that population sample is not random because only those outside of the senior center have an opportunity to participate, and as a result, the outcomes are skewed toward the elderly, who are most impacted by Social Security. On the other hand, a random sample polling of 1,000 people could represent the views of over 300 million Americans on the issue of Social Security.

- **Random digit dialing (RDD):** The most common means of obtaining a scientific sample for decades has been **random digit dialing**. Random sets of digits are added to known area codes to create a 10-digit phone number. Every person with a phone has an equal chance of those random digits being their phone number. The number is computer-generated, automatically dialed, and an interviewer takes over when someone answers. This process has become increasingly expensive because many of the phone numbers produced and called are non-working numbers; plus, the automated system does not work with cell phones, so interviewers must manually call cell numbers.

- **Registration-based sampling (RBS):** Registration-based sampling has proven to be a more efficient means of sampling and conducting a poll. A randomly selected sample is taken from voter registration lists, and phone numbers are then matched to those provided on the lists. While time isn't wasted on non-working numbers, there are some disadvantages: Not everyone provides a phone number, people may have moved so the phone number may no longer be valid, and those who plan to vote but have not yet registered don't have an equal chance of being selected.

- The issues with RDD and RBS are not the only problems pollsters can encounter. For example, their sample may indeed be random, but of the 1,000 randomly chosen for the sample, 600 may just happen to be men. Men do not make up 60 percent of the overall population, so how accurate would the result of the polling be? To be considered scientific, a poll must account for a **margin of error** (statistical uncertainty) to instill confidence that the results are accurate. The statistical variance is expressed as a "plus or minus" figure. The smaller the margin of error, the more confidence there is in the accuracy of the polling data as a measure of the broader population. For example, if a poll shows that 30 percent of Americans would like Congress to pass legislation that promotes transition to renewable energy sources and the margin of error is 3, then the expected results for the entire population could range from as low as 27 percent to as high as 33 percent. How confident can you be that the true response of the whole population would fall somewhere within the margin of error? For most pollsters, the confidence level used is 95 percent.

The bar graph that follows illustrates the results of a scientific poll showing statistically significant results that Americans support health insurance reform.

Americans Support a Public Option

Polls Continue to Find Significant Support for Health Insurance Reform with a Public Option

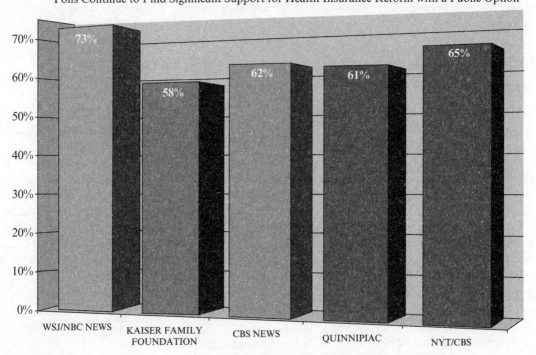

Source: Office of the Speaker Nancy Pelosi, "Americans Support a Public Option," 2009.

- **Unscientific polls** use **non-probability sampling** (sampling based on the subjective judgment of the researcher) and do not randomly select its participants. This type of polling is not scientifically reliable. It's important to consider the differences between scientific and unscientific polling because during election campaigns, news media outlets will sometimes report the "unscientific" results of in-house focus groups to influence the views of the American public. This type of polling is subject to **bias** (prejudice for or against) and does not necessarily reflect the opinions of the general population.

For example, if a radio station asks its listeners to call in to vote on whether or not they agree with healthcare insurance reform, the results of the poll are not statistically significant. Why? The listeners may already have biases because that particular station may appeal to people with specific social/political leanings. In addition, the listeners who happen to respond may be the only people listening to the radio during that particular show at that specific time. Not everyone was given the opportunity to answer the question. Therefore, the results are not representative of the population as a whole. Mail-in polls and text-in polls are also notoriously unscientific because they are targeted at a particular audience of readers, viewers, or listeners and only the most motivated of those are likely to respond. It simply would not be possible to interpret the data from such polls to draw any reasonably accurate conclusions about the general population and their thoughts regarding the polling questions.

TEST TIP: On the AP GOV exam, it is important to use the term *random sampling* in your free-response essays for questions about public opinion polling. Random sampling (sometimes called *probability sampling*) is the sampling process that allows every person within a defined population to have an equal chance of being selected. Because it is impossible to poll an entire population, random sampling techniques are vital to the process of collecting public opinion data.

Who conducts public opinion polls? Scientific political and social research polls are conducted by interviewers through independent organizations, television networks, and major newspapers. For example, in the United States, some of the most popular organizations include Pew Research Center, Gallup, CNN, ABC News, *The New York Times,* and *The Washington Post.*

How do public opinion polls work? Scientific polls use a systematic approach through controlled measures that randomly select *respondents* (citizens answering the questions) to answer survey questions. Questionnaires (surveys) are given to respondents in person, by telephone, by mail, or online (although most polls are given in person or by telephone).

In scientific polls, the following **demographic** factors are used for **respondent identification** for a random sample.

- Age
- Gender
- Race/ethnicity
- Income
- Geographic residence
- Religion

Two types of questions—open-ended and closed-ended—can be administered by the interviewer at the time of the poll. A **closed-ended question** requires the respondent to select from choices given— for example, "yes or no," multiple-choice: A, B, C, D, "satisfied or unsatisfied," or "agree or disagree." An **open-ended question** is more than a one-selection response. This type of question allows the respondent to develop their own unlimited response to the question.

Questionnaires can be administered by mass surveys or by focus groups. Both have benefits and weaknesses, but mass surveys are substantially more reliable. **Mass surveys** are cost-effective and are based on gathering quantitative data to form a generalized statement about a random sample population. Mass surveys are conducted by phone calls or in-person interviews and are typically the most common type of scientific survey. In **focus groups,** qualitative discussions are analyzed to draw conclusions about an issue or topic. Individuals who participate in focus groups are interviewed in the context of a group setting and are asked a series of questions. Open-ended questions provide the participants an opportunity to express their opinions in greater detail, as opposed to being restricted by a multiple-choice survey.

What are the main types of scientific polls? The main types of polls that you will need to know for the AP GOV exam are opinion polls, benchmark polls, tracking polls, entrance polls, and exit polls.

Types of Scientific Polls	
Poll	Description
Opinion polls	**Opinion polls** are exactly what the term denotes—nonbiased human research inquiries of a particular sample population. Opinion polls are designed to measure the public's views regarding political topics of interest. Surveys are conducted by a trained interviewer (called *pollster*) who asks a variety of questions in order to make generalizations about the population being studied. Many questions on the survey are ideologically pointed, though respondents are not always aware of the ideological motivation. One of the most common opinion polls is the **Gallup poll**. The Gallup poll tracks the most important political issues nationwide. It was developed by George Gallup, who used survey sampling techniques to correctly determine the outcome of the 1936 presidential race between Franklin D. Roosevelt and Alf Landon. Gallup predicted Roosevelt would win, and he did. The Gallup poll is used in more than 140 countries and is commonly cited by media personalities and political authorities as a reliable predictor of public opinion.
Benchmark polls	A **benchmark poll** is typically the first poll used in a campaign. It is used to gauge opinions just prior to the campaign or in the campaign's earliest stages. The results gathered are helpful to political candidates who are in the process of developing their political platform. The results provide the candidate an opportunity to decide which issues to focus on, which issues capture national attention, and how to formulate advertising strategies.
Tracking polls	**Tracking polls** measure the changes in opinion over a period of time. Tracking polls are shorter in length and are usually conducted during the final stages of a campaign to determine message resonance. Tracking polls also provide valuable information about both the candidate and the opponent. From the results of these polls, politicians can decide to alter their messages, use different means of appealing to the public, or make minor changes to their platforms.
Entrance polls	**Entrance polls** are taken before a voter enters a voting booth to cast a vote. Because the respondent is least likely to make a party switch prior to walking into the booth, entrance polls can be utilized to make election predictions, but exit polling is the more common means of gaining insight into voter preferences on election night.
Exit polls	**Exit polls** are surveys conducted immediately after voters cast votes. Exit polls are used to predict the outcome of the election before the voting ballots are officially tallied. The interviewer asks either one simple question about the voter's decision or asks questions related to the reasons the voter made his or her decision.

How does the format and type of questions impact public opinion polls? Writing and organizing good opinion questions is the most important part of the measurement process. Survey design biases must be considered when designing and administering any kind of polling survey. The questionnaire design must accurately identify relevant topics and pretest the questions before administering the surveys. How questions are worded and framed, including their order and overall presentation, can dramatically affect the results of the poll.

For example, it is human nature for some people to consider themselves aligned to a particular party or ideology, but their political views may not always correspond to the views of their political party. One way of guarding against this kind of self-assessment is for the questionnaire to ask a series of closed-ended questions that require the respondent to answer questions about specific political issues. Rather than asking respondents if they are "liberal" or "conservative," interviewers may ask whether respondents approve or disapprove of increasing military spending to determine ideological positions.

To prevent unreliable statistical results, researchers consider the qualities of responses on public opinion polls.

What are the qualities of public opinion and why are they important? Knowing how citizens think by answering "yes or no" questions may not be enough to achieve high predictive results on a scientific poll. How strongly a person feels about an issue, how long the person has held particular views, or if the person's views have changed over time due to changing circumstances can all influence an individual's responses.

Researchers have defined intrinsic characteristics that help to evaluate the context of the "yes or no" answers. On the AP GOV exam, you should be familiar with these public opinion qualities: direction, intensity, saliency, fluidity, stability, and latency.

Qualities of Public Opinion	
Direction	**Direction** describes the trends in answering survey questions. For example, conservative voters tend to lean toward the ideological Right on political issues (e.g., pro-life), and liberal voters tend to lean toward the ideological Left on political issues (e.g., pro-choice).
Intensity	**Intensity** describes how strongly people feel about important "hot button" issues (either positively or negatively). Some people feel an intense urgency to express their opinions about social or political issues.
Saliency	**Saliency** describes the degree to which an issue is important. It can be a degree of high priority or low priority.
Fluidity	**Fluidity** describes the change in an opinion over a short period of time. When political conditions change, it can dictate changes in political opinions. For example, at the beginning of the 2003 Iraq War, Americans were still gripped by the patriotic fervor generated by the 2001 terrorist attacks against the World Trade Center and the Pentagon. Convinced by information provided by the Bush administration about the future terrorist threat posed by Iraq, 90 percent of Americans agreed with the decision to invade Iraq. However, by 2008, revelations that the administration had lied about the terrorist threat posed by Iraq, the length of the conflict, and the rising number of U.S. casualties changed the public calculus about the justifications for conducting the war and fewer than 50 percent of Americans polled agreed with the original decision to enter the war.
Stability	**Stability** describes the consistency of public opinion. It is the likelihood that public opinion will be unchanged over a long period of time.
Latency	**Latency** describes underlying opinions that are not openly expressed but can be triggered by certain actions or events. Leaders tuned in to these latent opinions can use this knowledge to motivate large numbers of voters through their actions.

Did you know? Measuring public opinion has come a long way since the first recorded public opinion poll in the early 19th century. A local *straw poll* (informal survey accomplished by a show of hands) was conducted by the *Harrisburg Pennsylvanian* in 1824 to gauge political opinion in the presidential race between Andrew Jackson and John Quincy Adams. The poll showed that Andrew Jackson was favored over John Quincy Adams, 335 votes to 169. The 1824 poll was also the earliest indication that unscientific straw polls can be misleading when trying to draw conclusions about presidential elections: Andrew Jackson did indeed win the popular vote in the general election, but John Quincy Adams went on to win the presidency in a controversial Electoral College outcome.

What is the reliability of public opinion polls? The reliability of public opinion data is continuously being evaluated and scrutinized. While Gallup polls are generally conducted using reliable polling methods and media outlets, especially television broadcast news sources, which rely heavily on polls to make predictions on election night, voter behavior can be unpredictable, so relying on public opinion polling as an objective source of information can do more harm than good.

Exit polls present a number of problems. While they can give some reliable insight into election night outcomes, there are exceptions to their reliability. History has demonstrated that exit polls can be questionable, depending on factors such as the character or race of the candidates. In other words, voters might be not be forthright when revealing their candidate choices, a phenomenon known as the "Bradley effect" or *social desirability bias*. Tom Bradley, the African American former mayor of Los Angeles, ran for governor of California in 1982. The tracking polls as well as the exit polls all indicated Bradley would win. Based on the exit polls, major media outlets projected Bradley as the winner on election night, but the final tally revealed a narrow loss to his white opponent. When researchers looked at the polling, they concluded that a smaller percentage of white voters cast their votes for Bradley than the polls indicated. During polling, did some of these voters hope to appear socially acceptable by expressing a desire to vote for the African American candidate and then vote for the white candidate in the privacy of the voting booth, or was the polling itself flawed? The same effect can result with a candidate who has a less than savory personal reputation—supporters are reluctant to admit they will be casting their vote for such a candidate. There is also considerable evidence that exit polls can have an immediate and drastic effect on voter turnout. For example, if exit poll results allow networks to project winners soon after the polls close on the East Coast while polls are still open on the West Coast, this may impact the turnout for voters living in the west.

Public Opinion Case Study

One notable case study of public opinion that had a direct impact on legislative policy action was the Civil Rights Movement in the early 1960s. In the spring of 1963, when Martin Luther King Jr. decided to begin nonviolent protests that opposed segregation in Birmingham, Alabama, Police Chief Bull Connor commanded his unit to use any means necessary to break up the nonviolent demonstrations. Police officers unleashed police dogs and assaulted protesters with high-blast fire hoses. This incident was significant because it was televised. Americans witnessed the news coverage of the protest, along with brutal images of children being attacked by police dogs, and public outrage mounted. As a result, the Civil Rights Act of 1964 was passed by President Lyndon Johnson, not only as a means of preserving the pro-integration legacy of President Kennedy, but also as a direct response to the brutality that many African Americans had endured in 1963 while the country watched in horror. The powerful public

Source: Bill Hudson, *Associated Press*, July 15, 1963, in Birmingham, Alabama. Photo depicts firefighters turning their hoses full force on civil rights demonstrators.

response against the violent tactics used against peaceful demonstrators presented President Johnson an opportunity to use public opinion as leverage to get the Civil Rights Act through Congress.

Political Ideologies

Political ideology is a specific term used to describe consistent views about how a society, government, or economy should work. Political ideology is an important concept to understand because differences in ideological views are the major source of political polarization in the nation. While the shared values and beliefs that make up the American political culture exist, not all Americans agree on the scope and purpose of the government in upholding the culture and giving full support to those values and beliefs through their public policy decisions. The role of government is one of the most significant ideological rifts in American politics, dating back to the constitutional debates between the Anti-Federalists and Federalists. Today, the two sides of this debate are identified as liberals and conservatives. **Liberals** believe that the federal government can be a force for good and it should take an active role in ensuring the "general welfare" of the entire nation. **Conservatives,** on the other hand, believe that centralized policymaking by "big government" undermines the liberty of individuals, who are best served by decision making at the state and local levels.

Heads Up: What You Need to Know

The learning objectives that you must be able to accomplish are:

Explain how the ideologies of the two major parties shape policy debates.

Explain how U.S. political culture (i.e., values, attitudes, and beliefs) influences the formation, goals, and implementation of public policy over time.

Describe different political ideologies regarding the role of government in regulating the marketplace.

Explain how political ideologies vary on the government's role in regulating the marketplace.

Explain how political ideologies vary on the role of government in addressing social issues.

Explain how different ideologies impact policy on social issues.

TEST TIP: On the AP GOV exam, you may be asked to compare *Libertarian Party* ideologies to Democratic and Republican ideologies. Libertarianism is an economic and political platform that has gained momentum in recent years. Libertarians advocate for political freedom and individual rights in support of personal autonomy and vigilant restraint of government authority. Libertarians can find common ground with liberals on social issues, opposing government interference in choices about personal behavior. Conversely, they agree with conservatives regarding economic issues, favoring less government regulation and oversight of economic activities. Libertarianism is based on the philosophy of Englishman John Locke (1632–1704), who advocated *egalitarianism* (equality) through a social contract with the government to have rights of life, liberty, and property.

Democratic and Republican Ideological Differences

The two major parties that shape policy debates are the **Democratic Party** and the **Republican Party** (see Chapter 8). Democrat and Republican priorities have similarities on some key social and political issues, but they tend to be divided on many other issues based on contrasting ideological views (see the table that follows). Notice that the key priority issues for Democrats are the economy, education, poverty and homelessness, and healthcare policy. The key priority issues for Republicans are the economy, terrorism, the military and national defense, and healthcare policy.

Top Priority Issues, by Party Identification	
Question: How important is it to you that the president and Congress deal with each of the following issues in the next year?	
(% who believe issue is extremely/very important)	
Democrats/Democratic Leaners	**Republicans/Republican Leaners**
The economy (91%)	The economy (88%)
Education (91%)	Terrorism (77%)
Poverty and homelessness (82%)	The military and national defense (76%)
Healthcare policy (79%)	Healthcare policy (75%)
Social Security and Medicare (77%)	Education (70%)
Distribution of income/wealth (72%)	Taxes (69%)
Crime (71%)	Social Security and Medicare (67%)
The environment (71%)	Crime (65%)
Terrorism (68%)	Immigration (54%)
Gun policy (64%)	World affairs (53%)
	Poverty and homelessness (53%)

Source: Gallup poll, "Differences in Issue Priorities Between Democrats and Republicans," January 2014.

Both parties at one time embraced a broad coalition of supporters from left-leaning (liberal) to those who leaned right (conservative). However, in the post-1960s era of American politics, the parties have become increasingly polarized, with Democrats identified with liberalism and the Republican Party almost exclusively associated with conservatism.

Note: The chart below addresses ideological points of view in a general sense. Not every Democrat, Republican, or **Libertarian** adopts their party's ideological arguments in an absolute sense.

Compare and Contrast Selected Ideological Differences			
Issue	**Democrats (Liberal)**	**Republicans (Conservative)**	**Libertarians**
Abortion	Advocate the pro-choice position to preserve a woman's right to privacy and to make her own choices about her reproductive life. Because the consenting woman is of age and the fetus is not a legal person, the government is compelled to protect the woman's right to choose.	Take a pro-life stance against abortion on the grounds that a fetus is a person, and therefore is a life that warrants protection from the government. Conservatives believe that the government must protect the individual rights of the unborn fetus.	Favor individual privacy rights, which include the right of the mother to have an abortion.

Issue	Democrats (Liberal)	Republicans (Conservative)	Libertarians
Same-sex marriage	Support same-sex marriage as a union via marriage contract of two consenting adults. Allowing male/female couples the right to freely enter into a marriage contract while prohibiting same-sex individuals from doing likewise is a violation of their civil rights, as protected by the Equal Protection Clause.	Oppose same-sex marriage because such legally sanctioned unions violate their religious and moral consciences. Do not view same-sex marriage as a civil rights issue because it is not expressly protected by the Constitution, and the Tenth Amendment reserves marriage and family law to the states. Therefore, individual states should not be compelled by the federal government to recognize same-sex unions.	Favor same-sex marriage, although the government should not be overseeing marital unions. Marriage, like other issues, is fundamentally private, which should remove the government from the process in its entirety.
Separation of church and state	Support separation of church and state. Although not expressly stated, the Bill of Rights implies a separation of religion from government in the Establishment Clause, which forms a "wall of separation." As such, there is no room for religious expression within the context of government, including references in public buildings or prayer in school.	Oppose separation of church and state because the Constitution does not indicate such a separation in explicit words. While the government should not sanction a national church or religion, schools and public buildings can freely feature references to God or other religious figures. In doing so, the government reinforces freedom of religion.	Favor separation of church and state. Government should not be involved in either approving or disapproving a religious practice. To that end, the state itself should be nonreligious.
Government intervention	Favor government intervention to ensure social and economic equality. Social program spending, including healthcare, low income subsidies and assistance, and tax increases, are vital.	Mostly oppose government intervention to ensure social and economic equality. Government should not intervene by propping up social spending programs or providing continued assistance, including government-provided healthcare.	Oppose government intervention in its entirety. Sole purpose of government is to protect private property and individual liberty. Beyond those two tasks, government should not be involved in the private affairs of its people.

Political Ideological Roles in Market Regulations

Federal programs use regulatory practices to accomplish broad policy goals to place some constraints on businesses and promote fair competition. It is a powerful policymaking tool. The two main types of regulatory programs are social regulations and economic regulations. The Democrats want more regulatory policies to protect the interests of consumers and workers. They advocate for federal regulatory actions that protect workers' rights and safety, such as those that ensure equal opportunities, protect consumers from unsafe products and unfair competition, provide oversight of pharmaceutical testing and manufacturing, place some restrictions on gun ownership, and address the threat of global warming and other environmental dangers. The Republicans believe there is too much regulation, which inhibits free enterprise. Issues such as unsafe consumer products are best resolved by market forces, which ultimately lead consumers to reject faulty and dangerous goods. Republicans want to lift many of the regulations (deregulation) imposed by federal agencies to bring an end to "big government" and restore a more limited role of the federal government.

Republicans took control of Congress in the 1970s and began to deregulate businesses and industries (railroads, trucking, airlines, telecommunications, and the banking industry). Theoretically, deregulation would free small businesses to be more innovative and increase their competitive edge, allow the marketplace to determine price, and redirect business capital from regulatory compliance toward investment in modernization and efficiency.

When Congress passed the **Airline Deregulation Act** in 1978, some of the benefits anticipated did come to pass. More competition led to a decrease in airline fares, allowing more people to travel. However, smaller airlines or those that could not compete in the fare wars were forced to merge with more successful airlines, were bought out, or went bankrupt. With only four major carriers in the market, a near monopoly on airline travel has resulted. To pay for the cheaper fares, fewer services (e.g., ticket exchanges) and "freebies" (e.g., meals) are offered.

When the banking industry was deregulated in the 1980s, banks failed because they made unchecked risky investments and initiated new real estate lending practices, both of which had once been strictly regulated. These and other innovations in the financial markets promised by deregulation led to short-term profits in the late 20th and early 21st centuries, but the crisis created by the enormous risks taken caused the worst financial crash since the Great Depression. Magnifying the problem were the demands by some of the nation's biggest banks for a taxpayer "bailout"—billions of dollars to save them from bankruptcy, which they insisted would make the financial crisis even worse. Deregulation has proven to be a mixed bag, and Congress has yet to find an effective balance between freeing businesses from overly onerous regulations and providing necessary constraints on the worst of businesses practices.

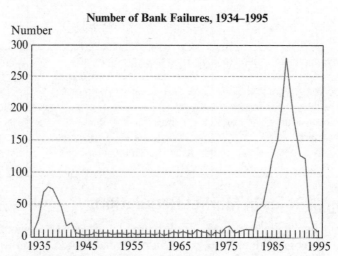

Number of Bank Failures, 1934–1995

Note: Data refer to FDIC-insured commercial and savings banks that were closed or received FDIC assistance.

Source: FDIC.

Heads Up: What You Need to Know

On the AP GOV exam, you should remember that liberal ideologies favor more government regulation of the marketplace, conservative ideologies favor fewer regulations, and libertarian ideologies favor little or no regulation of the marketplace beyond the protection of property rights and voluntary trade.

The Role of Government and Regulation	
Democrats	Democrats believe in more government regulations: The government should manage social welfare issues, including healthcare, aid and assistance, and environmental concerns. The higher tax rates passed on to citizens are justified to ensure a reasonable standard of living for low-income citizens and the disabled. The liberal view is more likely to support shared responsibility for healthcare.
Republicans	Republicans believe in fewer government regulations: The government's primary role is to ensure citizen safety, not social welfare. Lower tax rates are proposed to stimulate the economy by placing more disposable income in the hands of citizens. Private businesses and industries control the market, and thus excessive government regulation violates free market principles. Supply and demand will ensure equal opportunity.
Libertarians	Libertarians believe in little to no government regulations: A free market will regulate concerns. Unrestricted competition is necessary to preserve individual liberty. Even in the midst of a crisis, government bailouts are unacceptable, as they violate government's only role, which is to protect civil liberties.

Political Ideological Roles in Economic Policies

Democrats and Republicans have historically demonstrated diverging views regarding economic policies and practices. In the U.S. economic system, **free enterprise** is the right to freely pursue a business activity that operates for a profit, in competition with other businesses, and with limited government intervention—this is the basis of **capitalism**. Businesses can fail or succeed, depending on whether products or services are in demand in the marketplace. Products, services, and prices are determined by the marketplace, not by the government. America's free enterprise system is not written in the framework of the Constitution, but the Constitution did set up laws to protect individual rights, contracts, and business activities.

Key Facts about a Free Enterprise System

The Founders of the Constitution envisioned that all Americans could prosper with the basic freedoms spelled out in a free enterprise system.

The freedom to choose a business (private enterprise). In a free enterprise economy, everyone has the economic opportunity to enter into a business that is owned individually, in a partnership, or as a corporation.

The right to engage in competition. Business owners have an opportunity to compete in the marketplace. Competition is one of the key components of free enterprise that ensures a free market that benefits both consumers and the economy. Competition should create better-quality products, lower prices, and introduce new innovations.

The right to own private property. According to the laws that govern the United States, people have the right to acquire and own private property and make decisions about how that property is used or disposed of. Approximately 90 percent of the goods and services distributed in the United States are owned by private companies.

The right to make a profit. A key incentive to owning a business is the motivation to make a profit. In free enterprise, business owners can make decisions based on what will make a profit. Consumers (private citizens) can voluntarily make their own economic choices to spend money on certain goods or services. Instead of the government interfering to determine how the market should interact with citizens, including setting prices, free enterprise allows business owners to decide customer rates.

TEST TIP: Why does free enterprise matter? On the AP GOV exam, it is important to be familiar with the concepts of *free enterprise* and *capitalism.* The economic system in the United States supports our place in the world as "a land of opportunity" for enterprising individuals. The Constitution supports such enterprise by respecting private property rights, granting Congress the power to set up patent and copyright laws, which allow inventors and writers the exclusive right to profit from their discoveries and writings (Article I, Section 8), and guaranteeing the right of individuals to sue the government if their property or patent rights are violated (First Amendment). While, overall, the regulatory power of the government is limited, some level of government regulation is necessary to ensure safety, protect consumers, prevent fraudulent activity, and preserve the nation's shared environmental heritage from abusive business practices.

Economic Theories

Until the 20th century, the United States supported a free market without any intervention from the government based on the economic theories of Adam Smith. Smith proposed groundbreaking economic theories in his book *The Wealth of Nations* (1776). Smith argued that humans were self-interested individuals, and in order for a free market economy to prevail, the role of government and the relationship between business owners and their employees needed to change. Smith's theory changed the way that people understood economics and the role of government. Smith proposed two important economic concepts that the United States followed: *laissez-faire capitalism* (the government must not interfere in the economic system) and the *invisible hand* (based on invisible natural laws, people must be free to buy, sell, and compete without government interference—the unintentional impact is an economic benefit for everyone).

TEST TIP: The two 21st-century economic theories that you should be familiar with on the AP GOV exam are *demand-side economics* supported by the Democratic Party and *supply-side economics* supported by the Republican Party.

Demand-Side Economics

Demand-side economics (also known as **Keynesian economics**) was proposed by John Maynard Keynes in the 1930s during the Great Depression. Keynes argued that inefficiencies in an economy produce volatility in *aggregate demand* (all the goods and services demanded by all players in the marketplace). When demand is lagging, recession and unemployment result. Unemployment serves to magnify the drag on demand because consumers have no income to spend. On the other hand, in periods of economic boom, when unemployment levels are low and economic optimism is high, consumer and investment spending increases, leading to high levels of aggregate demand. The downside of low employment coupled with a high aggregate demand situation is that the supply of money circulating within the economy increases to such a high level that its value deflates, leading to inflated prices—what you could once buy with one dollar now costs you two. The ups and downs of an economy produced by erratic demand can be addressed by using **fiscal policy** (taxing and spending) and **monetary policy** (control of the money supply by the central bank) as tools to affect demand. According to Keynesians, when demand is low, leading to recession and unemployment, the government should spend more and simultaneously reduce taxes to drive up aggregate demand, which in turn increases productivity and jobs. On the monetary side, interest rates should be reduced to encourage more borrowing and spending to stimulate demand. If the nation is caught in an inflationary spiral, the government should do the opposite: reduce its own spending, raise taxes, and increase interest rates to withdraw some of the excess money out of the economy and stabilize its value.

The great test of **Keynesian theory** was the calamity faced by the nation during the Great Depression. President Franklin D. Roosevelt adopted the Keynesian approach, stimulating the economy with the New Deal and its many projects and programs aimed at raising aggregate demand and restoring the economy. Conservatives opposed FDR's New Deal because part of Keynesian theory called for *deficit spending* by the government; that is, during times of economic crisis, the government should resort to borrowing money if need be to fund the spending required to stimulate economic growth. Year-to-year deficits accrue into the national debt. Conservatives favor balanced budgets to avoid debt, so the deficits accrued to pay for New Deal programs alarmed them. Democratic allies in Congress supported the president in his Keynesian demand-side solution for the devastation caused by economic collapse.

What Roosevelt accomplished with the New Deal illustrated that it is necessary for the government to intervene to ensure that work is accessible during stagnant economic periods and that infrastructure projects like the New Deal's Tennessee Valley Authority massive dam-building initiative create jobs and increase orders for materials, thereby stimulating productivity and creating even more jobs. If the government is able to step in with a plan to provide jobs or reduce interest rates, the economy will improve because more people will be investing money back into the economy. President Barack Obama, among other Democratic leaders, was a supporter of demand-side economics.

Supply-Side Economics

Supply-side economics stands in contrast to demand-side economic theory. Supply-side economists argue that the economy is stimulated at the production end rather than the demand end of the economy. By lowering taxes and enacting government deregulation, private businesses will invest more in economic expansion and modernization, and can produce more goods, lower their prices, and increase employment. While there is little evidence that this approach has been successful, Republican presidents from Ronald Reagan to George W. Bush have embraced what has become known as "trickle-down economics." If the stimulus is provided at the top with producers, the benefits will eventually trickle down through the entire economy.

Proponents of supply-side economics assert that production and supply are essential for economic growth. This economic theory is often advocated as a response to financial declines, like unemployment, even today.

Did you know? Supply-side economics, as a system of economic thought, was at its most popular during the Reagan administration. It was so popular, in fact, that "supply-side" and "Reaganomics" are often used interchangeably. However, George H. W. Bush, Ronald Reagan's political rival before he became Reagan's vice president, famously referred to the practice of lowering taxes while maintaining high levels of government spending, particularly on the military, by a less flattering term—"voodoo economics."

Monetary Policies

The monetary system is regulated by the **Federal Reserve System**, the central bank of the United States. The Federal Reserve ("the Fed") is not regulated by the government, but members are appointed by the president and are confirmed by Congress.

The Federal Reserve was created by Congress to provide a secure monetary system to control the money supply (too much money in circulation can cause inflation, devaluing the dollar, and too little money in circulation can cause deflation). The Fed's role is to use the money supply to support economic stability by controlling inflation and unemployment. Through various means, such as control over interest rates, the reserve requirement placed on banks, the discount rate, and open market operations, the Fed can either prompt an increase or a decrease in the supply of money circulating in the economy. During high inflationary periods, the Fed acts to decrease the money supply; for example, an increase in interest rates would make borrowing more expensive, which would have a suppressive effect on spending. During periods of high unemployment, the Fed acts to increase the money supply to stimulate spending, which increases demand and raises productivity, leading to increased demand for labor. The Federal Reserve has a policymaking body within itself, the Federal Open Market Committee (FOMC). While the Federal Reserve is not involved in fiscal policy formation, the FOMC uses fiscal policy to understand the impact on monetary policy. For example, the FOMC reviews key economic initiatives and makes monetary decisions, like how employment and the GDP will be impacted by fiscal policies.

> **TEST TIP:** On the AP GOV exam, you should be familiar with the Federal Reserve System. Fiscal policy is determined by Congress and the president, but monetary policy is determined by the Federal Reserve. Monetary policy is important because it influences inflation and the economic direction of the country.

Political Ideological Roles—an Economics Case Study

Rigid ideological frameworks do not usually conform well to political reality and pragmatic governance. Democrat Bill Clinton was elected president of the United States in 1992 as the economy was tentatively emerging from a recession and the federal budget was amassing multibillion-dollar deficits every year. The policies encouraged by the Clinton administration and enacted by Congress led to the most extensive period of economic growth in the 20th century and paved the way for the globalization of the American economy. Clinton's approach was varied, and in several instances, stepped outside the ideological orthodoxy of Democratic Party politics.

In 1993, after an extensive lobbying effort in Congress and in spite of vehement opposition from supply-side Republicans, President Clinton signed the Omnibus Budget Reconciliation Act (also called the Deficit Reduction Act), which raised income taxes on the wealthiest 1 percent, placed a tax on Social Security benefits for the highest income earners, provided tax relief to the lowest income earners, and levied a new energy tax on all Americans. The income tax rate for top earners went from 28 percent to 36 percent, and rates for the richest corporations increased from 34 percent to 39 percent. These were the highest peace-time tax increases on high-income earners to date, helping to generate billions of dollars in revenue for the federal government. At the same time, the administration proposed a cut in defense spending. Did Clinton use fiscal policy in an energetic way, corresponding to Keynesian economic policy—austerity during periods of economic growth to eliminate deficits and control inflation? Some might argue he started a little early, when the economy was still vulnerable, yet his policies still managed to produce the first budget surplus since the late 1960s and stimulated further economic growth.

The "Clinton economy" did not rely entirely on tax increases and cuts in defense spending, however. He signed into law a reform of the open-ended welfare program once referred to as Aid to Families with Dependent Children. Recast as Temporary Aid to Needy Families (TANF), assistance was no longer open-ended, as TANF established a 2-year time limit on receiving aid, and funding allocated to the states through TANF block grants was dependent on states meeting federal requirements for establishing training and work programs to reduce recipient caseloads. The Clinton administration also negotiated the North American Free Trade Agreement (NAFTA), which eliminated tariffs and encouraged free trade between the U.S., Canada, and Mexico. In addition, the Clinton program promoted the deregulation of banks and financial markets, leading to an era of free-wheeling investment.

In the end, combining Keynesian principles beloved by liberals in the Democratic Party with free trade, social program cuts, and deregulation embraced by conservative Republicans, "Clintonomics" avoided a single ideological approach to economic growth. The Clinton years were unquestionably an economic boom time, but his legacy continues to be debated. In the light of growing poverty rates, job losses as a result of the new high-tech global economy, and the financial collapse of 2008 after decades of reckless activity in the deregulated financial sector, questions remain about the long-term effectiveness of Clinton's ideological balancing act.

Chapter Review Practice Questions

The practice questions show the types of questions that may appear on the exam. Practice questions are for instructional purposes only and may not reflect the format of the actual exam. On the actual exam, some questions may be grouped into sets containing one source-based prompt (document or image) and two to five questions. The questions and explanations that follow focus on essential knowledge, the learning objectives, and political science skills.

Multiple-Choice Questions

Question 1 refers to the following graph.

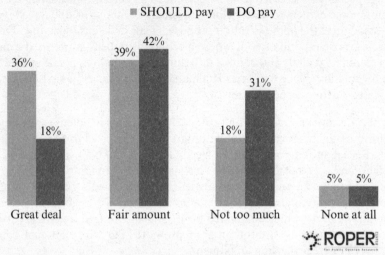

Attention Paid by Government Officials to Public Opinion Polls

Source: Henry J. Kaiser Family Foundation. Role of Polls in Policymaking Survey, Jan, 2001 [survey question]. USPSRA.01POLLS.R21F. Princeton Survey Research Associates [producer].Cornell University, Ithaca, NY: Roper Center for Public Opinion Research, iPOLL [distributor].

1. Based on the results shown in the graph, which of the following is an accurate statement?

    A. Public officials pay a great deal of attention to public opinion polls.
    B. Public officials pay a fair amount of attention to public opinion polls.
    C. Public officials should not pay more attention to public opinion polls than they already do.
    D. Public officials do not pay any attention to public opinion polls.

2. Which of the following political parties believes in the strictest interpretation of limited government?

    A. Democratic
    B. Republican
    C. Libertarian
    D. Socialist

3. Which of the following social groups is considered the primary agent of political socialization?

   A. Peers
   B. Family
   C. School
   D. Media

4. Which of the following polls would most benefit a first-time candidate running for political office to address important issues of the constituency?

   A. Entrance poll
   B. Exit poll
   C. Opinion poll
   D. Benchmark poll

5. Which of the following government agencies determines monetary policy?

   A. Office of Management and Budget
   B. The Treasury Department
   C. Congressional Budget Office
   D. Federal Reserve

Questions 6–7 refer to the following graph.

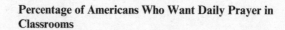

Percentage of Americans Who Want Daily Prayer in Classrooms

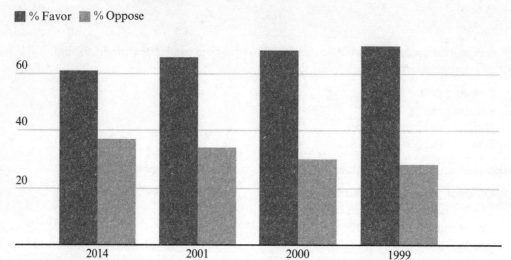

6. Based on the polling results shown in the graph, which of the following is an accurate statement?

   A. Support for prayer in the classroom has experienced incremental declines over time.
   B. Americans were the most polarized on the issue of prayer in the classroom in 2000.
   C. Opposition to prayer in the classroom experienced a sharp increase from 1999 to 2000.
   D. Americans are deeply divided over the issue of prayer in the classroom.

7. Which of the following is a reasonable conclusion to draw from the results of the polling in the graph?

   A. Most Democratic respondents supported prayer in the classroom, along with some Republicans.
   B. Ideology probably had little impact on the polling results.
   C. Most Republican respondents supported prayer in the classroom, along with some Democrats.
   D. All respondents in opposition to prayer in the classroom were likely Libertarians.

8. Which of the following statements is NOT true about opinion polls?

   A. The results are mostly reliable.
   B. They can be helpful to politicians.
   C. Televised news programs never rely on opinion polls.
   D. Policy is sometimes adjusted based on public opinion polling.

9. Which of the following statements most accurately describes Keynesian theory?

    A. It is most likely to be supported by Republicans.

    B. It can also be referred to as supply-side economics.

    C. It relies on the government to prop up the economy during recessionary periods.

    D. It favors lowering the tax rate on corporations to stimulate the economy.

10. Based on your knowledge of U.S. government and politics, which of the following government entities is LEAST influenced by public opinion?

    A. Presidential cabinet

    B. Congressional leaders

    C. Federal Reserve

    D. Supreme Court

Free-Response Question

1 question

40 minutes (suggested)

Directions: It is suggested that you take a few minutes to plan and outline your essay. Write your response on lined paper. You must demonstrate your understanding of course content, disciplinary practices, and reasoning processes. Your essay is considered a first draft and may contain some grammatical errors that will not be counted against you. However, to receive full credit, your essay must demonstrate defensible content knowledge with substantive examples where appropriate.

Question: Develop an argument that explains whether the nation's founding governing principles were derived primarily from collectivist or individualist ideas.

1. Articulate a defensible claim or thesis that responds to the prompt and establishes a line of reasoning.

2. Support your claim with at least TWO pieces of accurate and relevant information.

    (a) At least ONE piece of evidence must be from one of the following foundational documents:

        ■ The Declaration of Independence

        ■ The Articles of Confederation

        ■ The Constitution

    (b) Use a second piece of evidence from another foundational document from the list above or from your study of American democratic principles.

3. Use reasoning to explain why your evidence supports your claim/thesis.

4. Respond to an opposing or alternative perspective using refutation, concession, or rebuttal.

Answers and Explanations

Multiple-Choice Questions

1. **B.** According to the second set of bars in the graph, 39 percent of polled individuals believe that government officials should pay a fair amount of attention to public opinion polls, while 42 percent

believe that government officials actually do pay a fair amount of attention to public opinion polls. Therefore, it can be argued that public officials pay a fair amount of attention to public opinion polls, choice B. The first set of bars in the graph shows that 36 percent of individuals polled believe that government officials should pay a great deal of attention to public opinion polls, whereas only 18 percent of individuals believe they actually do pay a great deal of attention to public opinion polls. Therefore, it cannot be argued that public officials pay a great deal of attention to public opinion polls (choice A). Based on the third set of bars in the graph, those polled believe that public officials should pay more attention to public opinion polls than they actually do, eliminating choice C. The fourth set of bars in the graph shows that polled individuals believe that public officials pay a considerable amount of attention to public opinion polls, although they believe that they should pay more. Therefore, it cannot be argued that public officials do not pay any attention to public opinion polls (choice D).

2. **C.** Libertarians take the most extreme view of government's role. To a libertarian, government should exist only to preserve private property and individual liberty; government should never intervene in the economy and even defense spending should be either incredibly low or nonexistent, making choice C correct. Democrats (choice A) believe in expanded government for the purposes of promoting public welfare and ensuring a universally acceptable standard of living. Republicans (choice B) generally agree that government should be limited, although the question of defense spending, for example, removes Republicans from the absolute no intervention perspective. Socialists (choice D) favor perhaps the greatest level of government intervention, even beyond some non-Socialist Democrats.

3. **B.** The family, choice B, is the primary agent of socialization, which begins taking effect on an infant from the beginning of his or her life. Peer groups (choice A) are influential, but they are considered a secondary source of political socialization. School (choice C) plays an important early role, but like peer groups, it is a secondary role. The media (choice D) can only be influential if its message can be discerned and the individual is exposed to its mediums; the family controls the amount of media exposure in the beginning.

4. **D.** A benchmark poll, or tracking poll, would allow a first-time candidate to gauge his or her potential audience early and decide which issues require the most attention. Therefore, a benchmark poll is the best poll for this candidate, choice D. An entrance poll (choice A) is taken right before a voter enters the voting booth, so it is not relevant to a first-time campaigner. An exit poll (choice B) is taken after a voter leaves a voting booth, so again, it would not be relevant to a first-time campaigner. An opinion poll (choice C), while beneficial even early on, is not the most likely poll a first-time candidate needs to conduct.

5. **D.** The Federal Reserve, choice D, is the only entity that can determine monetary policy. While it sometimes does look to fiscal policy to determine its effect on monetary policy, no other entity beyond the Federal Reserve can change monetary policy. The Office of Management and Budget (choice A) and the Congressional Budget Office (choice C) can be eliminated because budgeting is a fiscal matter rather than a monetary one. The Treasury Department (choice B) is an executive department in charge of managing the nation's revenue and printing its currency; it does not control monetary policy.

6. **A.** The poll results demonstrate a decline in support for prayer in public schools over the 15 years represented on the graph. However, support only declined by approximately 9 percent. There was a reduction of about 1 percent from 1999 to 2000, another 1–2 percent from 2000 to 2001, and another 6 percent in the 13 years from 2001 to 2014, making choice A the correct response. Since nearly 70 percent of Americans supported prayer in schools in 2000, opinion in that year cannot be characterized as *polarized* (choice B). From 1999 to 2000, opposition to prayer in the classroom increased by approximately 2 percent, an increase that cannot be described as *sharp* (choice C). While Americans are deeply divided on many issues, prayer in the classroom is not one of them according to

these Gallup poll results, eliminating choice D. A clear majority of over 60 percent of the population consistently supported prayer in public schools in all of the polling years, indicating greater unity on this issue than division.

7. **C.** Ideological fault lines exist with nearly every public policy issue. Some issues demonstrate more unity in public opinion, and in this case one such issue is prayer in public schools. It is still reasonable to draw some conclusions about ideological/partisan responses given knowledge of political behavior in the United States. Support for prayer in public schools is very strong within the conservative evangelical base of the Republican Party; therefore, it is reasonable to assume that Republican Party respondents by and large demonstrated that support in the Gallup poll. However, Republicans do not represent over 60 percent of the population, and over 60 percent supported prayer in schools in every polling year. Therefore, it must be assumed that some Democrats lend their support to this issue, choice C. The same reasoning applies in assessing choice A, though it has an opposite effect. Democrats maintain a more Jeffersonian view of the First Amendment's Establishment Clause. That is, there is a clear "wall of separation" that must be maintained between the state and its involvement in religious matters in order to maintain religious liberty. The likelihood that most Democrats support prayer in public schools, with some Republican support, is not a reasonable conclusion to draw (choice A). Ideology impacts every public policy issue to some degree, so choice B is not a reasonable conclusion to draw from these polling results. Libertarians certainly oppose government intervention in the practice of civil liberties, and one could assume that many or most Libertarians would oppose prayer in the public schools, but to assert that "all" who expressed opposition to prayer in public schools in this poll were likely Libertarians is not a reasonable conclusion (choice D).

8. **C.** Televised news programs rely heavily on opinion polls to make predictions about elections. Polling is tracked relentlessly by broadcast news, forming the basis of political trend analysis by political reporters. Therefore, it is incorrect to state that televised news programs never rely on opinion polls, choice C. Opinion polls are mostly reliable (choice A), depending on the correct sample size, targeted demographic, and the margin of error. Opinion polls are incredibly helpful to politicians (choice B). Public policy is often affected by opinion poll outcomes (choice D).

9. **C.** Recall that Keynesian theory necessarily requires the government to intervene in times of crises. The government can initiate lower interest rates or start infrastructure programs designed to stimulate the economy, choice C. Republicans disagree with Keynesian theory, eliminating choice A. Keynesian theory is referred to not as supply-side economics (choice B), but rather as demand-side economics. Keynesian theory almost never favors lowering corporate tax rates to stimulate the economy (choice D); in fact, Keynesian proponents usually favor higher corporate tax rates.

10. **D.** While it cannot be argued that the Supreme Court is entirely insulated from a wave of public opinion on the most salient issues, the appointment rather than election of Supreme Court justices provides them the freedom to objectively interpret the Constitution and to be largely exempt from the influence of public opinion; therefore, choice D is the best answer. The president's cabinet (choice A), including the president, will always be swayed by public opinion. Congressional leaders (choice B), like the president, are impacted by public opinion; they are actually more impacted than the president because their terms can be shorter or their constituency may sporadically waiver and thus require message adjustment at various times. The members of the Federal Reserve Board (choice C) are appointed and their inner workings in determining monetary policy are largely shrouded in mystery to the American public. As such, it is largely free from public opinion, making it a possible correct response in the mind of test-takers. However, the decisions made by the Fed are largely subjective, and so public opinion and changing attitudes can have some impact on its choices regarding monetary policy.

Free-Response Question

Scoring Guide

This is an argument essay question. To achieve the maximum score of 6, your response must address the scoring criteria components in the table that follows.

Scoring Criteria for a Good Argument Essay		
Question: Develop an argument that explains whether the nation's founding governing principles were derived primarily from collectivist or individualist ideas.		
Scoring Criteria	Disciplinary Practice	Examples
A. THESIS/CLAIM		
(1 point) Presents a historically defensible thesis that establishes a line of reasoning. (Note: The thesis must make a claim that responds to *all* parts of the question and must *not* just restate the question.)	Practice 5.a	Developing a strong thesis for this question requires a thorough understanding of the philosophical concepts of individualism and collectivism. In addition, satisfying the demands of this domain requires an understanding of how the listed foundational documents relate to the development of individualism and/or collectivism. While you can posit an argument defending collectivism, the easier choice would be individualism. Note that in the opening paragraph of the sample response, the thesis is provided in a historical context. The sample response also clearly sets the stage for an alternative view, or counterclaim, by stating that "Although… pure forms of democracy are decidedly more collectivist in nature, the nation's founding governing principles…were primarily inspired by…individualism." This counterclaim is refuted in the concluding paragraph, after having clearly demonstrated how the founding principles, as illustrated by the Constitution and Declaration of Independence, were guided by a commitment to individualism.
B. EVIDENCE		
(3 points) Uses TWO pieces of specific and relevant evidence to support the argument (must be linked to the question). OR **(2 points)** Uses ONE piece of specific and relevant evidence to support the argument (must be linked to the question). OR **(1 point)** Describes one piece of evidence that is accurately linked to the topic of the question.	Practice 5.b	To receive the maximum of 3 points in this domain, you must include two pieces of specific and relevant information to support your thesis. In the provided prompt, you can select two of three of the foundational documents listed, or you can choose a concept or idea from your study of American democratic principles. The first founding document selected from the list provided is the Declaration of Independence. It is helpful to identify the connection between the Declaration of Independence and, in this case, individualism. The first way you can do this is by recalling the content of the Declaration of Independence. Consider the most memorable section—the Preamble. In the Preamble, you will find a few sentences that affirm the notion of individualism.

Scoring Criteria	Disciplinary Practice	Examples
(Note: To earn more than 1 point, the response must establish an argument and have earned the point for Claim/Thesis.)		The second founding document selected from the list provided is the Constitution. Because the Bill of Rights is the most memorable and perhaps most relevant to your study of the Constitution, it is helpful to include the Bill of Rights as direct evidence supporting your inclusion of the Constitution to support your thesis. This domain also allows for including concepts or ideas from your study of democracy beyond the foundational documents. For this section, it could be relevant to include how the formation of political beliefs, particularly libertarianism, represents the foundation of individualism as central to the nation's guiding principles.
C. REASONING		
(1 point) Uses reasoning to organize and explain how or why the evidence supports thesis or claim. (Note: To earn this point, you must have earned a point for Evidence.)	Practice 5.c	The reasoning for including the evidence will likely be embedded within the same paragraph as the evidence itself. Per the sample response: ❑ Declaration of Independence – self-evident rights, protection of those rights by the government. The government does not confer rights, but rather exists to protect them. When the government fails to do so, it betrays the trust of the people and requires a redress. Connects Jefferson's authorship to Enlightenment thinker and proponent of individualism, John Locke. ❑ Constitution – the Bill of Rights as a body of evidence supporting individual rights. The right to free speech, freedom of religion, freedom of the press, and privacy reveal the Founders' commitment to preserving individual liberties. Connects Madison's authorship of the Bill of Rights and former full alignment with the *Federalist Papers* to his commitment to individualism.
D. ALTERNATIVE PERSPECTIVES		
(1 point) Responds to an opposing or alternative perspective using refutation, concession, or rebuttal that is consistent with the argument. (Note: To earn this point, your response must have a claim or thesis.)	Practice 5.d	The concluding paragraph is a great place to respond to an opposing perspective or counterargument while closing out your essay. It is helpful to refer to your introduction, where it is most likely that you first referenced the counterargument. In the sample response, collectivism is addressed as a contributor to the nation's principled outworking, but not necessarily its underpinnings. As seen by virtue of statements like "The ideals of commitment to the 'preservation of the union' and 'the greater good,'..." and the passage of public policy in response to collective groups prevailing, collectivism obviously contributes to the ongoing development of American principles, but it is ultimately overshadowed by individualism.

Sample Student Response

While the terms "collectivism" and "individualism" were not expressly part of the American lexicon until the early to mid-19th century, these ideas find their fundamental roots in Enlightenment Thinkers like Thomas Hobbes and John Locke, both of whom were massively influential in the philosophical development of Thomas Jefferson and James Madison, developed conceptions of individualism. Although it can be argued that pure forms of democracy are decidedly more collectivist in nature, the nation's founding governing principles, as illustrated in the Declaration of Independence and the Constitution, were primarily inspired by the preservation of human independence—individualism. The founding documents that guided the republic revealed the immense commitment that our Founders had to preserve individual liberties, self-determination, and autonomy.

Some of the most quoted words from the Preamble of the Declaration of Independence are "life, liberty, and the pursuit of happiness." And, while these words are certainly important, it is the paragraph that comes immediately after these opening words that truly demonstrates where the Founders derived their conception of these "inalienable rights." The Preamble's second paragraph states that the government itself does not grant individuals certain rights, including the right to self-determination and liberty, but that the government merely ensures the ability of its people to retain those self-evident rights. If the government fails to ensure the rights of its naturally endowed people, effectively becoming destructive and oppressive, the people themselves must institute a new government. This idea of self-government, and more pointedly, the idea that the government must ensure the natural rights of its people, is firmly rooted in individualism. As previously mentioned, Thomas Jefferson was profoundly influenced by Enlightenment ideals, and particularly individualism. The same concept of divinely given individual liberties is also evident in another important document foundational to the United States' governing principles, the Constitution.

The Constitution, like the Declaration of Independence, also makes clear the individualist ties by which the nation's founding principles were derived and guided. More specifically, the Bill of Rights, or the first ten amendments to the Constitution, reflect the Founders' commitment to valuing individualism. While the Bill of Rights is not absolute in its promises of free speech, practice of religion, privacy, and other related liberties, meaning that there are legal abridgements permitted by government at certain times and places, it is an enumeration of pointed rights and liberties that cannot be wantonly circumvented by the government's discretion. James Madison, who authored the Bill of Rights (along with co-authoring the Federalist Papers), understood that American citizens required a codified list of rights that thoroughly protected them from the unlawful belligerence or invasion of government. Although Madison's initial alignment was with other Federalists in the assertion that the Constitution itself was an "entire bill of rights," his drafting of the eventually affirmed Bill of Rights recognized the acute need for citizens to be legally assured of their rights and the government assured of its limitations in circumventing self-endowed rights.

Admittedly, collectivist elements appear in the outworking of American democracy. The ideals of commitment to the "preservation of the union" and "the greater good," along with creating a state to combat Hobbes' "state of nature" mentality and way of life, demonstrate that U.S. citizens exhibit a sort of collectivist approach to governance, particularly in U.S. social programs such as public education, unemployment, and welfare programs. The U.S. is not a pure democracy, but the progression of public policy is shaped by certain voices and groups prevailing over others. To that end, collectivism is evident in the less formal institutions guiding civic participation. However, the underpinnings of the nation's earliest documents, including the Constitution and the Declaration of Independence, more robustly capture the spirit of individualism, of self-endowed liberties and freedoms, than the idea of submitting to the collective good at the expense of the individual.

Chapter 8

Unit 5: Political Participation

Unit 5 explores how governing is achieved directly and indirectly through voting and activities involving various linkage institutions, which serve as intermediaries between voters and their representatives in government.

- Voting
- Linkage Institutions
  - Political Parties
  - Interest Groups
  - Elections
  - Mass Media

Overview of AP U.S. Government and Politics Unit 5

The American system of democracy can only be achieved through the support of direct political participation by its citizens. The overarching concepts of voter behavior and linkage institutions will be discussed in this chapter, along with other topics that influence linkage institutions, including citizen beliefs about voting, campaigns, public opinion, and federal oversight.

The four main College Board content outlines for Unit 5 are as follows:

- **Linkage institutions.** Factors associated with political ideology, efficacy, structural barriers, and demographics influence the nature and degree of political participation.
- **Political parties and interest groups.** Political parties, interest groups, and social movements provide opportunities for participation and influence how people relate to government and policymakers.
- **Elections.** The impact of federal policies on campaigning and electoral rules continues to be contested by both sides of the political spectrum.
- **Mass media.** The various forms of media provide citizens with political information and influence the ways in which they participate politically.

AP U.S. Government and Politics Key Concepts

Success on the exam depends on your ability to make connections to the essential knowledge of the key concepts as described in the content outlines of the *AP U.S. Government and Politics Course Framework*. Remember that these concepts highlight the fundamental ideas that every student should take with them into the AP GOV exam and beyond.

Use the chart that follows to guide you through the specific knowledge that is covered in Unit 5. The information contained in this chart is an abridged version of the content outlines with topic examples. Visit https://apstudent.collegeboard.org/apcourse/ap-united-states-government-and-politics for the complete updated AP GOV course curriculum descriptions.

AP U.S. Government and Politics Key Concepts (Unit 5)	
Key Concept	**Content**
Big Idea 5: Methods of Political Analysis **Factors associated with political ideology, efficacy, structural barriers, and demographics influence the nature and degree of political participation.**	Legal protections found in federal legislation and the Fifteenth, Seventeenth, Nineteenth, Twenty-Fourth, and Twenty-Sixth amendments relate to the expansion of opportunities for political participation. Models explaining voting behavior include rational-choice voting, retrospective voting, prospective voting, and party-line voting. The impact of demographics and political efficacy can influence voter turnout, but structural barriers and the type of election can also influence voter turnout in state voter registration laws, procedures, and mid-term (congressional) or general presidential elections. Demographics and political efficacy are used to predict the likelihood of whether a person will vote. Factors influencing voter choice include party identification, ideological orientation, candidate characteristics, political issues, religious beliefs, gender, and race/ethnicity.
Big Idea 3: Civic Participation in a Representative Democracy **The impact of federal policies on campaigning and electoral rules continues to be contested by both sides of the political spectrum.**	The process and outcomes of U.S. presidential elections are impacted by incumbency advantage phenomenon, open and closed primaries, caucuses, party conventions, congressional and state elections, and the Electoral College. The winner-takes-all allocation of votes per state (except Maine and Nebraska) under the setup of the Electoral College compared with the national popular vote for president raises questions about whether the Electoral College facilitates or impedes democracy. The process and outcomes in U.S. congressional elections are impacted by the incumbency advantage phenomenon, open and closed primaries, caucuses, and general elections. The benefits and drawbacks of modern campaigns are represented by dependence on professional consultants, rising campaign costs and intensive fundraising efforts, duration of election cycles, and impact of and the reliance on social media for campaign communication and fundraising. Federal legislation and case law pertaining to campaign finance demonstrate the ongoing debate over the role of money in political and free speech as set forth in the Bipartisan Campaign Reform Act (2002) and *Citizens United v. Federal Election Commission* (2010). Debates have increased over free speech and competitive and fair elections related to money and campaign funding (contributions from individuals, PACs, and political parties). Different types of political action committees (PACs) influence elections and policymaking through fundraising and spending.

Key Concept	Content
Big Idea 4: Competing Policymaking Interests **Political parties, interest groups, and social movements provide opportunities for participation and influence how people relate to government and policymakers.**	Linkage institutions are channels that allow people to communicate their preferences to policymakers—parties, interest groups, elections, and the media.
	The functions and impact of political parties on the electorate and government are represented by mobilization and education of voters, party platforms, candidate recruitment, campaign management (fundraising), and the committee and party leadership systems in legislatures.
	Parties have adapted to candidate-centered campaigns, and their role in nominating candidates has been weakened.
	Parties modify their policies and messaging to appeal to various demographic coalitions.
	The structure of parties has been influenced by critical elections and regional realignments, campaign finance law, and changes in communication (data-management technology).
	Parties use communication technology and voter-data management to disseminate, control, and clarify political messages and enhance outreach and mobilization efforts.
	In comparison to proportional systems, winner-takes-all voting districts serve as a structural barrier to third-party and independent candidate success.
	The incorporation of third-party agendas into platforms of major political parties serves as a barrier to third-party and independent candidate success.
	Interest groups may represent very specific or general interests, and can educate voters and office holders, draft legislation, and mobilize membership to apply pressure on and work with legislators and government agencies.
	In addition to working within party coalitions, interest groups exert influence through long-standing relationships with bureaucratic agencies, congressional committees, and other interest groups (iron triangles) and issue networks and help interest groups exert influence across political party coalitions.
	Interest group influence may be impacted by inequality of political and economic resources, unequal access to decision makers, and the "free rider" problem.
	Single-issue groups, ideological/social movements, and protest movements form the goal of impacting society and policymaking.
	Competing actors such as interest groups, professional organizations, social movements, the military, and bureaucratic agencies influence policymaking, such as the federal budget process, at key stages and to varying degrees.
	Elections and political parties are related to major policy shifts or initiatives, occasionally leading to political realignments of voting constituencies.

Continued

Key Concept	Content
Big Idea 3: Civic Participation in a Representative Democracy **The various forms of media provide citizens with political information and influence the ways in which they participate politically.**	Traditional news media, new communication technologies, and advances in social media have profoundly influenced how citizens routinely acquire political information, including news events, investigative journalism, election coverage, and political commentary. The media's use of polling results to convey popular levels of trust and confidence in government can impact elections by turning such events into "horse races" based more on popularity and factors other than qualifications and platforms of candidates. Political participation is influenced by a variety of media coverage, analysis, and commentary on political events. The rapidly increasing demand for media and political communications outlets from an ideologically diverse audience has led to debates over media bias and the impact of media ownership and partisan news sites. The nature of democratic debate and the level of political knowledge among citizens is impacted by increased media choices, ideologically oriented programming, consumer-driven media outlets and emerging technologies that reinforce existing beliefs, and the uncertainty over the credibility of news sources and information.

Heads Up: What You Need to Know

As you study the topics related to Unit 5, it is important that you grasp the terms and concepts so that you can answer free-response questions that begin with one of these task verbs:

- **Explain.** What are the straightforward facts, details, data, principles, processes, and outcomes? For example, can you explain how cultural factors influence political attitudes and socialization?
- **Describe.** What is the relevant evidence or supporting examples to paint an overall picture? For example, describe the elements of a scientific poll.

Study Questions

Glance through the study questions before you start the review section. Take notes, highlight questions, and write down page number references to reinforce your learning. Refer to this list as often as necessary until you feel comfortable with your knowledge of the material.

1. What are voting rights protections in the Constitution and in legislation? (Hint: Fourteenth, Fifteenth, and Nineteenth amendments, along with the Voting Rights Act of 1965.)

2. What is the role of political parties in shaping the electorate, the government, and public policies? (Hint: Linkage institution.)

3. Why have political parties found it necessary to adapt and change over time? (Hint: Changing demographics.)

4. What are the election processes of a U.S. presidential election? (Hint: Primaries, caucuses, party conventions.)

5. How do the organization, finance, and strategies of campaigns impact the election process? (Hint: The FEC.)

6. How does the Electoral College impact elections? (Hint: Winner-takes-all format.)

7. What are the advantages and disadvantages of interest-group influences on the election process and policymaking? (Hint: Interest groups encourage participation but also hinder it.)

8. What are linkage institutions, and what is the media's role as a linkage institution? (Hint: Linkage institutions include political parties, interest groups, and elections.)

9. How have media and technology influenced political institutions and political behavior? (Hint: Social media and direct access.)

Important Terms and Concepts Checklist

This section is an overview of the terms, concepts, ideas, documents, and court cases that specifically target the AP GOV exam. Additional vocabulary is also included to aid in your understanding.

As you review the material covered in this chapter, remember that the required foundational documents and required Supreme Court cases (see the Appendix) are noted among the key academic terms, concepts, and language.

Note the abbreviations in the table that follows:

RFD – Required Foundational Documents
RSCC – Required Supreme Court Cases

As you study the terms and concepts, simply place a check mark next to each and return to this list as often as necessary to check your understanding. After you finish the chapter review section, reinforce what you have learned by working through the practice questions at the end of the chapter. Answers and explanations provide further clarification into perspectives of U.S. government and politics.

Term/Concept	Big Idea	Study Page	Term/Concept	Big Idea	Study Page	Term/Concept	Big Idea	Study Page
Bipartisan Campaign Reform Act	PRD	p. 279	Fundraising	PMI	p. 266	Political Action Committee (PAC)	PMI	p. 266
Campaign finance law	PRD	p. 277	Incumbency advantage	PRD	p. 274	Political parties	PMI	pp. 261–266
Caucus	PRD	pp. 276–277	Information and communications technology (ICT)	PRD	p. 266	Prospective voting	MPA	p. 252
Citizens United v. Federal Election Commission	RSCC; PRD	p. 279	Interest groups	PMI	pp. 267–270	Rational-choice voting	MPA	p. 251
Closed primary	PRD	p. 275	Linkage institutions	PMI	pp. 258–261	Republican Party	PMI	p. 265
Congressional elections	PRD	pp. 272–273	Mass media	PMI	pp. 284–285	Retrospective voting	MPA	p. 252
Critical election theory	PMI	p. 262	Muckrakers	PMI	p. 286	Social movements	PMI	pp. 270–271
Democratic Party	PMI	p. 265	Open primary	PRD2	p. 275	Voting Rights Act (1965)	PMI	p. 250
Electoral College	PRD	pp. 280–281	Party-line voting	MPA	p. 251	Winner-takes-all rule	PRD	p. 282
Federal Election Campaign Act (FECA)	PRD	pp. 278–279	Party platforms	PMI	p. 265	Yellow journalism	PMI	p. 285
Free-rider problem	PMI	p. 268						

Chapter Review

Heads Up: What You Need to Know

The learning objectives that you must be able to accomplish are:

Describe the voting rights protections in the Constitution and in legislation.

Describe different models of voting behavior.

Explain the roles that individual choice and state laws play in voter turnout in elections.

Much of this chapter focuses on the types of institutional systems that make it possible for citizens to connect with policymakers in government—these systems are called **linkage institutions.**

Before we discuss the four linkage institutions in detail, let's cover the history of American voting, voting laws, voting behavior, voter turnout, and influences on voting choices.

Voting

One of the founding principles of America is that the government gains its value from the consent of the governed. The democratic process of voting ensures that representatives are chosen by the will of the people. "Voting at elections is one of the most important rights of the subject, and in a republic ought to stand foremost in the estimation of the law" (Alexander Hamilton, 1782).

Voting is a feature of American democracy that demonstrates the federal nature of the republic. At the national level, Congress has passed four amendments ensuring equal access to voting (Fifteenth, Nineteenth, Twenty-Fourth, and Twenty-Sixth amendments), enacted the Voting Rights Act, passed campaign financing laws, and established the Federal Election Commission (FEC) to provide oversight of campaign donations and spending. The Supreme Court has also weighed in on campaign financing in various cases. The responsibilities of the states include voter registration and running elections.

> **TEST TIP:** On the AP GOV exam, you should be familiar with voting rights protections, different models of voting behavior, individual voting choices, and state laws that impact the nature and degree of political participation.

The History of American Voting

The expansion of voting rights was a long-fought struggle for women and African Americans.

Source: Harris and Ewing, "Suffragists Picketing the White House." Library of Congress, 1917.

Women's Right to Vote

Women fought for almost a century for the right to vote. Women were denied the right to vote until the Nineteenth Amendment was passed by Congress in 1919 (ratified in 1920). Before the women's suffrage movement, four states granted women the right to vote: Wyoming (1869), Colorado (1893), Idaho (1896), and Utah (1896), but even in these states women could not vote in federal elections until 1890, when

Wyoming allowed women to vote in all elections. From as early as the 1800s, women formally organized to protest the male-only system, with many marching and actively lobbying in various states to bring the issue to the forefront of the nation's consciousness. The Seneca Falls Convention (1848) was the first formal women's rights convention. While some opponents of the women's rights movement used violence to deter the movement's success, advocates were not hindered by the threat of imprisonment or, in some extreme cases, loss of life. In 1890, the two most influential organizations for women (the NWSA and the AWSA) united under the **National American Woman Suffrage Association** (NAWSA). Over the next two decades, the women's suffrage movement began to grow in numbers, with the common goal of seeking a constitutional amendment for women's right to vote. Meanwhile, a total of fifteen states had their own suffrage laws. Finally, bowing to public pressure and at the urging of President Wilson, Congress finally passed the Nineteenth Amendment in 1919. By August 18, 1920, Tennessee became the 36th state to ratify the amendment, and it was formally added to the Constitution.

African Americans' Right to Vote

African American men experienced *disenfranchisement* (deprived of the right to vote) until the Fifteenth Amendment was passed and ratified in 1870. Southern states, however, passed laws preventing African Americans from voting by requiring poll taxes, literacy tests, and an understanding of the U.S. Constitution. African Americans were mostly poor and unable to answer constitutional questions, given their restricted access to formal education and limited economic resources. The Fifteenth Amendment was more of a codified legality rather than a practical reality.

Throughout the 20th century, discrimination and intimidation continued in the South as exclusively white courts, juries, legislatures, and police agencies repeatedly rebuffed challenges to segregation and other violations of equal protection. Forces for change, progress, fairness, and equality coalesced in the 1950s and 1960s to produce the Civil Rights Movement, which provided African Americans with a specific historical context and opportunity to challenge the most fundamental inequality in a democracy: being denied the right to vote. It took the passage of the Voting Rights Act in 1965 to put the weight of enforcement behind the Fourteenth and Fifteenth amendments.

During the Civil Rights Movement, the Selma-to-Montgomery march across the Edmund Pettus Bridge discussed in Chapter 6 was the final straw that broke the back of African American disenfranchisement. The brutal assault by armed police and white mobs against unarmed peaceful protestors was televised to a national audience. The actions on the Edmund Pettus Bridge prompted action from the White House and Congress. The National Guard was federalized and sent by President Johnson to protect the marchers and in an address to a joint session of Congress, he urged passage of the **Voting Rights Act of 1965.** Shortly thereafter, the president signed the act into law.

The act empowered the federal government to:

- Provide oversight of state voter registrations where less than 50 percent of the non-white population was registered to vote.
- Banned literacy tests from being administered.
- Analyzed the legitimacy of poll taxes. The Twenty-Fourth Amendment banned poll taxes in federal elections (see *Harper v. Virginia Board of Elections,* which prevented poll taxes from being used in state elections).

On the AP GOV exam, you should be familiar with the following constitutional amendments affecting voting rights.

Voting Rights Constitutional Amendments	
Amendment	**Main Provisions**
Fifteenth Amendment (ratified in 1870)	Forbids federal and state governments from denying the right to vote based on an individual's "race, color, or previous condition of servitude." (Remember, however, that it took almost 100 years before African Americans in the South could vote due to barriers.)
Nineteenth Amendment (ratified in 1920)	Granted women the right to vote. "The rights of citizens to vote shall not be denied or abridged…by the United States or by any state on account of sex."
Twenty-Fourth Amendment (ratified in 1964)	Prohibited poll taxes that were used to prevent African Americans and poor whites from voting.
Twenty-Sixth Amendment (ratified in 1971)	Lowered the federal and state voting age from 21 years old to 18 years old.

Voting Behavior

The nature and function of elections depends on voter turnout, and voter turnout depends on voter behavior. For this reason, advances in mass communication have significantly increased political science research to study aspects of election strategies that characterize voter behavior. The extent to which citizens exercise their right to vote and participate in elections is determined by several short-term and long-term factors.

This section will discuss the theoretical models of voting behavior.

Models of Voting Behavior	
Type	**Description**
Party-line voting	Party-line voting is based on one's identification with a political party. Many people identify with one of the two main parties—Republican or Democratic—based on political socialization. Party loyalists vote a **"straight-ticket"**; that is, they go down the ballot and vote for every one of their party's candidates for every office. In the latter half of the 20th century, political analysts have noted a decline in straight-ticket balloting and an increasing number of Independents **"split-ticket"** voting, dividing their preferences between Democrats for some offices and Republicans for others. This development has changed campaign tactics as it takes minimal effort to woo party-line voters. It is the growing number of Independent voters that can make the difference between winning and losing; therefore, candidates campaigning for office frequently focus on moderating their ideological stands in order to entice these voters.
Rational-choice voting	Rational-choice voting is based on the premise that political choices are based on a candidate's record. This type of voter thinks rationally and deliberately to weigh the benefits and drawbacks prior to making a decision. In effect, a rational-choice voter ultimately chooses a candidate who best represents personal social, economic, ideological, and religious interests. This type of voting can also lead to split-ticket balloting.

Continued

Type	Description
Retrospective voting	Retrospective voters reflect on how a candidate, party, or administration has performed in the recent past and make a determination using these considerations. The focus of this type of voting behavior is actual policy outcomes, not promises of what might be in the future. Retrospective voters look at policies pursued and enacted that connect to their direct experiences and interests, such as the economy (often referred to as "kitchen table issues"—Do we have enough money to pay our bills? Can we afford healthcare?), war, and civil rights. These voters question whether or not they are materially and fundamentally better off due to policies supported by incumbents, the majority party in the government, or a presidential administration.
Prospective voting	Prospective voters have their eyes on the future. They listen to campaign rhetoric and make their ballot choices based on what is promised by a candidate and their level of trust that the candidate will follow through if they win.

Voter Turnout

The outcome of American elections is determined by who wins the popular vote, even in the case of the indirect selection of a presidential candidate via the Electoral College. Whether by a 1 percent margin or a 40 percent margin, the candidate who receives the most votes wins ("first past the post"). *Voter turnout* (a measure of those casting a ballot in a given election) is often a critical factor in determining who wins an election. If the registered voters in one party are highly motivated to turn out while the enthusiasm among opposition party voters is suppressed, the anticipated outcome of an election can be turned on its head.

Voter turnout can be expressed in a number of ways:

- Percentage of eligible voters
- Percentage of registered voters
- Percentage of voting-age population

Obviously, when comparing voter turnout in U.S. elections to turnout in other democratic countries, the measure used can skew the results. For example, the U.S. often uses the percentage of eligible voters, but not all those eligible to vote are registered, so the percentage of voter turnout is diluted by non-registered non-participants. It is also common to use the voting-age population, which includes all 18-year-old individuals counted in the last census. Not only are some of these individuals not registered, but also some are ineligible due to incarceration, felony convictions, or non-citizen status. Most other countries use the percentage of registered voters casting ballots. Voters who have made the effort to register are likely to vote, so voter turnout in other countries appears higher in comparison to voter participation in the U.S.

Regardless of the measure used, there is a general perception that civic participation in the United States has been declining since the 1960s, but a few statistics can demonstrate some nuances involved in analyzing voter turnout data:

Presidential Election Year	Republican	Democrat	Percent of Eligible Voters
2000	George W. Bush	Al Gore	54.2%
2004	George W. Bush	John Kerry	60.4%
2008	John McCain	Barack Obama	62.3%
2012	Mitt Romney	Barack Obama	57.5%
2016	Donald Trump	Hillary Clinton	56.0%

The data for the first five presidential elections of the 21st century indicate an overall downward trend, but voter turnout in all three presidential elections in the 1960s barely exceeded 60 percent, with the election of 1960 experiencing the highest turnout at 62.8 percent. Further, in no presidential election occurring from 1932–1948 did turnout exceed 60 percent. These numbers are consistent with the results in the elections held from 2000–2016.

Key Facts about 21st-Century Voter Turnout

Eligible voters do not vote. Regardless of the election year, in the 20th century and early 21st century a significant percentage of eligible voters do not participate in elections.

Turnout in presidential years, to a degree, is candidate-driven. In 1960, when turnout was 62.8 percent, there was a high level of interest in Democratic candidate John F. Kennedy. Young, charismatic, wealthy, and a war hero, he also represented a generational change in national leadership. The country eagerly followed news about Kennedy and his young family. Voters were motivated either by their enthusiasm for Kennedy or their Cold War fears that Kennedy was too young and inexperienced to deal effectively with the spread of Communism and the nuclear threat posed by the Soviet Union.

In 2008, when turnout again spiked (62.3 percent), one of the candidates, Barack Obama, was the first African American nominated by one of the major parties and, like Kennedy, represented a generational change. He was the first presidential candidate born after 1960 and was the youngest presidential candidate since Kennedy. Voter interest in the campaign and election was high and had a demographic appeal to groups such as African Americans and 18- to 25-year-olds, which historically experience low voter turnout.

War can impact voter turnout. While turnout was only 54.2 percent for the first election of George W. Bush, 60.4 percent of voters participated in his bid for reelection. The higher level of interest in the 2004 election was driven by President Bush's decision to invade Iraq in 2003. The war turned out to be highly unpopular among Democratic voters and motivated many of them to go to the polls.

Economic performance can impact voter turnout. A sluggish economy or an economic crisis drives more people to the polls. This factor undoubtedly contributed to the higher turnout in 2008, since beginning in 2007 and spilling over into 2008 the economy experienced its biggest collapse since the Great Depression.

Impact of low voter turnout. It is difficult to determine the will of the entire nation when well over 40 percent do not participate even in elections experiencing record turnout. Campaigns can be ideologically driven, but the disproportionate participation of certain demographic groups in low turnout elections cannot be ignored. For example, while ideologically conservative members of the Republican Party favor significant changes to Social Security and Medicare to balance budgets and deal with the debt crisis, Republican candidates for president do not suggest such major policy changes on the campaign trail due to the historically significant turnout of voters over the age of 65 (traditional retirement age).

In general, those who participate are motivated to do so by ideological goals, high-profile issues that appeal to a specific demographic within the populace, a geopolitical or economic crisis, and/or candidate appeal. A number of possible causes are suggested by low voter turnout throughout most of the 20th and early 21st centuries:

- Lack of real choice between the two parties
- Citizen indifference fueled by low *voter efficacy* (the feeling that one's vote doesn't really have an impact)
- Widespread complacency with the political/economic status quo
- Voter suppression targeting minority groups via state registration laws

Source: Mike Keefe, "Electronic Voting." *The Denver Post,* December 19, 2007. caglecartoons.com.

Key Facts about the Demographics Influencing Voter Turnout

Socioeconomic status. Citizens who make more money tend to vote more frequently than those with a lower income. A correlation between income and education indicates that the more education a person has achieved, the more likely that person is to vote.

Gender. Women are more likely to vote than men, although older women are less likely to vote when compared with older men.

Age. Voter turnout increases with age. Young people, ages 18 to 24 years old, are historically far less likely to vote when compared to their older counterparts, while older adults over 65 years old have the highest voter turnout.

Race. Voter turnout is highest among whites, as opposed to African American, Latino, or Asian American voters. While a number of factors may contribute to the higher turnout among white voters, there is a correlative relationship between participation of minority voters and socioeconomic status. Note: African American voter participation was intentionally suppressed until the Voting Rights Act of 1965 was passed. The psychological impact of a long history of intimidation against African American voters prior to its passage is difficult to assess, as is the feeling of efficacy among this group of voters who see few members of their community in the candidate pool of national office seekers. However, the candidacy of Barack Obama in 2008 and his campaign for reelection in 2012 motivated a record number of African Americans to go to the polls.

Black Voter Turnout Rate Rises

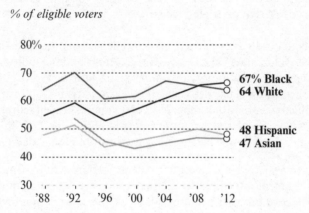

Registration Laws and State Voting Laws That Influence Voter Turnout

To vote in the United States, you must be an eligible citizen, meet the age requirement, register to vote, and meet the state's voting requirements at election time. While the "time, place, and manner" of holding elections for federal offices fall under the purview of the states according to the Elections Clause of the Constitution, the clause also allows Congress to alter laws impacting federal elections. Under this authority, Congress has taken action to improve voter turnout.

National Voter Registration Act ("Motor Voter Act"). Passed in 1993 and signed into law by President Bill Clinton, this law was designed to ensure fair and reasonably accessible registration procedures.

- Requires states to offer eligible voters the opportunity to register when applying for a driver's license, renewal of their license, or for public assistance through a state agency.
- States must accept federal voter registration forms from eligible voters.
- Only those states that do not require registration for voting (e.g., North Dakota) or allow election day registration (EDR) are exempted.

Help America Vote Act (HAVA). Passed and signed by President George W. Bush in 2002, the act provides federal funds to assist states in standardizing and modernizing voting procedures, voter registration, poll worker training, and voter education.

- Phase out use of punch-card and lever voting systems to be replaced by computerized voting machines.
- Make all polling places accessible to voters with disabilities and also provide at least one voting station at each polling site accessible to those with disabilities.
- Allow use of provisional ballots by those who do not appear on registration lists but believe they are eligible to vote (eligibility to be determined after the election, if eligible the voter's ballot is counted).
- Recruit college and high school students as poll workers and allocate some of the funding for mock elections held at school sites.
- Improve access to voting for members of the military and for citizens living overseas.
- Coordinate a single computerized list of registered voters in the state to avoid disqualifying ballots submitted by voters registered in multiple precincts.

Despite these federal efforts to boost voter participation, implementing the laws and running the elections is left to the states. Given this level of state sovereignty over elections and flexibility in implementing federal laws, registration and voting restrictions imposed by many states have served to suppress voter turnout. Research conducted by the political science department of University of California, San Diego (2008–2012) bears out the claim by political scientists that there is a voter suppression effect related to some of the strict guidelines implemented by states. Some states require voters to register no later than 30 days prior to an election, and other states that once allowed election-day registration have ended the practice.

Impact of state laws. Some states have employed photo identification requirements for voters. Most of these voter ID laws require a government-issued photo ID, such as a driver's license, military ID, or passport. Student IDs issued by a college or university do not qualify. Those who do not own a car or have a license, do not engage in foreign travel, or are not enlisted in the military—and thus do not have the required photo ID—can be turned away at the polls, even if they are properly registered. Voters without any of these forms of photo ID are encouraged to obtain a state photo ID. The cost of travel in rural areas to a location where such an ID can be obtained, plus fees associated with getting the ID, are often cost-prohibitive for low-income and elderly voters. Critics refer to voter ID laws as "voter suppression" laws, arguing that these laws are passed by Republican-controlled state legislatures for no other reason than to target demographic groups that traditionally vote Democratic. Supporters of voter ID laws claim their purpose is to eliminate voter fraud, although remarkably little evidence of such fraud exists. The University of California San Diego study once again supports what many critics have maintained, noting in their abstract that "strict identification laws have a differentially negative impact on the turnout of racial and ethnic minorities in primaries and general elections." Other factors that influence voter turnout include:

- The number and location of statewide polling sites
- Travel distance and time to arrive at balloting locations
- Limited hours of operation at polling locations
- The number of voting mode choices available (e.g., availability of mail-in, absentee, and early in-person balloting options)

Voter Choices

Agents of political socialization are discussed in Chapter 7 on pp. 215–217, but you should be familiar with the following factors that influence voter choices.

Factors That Influence Voter Choices	
Factor	**Summary**
Party identification	Party identification becomes a stronger determinant of voter choice later in adulthood, as ideology becomes more concrete. While many young voters identify as Independent due to disillusionment with the two-party system, they are somewhat dependent on party identification to form the political opinion and voting choices due to socialization and the tendency of young voters to lean more liberal.
Ideological orientation	Ideologically speaking, most people fall somewhere on the liberal-conservative continuum. Although the majority of American voters do not neatly align with one specific political party, individuals possess nuanced views that necessarily enable the formation of personal ideologies. These ideologies, which are created from a combination of subjective experience and educational background, practically translate to the development of political views that necessarily cohere with some party affiliation, either loosely or strongly.
Candidate characteristics	Candidate characteristics can influence voters in terms of personality, educational or work history, or individual choices. Broadly speaking, candidate charisma can profoundly impact voters who are far less ideologically bound than those who either possess party loyalty or more rigid political views that preclude an action of voting based on a personality assessment.
Political issues	Understandably, political issues affect how citizens vote. Most every person has an opinion on emerging issues and political debates dominating the media coverage. When an emerging issue trends, such as same-sex marriage or, more recently, the role of government in regulating minimum wage standards and providing healthcare services, individuals naturally form intense opinions that lead them to select a candidate based on his or her stance on a particularly controversial subject.
Beliefs	Voter identity, which includes religious (or nonreligious) orientation, race/ethnicity, and gender, impacts voter decisions. These personal characteristics shape individual consciousness and commonly extend into the realm of determining how distinct groups make collective decisions. Each subset of race, gender, or religious orientation generally aligns with one political party, though certainly a variance in individual decision making exists. Broadly speaking, most evangelical Christians are more conservative as a voting bloc and thus are more likely to be Republican. African Americans, however, tend to favor Progressive, Democratic candidates, as such candidates are more likely to advance social justice causes.

Voter Incentives and Voter Penalties

Although the government is not authorized to issue monetary incentives for voting, stickers with slogans like "I voted" are distributed at various polling locations on Election Day. Sometimes these stickers are honored by companies, particularly fast-food restaurants, that seek to reward customers for voting. However, offering any kind of reward for voting, even in the private sector, is a violation of election laws.

Similarly, imposing penalties or fines for not participating in the voting process is a violation of current election laws. Persons convicted of felonies may experience revocation of their voting privileges while incarcerated or on parole. Some state jurisdictions retain the right to permanently disenfranchise those convicted of felony offenses.

Linkage Institutions

Heads Up: What You Need to Know

The learning objectives that you must be able to accomplish are:

Describe linkage institutions.

Explain the function and impact of political parties on the electorate and government.

Explain why and how political parties change and adapt.

Explain how structural barriers impact third-party and Independent candidate success.

Explain the benefits and potential problems of interest-group influence on elections and policymaking.

Explain how variations in types of interest groups and their resources affect their ability to influence elections and policymaking.

Explain how various political actors influence public policy outcomes.

Linkage institutions serve as formal and informal entities outside of the government that provide the people access to policymakers, but also give the government information and insight into what the people want. The four linkage institutions that work together, sometimes as competing actors, are political parties, interest groups, elections, and the mass media.

In response to linkage institutions, citizens can directly respond to candidates through the voting process, including election primaries and caucuses. Candidates can adjust their messages to adapt to the shifts in cultural attitudes, technological advances, and public opinion. Candidates have direct access to potential voters through the media, and interest in political life is fueled by television, newspapers, social media, and the Internet.

Heads Up: What You Need to Know

On the AP GOV exam, you are required to understand how the structure of the government (separation of powers and the checks and balances system) impacts the political process and policymaking. It is important for you to not only define linkage institutions, but also to be able to explain this connection between structure and process. Linkage institutions are key elements in the process.

Linkage institutions provide voters and groups of citizens a variety of access points to influence policymakers because the branches of government are separate and guard their power prerogatives through the operation of checks and balances. You will be required to explain how separation of powers gives all the stakeholders (the people) within the policymaking process multiple access points to influence policymakers through examples. You don't have to know all the ways the multiple access points are utilized by stakeholders and interest groups, but you need to know some of those listed in the table below.

Linkage Institutions and the Political Process

Linkage Institution	Description	Activities/Impact
Political parties	Political parties provide an organizational framework and support for those who share a similar ideology. Their purpose is to achieve policy goals by getting members elected to office to impact policy outcomes. Political parties recruit, endorse, and fund candidates. Political parties disseminate information through mailings, phone calls, television, social media, and the Internet.	Political parties organize at the national level—e.g., the Republican National Committee **(RNC)** and the Democratic National Committee **(DNC)** for winning at the "top of the ticket" in a national presidential race. Control of the executive branch is critical to a party's success in getting its policy agenda enacted. The president's power to choose the heads of all the executive departments and agencies and to appoint judges to the federal courts can have a long-term impact that outlasts their term(s) in office. Further, a winning presidential candidate can use their "mandate" from the voters as well as their mandate from the Electoral College as leverage to push for the party's legislative agenda. Therefore, the national committees put a tremendous amount of time and resources into getting their respective candidates for president elected. The parties begin organizing immediately after a national presidential election to win the mid-terms. The "party in the government" (elected officials from each party) organize through the Democratic Congressional Campaign Committee **(DCCC)** and the National Republican Congressional Committee **(NRCC).** Their efforts include recruiting strong candidates and targeting congressional incumbents from the opposing party for defeat. A successful mid-term can mean the difference between the party in power holding on to its majority or the party out of power gaining ascendency and disrupting the president's policy agenda. State and local party organizations exist to get their candidates elected to statewide, city, and county offices. While the members of these organizations share the same party identification as those at the national level, given their local focus, they are independent from the national party organizations.

Continued

Linkage Institution	Description	Activities/Impact
Interest groups	Interest groups are a source of political influence and policymaking. In contrast to political parties, which focus on elections, interest groups do not nominate members to run for office, but rather, use a variety of means to impact policy. Types of interest groups include: ❑ Economic ❑ Public interest ❑ Intergovernmental ❑ Single issue ❑ Ideological ❑ Civil rights ❑ Grassroots	Interest groups provide campaign contributions to presidential and congressional candidates. Depending on their support or opposition, they can influence whether a president has a government unified under his or her party's control or a divided government in which a president must deal with the opposition holding a majority in Congress. They lobby lawmakers through direct contact (phone calls, meetings, etc.) can file lawsuits and *amicus curiae* (impartial adviser) briefs in the federal courts to achieve policy goals when Congress and/or the president fail to act. Interest groups also conduct demonstrations and protests that can draw media attention to an issue, placing political pressure on a chosen target (Congress, the president, or both); this tactic is usually, but not exclusively, associated with grassroots groups.
Elections	Elections give voters the power to impact policy outcomes by choosing candidates who most closely match their own ideological point of view. Elections make the most impact on the way in which citizens connect with government. The ballot box gives voice to the people's will at national, state, and local levels.	Mid-term elections occurring halfway through a presidential term traditionally result in a loss in seats for the party in power. Mid-terms can force a president to make concessions to the opposition in Congress to win their support for his or her policy initiatives. The *coat-tail-effect* (the tendency for the popular political leader to attract votes for other candidates of the same party) impacts candidates for Congress belonging to the same party as a popular president. This effect helps candidates win the election alongside the president. The coat-tail effect is most pronounced during a president's run for his or her first term in office. It can ensure that a newly elected president gets much of his or her agenda easily through Congress before the first mid-term election, and has put increasing attention and focus on a new president's "first hundred days." *Wave elections* (landslide elections) result in one party making major gains in Congress and are usually an indication of (1) widespread disconnect with policy outcomes associated with the party in power, or (2) desire in the electorate to have a stronger check on the president by electing candidates from the opposing party to a majority in the House, the Senate, or both chambers. Holding an edge in seats can result in a "veto-proof" majority for the opposition, more oversight of the executive branch, and, in cases of executive abuse of power, can increase chances of impeachment.

Linkage Institution	Description	Activities/Impact
Mass media	❑ Print media (newspapers, magazines, periodicals) ❑ Broadcast (radio, television, Internet) ❑ Social media (Facebook, Twitter, Reddit, blogs)	As a linkage institution, the media's role is to inform citizens, provide insight to government officials about public opinion on the major issues of the day. The media acts as a conduit for political candidates, party leadership, and government officials to communicate with the public. The various media platforms can have a major impact on framing issues and shaping public opinion through coverage of major legislation, the activities of party leadership and other government officials, policy outcomes, efforts by officials to communicate with the public, elections from primary season through the general election, and election results. Coverage of party leaders, policy failures and successes, scandals, and the private lives of political candidates can all impact voters' perceptions as they head to the ballot box. Media conducts and/or publishes public opinion poll results (e.g., Gallup, PEW, Quinnipiac, ABC News/*The Washington Post* poll, *The New York Times* poll). Polling informs politicians about levels of trust and support within the body politic for the institutions of government or for policy initiatives. Polling numbers can be used by Congress as leverage against the president or vice versa, depending on which institution or policy has higher poll numbers. Media provides a platform for speeches, debates, press conferences, interviews, and political commentary offered by "pundits."

Political Parties

As a linkage institution, a **political party** provides an opportunity for activists and rank-and-file voters to have their own ideologies expressed in the day-to-day work of creating public policy. The aim of political parties is to recruit and nominate candidates for office who will advance agendas prescribed by respective party platforms and carry out the party's legislative agenda. Any candidate hoping to make a legitimate run for a political office representing a major political party seeks that party's endorsement. Endorsement opens a flow of money and campaign support from party organizations. Political parties strive to elect as many of their represented candidates as possible to an office to fulfill the party's philosophical and ideological policy goals.

Political parties are responsible for **recruiting candidates,** fundraising, and providing campaign support. While once responsible for organizing and running campaigns, in recent years campaigns have become more candidate-centered, with the candidate hiring his or her own campaign managers, speech writers, and staff to organize appearances, frame the campaign message, run volunteer offices, and manage the candidate's time. This has weakened party coherence but has not entirely nullified the role of party organizations in elections. This section will cover the historical development of the two-party system, with emphasis on the two dominant political parties of the modern era—the Republican Party and the Democratic Party.

Political Parties in the Early Republic

Many early American leaders had a high regard for Enlightenment ideals—reason, debate, and deliberation. Leaders like George Washington and James Madison believed that these ideals should be the foundations of policymaking, not adherence to political factions or parties. Consequently, during Washington's two terms as president, the two dominant factions during the constitutional debates, Federalists and Anti-Federalists, remained simply that—factions, not organized political parties. Witnessing the growing divide between the two factions within his own administration (Secretary of State Thomas Jefferson leading the Anti-Federalists and Secretary of the Treasury Alexander Hamilton the spokesman for Federalists), Washington eschewed any affiliation that smacked of partisanship, and in his farewell address to the nation warned of the looming dangers of the nation dividing itself between two rival parties. Washington believed that unity behind constitutional principles would help to make our nation stronger, whereas petty differences over the policies and processes of the government would make it weaker in the eyes of the world. He asserted that organized parties would serve as a platform for men to conspire to fulfill their own agendas instead of staying focused on the will of the people.

Key Facts about the Political Parties from the Early Republic to the Present

As Washington departed the scene as the nation's elected executive in 1797, despite his warnings, Thomas Jefferson's adherents and those aligned with Alexander Hamilton proceeded to organize, with the electorate dividing itself. The two parties formed what became the **First Party System**—the **Federalist Party** led by Alexander Hamilton, and the **Democratic-Republican Party,** organized by the core of Anti-Federalist critics who sought to guard against vigorous use of federal power.

Federalists. Regionally, Federalists were concentrated in the manufacturing and commercial trading states of New England and the mid-Atlantic (New York and Pennsylvania). They believed the future of the nation lay in the development of a manufacturing-based economy and a robust federal government empowered to take actions promoting such activities for the benefit of the American people.

Democratic-Republicans. Led by Thomas Jefferson and James Madison, this party was strongest in the South and the emerging frontier states. Democratic-Republicans adhered closely to their belief in liberty and the need to ensure individual freedom by limiting the reach of the national government into the affairs of the states. Manufacturing, banking, and finance would corrupt democracy, but its virtues would be safeguarded in an agrarian nation inhabited by yeoman farmers. Ironically, given this vision, many of the leading Democratic-Republicans like Jefferson, Madison, and James Monroe owned large plantations dependent on slave labor. Nevertheless, they developed deep ties with the "common man" represented by yeoman farmers and the artisan class.

Election theory. From this point forward, American political party history is marked by **realigning elections** (Walter Dean Burnham) or the closely related **critical election theory** (V. O. Key Jr.). As issues change and new crises emerge that the old parties seem incapable of resolving, the coalition of voters supporting each of the major parties fracture and then realign with an emergent new party or with an ideologically redefined old one, thereby initiating a new party system. One party dominates during each period of alignment, controlling both the White House and Congress for significant periods of time.

Second Party System. When the limited regional appeal, loss of its most dynamic leaders, and lack of patriotic support for the War of 1812 fractured the Federalist party, causing its collapse, a single national party emerged by 1816, the National Republicans (Whigs). Factional differences over issues like tariffs and slavery divided the National Republicans. By 1828, a new alignment of parties emerged with southern and frontier supporters of Andrew Jackson coalescing to form the dominant **Democratic Party,** while a coalition of Jackson opponents remained within the **Whig Party.**

Third Party System. The Whig Party remained divided throughout most of the 1800s between free-soil, tariff-supporting northern Whigs and pro-slavery, anti-tariff southern Whigs. Their inability to bring their party together on the critical issues of the day led to the party's collapse and the emergence of a new anti-slavery **Republican Party,** with Abraham Lincoln becoming its candidate in the presidential election of 1860. Republican regional support was drawn exclusively from the North, while southern Whigs splintered between several rival small parties, but finally realigned with the **Democratic Party.** The Republicans dominated this era; while the Democrats maintained a stronghold in the South, several urban Democratic Party machines continued to control the political fortunes of northern cities.

Fourth Party System. After years of being the party of civil rights, passing through Congress the Thirteenth, Fourteenth, and Fifteenth amendments, Republican Party leadership was taken over by northern business interests and overseas expansionists. The emphasis on civil rights faded as Democratic "Redeemers" took over southern state governments and imposed Jim Crow segregation laws on African Americans, while weary northerners turned their attention away from the complexities of southern race relations. Republicans remained Progressive on issues of government reform and the fight against corruption, but the Democratic Party courted more conservative Progressives as well. The new alignment of big business **Republicans** and **Democrats** seeking Progressive reforms while giving tacit approval to racism and segregation was an outcome of the election of 1896. These loosely bound coalitions lasted until 1932, with the Republican Party dominating national politics.

Fifth Party System. The economic crash of 1929 and the onrush of the Great Depression blew the existing coalitions apart, with southerners, farmers, African Americans, northern and midwestern factory workers, unions, and political Progressives joining forces to elect Franklin Delano Roosevelt as president of the United States. FDR's "New Deal Coalition" strengthened the hand of the **Democratic Party** for decades to come and fundamentally changed the former party from one zealously guarding states' rights to one supporting a robust role for the federal government in solving national problems. Further, New Deal outreach to African Americans prompted a decades-long realignment. African American voters began to abandon the Republican Party, which no longer viewed racial justice and equality as a primary plank in their national political platform. Instead, they opted, in significant numbers, for adherence to the Democratic Party. The **Republican Party** limped along as the conservative party of big business and became the new champion of limited government intervention. It was strengthened during the Cold War through its conservative stands against Communism and for a strong national defense.

Era of Divided Government. Events in the last half of the 20th century and the early 21st century have pulled at the fabric of both party coalitions. The increase of voter dealignment from both major parties has sparked a rise in Independent voters whose tendency toward split-ticket voting has increased the frequency of divided government (one party controls the White House while the other controls one or both houses of Congress). No clear pattern of party dominance has yet emerged, and for this reason political scientists often refer to the period following the Fifth Party System as the Era of Divided Government. While this does not preclude the possibility of a clear Sixth Party System developing, only time will tell.

Impact of the Civil Rights Movement. The Civil Rights Act of 1964 and the Voting Rights Act of 1965, endorsed by and lobbied for by successive Democratic administrations in the 1960s, drove conservative Southerners away from the party and into the arms of the Republican Party. After the support of successive Democratic administrations for expansive civil rights protections (e.g., the Civil Rights Act of 1964 and the Voting Rights Act of 1965), the movement also marked the final shift of African American voters into the Democratic Party coalition first started during the New Deal. This realignment of a large voting bloc within the existing party coalitions simultaneously made the Democratic Party more liberal and the Republican Party more conservative.

Impact of Social issues. "Wedge issues" dividing the nation like abortion, feminism, and school prayer added evangelical Christians into the Republican fold.

Impact of Race. Both presidents Richard Nixon and Ronald Reagan played on the margins where racial politics and economic fear meet to appeal to traditional white working-class voters, famously called "Reagan Democrats." While the Democratic Party wooed many of these voters back during the 2008 election of Barack Obama, the populist appeal of Republican candidate Donald Trump in 2016, which again played on racial and ethnic fears, swung many of these voters back into the Republican camp.

Dealignment. The most notable change in party identification during this era is the **dealignment** rather than realignment of voters. Voters identifying as Independent (dealigned) have been an ever-growing voting bloc during this era, with many of those voting *split-tickets,* resulting in a succession of divided governments with no single party dominating. (See "Era of Divided Government," above.)

> **Did you know?** Political scientists consider the 1932 presidential election of Franklin D. Roosevelt the most definitive realigning election (or **critical election**) in the course of American politics. President Roosevelt's New Deal policy, which was a response to the disastrous Great Depression, contrasted greatly with Herbert Hoover's economic policies. Roosevelt's popular policies moved Republican strongholds to Democratic strongholds across the country, thereby reversing the trend of more than a century of single-party voting.

Political Parties of the 21st Century

The Two Main Political Parties in the United States.

The goal of political parties is to shape legislative policies based on ideological foundations. The functions of the parties include nominating and supporting candidates for political office, participating in political campaigns, creating and implementing policies, and gaining control of the government to implement policymaking.

In 21st-century American politics, several parties exist, but the two-party system consisting of the **Democratic Party** and the **Republican Party** continues to endure. While the number of voters identifying themselves as Independent has reached 42 percent of the electorate according to a 2016 Gallup poll, most of those voters continue to lean toward one party over the other, depending on the voter's ideology. An astonishing 90 percent of liberal-leaning Independents supported Barack Obama (D) in 2012, while 78 percent of conservative-leaning Independents supported Mitt Romney (R). In one form or another, the two-party system dominates American electoral behavior and policy outcomes.

Two-Party System

Despite disaffection with the two dominant parties as indicated by a dealigning electorate, the two-party system preserves itself through the **winner-takes-all** rule (see p. 282).

Democratic Party (DEM or D)

Democrats are often referred to as "liberals" and are symbolically represented by a blue donkey. Democrats tend to promote political and economic nationalism and a strong national government. In the mid-20th century, the Democratic Party became decidedly Progressive in its ideological alignment. Democrats became the champions of minority rights, social liberation, free thought, and the labor movement. With Roosevelt's "New Deal Coalition" forming the heart of the Democratic Party, it embraced socially liberal philosophies, but also greater government economic regulations to ensure the general welfare of society. As civil rights issues took center stage, the Democratic Party advocated for government intervention to gain approval for equal opportunity, and to sanction more Progressive policy changes.

Republican Party (GOP or R)

Republicans are often referred to as "conservatives" and are symbolically represented by a red elephant. Republicans adhere to a philosophy of minimal government intervention. Modern Republican conservatives oppose government intervention to ensure equality. The conservative coalition holds that the government's primary role is to be noninterfering, and if government is to interfere, it should only do so on the basis of preserving freedom. During the 20th century, the Republican Party became known as the party of lower taxes, fiscal conservatism, free-market economics, and family-centered values.

Political Party Platforms

Political **party platforms** share ideological ideals and interests that are designed to attain common political objectives through the electoral process. Decided upon every 4 years during presidential nominating conventions, congressional party leadership plays a major role in achieving the party's platform goals.

Party platforms make incremental shifts as changes in society necessitate policy modifications for future action. Even still, Democratic and Republican political parties have not altered their fundamental stance on many political and ideological issues in decades (see Chapter 7). While increasing issue polarization may seem to dominate political parties, the reality is that parties are similar in fundamental guiding principles, including the preservation of civil liberties, free market, and government limitations. Interpretations and the means to achieving these guiding principles is where party platforms begin to diverge.

Political Party Campaigns

Key Facts about Political Party Campaigns

Political parties recruit candidates. The main function of political parties is to formally recruit candidates for public office by means of nomination. A nominee is chosen for a variety of reasons, but the most important reason is that the selected candidate represents the party platform. Political parties and candidates have a two-sided relationship. A party that cannot recruit, nominate, and elect a candidate risks conceding political power. Depending on the type of election, the formality of selection and eligibility of a potential nominee can be rather lengthy, particularly during a presidential election.

Candidate-centered campaigns replace party control. Historically, political party organizations controlled the nomination process, guiding it toward a candidate of their choosing. In the 19th century, this process was often fueled by the rewards of the patronage system—government job offers in exchange for political support at the nominating convention. With the establishment of the merit system to hold civil service jobs within the government (Pendleton Civil Service Reform Act; 1883), the chipping away of party control of the nominating and campaign process began. However, it is the primary system for nominating candidates for federal and state offices that finally took the nomination process out of the hands of party organizations and put it in the hands of voters; this made the conversion to candidate-centered campaigns complete. Introduced sparingly during the Progressive Era of the early 20th century, by the late 1960s almost every state converted to the primary system for determining nominees for major offices. Candidates no longer had to make themselves appealing to party leadership, but instead had to sell themselves directly to voters. To do so, candidates make their own decisions about campaigning with the assistance of their own campaign managers and staffs. Party organizations play a secondary role, relegated to fundraising, organizing nominating conventions, and cheerleading both the party and its platform.

Political parties conduct fundraising. Political parties are organized nationally at federal, state, and local levels and dedicate considerable time to **fundraising.** Funds from individual party supporters, **PACs (Political Action Committees),** Super PACs, and other interest groups are funneled into pursuing media campaigns and other strategies to help get their candidates elected. Candidates also raise their own funds through direct contributions solicited using fundraising ads on television, in print media, and on social media sites and donor events. Within recent years, the use of social media has allowed lesser-known candidates to run direct fundraising campaigns without incurring the high cost of traditional media advertising.

Political parties modify messaging. The shifting demographic landscape of the U.S. necessarily requires the major political parties to adapt their platform messages accordingly. Minority voting populations are expected to increase substantially over the next several decades, and party platforms will undergo considerable reforms to stimulate a growing base of new voters.

Political parties' communication. ICT **(information and communications technology)** guarantees the best direct access from parties to individual voters. While television and radio overshadowed other forms of communication, ICT allows parties to communicate with a large database of U.S. citizens. Political parties can now quickly generate voter profiles and demographics to electronically target millions of Americans. Through social media platforms, users can comment, follow, or share content. Parties can immediately gauge the success, or lack of success, of any given message. More importantly, social media gives political parties direct access to citizens and party machines. Social media is an indispensable part of the political process. Social media serves to inspire citizen-to-citizen interaction with government and voters while encouraging other citizens to participate in the political process.

Source: Adam Zyglis, "Fake News." *The Buffalo News,* November 18, 2016.

Interest Groups

In Federalist No. 10, James Madison warned against organized interests that could threaten democracy. However, because coordinated sharing of interests is inevitable, banning such groups would not only not be possible, but would also hinder liberty. Consequently, the Founders hoped that the many interests present in a large and diverse republic would encourage a pluralist form of democracy in which many groups of organized collective voices would share in, but not dominate, public policy debate. Today, there are thousands of interest groups based on shared religious, environmental, labor, political, moral, or business positions that vary in goals, size, and procedures. There are questions about whether the Founders' vision has been realized given the differing nature of political, economic, and financial leverage exercised by the wide variety of interest groups in the United States today.

Interest groups serve as linkage institutions, providing a vehicle for individuals sharing the same or similar policy goals to pool their resources with the goal of making their political views known to policymakers and persuading them to act. For this purpose, they employ a variety of tactics. Interest groups are sometimes referred to as lobbying groups, although this is somewhat of a misnomer since lobbying is just one of many means used by interest groups to influence policy. Other references are advocacy groups or special interests. Regardless of what they are called, every interest group seeks to influence government policy.

Key Facts about Interest Groups

Lobbying and contributing to the draft of legislation. Members make direct contact with lawmakers through phone calls, meetings, and other forms of communication to provide pertinent information and persuade lawmakers to adopt legislation favorable to the group or block legislation that undermines the group's policy goals.

Campaign contributions. Interest groups form PACs to conduct political fundraising and collect donations. Following federal election guidelines, PACs use their money to make contributions to candidates for federal office who they believe will support their policy goals.

Litigation. When all else fails, sue! Interest groups often use class-action lawsuits and *amicus curiae* briefs to achieve policy goals through the courts when they meet legislative or executive resistance.

Iron triangles. Interest groups develop long-standing relationships with congressional committees and bureaucratic agencies directly responsible for policy areas most relevant to the group (e.g., pharmaceutical testing, air and water quality standards, energy exploration). Interest groups can also play a critical role in the formation of public policy. (For more on iron triangles, see pp. 147–148 in Chapter 5.)

Mobilized *grassroots* action. Grassroots activism is normally utilized by loosely organized groups of citizens interested in influencing policy but without the access to policymakers or the financial resources for media campaigns, PAC contributions, or lobbying. The goal is to attract media attention to put pressure on lawmakers by utilizing tactics such as demonstrations, boycotts, and letter writing/phone call campaigns.

Although the American democratic process is marked by *pluralist assumption* (the political theory of collective power instead of individual power) of competing voices, opposition, and debates, many political scientists argue that the rising influence of interest groups has served to counteract the benefits of pluralism. Political advocacy groups and other professional organizations have gained political traction out of proportion to the voice of the people. Inequality among interest groups has also contributed to the widening gap between citizens, interest groups, and the government. Depending on group contributions, membership, and the general socioeconomic status of participants, interest group influence can range from minimally potent to powerfully overwhelming. Professional organizations and PACs that draw on the contributions of millionaires to prop up their respective causes are more likely to wield substantial influence in the political process when contrasted with wider issue-based organizations that rely on a larger membership base (but actually have significantly smaller financial contributions).

Heads Up: What You Need to Know

The AP GOV exam frequently includes a question about the **free-rider problem.** What is the free-rider problem? An interest group relies on the participation of its members as well as its tangible financial support to maintain and advance the group's policy agenda. However, many people who are not members of an interest group and play no role in financially supporting its work receive the benefits of the group's political advocacy activities and influence. This is known as the free-rider problem. For example, all senior citizens benefit from legislation supported by the AARP (previously known as the American Association of Retired Persons), but only a small percentage of the senior population pay the membership dues that support AARP activities.

The benefit received by a free rider comes in the form of legislation or success in blocking laws that would negatively impact members of the group. To counteract the free-rider problem, interest groups encourage potential members to join by offering small tangible incentives, like magazine subscriptions or travel discounts.

Speaking of "Free Rider"!

Source: Jim Lange, "Speaking of Free Rider!" *The Daily Oklahoman*. The Oklahoman Archives.

Types of Interest Groups

Political scientists separate groups into two distinct political systems: *economic groups* that seek monetary advantages and *non-economic groups* that seek to promote issues that benefit society.

Types of Interest Groups			
Group	**Type**	**Description**	**Examples**
Public interest groups	Non-economic	Public interest groups are non-partisan and benefit the interests of the entire body politic, rather than a designated special interest. Many are joined together for a common cause of consumer advocacy or environmental protection.	❏ AARP ❏ Environmental Defense Fund (EDF) ❏ Mothers Against Drunk Drivers (MADD) ❏ National Alliance to End Homelessness ❏ Sierra Club

Continued

Group	Type	Description	Examples
Business-oriented groups	Economic	Business-oriented groups is a broad category to describe specific industries in business, labor, professions, or agriculture. For example, business interest groups promote employer interests, whereas labor interest groups represent workers.	❑ U.S. Chamber of Commerce (USCC) ❑ AFL-CIO ❑ Teamsters ❑ American Medical Association (AMA) ❑ American Bar Association (ABA)
Equity interest groups	Non-economic	Equity interest groups seek to advance the cause of a coalition for those who have faced discrimination based on gender, race, or sexual orientation.	❑ National Association for the Advancement of Colored People (NAACP) ❑ National Organization for Women (NOW) ❑ National LGBTQ Task Force
Single-issue interest groups	Non-economic	Single-issue interest groups are a type of citizen action group that is centered on a narrowly defined goal. This type of group is well-funded and employs the same tactics used by economic interest groups.	❑ National Rifle Association (NRA) ❑ National Abortion Rights Action League (NARAL)

The Nexus Between Social Movements and Interest Groups

Social movements often merge with the values of interest groups for the greater goal of enacting public policy changes. Generally, social movements fall into one of four broad categories:

- **Revolutionary:** Desire the alteration of every societal aspect
- **Resistant:** Literally resist changes within society
- **Alternative:** Seek to change personal beliefs and behaviors
- **Reform:** Point to seeking specific (usually political) changes

Social movements bring together a variety of groups and organizations sharing the same objective. Such movements hope to effect social change by mobilizing their members and other individuals with strong convictions for participation in mass demonstrations and protest. Social movements and interest groups often find their interests overlapping, and it is not uncommon to see interest groups becoming part of the larger coalition aimed at mass participation. While individual interest groups may be part of the coalition participating in the movement, the movement itself is not a formally organized interest group. A prime example of this type of movement is the Civil Rights Movement of the 1950s and 1960s. Disparate groups came together in a coalition focused on equal treatment under the law for African Americans. The Southern Christian Leadership Conference (SCLC), the Student Non-Violent Coordinating Committee (SNCC), and the Congress of Racial Equality (CORE) partnered with the National Association for the Advancement of Colored People (NAACP) to work together to end discrimination, segregation, and disenfranchisement.

While movement leaders like the SCLC's Martin Luther King Jr. frequently made direct contact with politicians to lobby for passage of the Civil Rights Act and the Voting Rights Act, and the NAACP focused on litigation (e.g., *Brown v. Board of Education of Topeka*), the real power to effect change came from the mass demonstrations and protests like the Montgomery Bus Boycott, the Selma-to-Montgomery marches, and the March on Washington.

Elections

Heads Up: What You Need to Know

The learning objectives that you must be able to accomplish are:

Explain how the different processes work in a U.S. presidential election.

Explain how the Electoral College impacts democratic participation.

Explain how the different processes work in U.S. congressional elections.

Explain how campaign organizations and strategies affect the election process.

Explain how the organization, finance, and strategies of national political campaigns affect the election process.

Elections serve as an important linkage institution. Through their votes, citizens inform government officials about general ideological and partisan shifts within the electorate which can be interpreted through the lens of public response to policy. Election results, particularly for "wave elections," can reflect public perception about the policy agenda, which policies actually get enacted, and how policies are implemented.

This section will review the process of becoming an elected official, starting with the nomination process, campaign process, and the election process. You should be able to explain how the different processes in a U.S. presidential election operate, including the Electoral College, and the relevance of campaign finance regulations on the election process.

Presidential and Congressional Elections

Election questions on the AP GOV exam focus on federal elections of two main types: presidential and congressional. Be prepared to explain the election process, including key factors such as the **incumbency advantage,** Electoral College, and how structural and non-structural elements within the election process support the perpetuation of the two-party system.

Similarities and Differences in Presidential and Congressional Elections

Presidential	Congressional
Held every 4 years	Held every 2 years, with every seat in the House contested and one-third of Senate seats up for grabs
Experience greater media coverage, more campaign contributions, and higher voter turnout	Receive less media coverage, campaign financing, and, during mid-term elections in non-presidential years, experience lower voter turnout
Races are more competitive than congressional races.	Gerrymandered single-member districts are often "safe" for one party's candidates, making elections for House seats less competitive.
There is an advantage to incumbency when running for reelection.	Congressional members have an incumbency advantage, with House members enjoying an even greater advantage than senators. Approximately 80 to 90 percent of congressional incumbents win congressional reelection (see graphs that follow).
Presidential elections rely on the Electoral College to determine the winner of the election. Votes in the Electoral College are allocated based on winner-takes-all outcomes in state-by-state elections. For example, Barack Obama took 60.24% of the popular vote in California in 2012; consequently, he received all 55 of California's electoral votes.	Congressional elections rely on the popular vote, with the candidate who is *first past the post* declared the winner of the election. ❑ House: Election by voters within a defined single-member district ❑ Senate: Election by voters within a state at large
Presidential candidates tend to represent the national policy goals of their party.	Congressional candidates must be more cognizant of local/state issues and constituents' needs and, therefore, tend to represent their own ideological views vs. national party goals.

U.S. House Reelection Rates, 1964–2016

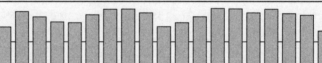

Election Cycle

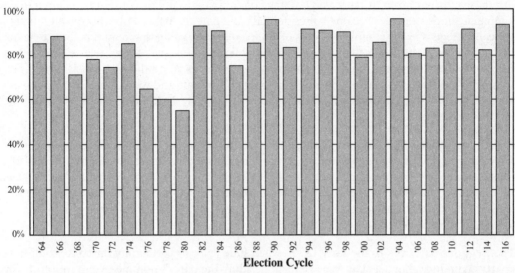

U.S. Senate Reelection Rates, 1964–2016

Election Cycle

> **Did you know?** **"First past the post"** is a term borrowed from horse racing. As horses approach the finish line, the one that crosses first, "by a nose" or by a mile, is the winner; the distance between the winner and second place does not matter. Likewise, in politics the distance between the winner and second place is irrelevant. The candidate with the most votes wins, whether by tenths of a percentage point or by amassing 80 percent of the ballots in an election win. Note, the hurdle that must be cleared is the MOST votes, not the majority of votes. If minor party candidates are on the ballot, the winning vote total may well fall below the majority mark of 50.1 percent of ballots cast.

Key Facts about Presidential Elections

Presidential constitutional prerequisites. The constitutional requirements for the presidential office are described in Article II of the Constitution. The person must be a natural-born citizen, must be at least 35 years old, and must have been a resident of the United States for 14 years. The Twenty-Second Amendment (1951) prevents anyone from being president more than twice (or one time, if the person completes at least 2 years of a presidential term in which someone else was elected).

Presidential intentions. Presidential candidates must announce their intention to run for office (sometimes as early as 1–2 years before the election) and then register with the Federal Election Commission.

Presidential campaigns. Presidential campaigning is a grueling process involving a nearly 24-hour, 7-days-a-week commitment to crisscross the country for public appearances, speechmaking, debate participation, attending fundraising events, and strategizing with campaign staff. These activities occur in two phases for those winning their party's nomination—the first phase involves the primary/caucus process and the second phase is the general election.

Presidential campaign consultants. With the rapid change in campaign communications that began in the 1960s with the explosive impact of television coverage of campaigns, political consultants hired to develop media communications strategies became a presidential candidate mainstay. Political consultants serve as the chief political strategists in the complex process of political campaigning that connects the public directly to the candidate. Political consultants manage candidate public relations, the sales of television or other communications advertisements, the dissemination of press releases, and other important candidate tasks. In modern history, Karl Rove was one of the most powerful consultants and was instrumental in the election of President George W. Bush in 2000 and 2004. In fact, President Bush explicitly named Rove as "the architect" of his election victories.

Political party conventions. Political party conventions are the end point of the nominating process. Organized by the national party committees, each party establishes the formal and informal rules of the convention. Conventions are held during the summer immediately prior to the November general election. Here, the formal nomination of a party's candidate takes place with a roll call of states, each in turn announcing the allocation of its delegate votes among the candidates. Delegates are apportioned proportionally to the states based on population.

Political conventions date back to the early 1830s, when state delegates attending the convention were chosen by state party committees but acted as free agents in deciding the party's nominee. Conventions before the primary/caucus system was in place were wild affairs with floor fights over delegates and backroom deals made to ensure support of a given candidate. The nominee could very often not be determined by the first balloting. Abraham Lincoln was only nominated after a dramatic floor fight and three ballots. A record 103 ballots occurred at the Democratic Convention of 1924 before candidate John W. Davis finally tallied the requisite number of delegates to win the nomination.

In modern history, conventions are not nearly as pivotal or exciting, with the winner predetermined by binding party primaries and caucuses that do not allow for delegate free agency. Today, during the 4 days of the convention, the platform is determined, and television coverage is used to acquaint the public with the nominee and his or her vice-presidential running mate, encourage party unity, rally support for the party platform, and introduce future stars in national party politics by assigning them as "keynote speakers" or allowing them to make the nominating speech.

Presidential campaigns and social media. Social media has made it possible for candidates to directly communicate their political platforms with potential voters relatively free of charge via a Facebook post or a tweet. This immediate access has enabled a more accessible and responsive political process and has further eroded party control over campaigns in favor of candidate-centered campaigning. Historically, candidates have had limited access to communication outlets.

Presidential incumbency advantage. Research shows that an incumbent will frequently win the second-term election even when the first presidential term is uneventful. Within modern history, especially since the Great Depression, most incumbent presidents, with the exception of Herbert Hoover, Jimmy Carter, and George H. W. Bush, have been elected for a second term. Notable reasons for this phenomenon include familiarity and name recognition, the incumbent's campaign experience, the ability to use the prestige of office to attract large campaign donations, access to free media coverage via press conferences and speeches, and, in the midst of a national emergency or crisis such as an economic crash or war, a desire to stick with the more experienced candidate.

Primaries and Caucuses

In the United States, three critical stages of presidential elections exist: the nominating process, the general election, and the Electoral College vote. Nominations are decided by the outcomes of a combination of party **primary elections** in most states and party **caucuses** held in 16 states. Primaries and caucuses determine how many of a state's delegates to party national nominating conventions will be allocated to each candidate. The first primary of the presidential campaign season is held in New Hampshire, while the first caucus is held in Iowa.

Primaries

A **primary election** is held to allow voters to cast their ballot for a candidate they want to be their party's nominee for office. Selection of a candidate is done by secret ballot, or "Australian ballot." Depending on state election rules, voting may be done via absentee ballot or mail-in ballot. Accommodations may also exist for early in-person voting. Any of these options or a combination of options increases voter participation, ensuring that as many voices as possible are heard during the nomination process. The types of primary elections are described in the table below. Note: More states continue to hold closed or semi-closed primaries rather than open primaries.

Compare and Contrast the Types of Primary Elections		
Closed Primary	**Semi-Closed Primary**	**Open Primary**
Voters must declare a party affiliation prior to Election Day (determined by voter registration) and can only vote in their party's primary.	For registered party members; follows the same process as a closed primary; Independent voters can cast their vote on either the Republican or Democratic primary ballot.	All voters have a chance to choose the party primary they want to participate in by requesting that party's ballot at the time of the election.
Pros: Supports freedom of association, allowing only fellow party members to choose the nominee who will represent them in the general election; allowing voters outside the fold of the party to participate in the choosing of their nominee completely undermines the purpose of voluntary association with people sharing ideological outlook and policy goals **Cons:** Allows party organizations to determine the rules and control the nominating process, thereby making it less transparent; allows no role for Independent voters in the nominating process	**Pros:** Gives Independent voters a chance to participate in the nominating process; may have a moderating influence on the choice of a nominee; encourages more open debate and coalition building **Cons:** Only voters formally associated with a party should be able to select the party's nominee; the party should be able to determine who participates in its primaries, rather than participation of outsiders being mandated by the states	**Pros:** Frees voters to cross party lines when highly motivated to do so; encourages coalition building; makes nominations more democratic by allowing all voters regardless of party to participate **Cons:** Only voters formally associated with a party should be able to select the party's nominee; creates opportunities for opposition party members to sabotage the rival party's nominating process by casting a ballot for weaker candidates

A fourth type of primary exists, known as a **blanket primary** or **Louisiana primary.** All nominees for all offices are listed on a blanket primary ballot. Voters are free to select a Republican candidate for one office and a Democratic candidate for another. Only one vote can be cast for each office on the ballot. Blanket primaries are less restrictive and give voters a maximum level of choice. However, opposition from the major parties concerned about the erosion of party loyalty and the opportunity for tactical voting against a party's strongest candidates led to a Supreme Court challenge. In *California Democratic Party v. Jones* (2000), the Court struck down blanket primaries in federal elections, citing violation of First Amendment freedom of association. Louisiana-style blanket primaries can still be adopted for use in statewide elections.

Did you know? Media coverage can impact the outcome of the primary and caucus process. (1) **Horse-race coverage** of only the top three finishers in each primary or caucus can drive lesser players out of the race before their campaigns have an opportunity to gain traction with the public. With the cost of campaigning so high, lesser-known candidates depend on the free media coverage they receive if they finish in the top three spots. The importance of this coverage is particularly true in the first primary, held in New Hampshire, and the first caucus, held in Iowa. A win or near-win in these two contests turns the media spotlight on, which attracts donor money, thus allowing candidates without a lot of resources to stay in the race. Finishing fourth in these two contests has caused many candidates over the years to drop out before any of the electorate in any other states have a chance to vote. (2) Press coverage of the primary/caucus season includes a tallying of the delegate count for each candidate immediately after a primary or caucus is held. Consequently, the public is informed when a candidate reaches the magic number of delegates needed to be nominated, at times months before voters in some states who are making their choices late in the primary season even have a chance to cast a ballot. This has led to the phenomenon known as **frontloading;** states deciding to move their primaries or caucuses up to a point earlier on the election calendar. The crowding of primaries to earlier points on the calendar has led to a greater focus on **"Super Tuesday"** primaries, in which a number of states hold their primaries or caucuses on the same day, with many delegates to nominating conventions up for grabs.

Caucuses

A **caucus** is literally a closed meeting of like-minded participants who gather to have a dialogue about a particular goal or interest. In the presidential nominating process, a caucus is an event held in a church, school, or private home. During the caucus, party members discuss and debate strengths and weaknesses of the candidates before conducting a show-of-hands vote or separating themselves into groups associated with the name of one of the candidates. The goal of the caucus is the same as that of the primary: the allocation of state delegates to party nominating conventions. As with most primaries, caucuses are either closed or semi-closed. While some states continue to hold caucuses, the majority of states have adopted the primary as their preferred means to allocate delegates to nominating conventions. While caucuses have their advocates, there are also significant drawbacks that have led most states to opt for a primary system.

Pros	Cons
Caucuses allow for an open and transparent selection process. They are a form of direct democracy in which citizens' voices are heard in a public forum. Only the most engaged in the process participate. Caucuses allow for serious deliberation before casting a vote. They allow participants to stand up for long-shot candidates who are only eliminated if they fail to reach a minimum level of support during the first round of voting, at which point participants have a second-choice option. However, if lesser-known candidates succeed in reaching the minimum level of votes (e.g., 15 percent in the Iowa caucus), they are awarded an appropriate portion of delegates, whereas in winner-takes-all primaries, only the candidate who is "first past the post" receives delegates, thus discouraging support for long-shot candidates.	Not truly democratic: Participants must show up at a specific time and place on a single day. Those who work, college students away from home, the elderly who no longer drive, or those in the military, etc. who cannot travel to the location at the appointed time have no option such as absentee balloting to ensure that their voices are heard. In addition, facilities may not be accessible to the disabled, thereby eliminating their voices as well. Without a system of secret balloting, participants may be subject to peer pressure or intimidation when choosing a candidate to support.

Campaign Financing

Heads Up: What You Need to Know

On the AP GOV exam, you should be familiar with **campaign finance law.** Over the years, the development and refinement of campaign finance law through legislation and Supreme Court decisions have fundamentally changed campaigning. Campaign finance is frequently the focus of questioning on the AP GOV exam. To understand the impact of campaign finance laws and Supreme Court decisions regarding campaign financing, students should be familiar with the vocabulary of campaign financing including hard money, soft money, PACs, independent expenditures, Super PACs, and 527s.

Key Facts about Campaign Financing

Hard money. Cash contributions made directly to candidates or their campaign committee by individuals or PACs. By law, hard money is currently limited to $2,500 per candidate or candidate committee per election cycle for individuals and $5,000 per candidate or candidate committee per election cycle for PACs.

Soft money. Contributions made by individuals or PACs to political parties for "electioneering activities." Party expenditures for electioneering were unregulated before the passage of the Bipartisan Campaign Referral Act (BCRA) in 2002, so soft money was funneled to candidates and candidate committees to bypass contribution limits set by the Federal Election Campaign Act (FECA) in 1974.

PACs. Structurally defined by the Federal Election Campaign Act as "separate segregated funds" explicitly set up by corporations and unions to collect voluntary campaign contributions solicited through fundraising. PACs keep corporate and union treasuries distinct from money raised specifically for donation to political campaigns.

Independent expenditures. Expenditures on campaign communications that advocate for or against a candidate by name (Super PACs) or for **issue advocacy** and **voter mobilization** (527s), but are separate and distinct from contributions made directly to any individual candidate or campaign committee. Generally, the amount of money used for independent expenditures is not limited by existing campaign finance laws. However, any communication or coordination directly with a candidate, a campaign, or party in the selection, use, or airing of independent expenditure ads violates federal election law.

Super PACs. Formed specifically as independent political action committees that solicit contributions from like-minded ideological or partisan donors. Contributions can be solicited from individuals, corporations, unions, or other associations. These funds cannot be contributed directly to campaigns but are instead used to influence campaign outcomes through spending on "attack ads" or ads supporting their candidates of choice. There is no limit on the amount Super PACs can spend in an election cycle.

527s. Tax-exempt non-profit groups organized under Section 527 of the Internal Revenue Service tax code. Considered an independent expenditure group, but unlike Super PACs, 527s are prohibited from advocating for or against a candidate by name. Instead, they focus on **issue advocacy** and **voter mobilization** ads. Like Super PACs, they tend to be ideological and/or partisan. There are no limits on the amount that can be contributed to a 527, on who can contribute, or how much money the group can spend. They are required by the IRS to publicly disclose their donors and file reports that account for contributions received and expenditures made.

Law/Court Decision	Content	Impact
Federal Election Campaign Act (FECA) (1971)	❑ Consolidated early-20th-century reform efforts focused on disclosure requirements for campaign donations and expenditures and regulation of corporate and union contributions to federal campaigns ❑ Prohibited union and corporate direct donations to federal candidates but allowed these groups to organize PACs ❑ Requires quarterly reporting of donations and expenditures by candidates, the parties, and PACs	FECA created the framework for PACs and established the reporting requirements that continue to be in force today.

Law/Court Decision	Content	Impact
FECA Amendments (1974)	❑ Created the **Federal Election Committee** (FEC) to enforce FECA ❑ Placed base limits on hard money donations made directly to candidates by individual donors and PACs, including a cap on aggregate (total) contributions per election cycle ❑ Placed limits on campaign expenditures	Donation and expenditure limitations were challenged in federal courts—*Buckley v. Valeo*.
Buckley v. Valeo (1976)	❑ Known for equating campaign expenditures with the First Amendment ("money is speech") ❑ Struck down FECA limits on independent campaign expenditures, but let limits on candidate expenditures and on individual and PAC contributions stand	With campaign donation limits remaining in place, special interest groups turned to "soft money" to influence elections. The use of independent expenditures increased.
Bipartisan Campaign Reform Act (BCRA) (also called the McCain-Feingold Act, 2002)	❑ Prohibited parties, candidates, and office holders from soliciting soft money contributions ❑ Banned corporations and unions from using money from their treasuries to pay for issue ads mentioning federal candidates by name 60 days prior to a general election or 30 days prior to primaries ❑ Increased limits on base individual and PAC contributions, including a cap on aggregate individual contributions	BCRA quickly lost its impact as special interests turned to forming 527 groups and Super PACs. Limits placed on corporate issue ad spending were challenged before the Supreme Court in *Citizens United v. Federal Election Commission*.
Citizens United v. Federal Election Commission (2010)	❑ Equated corporations with people, which were therefore deserving of First Amendment protections ❑ Majority opinion declared a ban on corporate and union spending from their treasuries on issue ads an unconstitutional violation of free speech	This highly controversial decision undermined what remained of the McCain-Feingold Act and opened the floodgates for unlimited independent corporate spending to influence federal elections. Limits on direct contributions by individuals and PACs remain in place.
McCutcheon v. Federal Election Commission (2014)	❑ Struck down aggregate cap on individual contributions per election cycle (the base contribution limit remains) ❑ While acknowledging a collective societal interest in curbing corruption in politics, (1) there is no evidence that aggregate caps effectively impact corruption, and (2) this concern cannot be used to justify restraint of free speech	The ruling increased organized Joint Fundraising Committees (JFCs), including individual donors, a group of candidates, party committees, and PACs. It also enabled wealthy individual donors to make one large contribution while adhering to the base contribution limit by adding together all base contributions made to each participant in the JFC.

The Electoral College

The **Electoral College** is the institution used for selecting the president and vice president of the United States established in Article II, Section I, of the Constitution.

Heads Up: What You Need to Know

On the AP GOV exam, you must be able to define and explain the Electoral College. It not only determines the winner of a presidential election, but has also become increasingly controversial and critics have called for it to be abolished. The debate over the Electoral College is often the focus of AP GOV exam questions.

History of the Electoral College

The process for electing the president was not an easy matter for the delegates at the Constitutional Convention. The debate highlighted a distrust of popular democracy and the will of the majority as well as the critical nature of the Founders' belief in the principle of separation of powers. James Madison's Virginia Plan served as the platform for debate. Madison suggested that the executive (president) should be elected by Congress. The Committee of Detail, which took over the drafting of the Constitution from the contentious Committee of the Whole, determined that election by Congress would not provide the president with sufficient independence from the will of the legislative branch. The Committee also rejected the idea of a popularly elected president because such a system would minimize the voice of smaller states in presidential elections and open the door to tyranny of the majority. The compromise Electoral College system, explained in Article II, Section I, of the Constitution, maintained a separation of the executive and legislative branches and a more proportional voice for the states. In addition, by giving to the states through their electors the power to choose the executive of the federal government, the Electoral College became an important and enduring feature of the Constitution's design.

The Electoral College Today

Today, in order to win an Electoral College victory, a candidate must reach the simple majority benchmark of 270 votes out of a total of 538 electoral votes. The 538 votes cast by electors are apportioned among the states based on the number of representatives a state has in the House, plus two senators. For example, according to the map on the next page, Minnesota has eight members in the House, plus two senators; therefore, Minnesota is apportioned 10 electoral votes. You will also note that the District of Columbia is allotted three electoral votes. While not a state, there is a significant number of American voters living in Washington, D.C.; therefore, the Twenty-Third Amendment granted the District three electors.

It is important to note the indirect nature of Electoral College voting. While the national popular vote is irrelevant to Electoral College outcomes (prompting one major criticism of the process), the people's will is not entirely ignored in today's electoral process.

- The statewide popular vote determines which candidate receives that state's electors: winner-takes-all.
- Maine and Nebraska are the exceptions. These two states employ the district split-elector system. The popular vote winner in each congressional district wins that district's electoral vote. The winner of the popular vote statewide takes the two electors allotted for the senators.
- Each state chooses its electors according to a process determined by the state political party committees.

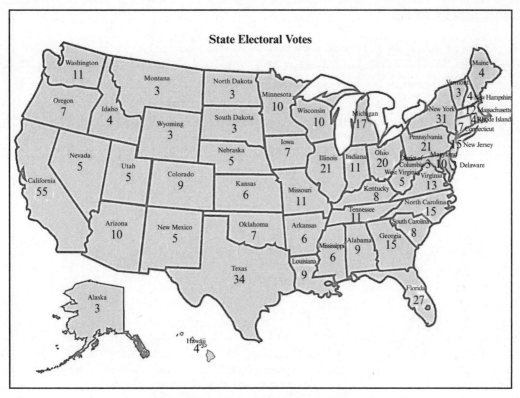

State Electoral Votes

The Electoral College Process

November	December	January	January 20
A general election is held on the first Tuesday in November.	Following the general election, electors in each state meet, and their votes are recorded on a "Certificate of Vote," which is forwarded to Congress.	The official Electoral College vote count is conducted before a joint session of Congress. The president of the Senate oversees the vote count and certifies the results.	The president-elect takes the oath of office and becomes president of the United States.

Did you know? It is important to note that there is no federal law or constitutional provision that demands that electors must vote in accordance with the popular vote outcome. Even still, the *faithless elector* (members of the Electoral College who do not vote for their party's candidate) law states that electors who do not vote as pledged may incur personal fines or may be disqualified from the elector process.

Generally, electors cast a ballot along the lines of the popular vote tally. In the history of U.S. elections, there have been only 167 faithless electors since the establishment of the Electoral College (71 electors were altered due to a candidate's death).

The Winner-Takes-All Rule

TEST TIP: On the AP GOV exam, you should know that the American electoral system is a *winner-takes-all system*, whereby each state has a number of electoral votes. Less-populated states have fewer electoral votes (see Chapter 7). The winner-takes-all aspect of the electoral system perpetuates the two-party system and makes it virtually impossible for third-party candidates to compete. Students should understand other structural and non-structural factors that undermine third-party efforts to win elective office (see "Winner-Takes-All and Third Parties").

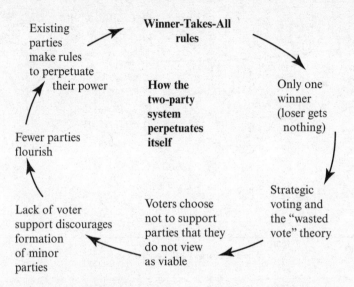

Winner-Takes-All Rules and Third Parties

Under the winner-takes-all rules adopted by most states, the candidate with the most votes (first past the post) wins the statewide popular election. The statewide popular vote victor wins all that state's electoral votes. While third-party candidates may certainly receive votes in statewide popular elections, it is nearly impossible for them to be first past the post; therefore, they receive no electoral votes. In the 2000 election, for example, Green Party candidate Ralph Nader received 2,822,995 popular votes nationwide, but he did not win the most votes in a single one of the 43 statewide contests in which his name appeared on the ballot. As a result, Nader was not awarded a single electoral vote.

Proportional district split-elector reform. Maine and Nebraska are the only two states to reject the winner-takes-all system as a means to distribute a state's electoral votes. The process adopted in these two states allows for a more proportional distribution of electoral votes while retaining a level of reward for the overall winner of the statewide popular vote.

- The popular vote within a single-member legislative district determines which candidate receives the electoral vote for that district. Theoretically, the candidate of one party can be first past the post in one district's popular vote count, while the opposition party's candidate wins the most votes in the neighboring district; therefore, the two electoral votes are split between the two candidates.
- The winner of the overall statewide popular vote receives the two electoral votes apportioned to each state for their two senators.

- Would a proportional system help third-party candidates? Conceivably a third-party candidate could have strong regional appeal, as did Populist Party candidates in the 1890s who won local elections in the midwestern farm belt. However, the traditional adherence of most voters to the two-party power structure remains persistent, making it very unlikely that a third-party candidate could win enough district popular votes across the nation to accumulate the requisite 270 electoral votes to become president.

Elimination of the Electoral College. If the Electoral College were to be eliminated, it would result in the following:

- The selection of the president would be based entirely on the popular vote outcome: First past the post wins.
- Based on the results in the 2000 election, eliminating the Electoral College would not help third-party candidates. Ralph Nader's popular vote total of 2,822,995 represented only 2.7 percent of the ballots cast. However, in the current winner-takes-all system, voters tend to opt for either of the two major party candidates, knowing that a ballot cast for a third-party candidate unlikely to win the statewide contest is a **wasted vote.** In addition, voters who have closer ideological ties to one of the two major parties, though preferring the third-party candidate, may want to avoid the **spoiler effect** by voting for the third party. Many critics of Nader's run for office in 2000 argue that Green Party voters would have voted for Democratic candidate Al Gore had Nader not been in the race. The votes for Nader made a difference in some of the statewide contests, handing George W. Bush the victories and therefore all those states' electoral votes, and thereby "spoiling" Gore's chances of becoming president. It is possible that by eliminating the Electoral College system of voting and relying instead on the national popular vote, more voters would vote their conscience without concern about wasting their vote or contributing to the spoiler effect. Presidential contests would also be more competitive, motivating more voters to participate.
- The biggest challenge to this reform is that it cannot be legislated; rather, it must be accomplished by passing a constitutional amendment. The process of amending the Constitution can be long and complicated. In addition, the Electoral College maintains a voice for smaller states in the presidential election. Reliance simply on the popular vote would allow the largest states to dominate the choice of the nation's executive. This being the case, the legislatures in small states would resist ratification of such an amendment.

Additional structural and non-structural barriers for third parties:

- The persistence of the two-party system has traditionally undermined third-party candidates in national elections. The United States has been dominated by a two-party political system since 1797, and, consequently, the majority of voters continue to register as members of one of the two major parties and vote for major party candidates. Party loyalty has always been the foundation of this system, so with increased dealignment of Independent voters in recent decades it would be reasonable to assume that the chances for third-party candidates would increase; however, while they are not aligned with either party, Independent voters continue to cast their ballots for one of the two major party candidates.
- Limited **ballot access** keeps third parties off many state ballots. Since states set the rules for elections, they have the option to determine what qualifies a candidate to be placed on the ballot. Many of these ballot access laws require first-time third- or minor-party candidates to obtain a set number of legitimate signatures on a petition. If they meet the signature requirement to have their name placed on the ballot, they must then win a set percentage of the popular vote (15 percent is common) to have their party's candidates placed on future ballots. No comparable requirements exist for candidates from the two major parties.

- **Media coverage** during elections focuses on the **"horse race"** (i.e., who's ahead?). Horse-race news coverage often results in events and speeches delivered by third-party candidates to be ignored by major media outlets as they chase down stories about the major party front-runners.

- **Debate access** is also denied to third-party candidates. The Commission on Presidential Debates sponsors and produces the debates; its responsibilities include determining who gets to participate. The commission is jointly sponsored by the two major parties, so it continues to deny a national televised platform for third-party candidates to increase their name recognition among voters or to present their views and ideas regarding the most salient issues in an election.

Did you know? The popular vote usually results in the same winner as the Electoral College vote, but not always. Five times in American history the candidate who won the Electoral College vote did not win the national popular vote: John Quincy Adams (1824), Rutherford B. Hayes (1876), Benjamin Harrison (1888), George W. Bush (2000), and Donald Trump (2016). The most recent of these elections have raised questions about the legitimacy and necessity of the Electoral College. Critics have frequently taken issue with the Electoral College, arguing that it subverts the will of the people by disregarding the popular vote and impacts campaigning, forcing candidates to focus their efforts on **"swing states"** (also known as "battleground states"), with substantial electoral votes and a popular vote that could go either way. Currently, Ohio, Florida, and Virginia are considered key swing states. Abolishing the Electoral College would prompt candidates to run a national campaign addressing all the people.

Mass Media

As a linkage institution, the media plays a major role in informing the public about issues, policy, and government actions. In turn, by means such as polling, focus group interviews, and coverage of demonstrations, the media informs policymakers about the public response to their actions (or their inaction!).

Heads Up: What You Need to Know

The learning objectives that you must be able to accomplish are:

Explain the media's role as a linkage institution.

Explain how increasingly diverse choices of media and communication outlets influence political institutions and behavior.

On the AP GOV exam, you must be able to explain the impact of media choices and the options of political participation.

Types of Mass Media

Multiple media outlets provide continuous political commentaries and information that shape the increasingly fluid public opinion. Mass media includes *print media* (newspapers, magazines, books, posters, and bulletins), *broadcast media* (radio and television), and *electronic media* (the Internet and social media).

It is through mainstream media that the "information highway" of cable television news networks, social media, and even radio personalities is able to quickly report information and comment on unfolding political events. Cable news networks like CNN and Fox News, for example, offer 24/7 coverage, with featured political analysts and pundits receiving dedicated airtime. These news networks retain White House correspondents, whose jobs concern the constant monitoring of events, information, and press releases delivered on behalf of government officials.

The distribution of mass media has three outlets: national, mid-range, and local.

Structure	Description
National outlets	The national media outlets are those that are widely circulated or viewed, including nationwide newspapers (*The Wall Street Journal, The Washington Post, The New York Times,* and *Los Angeles Times*), major television networks (ABC, NBC, and CBS) and cable news stations (CNN, CNBC, and Fox), and nationwide magazines and wire services (Associated Press, *U.S. News & World Report, Newsweek,* and *Time*).
Mid-range outlets	The mid-range outlets center on circulation newspapers and partisan publications like *Chicago Tribune, USA Today, The Christian Science Monitor* (conservative), *National Review* (conservative), *The Nation* (liberal), and *The New Republic* (liberal).
Local outlets	Local outlets consist of newspapers, television stations, and radio stations that broadcast news from the local community.

Yellow Journalism

The first American newspapers were published with media biases for the purpose of promoting partisan politics. The Federalists published the *Gazette of the United States*, and the Anti-Federalists published the *National Gazette*. By the late 19th century, **yellow journalism** emerged (a type of journalism that referred to sensational reporting, rather than reporting well-researched facts). It was during the rise of yellow journalism that the fires for the Spanish-American War were ignited.

William Randolph Hearst, who owned the *New York Journal* during the Spanish-American War, used yellow journalism to sell newspapers. In 1895, revolutionaries in Cuba overthrew their Spanish imperialist rulers. Journalists who wrote stories that twisted facts to influence the public, like those hired by Hearst and Joseph Pulitzer's *New York World,* encouraged U.S. politicians to enter the war. Journalists attacked politicians when politicians hesitated to assist the fledgling nation of Cuba. The departure from traditional reporting during the tense time is actually blamed for contributing, at least in part, to the U.S. entering the war with Spain.

After the battleship *Maine* was sunk in Cuba's Havana Harbor and 260 soldiers were killed, Hearst's journalists blamed Spain, as illustrated on the front page of the *New York Journal* on the next page. Drawing attention to the speculation that the Spanish sunk the American ship, U.S. citizens began to cry for war. Public opinion had instantly shifted due to the influence of yellow journalism reporting.

Source: *New York Journal,* "Destruction of the War Ship Maine Was the Work of an Enemy." February 17, 1898.

Muckrakers

During the Progressive Era in the late 1890s to early 1900s, a new style of reporting emerged. This new wave of investigative journalism focused on reform became synonymous with the term **muckraker** (a journalist who was committed to reporting on political and corporate corruption). The origin of the term first came from writer John Bunyan, but was widely popularized with a speech Theodore Roosevelt delivered: "The men with the muck rakes are often indispensable to the well-being of society; but only if they know when to stop raking the muck."

Today, the term is used to refer to any kind of investigative journalism. Investigative journalists, like muckrakers of the Progressive Era, expose and report instances of fraud and abuse, particularly within government and politics.

Advances in Mass Communication Technologies

Advances in rapid communication, like the smartphone, serve as conduits for increasing speed and maximizing message resonation. As more Americans own smartphones, citizens are instantly linked to government and political news, unlike any time in our nation's history. Citizens can now access an overwhelming amount of information from multiple sources and multiple ideological perspectives, making it difficult to untangle credible sources from unreliable sources.

Increased communication heightens the desire for not only journalistic transparency, but also government transparency. With the advent of the Internet and social media, credibility has become a major issue. Anyone can initiate a website and use it to disseminate information. Stories from these sites are viewed and shared instantaneously via Facebook and Twitter whether the sources are credible or not and when "facts" reported are demonstrably false. This places a burden on citizens to "fact check" their news and ask critical questions about the information they receive. While some outlets like National Public Radio (NPR) are purportedly among the most centrist, others have political allegiances to the Left or the Right.

Chapter Review Practice Questions

The practice questions show the types of questions that may appear on the exam. Practice questions are for instructional purposes only and may not reflect the format of the actual exam. On the actual exam, some questions may be grouped into sets containing one source-based prompt (document or image) and two to five questions. The questions and explanations that follow focus on essential knowledge, the learning objectives, and political science skills.

Multiple-Choice Questions

Questions 1–2 refer to the following graph.

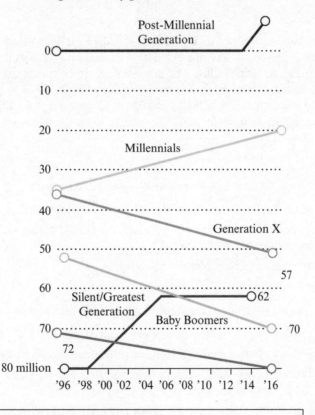

Number of Millennials Eligible to Vote Approaching that of Boomers

Eligible voters by generation, 1996–2016

Post-Millennial Generation (those born after 1996)
Millennials (ages 20 to 35 as of 2016)
Generation X (ages 36 to 51)
Baby Boomers (ages 52 to 70)
Silent/Greatest Generation (ages 71 and older)

1. Which of the following conclusions is reflected in the graph?

    A. The percentage of eligible voters among Baby Boomers has dramatically increased since the 2008 election.

    B. Post-Millennials have the lowest percentage of voter turnout.

    C. The number of eligible voters age 35 and under will outnumber those 52 and older by 2016.

    D. The number of eligible voters among Post-Millennials increased 7 percent from 2014 to 2016.

2. Which of the following is a likely outcome of the trends shown on the graph?

    A. The existing gap between registered Democrats and registered Republicans will continue to grow.

    B. Voter turnout among those 18 to 24 years of age will increase.

    C. The nation at large will become more ideologically conservative.

    D. Voter efficacy will increase.

Questions 3–4 refer to the following excerpt.

> Let's examine how the duopolists try to keep so-called spoilers out of competition.
>
> Starting at the beginning of the process: They've enacted state laws that make it exceedingly difficult for outsiders to even get on the ballot. In California, would-be third-party candidates must submit valid signatures of at least 1% of registered voters (roughly 177,000) 88 days prior to an election. But that's just the technical requirement; practically speaking, it's necessary to submit roughly twice that because state officials jettison so many names.

> —Ralph Nader, *Los Angeles Times*, June 10, 2016.

3. Which of the following statements best reflects Nader's argument?

    A. Federal election laws are used to keep third-party candidates off state ballots.

    B. Third-party candidates cannot be considered "spoilers" because it's impossible for them to get on ballots in large states like California.

    C. California is unfair to minor party candidates.

    D. The two major parties manipulate the system to keep third parties out of the election process.

4. Which of the following assertions would provide additional support to Nader's argument?

    A. Actual third-party "spoilers" are rare in presidential election history.

    B. Nearly 60 percent of Americans favor having a viable third-party option.

    C. Major party sponsorship of the Commission on Presidential Debates ensures that third-party candidates can't participate in national televised debates.

    D. Political elites oppose third-party candidates by denying them access to the public funding option.

Questions 5–6 refer to the following graph.

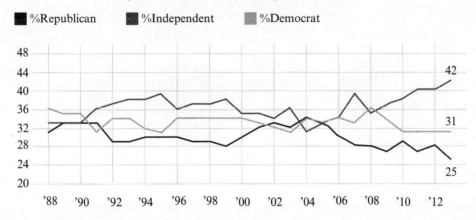

Party Identification, Yearly Averages, 1988–2013

Based on multiple-day polls conducted by telephone

5. Which of the following statements can be supported with data from the graph?

    A. From 1988 to 2013, the number of voters identifying as Republican increased.
    B. The number of voters identifying as Independent spiked in 2013.
    C. The decline in Democratic Party affiliation over time was significantly greater than affiliation with the Republican Party.
    D. The electorate was more polarized on a partisan basis in 1988 than in 2013.

6. Which factor is most likely associated with the party identification data from 2013?

    A. State voter registration laws
    B. Dealignment
    C. Realignment
    D. Aging of the population

Question 7 refers to the following excerpt.

> The fact that Mrs. Clinton won the popular vote may console Democrats, but if that were the measure of victory we would have had a different campaign. Both candidates would have parked themselves in populous states like New York, and Mr. Trump would have spent weeks in Texas. As it is, the Republican nominee didn't compete in Illinois or California, allowing Mrs. Clinton to pile up big majorities. Mrs. Clinton's advantage in California alone—more than 2.7 million votes—accounts for more than her projected margin of victory of about two million.

> —*The Wall Street Journal,* November 2016.

7. Which of the following arguments for retaining the Electoral College is supported by this excerpt?

    A. The process for eliminating the Electoral College is too complex and time-consuming.
    B. The Electoral College ensures broad national support.
    C. The Electoral College supports the traditions of the two-party system.
    D. The popular vote favors Democratic candidates who always win in the largest states.

Question 8 refers to the following two graphs.

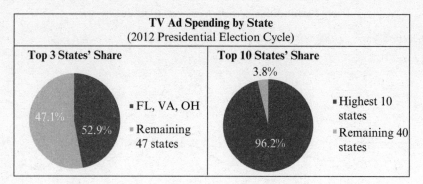

8. Which of the following conclusions can be drawn from the graphs?

    A. Television ad spending decreased during the 2012 presidential election.
    B. Television ad spending was relatively the same for each state during the 2012 presidential election.
    C. Television ad spending increased during the 2012 presidential election.
    D. Television ad spending was highly targeted on battleground states during the 2012 presidential election.

Questions 9–10 refer to the following excerpt.

While both parties, especially Democrats, have altered their primary process and calendar often since the late 1960s, one trend remains constant: campaigns start with the Iowa caucuses, followed by the New Hampshire primaries... The highest number of votes went to front-runner Edmund Muskie and insurgent candidate George McGovern. McGovern's better than expected showing in Iowa boosted his candidacy, and his second place showing in New Hampshire provided more momentum. In 1976, Jimmy Carter won the most votes of any Democratic candidate in Iowa and used this to boost his campaign as he headed to New Hampshire. Carter won New Hampshire before capturing the Democratic Party nomination and, ultimately, the presidency.

—Northeastern University, Boston; U.S. Political Conventions & Campaigns.

9. Which of the following summarizes the central argument of this excerpt?

    A. The Iowa caucus and New Hampshire primary are critical for Democratic candidates seeking the presidency.
    B. The Iowa caucus first became important to the nomination process in 1976.
    C. Victories early in the primary season can elevate lesser-known candidates to front-runner status.
    D. Candidates who win in New Hampshire go on to win the presidency.

10. The factor most associated with the central argument of the excerpt is

    A. Frontloading
    B. Horse-race media coverage
    C. Winner-takes-all
    D. Plurality voting

Free-Response Question

1 question

20 minutes (suggested)

Directions: Write your response on lined paper. You are not required to develop and support a thesis statement. Use complete sentences—bullet points or outlines are unacceptable. Answer **all** parts of the question to receive full credit.

Question 1. Use the graph below to answer all parts of the question that follows.

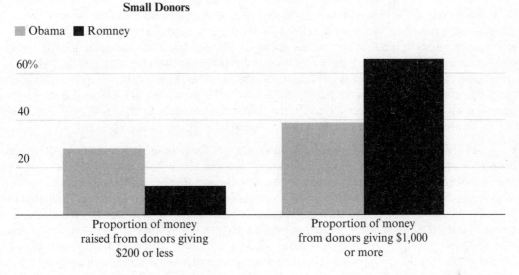

2012 Presidential Election: Percent of Money Raised from Small Donors

1. Using the graph, answer (a), (b), and (c).

   (a) Identify the percentage of money each candidate received from the two donor categories.

   (b) Analyze and describe the difference in donor contributions for Democratic candidate, Obama, and Republican candidate, Romney. Draw a conclusion about why the differences, based on party lines, exist.

   (c) Explain how the graph reflects the ongoing debate about campaign finance reforms.

Answers and Explanations

Multiple-Choice Questions

1. **C.** According to the graph, the population of eligible voters among Millennials by 2016 reached 62 million; Generation X, 57 million; and Post-Millennials, 7 million, for a total of 126 million eligible voters. Conversely, the population of eligible voters among Baby Boomers declined slightly by 2016 to 70 million, and the Silent/Greatest Generation declined precipitously to 28 million by 2016 for a total of 98 million eligible voters. Eligible voters under the age of 35 clearly outnumbered those 52 and older by 2016, choice C. The graph measures the population in the millions of individuals, not by the percent, so neither choice A nor B can be correct. While the youngest range of voters (ages 18–24) tends to have the lowest voter turnout historically, one could assume their turnout in 2016 would be

low as well. However, the data simply provides information about eligible voting numbers and does not address assumptions about voter turnout, so choice D is incorrect.

2. **A.** Generally, in terms of voting behavior, younger voters tend to be more liberal and become more conservative as they age. Since the Republican Party is ideologically conservative and the Democratic Party is more ideologically liberal, the Democrats stand to benefit from the large numbers of young people meeting voter eligibility age, choice A. Whether turnout among any age group will increase (choice B) would be difficult to conclude, particularly with the 18–24 demographic, whose turnout is traditionally low. Since younger citizens tend to be more ideologically liberal and the younger demographic is increasing its presence in the population of eligible voters, it is very unlikely that the nation at large will become more ideologically conservative (choice C). There is no correlation between population increase within certain demographic groups and the level of voter efficacy (choice D).

3. **D.** Nader asserts in the first sentence of the excerpt that Republicans and Democrats ("the duopolists") proactively sabotage the efforts of third-party candidates to compete fairly. One piece of evidence he points to is ballot access laws, using California's law as an example, making choice D the correct answer. States establish their own laws and rules regulating elections, not the federal government (choice A). Nader is not making a case in this excerpt for why third-party candidates cannot be considered spoilers (choice B). While the ballot access law in California does discriminate against third-party candidates (choice C), that is not the overarching argument Nader is making; rather, he uses it as evidence of major party manipulation of the election process.

4. **C.** Nader argues that the "duopolists" (Republicans and Democrats) deliberately sabotage the efforts of third-party candidates. As evidence, he points to ballot access laws, using California's law as an example of requirements placed on minor party candidates that are difficult to attain. Another piece of evidence Nader could use would be the Commission on Presidential Debates, which denies minor party candidates a chance to participate in debates with the major party candidates, choice C. While it is true that third-party spoilers are rare in presidential election history (choice A) and it is also true that nearly 60 percent of Americans want to have the option of voting for third parties (choice B), neither of these responses provides evidence of major party manipulations to keep third parties from competing in elections. The two major parties have no control over which candidates qualify for public funding of their campaigns (choice D).

5. **B.** By 2013, 42 percent of voters identified as Independent, an increase of 10 percent from 1988 and the highest percentage over the 25-year timespan represented on the graph (choice B). The number of Republicans decreased, rather than increased, so choice A is incorrect. While both major parties lost ground over the 25 years shown on the graph, the losses experienced were similar—a 6 percent loss for the Republican Party and a 5 percent loss for the Democratic Party, so choice C is incorrect. The degree of polarization, which is an effect of ideology, is difficult to assess from raw data focused simply on party identification. What is clear is that dealignment of voters from affiliation with either of the two major parties increased over time, which may indicate disenchantment among voters with both parties rather than an ideological shift within the parties, so choice D is also incorrect.

6. **B.** Dealignment refers to decisions reached by voters to end their affiliation with the major parties. It affects both major parties and may be the result of frustration with hyper-partisanship and the inability of office holders from the two major parties to get anything done (gridlock), declining trust in government, or disillusionment with a political process that doesn't seem to serve the interests of the average American. Whatever the reasons, an increase in the number of voters registering as Independent is a signal that voters are dealigning. According to the graph, by 2013, 42 percent of

voters identified as Independents, 31 percent identified as Democrats, and only 25 percent identified as Republicans, so choice B is correct. While there is some speculation that restrictive registration requirements impact traditionally Democratic voters, that hasn't translated into more voters identifying as Republican. Instead, the number of Independent voters reached its highest point in 2013, while voters identifying as Republican reached an all-time low, so choice A can be eliminated. Realignment is marked by large numbers of voters traditionally part of a coalition supporting one of the major parties switching their affiliation to the opposition party. It is a term associated with critical elections and changes in party systems, rather than an abandonment of both major parties in favor of Independent status; thus, choice C can also eliminated. Aging of the population would not necessarily lead to a rise in the number of voters identifying as Independent. To the contrary, older voters are more traditional and tend to adhere to the identification with either of the two major parties, so choice D is also incorrect.

7. **B.** The excerpt addresses the size of the popular vote in large states like New York, Texas, and, more specifically, California. If elections were just determined by the popular vote, then candidates would only spend time trying to curry the favor of voters in those states. Since the Electoral College is designed to maintain a voice for smaller states in the selection of the president, candidates must seek a broader base of national support, choice B. No argument is made in the excerpt about the difficulties involved in eliminating the Electoral College (choice A) or the traditions of the two-party system (choice C). While it is noted that Democratic candidate Hillary Clinton received 2.7 million votes in California, clearly by inference Republican candidates perform better in Texas than do Democrats, and voter demographics are fluid enough to make any absolute statement ("always") about voter outcomes in any particular state incorrect, eliminating choice D.

8. **D.** The two graphs show that 96.2 percent of all campaign spending focused on 10 states, and more importantly for this question, 52.9 percent of all spending focused on only three states—Florida, Virginia, and Ohio, three key swing states, or "battlegrounds," choice D. The graphs provide no data on the amounts spent in the 2012 campaign, so choices A and C cannot be correct. Nor do the graphs indicate a balanced approach to spending since the lion's share of campaign ad spending went to 10 states, eliminating choice B.

9. **C.** George McGovern, an insurgent candidate rather than the front-runner at the beginning of the 1972 campaign, outperformed expectations in the Iowa caucus and came in second in New Hampshire, giving his campaign momentum; he ultimately became the Democratic Party's nominee. The same results happened for little-known candidate Jimmy Carter in 1976. He went from unknown to front-runner by winning both the Iowa caucus and the New Hampshire primary. Since Iowa holds the first caucus and New Hampshire the first primary, choice C is the correct answer. While the examples used are both Democratic candidates, no argument is made that winning in New Hampshire and Iowa is only important to Democrats (choice A), nor is there any assertion that the Iowa caucus only became important after 1976 (choice B). While many candidates who do win in New Hampshire go on to win the presidency, nothing in the excerpt makes the claim that all candidates who win in New Hampshire win the presidency (choice D).

10. **B.** Horse-race media coverage of the top three finishers in primaries and caucuses gives lesser-known or "dark horse" candidates who finish first, second, or third in the first primary and caucus of the campaign season name recognition, free media coverage, and the ability to attract donors, so choice B is the correct answer. Frontloading (choice A) involves states moving their primaries to positions earlier on the campaign calendar and is not the subject of the excerpt, nor is winner-takes-all (choice C) or plurality voting (choice D).

Free-Response Question

The quantitative analysis question asks you to interpret the information provided in the graph. You must analyze the data in the graph to determine what it tells you about the spending profiles of donor categories, political parties, and campaign finance reforms. Based on your knowledge of these three topics, you should be able to plan an appropriate response.

To receive full credit of 4 points, you must address all parts. A good response should:

- Identify the percentage of money each candidate received from the two donor categories. (0–1 point)
- Analyze the difference in donor contributions for Democratic candidate, Obama, and Republican candidate, Romney (0–1 point). Draw a conclusion about why the differences, based on party lines, exist. (0–1 point)
- Explain how the graph reflects the ongoing debate about campaign finance reforms. (0–1 point)

Note: The sample responses for parts (a), (b), and (c) in the table below are for instructional purposes only. On the actual exam, you must write ONE complete essay.

Part	Task	Explanation	Examples
(a) (1 point)	Identify the percentage of money each candidate received from the two donor categories.	Part (a) asks you to make an accurate reading of the data in the graph in relation to the percentage of campaign funds provided by small donors to the two candidates in the 2012 presidential campaign—Barack Obama (D) and Mitt Romney (R).	According to the data in the graphic, of the campaign funds raised by the two candidates in the 2012 presidential election, approximately 30% of money amassed by Barack Obama came from donors giving $200 or less, while only 10% of Mitt Romney's campaign war chest was donated by this same group. On the other hand, Romney raised 68% of his money from donors giving $1,000 or more, while approximately 39% of Obama's funds came from the $1,000 or more group of donors.
(b) (1 point) (1 point)	Analyze and describe the difference in donor contributions for Democratic candidate, Obama, and Republican candidate, Romney. Draw a conclusion about why the differences, based on party lines, exist.	Part (b) asks you to describe the comparative differences in small donor contributions to Barack Obama (D) and Mitt Romney (R) in the presidential campaign of 2012, and to draw a conclusion about the differences which may stem from partisan identification.	Democrats have traditionally garnered support from the working class and the lower middle class, while wealthier Americans, particularly corporate donors, have supported the Republican Party. The numbers seem to conform with this socioeconomic profile of the parties and their candidates, with 68% of Romney's donations drawn from those with disposable incomes, allowing them to give $1,000 or more to political campaigns, while only 39% of Obama's donations came from this group. Conversely, Obama collected 30% of his campaign contributions from the smaller donor group ($200 or less), while Romney acquired only 10% of his funds from this group.

Part	Task	Explanation	Examples
(c) (1 point)	Explain how the graph reflects the ongoing debate about campaign finance reforms.	Part (c) requires knowledge of efforts in support of campaign finance reforms and how data supplied in the graph relate to this issue.	FECA (1971 and 1974) placed limits on individual and PAC donations, but the limits still allow those with higher disposable incomes to have a proportionately larger impact on campaign fundraising than those with lower disposable incomes. With 30% of Obama's donations coming from small donors ($200 or less), while only 10% of Romney's donations came from this group, the data seem to support the traditional view of the Democratic Party as the party of the working class and lower-income middle-class voters and the Republicans as the party of "big business." A recognition of the impact of *Citizens United v. Federal Election Commission* in removing campaign donation limitations by other means (Super PACs and 527 groups) would strengthen the written response; that is, Democrats must rely not only on Super PACs and 527 groups, but must focus more attention on the base of lower-income donors in keeping with their traditional socioeconomic alliances within the electorate.

Sample Student Response

According to the graphic, Democratic candidate Obama received roughly 30% of campaign funds from donors giving $200 or less. On the other hand, Republican candidate Romney received roughly 10% of campaign funds from donors giving $200 or less. For the proportion of money received from donors giving $1,000 or more, Obama received roughly 40% of funds, while Romney received about 70% of campaign funds.

Although the totals for each candidate do not equal 100%, and thus there must be an alternative donor category, the majority of funds are reported in the graphic and show a clear trend within the Romney campaign of raising funds from those donors providing $1,000 or more. While Obama also received a considerable amount of funds from this spending category, the percentage coming from the $200 or less group to the $1,000 or more donor group increased by only 9%. The contrast for Romney was much more significant: the percentage coming from larger donations increasing by approximately 58% over smaller donations. Consequently, it is reasonable to conclude that wealthy benefactors provided much more financial support to Romney than to Obama, who attracted more support among working-class and middle-class individuals than Romney.

The Republican and Democratic parties have historically represented specific demographics, and, as such, have been supported by individuals defined not only by ideology, religion, or ethnicity, but also by socioeconomic status. Socioeconomic status is impacted by a variety of factors, including, but not limited to, relative income and disposable income. Generally, the working class (blue-collar workers) has less disposable income than other socioeconomic groups, and this group aligned with the Democratic Party dating back to the days of the New Deal coalition. Many lower middle-class voters also identified with the economic equity message of the Democratic Party. Alternatively, the Republican Party has been viewed as the party of "big business," adopting policies that favored more wealthy Americans. While the Republican Party made inroads into the Democratic socioeconomic base, a group often referred to as "Reagan Democrats," they retain an identification as the party of wealth and privilege. It is reasonable to conclude, therefore, that the graphic donor data for the Republican candidate Romney and the Democratic candidate Obama is rightly representative of the donor profiles more likely to conform to their respective political party platforms.

The Federal Election Campaign Act of 1971 and subsequent amendments in 1974 placed donation caps on individual and PAC hard money donations given directly to candidates and created the Federal

Election Commission (FEC) to oversee the regulation of campaign donations and expenditures. Indexed to inflation, the limitations currently sit at $2,700 per candidate for individuals and $5,000 per candidate for PACs. The purpose of these limitations was to prevent the wealthiest Americans, and special interests they represent, from dominating the political process. In reality, few working- and middle-class Americans, or more broadly, average Americans, can afford to donate $2,700 to a candidate or even the $1,000 ceiling reflected in the graph. Thus, the data in the graph brings up an important question about the influence of campaign finance in politics. Because the disparity in spending categories is so pronounced with respect to Obama and Romney, it lends credence to socioeconomic demographics playing a role in which candidate donors support. Due to the Citizens United decision delivered by the Supreme Court in 2010, which eliminated any attempts to control the flow of individual and/or corporate donations into Super PACs and 527 groups, it was incumbent on the Obama campaign to broaden its base among small donors to compete with the narrower but wealthier donor class supporting the Republican candidate.

Chapter 9

Full-Length Practice Exam

This chapter contains a full-length practice exam that will give you valuable insight into the types of questions that may appear on the AP GOV exam. As you take this practice exam, try to simulate testing conditions and time limits for each of the following sections:

Section	Questions	Time
Section I: Multiple-Choice Questions	55 questions	80 minutes
Section II: Free-Response Questions		
Concept Application Question	1 question	20 minutes (suggested)
Quantitative Analysis Question	1 question	20 minutes (suggested)
SCOTUS Comparison Question	1 question	20 minutes (suggested)
Argument Essay Question	1 question	40 minutes (suggested)

Answer Sheet for Section I: Multiple-Choice Questions

1	A	B	C	D
2	A	B	C	D
3	A	B	C	D
4	A	B	C	D
5	A	B	C	D
6	A	B	C	D
7	A	B	C	D
8	A	B	C	D
9	A	B	C	D
10	A	B	C	D
11	A	B	C	D
12	A	B	C	D
13	A	B	C	D
14	A	B	C	D
15	A	B	C	D
16	A	B	C	D
17	A	B	C	D
18	A	B	C	D
19	A	B	C	D
20	A	B	C	D
21	A	B	C	D
22	A	B	C	D
23	A	B	C	D
24	A	B	C	D
25	A	B	C	D
26	A	B	C	D
27	A	B	C	D
28	A	B	C	D
29	A	B	C	D
30	A	B	C	D

31	A	B	C	D
32	A	B	C	D
33	A	B	C	D
34	A	B	C	D
35	A	B	C	D
36	A	B	C	D
37	A	B	C	D
38	A	B	C	D
39	A	B	C	D
40	A	B	C	D
41	A	B	C	D
42	A	B	C	D
43	A	B	C	D
44	A	B	C	D
45	A	B	C	D
46	A	B	C	D
47	A	B	C	D
48	A	B	C	D
49	A	B	C	D
50	A	B	C	D
51	A	B	C	D
52	A	B	C	D
53	A	B	C	D
54	A	B	C	D
55	A	B	C	D

Section I: Multiple-Choice Questions

Directions: Read each item and select the best answer.

55 questions
80 minutes

Questions 1–3 refer to the following political cartoon.

Source: Herblock, "What do they expect us to do—listen to the kids pray at *home*?" *The Washington Post,* June 18, 1963.

1. Which of the following Supreme Court cases is reflected in Herblock's political cartoon?

   A. *Engel v. Vitale* (1962)
   B. *Tinker v. Des Moines Independent Community School District* (1969)
   C. *Wisconsin v. Yoder* (1972)
   D. *Roe v. Wade* (1973)

2. Which of the following provisions of the Constitution is reflected in Herblock's political cartoon?

   A. Free Exercise Clause
   B. Due Process Clause
   C. Necessary and Proper Clause
   D. Establishment Clause

3. Which of the following amendments is relevant to Herblock's cartoon?

   A. First Amendment
   B. Second Amendment
   C. Third Amendment
   D. Fourth Amendment

Question 4 refers to the following table.

Presidential Elections of 1824 and 1888				
		Popular Vote		Electoral College
Year	Candidate	Total	Percent	Vote
1824	Adams*	115,696	31.9%	84
	Jackson	152,933	42.2%	99
	Crawford	46,979	13.0%	41
	Clay	47,136	13.0%	37
1888	Harrison*	5,445,269	47.8%	233
	Cleveland	5,540,365	48.65%	158
	Fish	250,122	2.2%	—
	Streeter	147,606	1.3%	—
*Won the election and became president.				

4. Which of the following is a correct inference based on the information presented in the table?

   A. The popular vote directly determined the presidential elections of 1824 and 1888.
   B. In 1824, the House of Representatives determined the winner of the election.
   C. Cleveland should have won the 1888 election.
   D. Andrew Jackson and Grover Cleveland both became presidents after losing an election.

Questions 5–6 refer to the following passage.

Among the numerous advantages promised by a well-constructed Union, none deserves to be more accurately developed than its tendency to break and control the violence of factions. The friend of popular governments never finds himself so much alarmed for their character and fate, as when he contemplates their propensity to this dangerous vice. He will not fail, therefore, to set a due value on any plan which, without violating the principles to which he is attached, provides a proper cure for it. The instability, injustice, and confusion introduced into the public councils, have, in truth, been the mortal diseases under which popular governments have everywhere perished; as they continue to be the favorite and fruitful topics from which the adversaries to liberty derive their most specious declamations.

—James Madison, Federalist No. 10,
"The Unity of the Union as a Safeguard against Domestic Faction and Insurrection," 1787.

5. Which of the following current political issues is most related to Madison's concerns outlined in Federalist No. 10?

   A. Polarization of the electorate
   B. Politicization of the judiciary
   C. Military spending
   D. Internet regulations

6. Which of the following is the best resolution to the issue of factions, as described in Federalist No. 10?

   A. Controlling political parties
   B. Limiting private property ownership
   C. Suppressing religious expression
   D. Establishing a constitutional republic

Questions 7–8 refer to the following passage.

The first question that presents itself on the subject is, whether a confederated government be the best for the United States or not? Or in other words, whether the thirteen United States should be reduced to one great republic, governed by one legislature, and under the direction of one executive and judicial; or whether they should continue thirteen confederated republics, under the direction and control of a supreme federal head for certain defined national purposes only?

This enquiry is important, because, although the government reported by the convention does not go to a perfect and entire consolidation, yet it approaches so near to it, that it must, if executed, certainly and infallibly terminate in it.

—Excerpt from Brutus No. 1, 1787.

7. Which of the following political factions most likely supported the arguments made by the author of Brutus No. 1?

   A. Federalist
   B. Anti-Federalist
   C. Republican Whig
   D. Tories

8. Based on your knowledge of U.S. government and politics, what is the author's central concern?

   A. The principles of a free people
   B. The concentration of power in a central government
   C. The strength of the states' power
   D. The establishment of political parties

Questions 9–10 refer to the following graph.

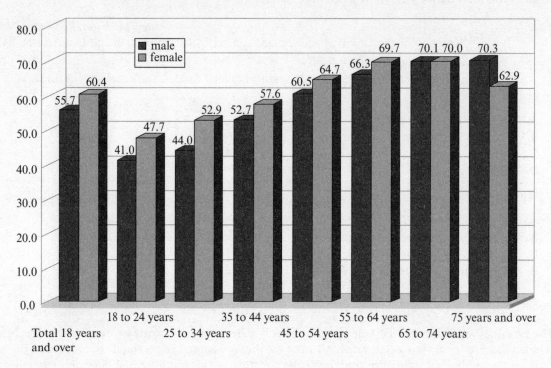

Percentage of Voter Turnout by Sex and Age, 2008 U.S. Presidential Election

9. Which of the following statements can be supported by the data presented in the graph?

   A. Voter turnout in 2008 was greater among males than females in the youngest age demographic groups.

   B. Age had no effect on voter turnout in 2008.

   C. Voter turnout in 2008 was highest among women across most age demographics.

   D. In 2008, gender had the greatest impact on voter turnout in the 55–64 and 65–74 age demographics.

10. Based on the data, which of the following would have been a reasonable conclusion to draw regarding future campaigns for the presidency?

    A. Candidates for the presidency should focus on foreign policy issues.

    B. Social Security and Medicare should be the focus of campaigning in future elections.

    C. To win a party's nomination for the presidency, candidates should focus on motivating younger voters.

    D. Presidential candidates should support policy proposals emphasizing social and economic equality.

Question 11 refers to the following political cartoon.

Source: Adam Zyglis, "We the Corporations." *The Buffalo News,* January 22, 2010.

11. Which of the following Supreme Court cases is depicted in this political cartoon?

   A. *New York Times Co. v. United States*
   B. *United States v. Lopez*
   C. *Citizens United v. Federal Election Commission*
   D. *McDonald v. Chicago*

Questions 12–13 refer to the following excerpt.

No State shall be represented in Congress by less than two, nor more than seven members; and no person shall be capable of being a delegate for more than three years in any term of six years; nor shall any person, being a delegate, be capable of holding any office under the United States, for which he, or another for his benefit, receives any salary, fees or emolument of any kind.

Each State shall maintain its own delegates in a meeting of the States, and while they act as members of the committee of the States.

In determining questions in the United States in Congress assembled, each State shall have one vote.

Freedom of speech and debate in Congress shall not be impeached or questioned in any court or place out of Congress, and the members of Congress shall be protected in their persons from arrests or imprisonments, during the time of their going to and from, and attendence on Congress, except for treason, felony, or breach of the peace.

—Excerpt from the *Articles of Confederation,* March 1, 1781.

303

12. Which of the following proposals adopted at the Constitutional Convention redefined representation as practiced according to this excerpt?

    A. Virginia Plan
    B. Great Compromise
    C. New Jersey Plan
    D. Three-Fifths Compromise

13. Which of the following problems with representation reflected in this excerpt did the agreement reached at the Constitutional Convention rectify?

    A. Disproportionate representation
    B. Lack of term limits
    C. The unchecked sovereignty of the people in selecting representatives to Congress
    D. No specificity on representation for new states entering the Union

Question 14 refers to the following table.

State	Eligible Voters	Florida Votes per Voter	Change to State's Electoral Impact
Wyoming	431,011	3.50	+94%
Vermont	496,439	3.04	+56%
Washington, D.C.	516,771	2.83	+46%
Alaska	519,501	2.85	+44%
North Dakota	582,534	2.59	+18%
Rhode Island	786,111	2.55	+15%
California	25,278,803	1.10	–8%
Texas	17,514,961	1.09	–8%
Michigan	7,431,589	1.08	–9%
Virginia	6,061,032	1.08	–9%
New York	13,593,128	1.07	–10%
Ohio	8,753,269	1.04	–13%
Pennsylvania	9,737,690	1.03	–13%
North Carolina	7,317,507	1.03	–13%
Florida	14,601,373	1.00	–16%

14. Which of the following conclusions can be drawn from the data provided, assuming participation of all voters?

    A. A single voter in Florida has a potentially greater impact on the Electoral College than a single voter in Wyoming.
    B. Florida is underrepresented in its impact on the Electoral College compared to both large and small states.
    C. Individual state size, as measured by eligible voters, is irrelevant to its electoral impact.
    D. Florida's population of eligible voters is decreasing due to massive voter relocation.

Questions 15–16 refer to the following pie chart.

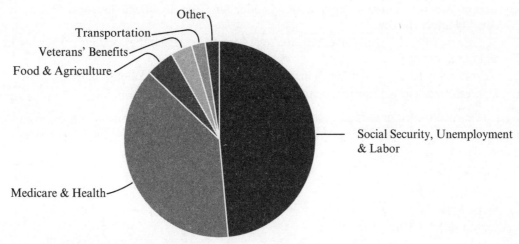

Source: OMB; National Priorities Project.

15. Which of the following expenditures within the federal budget is represented on this graph?

    A. Discretionary spending
    B. Mandatory spending
    C. Authorized spending
    D. Subsidy spending

16. Which of the following conclusions can be drawn from the data in the chart?

    A. U.S. highway funding is a priority.
    B. The Food and Drug Administration receives more from the federal budget than does the Department of Health and Human Services.
    C. The government considers support for aging and low-income populations vital.
    D. Entitlement programs are underfunded relative to other federal programs.

Questions 17–19 refer to the following excerpt.

We know through painful experience that freedom is never voluntarily given by the oppressor; it must be demanded by the oppressed. Frankly, I have yet to engage in a direct action campaign that was "well timed" in the view of those who have not suffered unduly from the disease of segregation. For years now I have heard the word "Wait!" It rings in the ear of every Negro with piercing familiarity. This "Wait" has almost always meant "Never." We must come to see, with one of our distinguished jurists, that "justice too long delayed is justice denied."

—Martin Luther King Jr., *Letter from Birmingham Jail*, 1963.

17. Which of the following statements best summarizes Dr. King's message in this excerpt?

    A.   African Americans have suffered too long under Jim Crow and are no longer willing to wait for equality under the law.

    B.   His release from jail would give African Americans a signal that they no longer had to wait for an end to segregation.

    C.   He was ready to start a new social justice campaign focused on economic equality.

    D.   Oppression can only be overcome through direct action.

18. Based on your knowledge of the Constitution, the quote attributed to "one of our distinguished jurists" is the principle underlying which of the following amendments included in the Bill of Rights?

    A.   First Amendment

    B.   Fourth Amendment

    C.   Sixth Amendment

    D.   Eighth Amendment

19. Which of the following protections extended to citizens by the Constitution is most consistent with Dr. King's message?

    A.   Civil liberties

    B.   Civil rights

    C.   Free exercise

    D.   Due process

Questions 20–22 refer to the following political cartoon.

Source: Paul Tuma, "We Founders call this one The Theory of 'DUH.'" Benjamin Franklin, one of the Founders of our country, critiquing the slogan "Disarming Innocent People Does Not Protect Innocent People."

20. Which of the following Supreme Court cases is illustrated in this political cartoon?

    A. *McCulloch v. Maryland* (1819)
    B. *Wisconsin v. Yoder* (1972)
    C. *Shaw v. Reno* (1993)
    D. *McDonald v. Chicago* (2010)

21. Which of the following interest groups is most likely to support the political message in this cartoon?

    A. NARAL
    B. NOW
    C. NRA
    D. NAACP

22. Based on your knowledge of U.S. government, which of the following amendments does this political cartoon address?

    A. First Amendment
    B. Second Amendment
    C. Third Amendment
    D. Fourth Amendment

Question 23 refers to the following passage.

    Each judge, when deciding a matter before him or her, selects the prior cases on which to rely. Only the holding...of a case can be binding; any remarks unnecessary to the result are non-binding dicta.

    A prior case must meet two requirements to be considered binding precedent. First...the prior case must address the same legal questions as applied to similar facts. The higher the degree of factual similarity, the more weight the judge gives the prior case when deciding the present matter. The second requirement for a case to be considered binding precedent is that it must have been decided by the same court or a superior court within the hierarchy to which the court considering the case belongs.

        —Hon. John M. Walker Jr., Senior Circuit Judge, U.S. Court of Appeals for the Second Circuit; 2016.

23. Which of the following best identifies the judicial principle explained in the excerpt?

    A. *Stare decisis*
    B. Judicial restraint
    C. Writ of *certiorari*
    D. Judicial review

24. Based on your knowledge of U.S. government and politics, which of the following is NOT included among the models of modern democracy?

    A. Participatory democracy
    B. Mass democracy
    C. Pluralist democracy
    D. Elite democracy

25. Which of the following provisions in the Constitution is the foundation for the "preemption doctrine"?

    A. Supremacy Clause
    B. Elastic Clause
    C. Implied powers
    D. Necessary and Proper Clause

26. Based on your knowledge of U.S. government and politics, why was state sovereignty a central feature of the Articles of Confederation?

    A. Elected officials in the former colonies had no experience in governing a nation.
    B. Smaller states feared the power of larger states over issues of national importance.
    C. It was believed that liberty was best ensured by local governance rather than centralized governance.
    D. States did not want to co-mingle their revenues for the purpose of funding a central government.

27. The Electoral College reflects the Founding Fathers' belief in

    A. The wisdom of popular democracy
    B. The potential threat of tyranny when relying on the will of the majority
    C. The limits of state sovereignty in national elections
    D. Control of all political processes by elites

28. Which of the following applies to evidence that is illegally obtained, rendering it unusable against a defendant in a criminal case?

    A. Time, place, manner restrictions
    B. Right to privacy
    C. Exclusionary rule
    D. Selective incorporation

29. Which of the following would a social conservative most likely oppose?

    A. Same-sex marriage
    B. Pro-life movement
    C. Limited discretionary spending
    D. Religious-oriented school activities

30. Based on your knowledge of U.S. government and politics, which of the following qualifications must a prospective senator possess?

    A. Minimum 25 years old
    B. U.S. citizen for at least 9 years
    C. Resident of the state he or she wishes to represent for at least 10 years
    D. An advanced degree in law

31. Which of the following scenarios lends itself to the characterization of a sitting president as a "lame duck"?

    A. Richard Nixon's impeachment by Congress
    B. Franklin D. Roosevelt's fourth term as president
    C. Dwight D. Eisenhower's election to the presidency in 1952 following military service
    D. Incumbent Jimmy Carter's defeat for reelection in 1980 by Ronald Reagan

32. Based on your knowledge of U.S. government and politics, which of the following federal agencies oversees cyberspace safety?

    A. Securities and Exchange Commission (SEC)
    B. Federal Election Commission (FEC)
    C. Department of Homeland Security (DHS)
    D. Environmental Protection Agency (EPA)

33. Based on your knowledge of U.S. government and politics, the Nineteenth Amendment

    A. Grants women the right to vote
    B. Enables private citizens to directly elect senators
    C. Eliminates poll taxes
    D. Alters the minimum age to vote in federal elections

34. The *Federalist Papers* were instrumental in developing support for the government formed by the Constitution. Which of the following was the central theme of the *Federalist Papers*?

    A. The need for a Bill of Rights to protect the rights of the people
    B. The need for a strong central government to govern the country effectively
    C. The need to protect small states against the tyranny of the majority
    D. The need to strengthen the Articles of Confederation but still protect states' rights

35. Based on your knowledge of U.S. government and politics, which of the following is NOT classified as a linkage institution?

    A. Interest groups
    B. Mass media
    C. Elections
    D. Congress

36. Based on your knowledge of U.S. government and politics, which of the following statements reflects what the Founding Fathers believed about political parties?

    A. They are necessary for the healthy function of a democracy.
    B. They create a plurality of ideas.
    C. They foster disunity and hinder the decision-making process.
    D. They ensure transparency in the processes of governing.

37. Which of the following incentives would an interest group be most likely to use in order to overcome its "free-rider" problem?

    A. Offer publication subscriptions to members
    B. Host public raffles
    C. Promise legislative jobs to members
    D. Hold monthly telethons

38. Based on your knowledge of U.S. politics, which of the following best describes the term "hard money"?

    A. Cash given to political candidates by corporations
    B. Direct contributions to political candidates
    C. Donations used for specific party-building activities
    D. Money given to advance a particular law

39. Which of the following best identifies the issue that was resolved by reaching the Three-Fifths Compromise in 1787?

    A. Authority over interstate commerce
    B. Property qualifications for voting rights
    C. The importation of slaves
    D. Representation in Congress

40. Which of the following federal institutions can check an executive order?

    A. The House of Representatives
    B. The Senate
    C. The Supreme Court
    D. The federal bureaucracy

41. Which of the following is NOT considered a political effect associated with third-party candidacies in national elections?

    A. An increase in voter interest and turnout
    B. The possibility of taking votes away from one of the major party candidates and spoiling their chances for victory
    C. Greater bipartisanship within the two major governing parties
    D. The adoption of sideline agendas into the main platforms of the two major parties

42. Which one of the following played a key role in John F. Kennedy's defeat of Richard Nixon in the election of 1960?

    A. JFK's wartime service
    B. Nixon's ties to McCarthyism
    C. The televised debates between the two candidates
    D. Their widely diverging views on how to deal with the Soviet Union

43. Which of the following is an accurate comparison of the roles of the judicial and executive branches?

	Judicial Branch	Executive Branch
A.	Justices serve a for a fixed term	President appoints federal justices
B.	Can declare laws unconstitutional	Can issue executive orders
C.	Checks itself	Is checked by the legislative branch
D.	District judges are self-appointed	Can impeach justices

44. Which of the following is an accurate comparison of Federalist and Anti-Federalist views on government?

	Federalist	Anti-Federalist
A.	Strong state governments	Strong central government
B.	Articles of Confederation	Constitution
C.	Limit state power	Expand state power
D.	Bill of Rights	No Bill of Rights

45. Which of the following is an accurate comparison of the two Supreme Court cases?

	Baker v. Carr (1962)	*Shaw v. Reno* (1993)
A.	Determined Tennessee did not violate Equal Protection Clause	Determined North Carolina violated Equal Protection Clause
B.	Invoked Article II of the Constitution	Invoked standard of strict scrutiny
C.	Judiciary excluded itself from overseeing redistricting	Reversed district court ruling
D.	Each individual must be rightly represented in legislative appointment	Redistricting according to race is unconstitutional

46. Which of the following is an accurate comparison of Federalist No. 51 and Federalist No. 78?

	Federalist No. 51	Federalist No. 78
A.	Central idea is checks and balances	Central idea is the judicial branch
B.	Advocates for a unicameral Congress	Sees the judicial branch as weak
C.	Argues for the ratification of the Constitution	Argues for a single executive (president)
D.	Written by Hamilton	Written by Madison

47. Which of the following is an accurate comparison of the Articles of Confederation and the U.S. Constitution?

	Articles of Confederation	U.S. Constitution
A.	Bicameral Congress	Unicameral Congress
B.	1-year term for all office holders	2-year terms for representatives 6-year terms for senators
C.	Strong central government	State sovereignty above centralized federal authority
D.	Congress can regulate interstate trade	Congress can tax individuals

48. Based on your knowledge of U.S. government and politics, which of the following was the Founding Fathers' primary purpose in establishing checks and balances?

A. To keep one branch from becoming too popular
B. To avoid the concentration of power in a single branch of government
C. To make government accountable
D. To place ultimate sovereignty in the people

49. Which of the following political ideologies supports limiting government economic intervention to the protection of property rights and instituting policies promoting voluntary trade?

A. Liberal
B. Conservative
C. Libertarian
D. Keynesian

50. Which of the following forms of mass communication is increasingly favored by 21st-century political parties to increase popularity?

    A. Television
    B. Radio
    C. Newspaper
    D. Internet/social media

51. Which of the following forms of political participation would be considered a "competing actor" with interest groups?

    A. Social movements
    B. Membership in non-governmental organizations (NGOs)
    C. Partisan electioneering
    D. Conducting voter registration drives

52. Which of the following impacts on the policymaking process was an intentional outcome of a constitutional foundation that emphasized the separation of powers?

    A. Public policy results from a competitive democratic process.
    B. Public policy is a collaborative result of contributions by all three branches.
    C. Public policy is always a reflection of what is best for the common good.
    D. The machinery of policymaking develops and implements public policy efficiently.

53. Which of the following best describes the *Brown v. Board of Education of Topeka* (1954) ruling?

    A. The busing of students to achieve desegregation in schools was legal.
    B. The Board of Education of Topeka could not fairly allocate resources to its schools because African Americans were prohibited from seeking elected positions on the board.
    C. Separate facilities based on race were inherently unequal, and desegregation of public schools must commence immediately.
    D. Black students should be provided with additional opportunities to prepare for standardized testing, which was determined to have inherent cultural biases.

54. The advancement of civil rights legislation is most impacted by citizen-state interactions and which of the following?

    A. Political party influences
    B. Social movements and interest groups
    C. Interpretation of the Constitution over time
    D. Media's representation of institutionalized racism

55. Which of the following was the result of the decision rendered by the Marshall Court in *Marbury v. Madison*?

    A. The extension of the federal government's power to define and regulate interstate commerce
    B. A prohibition against federal laws affecting gun control in public schools
    C. An endorsement of the implied powers doctrine
    D. The establishment of the Court's power of judicial review

IF YOU FINISH BEFORE TIME IS CALLED, CHECK YOUR WORK ON THIS SECTION ONLY. DO NOT WORK ON ANY OTHER SECTION IN THE TEST.

Section II: Free-Response Questions

Question 1

20 minutes (suggested)

Directions: Write your response on lined paper. The question will not require that you develop and support a thesis statement. Use complete sentences—bullet points or outlines are unacceptable. Answer **all** parts of the question to receive full credit.

Question 1. Use the scenario below to answer all parts of the question that follows.

> The winners of Tuesday's elections—Republican or Democrat, for governor, mayor or dogcatcher— all have one thing in common: They received more votes than their opponent. That seems like a pretty fair way to run an electoral race, which is why every election in America uses it—except the most important one of all. Was it just a year ago that more than 136 million Americans cast their ballots for president, choosing Hillary Clinton over Donald Trump by nearly three million votes, only to be thwarted by a 200-year-old constitutional anachronism designed in part to appease slaveholders and ratified when no one but white male landowners could vote? It feels more like, oh, 17 years—the last time, incidentally, that the American people chose one candidate for president and the Electoral College imposed the other.
>
> —"Let the People Pick the President." Editorial Board, *New York Times*; November 7, 2017.

1. After reading the scenario, respond to (a), (b), and (c) below:

   (a) Describe how this scenario reflects the allocation of Electoral College votes after the general election.

   (b) In the context of the scenario, explain how the allocation of votes described in part (a) can impact political behavior, including voter turnout.

   (c) In the context of the scenario, explain a possible remedy to the situation referenced in parts (a) and (b).

IF YOU FINISH BEFORE TIME IS CALLED, CHECK YOUR WORK ON THIS QUESTION ONLY. DO NOT WORK ON ANY OTHER QUESTION IN THE TEST.

Question 2

20 minutes (suggested)

Directions: Write your response on lined paper. The question will not require that you develop and support a thesis statement. Use complete sentences—bullet points or outlines are unacceptable. Answer **all** parts of the question to receive full credit.

Question 2. Use the infographic below to answer all parts of the question that follows.

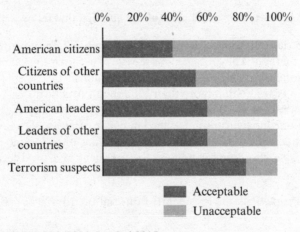

Listening In

Opinions of U.S. adults on whether it is acceptable or unacceptable for the American government to monitor communications from:*

*Nov 26th 2014–Jan 3rd 2015

2. After reviewing the infographic, respond to (a), (b), and (c) below:

   (a) Identify the attitude that American citizens have toward government monitoring of communications of American citizens and various other groups.
   (b) Describe the difference in attitudes between the government monitoring potential terrorism suspects vs. the government monitoring American citizens. Draw a conclusion about why the differences in attitudes are justifiable.
   (c) Explain how the infographic reflects the ongoing debate about the role of central government and the rights of individuals.

IF YOU FINISH BEFORE TIME IS CALLED, CHECK YOUR WORK ON THIS QUESTION ONLY. DO NOT WORK ON ANY OTHER QUESTION IN THE TEST.

Question 3

20 minutes (suggested)

Directions: It is suggested that you take a few minutes to plan and outline your essay. Write your response on lined paper. You must demonstrate your understanding of course content, disciplinary practices, and reasoning processes. Your essay is considered a first draft and may contain some grammatical errors that will not be counted against you. However, to receive full credit, your essay must demonstrate defensible content knowledge with substantive examples where appropriate.

Question 3. Use the passages below to answer all parts of the question that follows.

Passage 1

Under our Constitution, free speech is not a right that is given only to be so circumscribed that it exists in principle, but not in fact. Freedom of expression would not truly exist if the right could be exercised only in an area that a benevolent government has provided as a safe haven for crackpots. The Constitution says that Congress (and the states) may not abridge the right to free speech. This provision means what it says. We properly read it to permit reasonable regulation of speech-connected activities in carefully restricted circumstances. But we do not confine the permissible exercise of First Amendment rights to a telephone booth or the four corners of a pamphlet, or to supervised and ordained discussion in a school classroom.

—*Tinker v. Des Moines Independent Community School District* (1969).

Passage 2

Words which would ordinarily be within the freedom of speech protected by the First Amendment may become subject to prohibition when of such a nature and used in such circumstances as to create a clear and present danger that they will bring about the substantive evils which Congress has a right to prevent. The character of every act depends upon the circumstances in which it is done.

—*Schenck v. United States* (1919).

3. Using the passages above, answer (a), (b), and (c).

   (a) Identify the principle enshrined in the Bill of Rights that is common to both *Tinker v. Des Moines Independent Community School District* and *Schenck v. United States*.
   (b) Based on the constitutional principle identified in part (a), provide facts from the Supreme Court cases and explain why the circumstances surrounding *Schenck v. United States* led to a different holding than the ruling in *Tinker v. Des Moines Independent Community School District*.
   (c) Explain how the Court has refined its opinion over the years since *Schenck v. United States*.

IF YOU FINISH BEFORE TIME IS CALLED, CHECK YOUR WORK ON THIS QUESTION ONLY. DO NOT WORK ON ANY OTHER QUESTION IN THE TEST.

Question 4

40 minutes (suggested)

Directions: It is suggested tthat you take a few minutes to plan and outline your essay. Write your response on lined paper. You must demonstrate your understanding of course content, disciplinary practices, and reasoning processes. Your essay is considered a first draft and may contain some grammatical errors that will not be counted against you. However, to receive full credit, your essay must demonstrate defensible content knowledge with substantive examples where appropriate.

Question 4. Develop an argument that analyzes how the Founding Fathers' concern about the influence of political factions impacted the constitutional framework.

In your essay, you must:

1. Articulate a defensible claim or thesis that responds to the prompt and establishes a line of reasoning.
2. Support your claim with at least TWO pieces of accurate and relevant information:
   (a) At least ONE piece of evidence must be from one of the following foundational documents:
   - U.S. Constitution
   - Federalist No. 10
   (b) Use a second piece of evidence from other foundational documents listed or from your study of the foundations of constitutional democracy.
3. Use reasoning to explain why your evidence supports your claim/thesis.
4. Respond to an opposing or alternative perspective using refutation, concession, or rebuttal.

IF YOU FINISH BEFORE TIME IS CALLED, CHECK YOUR WORK ON THIS QUESTION ONLY. DO NOT WORK ON ANY OTHER QUESTION IN THE TEST.

Answer Key for Section I: Multiple-Choice Questions

1. A	12. B	23. A	34. B	45. D
2. D	13. A	24. B	35. D	46. A
3. A	14. B	25. A	36. C	47. B
4. B	15. B	26. C	37. A	48. B
5. A	16. C	27. B	38. B	49. C
6. D	17. A	28. C	39. D	50. D
7. B	18. C	29. A	40. C	51. A
8. B	19. B	30. B	41. C	52. A
9. C	20. D	31. D	42. C	53. C
10. D	21. C	32. C	43. B	54. C
11. C	22. B	33. A	44. C	55. D

Answer Explanations

Section I: Multiple-Choice Questions

1. **A.** *Engel v. Vitale* was the Supreme Court case regarding prayer in public schools, choice A. The Supreme Court decided that prayer in public schools violated the First Amendment, which prohibits state-sanctioned religion in public schools. *Tinker v. Des Moines Independent Community School District* (choice B) addressed First Amendment rights (freedom of symbolic speech) and the right of students to wear black armbands at school to protest the Vietnam War. In *Wisconsin v. Yoder* (choice C), the Court ruled that compulsory education for Amish students past eighth grade was unconstitutional based on the free exercise of religion. *Roe v. Wade* (choice D) affirmed that women have the constitutional right to have an abortion under the Fourteenth Amendment (the right to privacy under the Due Process Clause).

2. **D.** The subject of the cartoon is the Supreme Court's ruling in *Engel v. Vitale*. The Court's decision struck down laws allowing use of a school-sanctioned prayer in public school classrooms even if the prayer is non-denominational and participation is voluntary. When the New York Board of Regents authorized the recitation of a prayer to start the school day, it violated the "wall of separation" between church and state created by the Establishment Clause, choice D. This was not a case involving the Free Exercise Clause (choice A) because the question at hand did not involve an agency of the state denying a citizen the right to freely exercise the tenets of their faith. The Due Process Clause (choice B) is embedded in the Fourteenth Amendment and prohibits any state from denying to its citizens due process of the law. Clearly the Due Process Clause has no relevance to the cartoon or school prayer. The Necessary and Proper Clause (choice C) is also irrelevant to prayer in school. This clause authorizes Congress to make any laws "necessary and proper" to the carrying out of its powers and duties enumerated in the Constitution.

3. **A.** The First Amendment states that Congress shall not establish a religion in a separation of church and state, choice A. The Second Amendment (choice B) states that citizens have the right to bear arms. The Third Amendment (choice C) addresses the quartering of soldiers. The Fourth Amendment (choice D) protects citizens against unreasonable searches and seizures.

4. **B.** The Electoral College is established in Article II of the Constitution and also in the Twelfth and Twenty-Third amendments. The Electoral College is based on state representation (House and Senate) in Congress. The Twelfth Amendment included the provision that the House of Representatives elects the president if a candidate does not receive an absolute majority of the electoral vote. An absolute majority is one more than half of the total electoral vote. The Twenty-Third Amendment, passed in 1960, added three electoral votes for the District of Columbia. In the elections of 1824, 1876, 1888, and 2000, the losing candidate received more popular votes but still lost the election. When a candidate fails to win an absolute majority of the electoral vote, the House determines the presidency, with each state receiving one vote. In the election of 1824, the House voted for Adams, making choice B correct. The election of 1824 is unique in that Jackson received more electoral and popular votes but still lost the election since he did not receive an absolute majority of the electoral vote, thus making choice A incorrect. Choice C is an opinion, and choice D is a correct statement but does not address the question. Note: Cleveland is the only president in U.S. history to serve two nonconsecutive terms (1884 and 1892).

5. **A.** In Federalist No. 10, Madison addresses his concerns about the violence of factions ("a number of citizens"). The key to understanding this excerpt is his reference in the subtitle of the essay to unity as the safeguard against instability and insurrection. The increased level of polarization in the electorate has led to the breakdown of public discourse on issues and politicians using the situation to drive further wedges between citizens rather than uniting them. The gridlock resulting in Washington as the two major parties refuse to cooperate and compromise with one another undermines the people's faith in the government and contributes to rising anger in the electorate. Consequently, polarization of the electorate, choice A is the most appropriate answer. While many citizens and political scientists have raised concerns about the politicization of the judiciary (choice B), judicial independence from partisan politics is not an issue addressed by Madison. Military spending (choice C) is an implausible option despite direct references to "violence" and "insurrection" in the excerpt. Madison's words do not address a relationship between instability and the military since no standing army existed at the time Madison wrote his essay. His reference is to a faction-driven insurrection of citizens, with one faction trying to wrest control from another. Although federal agencies monitor the transmission of information over the Internet (choice D), modes of communication and how to regulate them are not relevant to the excerpt.

6. **D.** The only possible option to remedying the issue of factions, as evidenced in Federalist No. 10, is through the establishment of a large, diverse republic such as the one proposed in the Constitution, choice D. Madison saw the Constitution as forming a happy combination of a republic and a democracy. The word "control" indicates that the government should somehow be involved in political parties, which is not what the Founding Fathers had intended, eliminating choice A. Limiting private property ownership (choice B) is not a viable resolution to factions. The suppression of religious expression (choice C) would violate individual liberty, the protection of which the Founding Fathers believed was the whole purpose of government.

7. **B.** The republican Whigs (choice C) and Tories (choice D) were colonial factions taking sides with either the revolutionaries (Whigs) or the loyalists (Tories). The Federalists (choice A) and Anti-Federalists (choice B) were the two post-revolution factions whose principle point of contention was the proposed centralization of power in a new constitutional government which would replace the Articles of Confederation. The excerpt expressly discourages the consolidation of powers granted to 13 sovereign states into one republic, clearly putting "Brutus" in the Anti-Federalist camp, so choice B is correct. The Federalist opposition supported the consolidation "Brutus" questions, so they would not have supported his views.

8. **B.** The main idea of the passage is that a large republic that centralizes power, as proposed in the Constitution, is an unacceptable proposition, choice B. The principles of a free people (choice A) are outlined in the U.S. Constitution, and therefore, not relevant to this passage. The strength of the states is what an Anti-Federalist would support, eliminating choice C. The establishment of political parties (choice D) is not relevant to the passage since Federalists and Anti-Federalists focused their debate on the form the new constitutional government would take at a time when organized political parties did not exist.

9. **C.** Based on the data provided in the 2008 voter turnout graph, voter turnout was greater among females in all of the age demographics except age 65–74 and over age 75; consequently, choice C is the correct answer. Turnout among female voters was greater than turnout among males in the first three demographic age groups on the graph representing younger voters, so choice A is clearly incorrect. Looking at age without regard to gender, there is a clear trend on the graph indicating that voter turnout increases with age, so choice B is also incorrect. In the 55–64 and 65–74 age groups, the turnout gap between females and males was 3.4 percent and 0.1 percent, respectively, indicating that gender had the least impact rather than the greatest impact on voter participation, making choice D incorrect.

10. **D.** Since turnout among female voters is greater in nearly every age demographic, it would be reasonable for candidates to assume that support for issues of equality would be highly relevant and motivating for these voters (choice D). While some female voters can be motivated on foreign policy issues (choice A), particularly war, most tend to be more interested in "kitchen table" economic issues (those policy issues that have the greatest impact on the financial stability of their families) and social issues, particularly those impacting their standing as equal members of society; therefore, choice A would not be a reasonable conclusion to draw. Social Security and Medicare (choice B) are policy issues with a high degree of voter intensity among voters in the older age demographics, but not among all age groups. Candidates for the presidency hoping for success wouldn't focus on a single age or gender demographic, but rather, would support issues highly relevant across age and gender lines. While motivation of younger voters (choice C) might be considered beneficial, the graph gives no indication of the raw numbers of voters turning out in each age group. Given the growing numbers of voters in the youngest demographics and those reaching voting age within the next decade, all candidates should consider an appeal to younger voters, but this data is not available on the graph. More critically, given the history of voting behavior, motivating younger voters would help Democratic candidates more than Republican candidates, so Republican candidates would not necessarily draw a conclusion that getting more younger voters to participate is a good idea.

11. **C.** This cartoon references the Supreme Court's decision in *Citizens United v. Federal Election Commission* (choice C), in which a majority on the high court ruled that corporations are the equivalent of people with the same free speech rights guaranteed for individuals. Accordingly, the free speech rights of corporations cannot be infringed by limiting their independent expenditures during elections. The constitutional issue in the *New York Times Co. v. United States* case (choice A) was freedom of the press, not the free speech rights of corporations. The extent of congressional authority under the Commerce Clause was the issue in *United States v. Lopez* (choice B) and had nothing to do with the constitutional protections for corporations under the Bill of Rights. The Second Amendment and whether this amendment protected an individual's right to possess a firearm for self-defense was the focus in *McDonald v. Chicago* (choice D), so there is no relevance to the cartoon.

12. **B.** The Great Compromise (choice B) redefined representation as practiced under the Articles of Confederation. As the excerpt makes clear, the Confederation Congress was unicameral (a single chamber), with each state apportioned a number of delegates according to its population, and each delegate granted a single vote. The Great Compromise created a bicameral Congress, with each state apportioned representatives in the House of Representatives based on population and each state apportioned an equal number of two Senators in the upper chamber. The Virginia Plan (choice A) was James Madison's proposal for representation, but it was not adopted by the Constitutional Convention; the same is true of the New Jersey Plan (choice C). The Three-Fifths Compromise (choice D) addressed how slaves should be counted for the purposes of representation and taxation.

13. **A.** Representation under the Articles of Confederation was disproportionate (choice A) because by granting only one vote to each state, small states had the ability to support or block legislation that the majority of the population living in large states had no proportionate ability to counteract. Term limits (choice B) were actually imposed in a roundabout way in the Articles of Confederation by allowing state delegates to serve only 3 years of a 6-year term. It was the Constitution that placed no term limits imposed on members of Congress, rather than the other way around. The excerpt indicates that the choice of delegates to the Confederation Congress was left to the states and makes no explicit provision for selection by popular vote, so choice C is incorrect. The issue of representation for new states entering the Union (choice D) is not included in the excerpt and was also not addressed in the Constitution.

14. **B.** This question requires students to apply their knowledge of reapportionment and its impact on the Electoral College to understanding the table provided. The 2010 census showed enough of an increase in Florida's population to increase its number of representatives in the House by two. Since the number of representatives apportioned to states in Congress determines their number of electoral votes, Florida also increased its electoral votes by two. Despite increasing its electoral votes by two, Florida remains underrepresented compared to small states but also compared to other underrepresented large states like California and New York. A single vote in those states is worth 1.10 and 1.07, respectively, compared to a single vote cast in Florida; therefore, choice B is correct. Florida voters lag far behind Wyoming (choice A) with votes in this sparsely populated state worth 3.5 votes compared to a single vote cast in Florida when divided by its allotted electoral votes; clearly, choice A is incorrect. The population of a state clearly matters in terms of impact on the Electoral College since even the smallest state is guaranteed at least three electoral votes. At the same time, the largest states are limited in their ability to expand their electoral impact since membership in the House is limited to 435 and the number of electoral votes is based on this number plus 100 (for the Senate). Five hundred and thirty-five electoral votes divided among the states restricts the largest states in acquiring representation and electoral votes commensurate with their actual size; consequently, choice C is incorrect. Florida's population of eligible voters is increasing, not decreasing, and the causative factors behind population changes are not discernable from the data provided on this table, so choice D is also incorrect.

15. **B.** The two forms of spending used as classifications in the federal budget are mandatory and discretionary. The pie chart represents mandatory spending, choice B, on entitlements such as Social Security, disability, and Medicare as well as SNAP (food stamps), agricultural subsidies, and certain transportation infrastructure projects. Discretionary programs (choice A), which require congressional appropriations and authorizations, are not included. Authorized spending (choice C) and subsidy spending (choice D) are not classifications used in representing federal budget spending.

16. **C.** Based on the information provided, it can be reasonably concluded that the government considers aging and low-income populations important, as evidenced through the large allocations for Social Security, unemployment, and Medicare, choice C. Transportation is a small part of the federal budget, eliminating choice A. Health and Human Services oversees the largest portion of the budget, eliminating choice B. Entitlement programs (choice D) are heavily funded.

17. **A.** Dr. King makes clear that waiting for an end to segregation imposed by Jim Crow laws was not an option because oppressors never give up their power over the oppressed voluntarily, so the clear answer is choice A. King's *Letter from Birmingham Jail* was not focused on his release from jail (choice B), but on the compelling reasons for the justice protests taking place in Birmingham. King's social justice crusade for economic equality (choice C) was not fully launched until the last year of his life (1968), and the focus of the excerpt is segregation, not economic inequality. That oppression can only be overcome through direct action (choice D) is certainly a statement with which King would have probably agreed, but it is not the central point of this excerpt.

18. **C.** This question requires students to demonstrate their knowledge of the Bill of Rights, which is included in the Constitution, a required foundational document for the AP GOV exam. The Sixth Amendment (choice C) guarantees a speedy and public trial to an accused person. This guarantee stems from the principle that justice delayed is justice denied, making choice C correct. The First Amendment (choice A) extends protections for the free expression of ideas via speech, religion, press, assembly, and petitioning the government for redress of grievances; it does not involve issues of justice. The Fourth Amendment (choice B) involves due process and could be interpreted as being related to justice; however, this amendment establishes the warrant requirement for a reasonable search of a person and does not address delaying justice. The Eighth Amendment (choice D) addresses prohibitions about cruel and unusual punishment rather than the delay of justice.

19. **B.** This question requires an understanding of civil rights vs. civil liberties. Civil rights (choice B) protect citizens from unequal treatment based on gender, race, or disability. Since Dr. King addressed injustice related to racial segregation, the excerpt is related to civil rights. Civil liberties (choice A) are rights guaranteed to the individual as protections against abridgment of liberty exercised by the federal government. Civil liberties are enshrined in the Bill of Rights. Free exercise (choice C) prevents the government from interfering with religious practices based on the First Amendment, not racial discrimination addressed by Dr. King. While Dr. King was in jail when he wrote the letter, his message is not concerned with his own rights of due process or the Due Process Clause of the Fourteenth Amendment in general (choice D); instead, his focus is on the Equal Protection Clause, which is relevant to the protection of civil liberties.

20. **D.** *McDonald v. Chicago* addresses the issue of the right to bear arms, which is protected under the Second Amendment, choice D. *McCulloch v. Maryland* (choice A) is based on the Supremacy Clause, which declares that state law is unconstitutional if it conflicts with a law passed by Congress under the authority of its implied powers. *Wisconsin v. Yoder* (choice B) addresses the issue of compulsory school attendance and prevents the government from compelling students to attend school past the eighth grade, citing First Amendment rights. *Shaw v. Reno* (choice C) addresses the issue of voter redistricting.

21. **C.** This political cartoon is particularly relevant to the NRA (National Rifle Association), which would likely support its message and the right to bear arms, choice C. NARAL (National Association for the Repeal of Abortion Laws) is a pro-choice organization (choice A). NOW (National Organization for Women) is an American feminist organization (choice B). The NAACP (National Association for the Advancement of Colored People) ensures the equal rights to advance African Americans, including national initiatives for political, educational, economic, and social advancements (choice D).

22. **B.** The Second Amendment is relevant to the right to bear arms, which is the central focus of the cartoon, choice B. The First Amendment (choice A) is relevant to freedom of speech, religion, the press, and assembly. The Third Amendment (choice C) is relevant to the quartering of soldiers. The Fourth Amendment (choice D) is relevant to the rights of citizens to be free from unreasonable search and seizure.

23. **A.** *Stare decisis* literally means to "let the decision stand; do not disturb settled matters," which was established by the highest courts in setting legal precedents for the lower courts to follow, choice A. Judicial restraint (choice B) is the legal concept of a judge limiting his or her power to allow the legislative branch and states to resolve an issue (unless the case necessitates striking down a law). A writ of *certiorari* (choice C) is an order from a superior court for the transcripts of a case decided by a lower court and is an essential element in the appeals process. It does not address the rule of precedent described in the excerpt. Judicial review (choice D) empowers the judiciary to review the actions of the legislative and executive branches and is a concept unrelated to this excerpt.

24. **B.** Mass democracy is not a model of democracy, choice B. Mass democracy is defined as society choosing and voting for its political leaders, rather than partaking in a democratic election. For example, President Andrew Jackson was in office from 1829 to 1837. Participatory democracy (choice A) emphasizes citizen participation in political decision making and the implementation of policy decisions. Pluralist democracy (choice C) emphasizes the role non-governmental interest groups play in influencing public policies; no one group dominates political decision making. Elite democracy (choice D) is a form of representative democracy in which a small group of well-educated people make policy decisions. These representatives are elected and act as trustees.

25. **A.** The Supremacy Clause in Article VI is the foundation for the preemptive doctrine, which allows the federal courts to invalidate state laws in conflict with the Constitution, federal laws, and treaties, choice A. The Elastic Clause (choice B) is the same as the Necessary and Proper Clause (choice D), which grants Congress the power to pass laws that are necessary and proper to carry out powers. The Necessary and Proper Clause in Article I established the foundation for the implied powers doctrine (choice C) as ruled in *McCulloch v. Maryland* (1819). The Court ruled that Congress had the power to establish a national bank and carry out necessary functions (e.g., collecting taxes and regulating commerce).

26. **C.** The Articles was a wartime government designed to unify the states in the revolution against British control, but those who designed the framework did not trust a centralized, unitary government. It was such a government based in London, remote from the needs and concerns of its colonies, which the revolution was designed to expel. For this reason, sovereignty over local affairs was considered essential to defending the liberty of the people against the tyranny of monolithic centralized power; therefore, choice C is the correct answer. While the inexperience of colonial officials with running a national government (choice A), fear among the smaller states that they would be overpowered by larger states in a centralized government (choice B), and the co-mingling of state revenues (choice D) may have all been matters of concern, they did not serve as the organizing principle behind a confederation of sovereign states.

27. **B.** The Founding Fathers were aware of the dangers posed by a system based on direct participation by all citizens and relying on the will of the majority. This was one of the clear warnings James Madison sounded in his Federalist No. 10. There existed a distrust of the majority, who could use their considerable power to suppress the rights of the minority. Most of the Founding Fathers held little faith in the masses to make rational political decisions and trusted themselves much more. Therefore, the Electoral College is a model for indirect democratic decision making, with the popular vote for the presidency counting for nothing in the original constitutional design. Instead, experienced electors would be selected by state legislatures to make the decision regarding who would be president. The system also ensured that states with the largest populations couldn't minimize the voice of smaller states in the election of a president. Alexander Hamilton proposed the Electoral College in Federalist No. 68. He argued that it was important for people to choose their candidate, but it was also important that "electors" could ensure that each state had an equal chance to choose a candidate. Therefore, choice B is correct. This rationale for the Electoral College reflects a belief in total contradiction with popular democracy (choice A). The limits placed on state sovereignty (choice C) are not relevant to the Electoral College, and while the Founding Fathers had greater faith in the elite (choice D) than in the masses, they did provide for an element of popular democracy in the election of members of the House of Representatives.

28. **C.** The Due Process Clause prevents infringements of basic civil liberties and privacy. The Due Process Clause provides the basis for the exclusionary rule, which prevents evidence that is illegally acquired to be used against a defendant in a criminal case, choice C. Time, place, and manner restrictions (choice A) concern the issue of free speech. The right to privacy (choice B) is a Fourth Amendment protection. Selective incorporation (choice D) prevents state lawmakers from enacting laws that violate personal liberties, as detailed in the Bill of Rights.

29. **A.** A social conservative would most likely oppose same-sex marriage, choice A. A social conservative would most likely favor the pro-life movement (choice B). A social conservative is not necessarily a fiscal conservative, although the issue of limiting discretionary spending may be relevant (choice C). A social conservative would most likely be in favor of including religious-oriented school activities (choice D).

30. **B.** A senatorial candidate must be a U.S. citizen for at least 9 years before running for office, choice B. A prospective senator must be at least 30 years of age and be a resident of the state he or she wishes to represent at election time, eliminating choices A and C. The candidate is not required to have an advanced law degree (choice D), although many senators do have advanced law or business degrees.

31. **D.** In politics, a *lame-duck* president is a reference to an incumbent president who runs for reelection and loses. The final months of their presidency between the general election in November and the inauguration of a new president in January is referred to as the lame-duck period. A president can also be considered a lame duck during the final months of their second term when the nation's attention is captured by the newly elected president. Ronald Reagan's election in November 1980 made the incumbent president Jimmy Carter a lame duck until January 1981, choice D. President Nixon resigned from office, so Congress did not pursue impeachment, eliminating choice A. Franklin D. Roosevelt held the presidency from 1933 to 1945, but died while he was in office, eliminating choice B. Dwight D. Eisenhower (choice C) was in office from 1953 to 1961. He successfully won two terms in office, but his initial victory, built largely on his military reputation, is not relevant to the term "lame duck."

32. **C.** The Department of Homeland Security watches over and protects activity on the Internet and the data superhighway, choice C. The Securities and Exchange Commission (SEC) manages the financial market and protects investors, choice A. The Federal Election Commission (FEC) oversees elections and enforces campaign finance laws, choice B. The Environmental Protection Agency (EPA) protects health and the environment, choice D.

33. **A.** The Nineteenth Amendment granted women the right to vote and prohibited American citizens from being denied the right to vote based on sex, choice A. The Seventeenth Amendment allowed citizens to directly elect senators so that "the Senate shall be composed of two senators from each state" (choice B). The Twenty-Fourth Amendment abolished poll taxes aimed at denying African Americans the right to vote (choice C). The Twenty-Sixth Amendment lowered the minimum voting age from 21 years old to 18 years old (choice D).

34. **B.** In the Federalist Papers, James Madison, Alexander Hamilton, and John Jay argued in support of a strong central government, choice B. Their 85 essays, most of which were written by Madison, were published collectively as The Federalist (1788) and were designed to convince the influential "laggard states" of New York and Virginia to ratify the Constitution. The authors convincingly argued for a strong national government with enough power to protect the liberty of the people at home and defend the interests of the country abroad. They also pointed out the limitations and weaknesses of the Articles of Confederation, justifying rejection of the entire framework in favor of the Constitution, so choice D is incorrect. An objection to the proposed new government was that individual liberties were not protected. This was corrected by adding the Bill of Rights as the first 10 amendments to the Constitution (choice A), but these were not added until after the Federalist Papers were published and the Constitution ratified. While tyranny of the majority (choice C) was a concern of the authors and Madison addressed it in Federalist No. 10, it was not the central organizing theme of the entire body of work.

35. **D.** A linkage institution connects the people to the government. Congress, choice D, is not a linkage institution, but is part of the government (executive, congressional, and bureaucratic). Interest groups (choice A), mass media (choice B), and elections (choice C) serve to connect (or link) people to the institution of government. Therefore, the only choice that is not a linkage institution is choice D.

36. **C.** The Founding Fathers believed that the formation of political parties (the formal organization of rival factions) would undermine unity within the republic and thereby hinder decision making by the government, choice C. John Adams wrote, "There is nothing which I dread so much as a division of the republic into two great parties." George Washington's farewell address warned fellow Americans about the dangers of political parties. Although the Founders believed that free thought was necessary, the partisan format of political parties today is an accurate reflection of what the Founders imagined would happen in the U.S., so choice A is clearly incorrect. The Founding Fathers' beliefs about political parties involved the threat to civic unity and the dangers of the emergence of a popular majority, which would potentially threaten the rights of minority interests. Their discussion of this issue did not involve a "plurality of ideas" (choice B) or the transparency of government processes (choice D).

37. **A.** Interest groups are mostly voluntary associations that set out to accomplish political policy goals. A free-rider problem refers to the problem of getting members when people can gain benefits without membership. One of the most common ways that interest groups overcome their free-rider problem is by offering publication subscriptions to members. Publications are a relatively inexpensive, yet a tangible, incentive that encourages some people to join interest groups, choice A. Hosting public raffles (choice B) can be a tactic used by interest groups to overcome the free-rider problem, although it is not one of the most economical and impactful activities. Promising legislative jobs to members (choice C) would be a conflict of interest for interest groups and therefore would not be considered an adequate response to the free-rider problem. Monthly telethons (choice D), like public raffles, are sizeable events that cost time and money for the interest group to establish, and are therefore an ineffective solution to combat the free-rider problem.

38. **B.** Hard money in politics is the direct monetary donations given to a political candidate and is strictly regulated by the Federal Election Commission (FEC), choice B. Soft money, on the other hand, includes indirect cash contributions given to political candidates by corporations (choice A), donations used for specific party-building activities (choice C), and money given to advance a particular law (choice D). Soft money is donated in a way that leaves the contribution unregulated.

39. **D.** The Three-Fifths Compromise was reached at the Constitutional Convention in 1787 to address the issue of state representation between larger states and smaller states (and particularly between northern and southern states), choice D. To appease delegates from states with large populations of slaves, delegates reached a compromise to count slaves as "three-fifths" of a person to apportion U.S. representatives, presidential electors, and taxes. Although the issue of slavery is at the heart of the compromise (choice C), the compromise was reached to solve the issue of state representation. This issue was not commerce (choice A) or property (choice B).

40. **C.** The president can issue executive orders, but only the Supreme Court (choice C) can declare such actions unconstitutional. Neither the House (choice A) nor the Senate (choice B) has the authority to reverse an executive order, nor does any agency of the federal bureaucracy (choice D).

41. **C.** Third-party insurgencies are not common in American politics, nor are they often successful, but when they occur, they can impact elections and have political consequences. One complaint about the "duopoly" of the party system is that elections lack a competitive edge, which suppresses voter interest. Third-party candidates often provide a level of competition that increases voter interest and voter turnout on Election Day (choice A). Third-party candidates, such as Theodore Roosevelt in 1912 and Ralph Nader in 2000, have a tendency to attract more voters from one major party than the other. By peeling off these voters, the chances for victory for the one major party candidate are diminished, if not ruined, in what is referred to as the "spoiler effect" (choice B). To win back voters wooed by third-party candidacies, major parties often adopt some of the third party's policy proposals and incorporate them into their own platforms (choice D). There is no evidence that third-party candidacies compel a greater degree of bipartisanship among major party officials in their approach to governing, so choice C is the correct answer

42. **C.** The Kennedy-Nixon debate was the first televised presidential debate in U.S. history. While radio listeners declared Nixon to be the unequivocal winner, television viewers said that Kennedy unquestionably won the debate. Nixon's disheveled appearance, when contrasted to Kennedy's polished looks, cost him the debate and, many political scientists believe, ultimately, the election, choice C. JFK's wartime service (choice A) was not a central issue in the 1960 election. Nixon's ties to McCarthyism (choice B) did not necessarily hurt his chances for the presidency during the 1960 election. While both Kennedy and Nixon had varying views on how to deal with the Soviet Union (choice D), this was not the most overwhelming reason contributing to Nixon's defeat.

43. **B.** The judicial branch can declare laws unconstitutional, and the executive branch can issue executive orders, choice B. Justices serve for life, not a prescribed amount of time (eliminating choice A); the president appoints federal justices. Each branch is checked; therefore, the judicial branch does not check itself (eliminating choice C), and the executive branch is checked by the legislative branch. District court judges are not self-appointed, but rather are nominated by the president and confirmed by the Senate (eliminating choice D); the legislative branch, not the executive branch, can impeach justices (further eliminating choice D).

44. **C.** Federalists wanted to limit state power, and Anti-Federalists wanted to expand state power, choice C. Federalists advocated for a strong central government; Anti-Federalists advocated for strong state governments, eliminating choice A. The Articles of Confederation was preferred by Anti-Federalists because the Articles limited the central government, and the Constitution was preferred by Federalists, eliminating choice B. The Federalists argued against a Bill of Rights, and the Anti-Federalists argued for a Bill of Rights, eliminating choice D.

45. **D.** *Baker v. Carr* determined that each individual must be rightly represented in legislative appointment, and *Shaw v. Reno* determined that redistricting according to race is decidedly unconstitutional, choice D. The outcome of *Baker v. Carr* determined Tennessee to be in violation of the Fourteenth Amendment's Equal Protection Clause (eliminating choice A); *Shaw v. Reno* did determine North Carolina to be in violation of the Equal Protection Clause. *Baker v. Carr* invoked Article III of the Constitution (rights of the federal government), not Article II (eliminating choice B); *Shaw v. Reno* did invoke a standard of strict scrutiny. In *Baker v. Carr*, the judiciary did not exclude itself from overseeing redistricting (eliminating choice C); *Shaw v. Reno* was remanded back to the district court (further eliminating choice C).

46. **A.** In Federalist No. 51, the central idea is checks and balances; in Federalist No. 78, the central idea is the judicial branch, choice A. Federalist No. 51 advocates for a bicameral, not a unicameral, Congress (eliminating choice B); Federalist No. 78 views the judicial branch as inherently weak. Federalist No. 51 argues for the ratification of the Constitution; Federalist No. 78 is concerned with the judiciary, not the executive branch (eliminating choice C). Federalist No. 51 was written by Madison, and Federalist No. 78 was written by Hamilton (eliminating choice D).

47. **B.** The Articles of Confederation provided for a 1-year term, while the Constitution stipulated 2-year terms for representatives and 6-year terms for senators, making choice B an accurate comparison. The Articles of Confederation stipulated a unicameral Congress, while the Constitution provided for a bicameral Congress (eliminating choice A). One of the problems of the Articles of Confederation was that the central government was weak, so the Constitution was designed to combat the issue of central government impotency by preventing state sovereignty from superseding the power of the federal government (eliminating choice C). In the Articles of Confederation, Congress could not regulate interstate trade (eliminating choice D), but in the Constitution, Congress can tax individuals.

48. **B.** The Founding Fathers established checks and balances to maintain the separation of powers between the three branches and thereby avoid a concentration of too much power in a single branch, choice B. Without specific powers granted to each branch for restraining the actions of the others, simply separating the branches would be insufficient to avoid the tyranny the Founding Fathers feared. The popularity of any given branch was not a concern (choice A). While one might view government accountability (choice C) as one of the goals of checks and balances, accountability is more often associated with elections and it was not the primary purpose of the Founding Fathers in creating the system of checks and balances. The sovereignty of the people (choice D) is unrelated to the system of checks and balances.

49. **C.** According to Libertarians, the only role of government intervention should be protecting private property rights, settling disputes, and providing a legal framework to protect voluntary trade, choice C. The platform of the Libertarian party promotes civil liberties, no government intervention, no welfare, and laissez-faire capitalism. Libertarians are in favor of the free enterprise system (the rights to choose a business, own private property, engage in competition, and make a profit). Liberals (choice A) generally favor more government economic intervention. Conservatives (choice B) generally favor less government economic intervention but do not limit intervention as strictly as do Libertarians. Keynesian economic theory proposes proactive government intervention in the economy to maintain growth and stability, but it is not a political ideology, eliminating choice D as a possible answer.

50. **D.** In the 21st century, mass media has taken a popular role of influencing political socialization and public opinion. Political socialization is shaped by all forms of mass media, but the Internet and social modes of communication (Twitter, Facebook, etc.) have become increasingly popular for political parties to spread ideologically oriented platforms, choice D. Candidates can easily communicate to potential voters, and political messages can easily be disseminated without additional campaign costs. Television (choice A), radio (choice B), and newspapers (choice C) are important platforms for political candidates, but are not favored over Internet/social media.

51. **A.** Social movements can often give rise to the development of interest groups, but are commonly considered competing actors of interest groups, choice A. Social movements are much larger than interest groups and are in partnership with many different groups, including interest groups, which have the shared intention of influencing the government and policies. On the other hand, interest groups have broad alliances and have more organization, money, and power to shape legislative policy preferences. One concern about interest groups, however, is that they promote self-interest at the expense of what is good for society, causing social movements to organize. Non-governmental organizations, or NGOs (choice B), are international non-profit groups that are not affiliated with or directed by any government. Generally, they focus their efforts on humanitarian assistance, human rights, healthcare, and environmental issues. Membership in these organizations is unrelated to domestic political maneuvering and is, therefore, not considered a "competing actor" in the political arena. Partisan electioneering (choice C) is a form of political participation in which members of interest groups often take part, but the action itself is not a "competing actor." As with choice C, conducting voter registration drives (choice D) is a form of political participation, but such drives are often conducted by interest groups themselves, so would not be considered a "competing actor."

52. **A.** By separating powers, the Founding Fathers created multiple points of access for American citizens to have their voices heard and influence public policy. Through a variety of linkage institutions that serve to connect citizens to their government, through individual participation, or through collective action via interest groups, Americans compete for influence over the policymakers who hold elective office, so choice A is the correct answer. Collaboration between the three branches (choice B) was not the intent of the Founding Fathers in separating powers between three branches; in fact, their intent was to keep them from collaborating and to act as a check on one another. Public policy does not always result in the public good (choice C). While that might be the expectation, because policymaking is competitive, the loudest voices (through activism or the donation of large sums of money to campaigns) often exert the greatest influence over public policy. This can result in policy that serves narrow interests rather than the public good. The machinery of policymaking does not develop and implement public policy efficiently, eliminating choice D. It often takes many months, if not years, for the machinery of government to finally decide upon and implement a policy. In the 1960s, for example, African American activists began their pressure to pass a comprehensive civil rights bill as John F. Kennedy was inaugurated in 1960. Due to opposition from many quarters, a bill was not developed by the Kennedy administration until 1963, and it was not signed into law (the Civil Rights Act of 1964) by President Johnson until a year after President Kennedy's assassination. The competing voices on this issue made the process of policymaking protracted, bitter, and hardly efficient.

53. **C.** A class action lawsuit brought by 13 parents, led by Oliver Brown, again the Board of Education of Topeka, Kansas, for racial discrimination ended with a landmark unanimous decision by the U.S. Supreme Court. The Court ruled that the segregation enforced in Topeka schools denied African American students equal educational opportunities and was thus a violation of the Equal Protection Clause of the Fourteenth Amendment, choice C. This decision overturned *Plessy v. Ferguson,* which first endorsed the concept of "separate but equal" in 1896. Busing (choice A) as a remedy for segregation was part of the *Swann v. Charlotte-Mecklenburg Board of Education decision, not Brown v. Board of Education of Topeka.* The racial

makeup of the Topeka School Board (choice B) was not at issue in *Brown v. Board of Education of Topeka*. Standardized testing (choice D) was not at issue in 1954, or in this case.

54. **C.** How the Constitution is interpreted over time, particularly how decisions are handed down from the Supreme Court, carries the most political influence to advance civil rights legislation, choice C. Political party influence (choice A) can either negatively hamper or positively impact civil rights legislation. Citizen-state interactions can be illustrated by citizen participation in social movements and interest groups. In this way, social movements and interest groups exist within the sphere of citizen-state interactions, but this is not the best choice from the answers listed, eliminating choice B. The media's representation of racial disparities (choice D) can help viewers' perceptions, but it is not the best choice.

55. **D.** By striking down the Judiciary Act of 1789 as unconstitutional, the Marshall Court marked *Marbury v. Madison* (1803) as a landmark case that formed the basis of the Court's power of judicial review under Article III of the Constitution, choice D. The federal government's authority over interstate commerce (choice A) was established by another Marshall case, *Gibbons v. Ogden*. The issue of federal authority to pass laws affecting gun control in public schools (choice B) was decided in 1995 by a ruling handed down by the Rehnquist Court in *United States v. Lopez*. An endorsement of the implied powers doctrine (choice C) was a result of the Marshall Court ruling in *McCulloch v. Maryland*.

Section II: Free-Response Questions

Question 1

This concept application question asks you to interpret the information provided in the scenario. You must analyze the scenario to determine what it tells you about the Electoral College. Based on your knowledge of the Electoral College, you should be able to narrow down your topic considerably.

To receive full credit of 3 points, you must address all three parts. A good response should:

- Describe how this scenario reflects the allocation of Electoral College votes after the general election (0–1 point).
- In the context of the scenario, explain how the allocation of votes described in part (a) can impact political behavior, including voter turnout (0–1 point).
- In the context of the scenario, explain a possible remedy to the situation referenced in parts (a) and (b) (0–1 point).

Sample Student Response

The Electoral College operates on the basis of winner-takes-all. All states are apportioned a number of electoral votes out of a fixed total of 538 electors. The number of electors each state receives corresponds to the number of seats they hold in the House of Representatives, plus their two Senate seats. The Twenty-Third Amendment also gave Washington, D.C., three electoral votes. In the winner-takes-all system, the candidate who wins the most votes in any given state takes all of that state's allocated electors. The only exceptions to the winner-takes-all rule are Maine and Nebraska. The scenario presented is at the heart of the ongoing debate regarding the validity and necessity of the Electoral College as a winner-takes-all system. As mentioned in the scenario, the current setup of the Electoral College seems to violate the notion of "one person, one vote." According to the presented scenario, a vote in Wyoming during the 2012 election was worth 2.87 California voters in terms of respective state electoral votes. Clearly, this winner-takes-all system violates the constitutional principle of "one person, one vote," with voter representation skewed to advantage voters in Wyoming, for example, as opposed to those in California.

The immediate impact on voter behavior can be directly seen in voter turnout. With television news outlets offering minute-by-minute coverage of presidential elections, how voters interpret those messages matters greatly. Due to time zone differences, the results of statewide voting in east coast and Midwestern states are being reported, along with an Electoral College vote countdown, before polls have closed on the west coast. If a media reports that one candidate has clinched the magic number of 270 Electoral votes by winning enough of the early statewide elections, voters in the west, Hawaii, and Alaska may not be motivated to get out and vote. If the election of a president relied on the popular vote, absent a landslide, the winner could not be declared until after the last polls closed.

Turnout in midterm congressional elections is consistently and predictably lower than it is in presidential elections. The reasons for this are varied (e.g., media coverage of presidential elections is more intense; voter interest in presidential elections is higher) but has little or nothing to do with Electoral College and winner-takes-all.

According to the scenario, the setup of the Electoral College is inherently designed to reward certain voters while punishing other voters. Ongoing debates centered around the validity of "one person, one vote" can affect voter behavior and their faith in the democratic process. One possible remedy is already used by Maine and Nebraska, the two exceptions to winner-takes-all. These two states use the proportional district system. The popular vote in each district determines which candidate receives the state's electoral votes. If one candidate wins the popular vote in a district, they get the electoral vote associated with that district. If the opposition candidate wins the popular vote in a neighboring district, they get that electoral vote. The overall popular vote winner in statewide voting receives the two electoral votes allocated for the state's two Senate seats. While this system gets closer to the "one man, one vote" principle, it still dismisses the voice of some voters. A candidate in a given district might receive 40% of the vote in that district, but the electoral vote will go to the opposition's candidate if that candidate gets even 41% of the vote. If the remaining votes go to a third-party candidate, these voters also have their voices ignored. This also raises the problem of gerrymandering and how it could impact presidential voting. Partisan gerrymandering of districts by state legislatures could unfairly skew the overall electoral vote allocation for the state. As the title of the excerpt suggests, the people should choose the president through the popular vote rather relying on an outdated system that undermines faith in democracy. Getting rid of the Electoral College would automatically end "winner-takes-all" because there wouldn't be any electors to allocate. In a simple contest determined by who gets the most votes, voters nationwide would know that every vote counts and would be more motivated to turn out.

Question 2

This quantitative analysis question asks you to interpret the information provided in the graph. You must analyze the data in the graph to determine what it tells you about American attitudes toward communication monitoring. Based on your knowledge of U.S. government and politics, you should be able to narrow down your topic considerably.

To receive full credit of 4 points, you must address all parts. A good response should:

- Identify the attitude that American citizens have toward government monitoring of communications of American citizens and various other groups (0–1 point).

- Describe the difference in attitudes between the government monitoring potential terrorism suspects vs. the government monitoring American citizens (0–1 point). Draw a conclusion about why the differences in attitudes are justifiable (0–1 point).

- Explain how the infographic reflects the ongoing debate about the role of central government and the rights of individuals (0–1 point).

Sample Student Response

According to the graphic, only 40% of U.S. adults believe that it is acceptable for the American government to monitor American citizens. On the other hand, the polled individuals, by an average of nearly 60%, believed that it is acceptable to monitor citizens of other countries, American leaders, and leaders of other countries. Finally, over 80% of polled U.S. citizens believed it was acceptable to monitor terrorism suspects. Presumably, the category of monitored terrorism suspects could include both suspected domestic or international terrorists.

Following the terrorist attacks perpetrated on September 11, 2001, the U.S. government passed a series of laws enabling agencies to monitor communications information, including telephone calls and Internet activity. This was later translated into the bulk collection of telecommunications data by the National Security Agency (NSA), made possible by Section 215 of the USA PATRIOT Act. This enabled the government to gather metadata related to telecommunications of all Americans in an attempt to identify potential terrorist suspects, hence the term "bulk collection."

The bulk collection of data raised a red flag with the American Civil Liberties Union. The ACLU concern is supported by the data from the public opinion infographic polled at the end of 2014 and early 2015. The vast majority of the American people felt it was either unnecessary, or more critically, unconstitutional for the government to collect communications data from American citizens without the probable cause to do so. On the other hand, over 80% of polled individuals felt that it is entirely acceptable for the government to monitor terrorism suspects.

The attitudes depicted in the infographic clearly reflect the ongoing debate about the role of central government intervening in the lives of individuals. The question of privacy intrusion is not a minor one; from the inception of the country, the courts have repeatedly addressed questions as to the role of the government in monitoring and overseeing activity that could potentially be deemed a "clear and present danger," with some cases stepping over into the free speech arena as well. The Fourth Amendment to the Constitution protects an individual's right to privacy, which is particularly relevant in the case of communications collection. For example, in Carpenter v. United States (2018), the Supreme Court ruled that the government needs a warrant before having access to cell phone location data, citing the Fourth Amendment. Although the government's interest in intercepting or overseeing information must be entirely compelling, there have been times that the government has unilaterally invaded citizen privacy for the sake of preserving the good of the nation as a whole.

This is perfectly illustrated in the passage of the USA PATRIOT Act, Section 215, which enabled the government to collect phone records in bulk. However, it was struck down when the court of appeals found, in May 2015, that the systematic collection of Americans' phone records in bulk was unconstitutional. The disparity in attitudes in monitoring communications between American citizens in general vs. suspected terrorists reflects the idea that, while Americans value safety, they also value privacy, unless absolutely warranted.

Question 3

This SCOTUS comparison question asks you to identify the principle of free speech and compare two relevant cases, *Tinker v. Des Moines Independent Community School District* and *Schenck v. United States*. In these cases, was freedom of speech protected under the First Amendment? What considerations distinguished the similarities and/or differences in the rulings? Based on your knowledge of judicial decision making, how has the Court changed its opinion over time?

To receive full credit of 4 points, you must address all parts. A good response should:

- Identify the principle enshrined in the Bill of Rights that is common to both *Tinker v. Des Moines Independent Community School District* and *Schenck v. United States* (0–1 point).

- Based on the constitutional principle identified in part (a), provide facts from the Supreme Court cases, and explain why the circumstances surrounding *Schenck v. United States* led to a different holding than the ruling in *Tinker v. Des Moines Independent Community School District* (0–1 point).
- Explain how the Court has refined its opinion over the years since *Schenck v. United States* (0–1 point).

Sample Student Response

The constitutional principle common to both <u>Tinker v. Des Moines Independent Community School District</u> and <u>Schenck v. United States</u> is free speech. Free speech, which is guaranteed to all American citizens under the Bill of Rights, was the central concern in both of the Supreme Court cases. It is important to note, however, that the right to free speech is not absolute. As demonstrated in <u>Tinker</u> and <u>Schenck</u>, the Court has always reserved the right to interpret, under the Constitution, what actually qualifies as "protected free speech." This demonstrates the idea that the provisions of the Bill of Rights are continually being interpreted to balance the power of government and civil liberties of individuals.

During the Vietnam War, students from Des Moines, Iowa, gathered at another student's home to plan revealing their support for a ceasefire in Vietnam by wearing black armbands to school as a symbol of their solidarity. However, the principals of their school intercepted the students' plan and preemptively established a policy that was designed to prevent those students from wearing the armband; they were asked to remove their armbands. Even still, the students came to school with their armbands and were sent home. This action was repeated and ultimately ended with the parents of the students suing the school district for violating their right to free speech via expression in <u>Tinker v. Des Moines Independent Community School District</u> (1969). Ultimately, the Court ruled on the side of the students. In the landmark ruling, the Court determined that students did not "shed their constitutional rights to freedom of speech or expression at the schoolhouse gate" because the students' expression was "pure speech" and not aggressive.

In another case, <u>Schenck v. United States</u> (1919), Schenck, a protester of World War I, developed leaflets to be distributed to those being drafted for war. In the leaflet, Schenck expressly encouraged potential draftees to actively pursue, through peaceful action, a petition to appeal the Selective Service Act of 1917, which enabled the government to draft individuals for World War I via conscription. Further, invoking the Thirteenth Amendment, Schenck declared via the leaflet that individuals were not required to submit to involuntary servitude and, as such, could freely refute the mandatory draft. After sending out more than 15,000 leaflets, Schenck was arrested and sentenced to 30 years in prison. Following his conviction, Schenck appealed to the Supreme Court on the grounds that his First Amendment right to free speech was violated. The Court heard the argument and affirmed the lower court's conviction of Schenck. Famously citing Schenck's actions as posing a "clear and present danger," Oliver Wendell Holmes delivered the majority opinion.

While <u>Tinker</u> and <u>Schenck</u> both, at least on the surface, present the issue of First Amendment violations, the difference between the two, as evidenced in the differing rulings by the Court, is that the case involving Tinker did not include actions that seemed to pose a "clear and present danger," which was the case with Schenck's actions. However, this difference in outcome may be one reflected by the times. That is, following Schenck's case in the 1920s, the same justice, Oliver Wendell Holmes, effectively redacted his precedented "clear and present danger" test and replaced it with the "bad (or dangerous) tendency" test, as evidenced in the case of <u>Gitlow v. New York</u> (1925). By the 1930s, the Supreme Court substantially altered its conception of government suppression of free speech. In fact, it subjected cases that punished free speech to strict scrutiny. Although the ruling in <u>Tinker</u> was not directly related to the "bad (or dangerous) tendency" test and was instead related to practical interference during the course of the school day, the previous cases, including that of <u>Schenck</u>, certainly paved the way for subsequent cases regarding the Court's opinion on free speech.

Question 4

To achieve the maximum score of 6, your response must address the scoring criteria components in the table that follows.

Scoring Criteria for a Good Argument Essay		
Question 4: Develop an argument that analyzes how the Founding Fathers' concern about the influence of political factions impacted the constitutional framework.		
Scoring Criteria	**Disciplinary Practice**	**Examples**
A. THESIS/CLAIM		
(1 point) Presents a historically defensible thesis that establishes a line of reasoning. (Note: The thesis must make a claim that responds to *all* parts of the question and must *not* just restate the question.)	Practice 5.a	A good response to this question has a central thesis that articulates how the Founders' concern with factions translated itself into their decisions about the structure of the constitutional government and how it had an explicit effect on the constitutional framework. **Purpose:** To demonstrate how the Founders' fear of factionalism had an explicit impact on the framework of government established by the Constitution. **Defensible claim:** The Founders' fear of a majority faction threatening the rights of minority interests led to many of the decisions reached about the framework of government.
B. EVIDENCE		
(3 points) Uses TWO pieces of specific and relevant evidence to support the argument (must be linked to the question). OR **(2 points)** Uses ONE piece of specific and relevant evidence to support the argument (must be linked to the question). OR **(1 point)** Describes one piece of evidence that is accurately linked to the topic of the question. (Note: To earn more than 1 point, the response must establish an argument and have earned the point for Thesis/Claim.)	Practice 5.b	Remember to aim for the most possible points. To accomplish this, you must address at least two pieces of relevant evidence to support your argument. First, select a founding document from the list, then select a second founding document from the list or from your study of the electoral process. In this case, Federalist No. 10 and the U.S. Constitution were selected. **Federalist No. 10:** What is the purpose of the document? What evidence directly supports the claim that concern about factions impacted the constitutional framework? ■ Madison's argument that factions undermine civic unity and the possibility of a majority emerging put the rights of minority interests at risk. ■ The unequal distribution of property is the leading cause of factionalism and resentment.

Scoring Criteria	Disciplinary Practice	Examples
		U.S. Constitution: ■ How does the wording of the Constitution lead to a conclusion that the Founders hoped to avoid the possibility of organized factions? ■ Organized factions in the form of political parties are granted no role in the wording of the Constitution. The role that parties play in the organization and leadership of Congress developed over time. For example, the committee system is not articulated in the Constitution, nor is the practice of the position of Speaker of the House going to the leader of the majority party articulated. Federalist No. 10 and the U.S. Constitution reveal the Founders' concern about the rights of the minority elite faction in the face of organized opposition by the popular majority faction.
C. REASONING		
(1 point) Uses reasoning to organize and explain how or why the evidence supports the claim or thesis. (Note: To earn this point, you must have earned a point for Evidence.)	Practice 5.c	Federalist No. 10 conveyed the deep hesitation Madison felt about factions, particularly factions driven by the unequal distribution of property. He argues that the creation of a large, diverse republic would mitigate against the emergence of a single majority faction that might result in the oppression of religious, ethnic, or economic minority factions.
D. ALTERNATIVE PERSPECTIVES		
(1 point) Responds to an opposing or alternative perspective using refutation, concession, or rebuttal that is consistent with the argument. (Note: To earn this point, your response must have a claim or thesis.)	Practice 5.d	After determining which foundational documents to use, tie those together in a coherent, persuasive argument that articulates a solid defense of your thesis. You must also be able to use an alternative perspective that is consistent with the argument. Explain how the Constitution promotes popular sovereignty.

Sample Student Response

The Founders had deep concerns about the influence of factions, and this concern was foundational not only to many of the debates at the Constitutional Convention but to the ultimate framing of the Constitution itself. Though grounded in Enlightenment thinking about "consent of the governed," the Founders believed that factional divisions would provide opportunities for the popular majority to overwhelm the interests of minority factions. The importance of this issue is evidenced in Federalist No. 10. Madison's entire essay is dedicated to the pernicious effects of factions and how the Constitution creates safeguards against popular majoritarianism. While in Federalist No. 10 Madison focuses on the creation of a large, diverse republic as one of these safeguards, his Madisonian model for constitutional government affected many other important features of the constitutional framework.

Federalist No. 10 details the issue of factions as related to the distribution of property. Rightly so, Madison pointed out that unequal distribution of property is the most common factor undermining civic unity by driving wedges between the "haves" and the majority who were counted among the "have nots." While Madison points out that religion and other differences can drive populations into factional divides, he argued that the great diversity of one large republic would minimize the possibility of say, one religious faction oppressing another. Concern still remained, however, about economic disparity since, according to Madison, this factor compels envy and animosity more than any other. The fact that the Constitution makes no provision for the role of factions in the form of political parties attests to the Founders' aversion to the possibilities of organized majority opposition to minority interests. Instead, the Founders relied on the framework of government itself to incorporate "consent of the governed," grounded in the principle of popular sovereignty, but to moderate the impact of majority factions by decisions reached regarding a bicameral Congress, the election of senators and the president, and removing the judicial branch from popular accountability altogether. While members of the House of Representatives were to be elected by popular vote in keeping with the principle of popular sovereignty, senators were to be chosen by state legislatures. The assumption was that state legislatures would choose from among political elites to act as senators, and the Senate would serve as the "cooling saucer" to the unrestrained voice of the popular will as expressed in the House. The creation of the Electoral College also removed the president from direct choice by the popular will. Electors, like senators, were originally to be selected by state governments in the belief that the elite would be chosen and the selection of the president would be decided by those with experience and education rather than by the passions of the popular will. The choice of Supreme Court justices was removed from the elective process completely and was turned over to the president and the Senate.

It might be argued that the Constitution is, by its wording in the Preamble and by definition, a social contract in recognition of the value and faith the Founders placed in the will of the people. The principle of popular sovereignty enshrined in the Preamble indicates that the Founders had no fear of the popular majority. However, the Preamble is simply an expression of the Enlightenment philosophy of the time, not the actual framework of the government. The framework that follows, allowing the popular will to prevail only in the election of House members, clearly demonstrates the high level of concern among the Founding property owners, slave holders, and wealthy merchants that formation of a popular majority faction could threaten the rights and privileges of the elite minority faction. Of course, this framework protects not just economic minorities from the will of the majority but other minority factions as well.

Required Foundational Documents and Supreme Court Cases

Required Foundational Documents

On the AP GOV exam, you must be able to respond to questions about the principles of America's founding documents that remain a vital part of U.S. government and politics. In the table that follows, chapter references are provided at the end of the Summary column for further reading. In addition, information about constitutional issues is located at the National Constitution Center at the following website: http://constitutioncenter.org/interactive-constitution.

Required Foundational Documents		
Document	**Main Point**	**Summary**
The Declaration of Independence (1776)	America's founding document for the original 13 colonies.	The American colonies' justification to the world for their revolutionary act of severing ties with England. The task of writing this declaration was originally given to a committee including Thomas Jefferson, John Adams, and Benjamin Franklin, but Thomas Jefferson emerged as its primary author. Jefferson spoke to the philosophical principles, values, and fundamental beliefs that inspired not only American colonial revolutionaries but revolutionaries throughout the world to seek a government of their own consent. It is considered a founding document in American history that established the United States as a nation. It contains four sections: (1) the Preamble, explaining why the document was written; (2) the declaration of natural rights (basic rights of man that cannot be taken)—life, liberty, property; the consent of the governed; and limited government; (3) the list of grievances—complaints against the King of England and the British government; and (4) the declaration that the 13 colonies were independent and free. (Chapter 4)
The Articles of Confederation (1777)	The first government framework for the newly independent United States.	Following their declared independence, Americans had to create a government that could act on behalf of the new nation during the American Revolution with Britain. Harboring strong fears that a strong centralized government would threaten their newly claimed freedom, the members of the Second Continental Congress formulated a plan of government that they believed was adequate to guide the nation through the war, but protected the people and their rights by granting sovereignty to the states. After the conclusion of the revolution, the United States faced the challenges of building a new nation and many Founding Fathers questioned whether the fragmented, decentralized government under the Articles was too weak and powerless to meet these challenges successfully. (Chapter 4)

Continued

Document	Main Point	Summary
The Constitution of the United States (1787, ratified in 1788)	The U.S. Constitution was a blueprint for a new U.S. government designed to replace the faltering Articles of Confederation.	Drafted by delegates from every state except Rhode Island, the Constitution was finally ratified in 1788. The Constitution was designed to replace the Articles of Confederation with a new federal design that included a central government empowered to act on behalf of the national interest and to enforce its decisions. It is the foundation for our political system today and features a government of separated powers (executive, legislative, and judicial branches) and safeguards against the concentration of power in any one branch—referred to as the system of checks and balances. The fight over its ratification revealed a philosophical rift that persists to the present day. Regardless of the ongoing debate over its interpretation and the application of its provisions, the Constitution avoided tyranny and allowed the constitutional government to last for more than 230 years. (Chapter 4)
The Bill of Rights	The Bill of Rights consists of the first 10 *amendments* (changes) to the Constitution.	The first 10 amendments put in place protections for the rights and civil liberties of individuals against the authority of the central government and included assurances to the states of their continued sovereignty over state and local issues. **First Amendment.** Prohibits the government from making any law that infringes on freedom of religion, freedom of speech, freedom of the press, and the right to peaceably assemble, and prohibits the petition of a governmental grievance. **Second Amendment.** Protects the right of people to keep and bear arms. **Third Amendment.** Prohibits soldiers from temporarily residing in private homes during peacetime without getting the consent of the owner. **Fourth Amendment.** Prohibits unreasonable searches and seizures of individuals and property. **Fifth Amendment.** Protects a person from being compelled to be a witness against himself/herself in a criminal case. **Sixth Amendment.** Guarantees rights to criminal defendants (i.e., the right to a public trial without delay, the right to a lawyer, the right to an impartial jury, the right to know your accusers, the right to know the nature of the charges and evidence against you). **Seventh Amendment.** Guarantees the right to a jury trial in certain civil cases and inhibits courts from overturning a jury's findings of fact. **Eighth Amendment.** Prohibits the government from imposing excessive bail, excessive fines, or cruel and unusual punishment, including torture. **Ninth Amendment.** States that any rights not specifically granted to the people by the Constitution are not necessarily denied to them, either. **Tenth Amendment.** Defines the concept of *federalism* and the relationship between the federal and state governments by differentiating between the delegated power of the federal government and those powers reserved to the states. (Chapter 5)

Document	Main Point	Summary
Federalist No. 10 (1787) **James Madison**	A large republic, such as the United States, under the Constitution would be so diverse that it would be the best means of avoiding "tyranny of the majority" through formation of a majority faction which would use its power to oppress minority interests.	Federalist No. 10 focused on the superiority of a large republic in controlling the "mischiefs of faction," delegating authority to elected representatives and dispersing power between the states and national government. Madison argued that the formation of factions was natural in any group of people. Trying simply to eradicate factions was impossible; therefore, civil societies must attempt to control their effects. The Constitution was one such attempt (Chapter 4)
Federalist No. 51 (1788) **James Madison**	The importance of establishing checks and balances between different departments.	Madison's essay argues that "If men were angels, no government would be necessary." The essay argues in favor of the constitutional structure of the government into separate branches and the importance of checks and balances in a scheme to use the internal workings and interactions of the three branches to avoid the concentration of power in the hands of a few. It embodies a commonly held Enlightenment-Era belief that men are driven by self-interest; self-interest, in fact, drives human impulse. (Chapter 4)
Federalist No. 70 (1788) **Alexander Hamilton**	The importance of establishing an executive branch for a unified government.	Alexander Hamilton wrote about the power of the executive branch of government. Hamilton argued that a strong unitary executive is necessary as a source of energy, rather than a plural executive branch, as a protection against the self-interest of factions. (Chapter 5)
Federalist No. 78 (1788) **Alexander Hamilton**	The importance of a judicial branch of government.	Federalist No. 78 discusses the power of the judicial review process. Hamilton's essay argues that the judicial branch determines the lawfulness of proposed statutes. Instead of vesting sole power in the legislature to decide what is legal, the judicial branch is charged with the task of defending the rights of the people and, in effect, protecting them from any potential abuse from the hands of unconstitutional legislation. Hamilton's argument planted the seed for the Supreme Court to exercise the power of judicial review. (Chapter 5)

Continued

Document	Main Point	Summary
Brutus No. 1	Anti-Federalist writings that emphasized the benefits of a small decentralized republic.	Brutus No. 1 was a powerful articulation by an anonymous Anti-Federalist author who argued against immediate ratification of the Constitution as a replacement for the Articles of Confederation. While acknowledging problems with the Articles, "Brutus" argued that the potential for tyranny in such a design was far too great. The essay adhered to popular democratic theory that warned of the dangers to personal liberty from a large, centralized government. The author questioned whether the formation of one large republic with executive, legislative, and judicial branches exercising expansive powers over tremendously diverse populations in each of the states was a good remedy. (Chapter 4)
***Letter from Birmingham Jail* (1963)** **Dr. Martin Luther King Jr.**	Dr. King wrote about inequality in the United States stemming from racial segregation and the imperative nature of African American demands for civil rights and an end to racial practices that violate the U.S. Constitution.	Dr. Martin Luther King Jr. wrote the *Letter from Birmingham Jail* when he was wrongly imprisoned as a participant in a nonviolent march. Dr. King was laboring over equal treatment of all American citizens, regardless of race or ethnic identity, under the law. King sought an explanation for the violation of statutes in U.S. founding documents, which promised "all" citizens inalienable, natural rights defined in the U.S. Constitution and the Declaration of Independence. (Chapter 6)

Required Supreme Court Cases

On the AP GOV exam, you must know the facts, issues, holdings (including dissenting opinions), and reasoning behind decisions for 15 required Supreme Court cases. The SCOTUS free-response question will require that you apply real-world scenarios to a case listed in the table or compare the similarities and differences to another Supreme Court case. The table that follows also provides relevant non-required cases for your reference where applicable.

Chapter references are included at the end of the Facts and Summary column for further reading. Visit the following websites for more information about important Supreme Court cases.

http://www.uscourts.gov/about-federal-courts/educational-resources/supreme-court-landmarks

https://www.supremecourt.gov/

Required Supreme Court Cases			
Case	Key Issue	Facts and Summary	Relevant Non-Required Cases
***Marbury v. Madison* (1803)**	Judicial review	The Court established the principle of judicial review and affirmed the Court's authority to nullify legislation or executive actions that violate the Constitution. The decision changed the relationship between the judiciary and the other branches by firmly asserting the power of judicial review; this is still reflected in the Court today. *Marbury v. Madison* was relevant because it declared the Judiciary Act of 1789 unconstitutional (see Chapter 5).	
***McCulloch v. Maryland* (1819)**	Article I— Necessary and Proper Clause (Supremacy Clause and implicit powers)	The Court determined supremacy of Constitution and federal laws over state laws. The Court declared a state law to be unconstitutional, null and void, if it conflicted with a law passed by Congress under the authority of its implied powers. Under the leadership of Chief Justice John Marshall, it was the first test case of the Supremacy Clause and an early example of the "preemption doctrine" that allows federal courts to intervene in state attempts to nullify federal law (see Chapter 4).	*Gibbons v. Ogden* (1824). The Court held that Congress had the sole authority to regulate interstate commerce (granted to Congress by the Commerce Clause).
***Schenck v. United States* (1919)**	First Amendment— freedom of speech (civil liberties)	The Court ruled that the First Amendment's free speech is not protected by the "clear and present danger" doctrine. The Court distinguished between dangerous "expressions" and dangerous "acts" (as in the Espionage Act of 1917). A person cannot "falsely shout fire in a theater and cause panic" (see Chapter 6).	*Gitlow v. New York* (1925). In a case involving calls by Socialist activist Benjamin Gitlow for strikes and other forms of direct action against the government that violated New York's anti-anarchy law, the Court ruled that freedom of speech is incorporated to include the states under the Fourteenth Amendment. This is known as the *incorporation doctrine,* or *selective incorporation.* Despite the Court's ruling on free speech, unfortunately for Gitlow, the Court also upheld his New York conviction based on the Court's "clear and present danger rule" established in *Schenck v. United States.* *Brandenburg v. Ohio* (1969). The Court held that the government cannot punish inflammatory speech unless that speech incites or produces an imminent lawless action.

Continued

Case	Key Issue	Facts and Summary	Relevant Non-Required Cases
Brown v. Board of Education of Topeka (1954) (Brown I)	Fourteenth Amendment—Equal Protection Clause (equality)	The Court ruled that school segregation based on race violates the Equal Protection Clause and thereby set aside the *Plessy v. Ferguson* (1896) "separate but equal" doctrine. State laws that established separate public schools for white and black students were ruled unconstitutional. The case also sparked the Civil Rights Movement in the 1950s and 1960s (see Chapter 6).	*Plessy v. Ferguson* (1896). The Court upheld "separate but equal" racial segregation by the states. *Brown v. Board of Education of Topeka* (1955; *Brown II*). School districts and federal courts must implement the Court's decision in *Brown v. Board of Education of Topeka* (1954; *Brown I*) "with all deliberate speed."
Baker v. Carr (1962)	Fourteenth Amendment—Equal Protection Clause (redistricting and gerrymandering)	The Court established an equitable system of representation, ruling that the "one man, one vote" principle applied to legislative districts as well; that is, all votes within each district must be weighted equally. The Court based its ruling on the Fourteenth Amendment's Equal Protection Clause. The Court's decision to hear this case paved the way for the federal courts to hear other cases challenging legislative redistricting (see Chapter 5).	*Shaw v. Reno* (1993). The Court ruled that redistricting must be mindful of race to guarantee compliance with the Voting Rights Act of 1965.
Engel v. Vitale (1962)	First Amendment—Establishment Clause (civil liberties)	The Court ruled that prayer in public schools violates the First Amendment. The public school sponsorship, endorsement, and encouragement of religious activities violates the Establishment Clause. Prayer in public schools is permitted if it is student-initiated, student-led, or voluntary (see Chapter 6).	*Everson v. Board of Education* (1947). The Court held that the state of New Jersey did not violate the Establishment Clause when reimbursing parents for transportation. *Lemon v. Kurtzman* (1971). The Court held that reimbursing nonpublic schools was in violation of the Establishment Clause because of the entanglement between a private, religious school and the state.
Gideon v. Wainwright (1963)	Fourteenth Amendment—Due Process Clause	Under the Fourteenth Amendment, criminal defendants are guaranteed the right to an attorney in their defense and protection from unreasonable searches based on the Due Process Clause. The Court held that it was unreasonable to expect that people who could not afford an attorney could receive a fair trial (see Chapter 6).	*Betts v. Brady* (1942). The Court decided that the right to an appointed attorney was not required in all cases in order to receive a fair trial. It was up to the states to decide the right to an attorney.

Case	Key Issue	Facts and Summary	Relevant Non-Required Cases
Tinker v. Des Moines Independent Community School District (1969)	First Amendment—freedom of speech (civil liberties)	The Court ruled that a student wearing a black armband to protest the Vietnam War is protected under freedom of "symbolic" free speech expression, as long as it does not cause a "material disruption or substantial interference" (see Chapter 6).	*Texas v. Johnson* (1989). The Court determined that the burning of an American flag was protected under the First Amendment.
New York Times Co. v. United States (1971)	First Amendment—freedom of the press (civil liberties)	The Court ruled that *The New York Times* had the right to publish the Pentagon Papers, classified government materials about the United States' involvement in the Vietnam War. The government failed to meet the requisite of "burden of proof"; therefore, the printed material did not infringe on national security. The decision bolstered the freedom of the press, establishing a "heavy presumption against prior restraint" even in cases of national security (see Chapter 6).	*New York Times Co. v. Sullivan* (1964). The Court held that news publications could not be sued by public officials unless the plaintiffs were able to establish malice. The Court supported freedom of the press.
Wisconsin v. Yoder (1972)	First Amendment—Free Exercise Clause (civil liberties)	Under the Free Exercise Clause, compelling Amish students to attend school past the eighth grade violates the Constitution. Based on religious beliefs, public schools are not mandatory after a child is 14 years old (see Chapter 6).	
Roe v. Wade (1973)	Fourteenth Amendment—Due Process Clause (right to privacy)	The Court extended the constitutional right to privacy to a woman's right to decide to have an abortion in the first trimester of pregnancy. The state can impose restrictions in the second and third trimesters of pregnancy (see Chapter 6).	*Planned Parenthood of Southeastern Pennsylvania v. Casey* (1992). The Court upheld *Roe v. Wade*'s decision that women have a right to an abortion, but the Court rejected the trimester framework, holding that states can impose regulations on abortion as long as "undue burden" is not placed on women (e.g., counseling, 24-hour waiting period).
Shaw v. Reno (1993)	Fourteenth Amendment—Equal Protection Clause	The Court ruled that legislative redistricting based on race must be held to a standard of *strict scrutiny* under the Equal Protection Clause. The Court ruled against racial gerrymandering to ensure the election of an African American representative (see Chapter 5).	*Miller v. Johnson* (1995). The Court ruled against a North Carolina redistricting plan that created a majority/minority legislative district. Based on the *Shaw v. Reno* decision, the states' eleventh district failed to pass the strict scrutiny test required whenever race is an overriding, dominant force in the decision to draw the district's boundaries.

Continued

Case	Key Issue	Facts and Summary	Relevant Non-Required Cases
United States v. Lopez **(1995)**	Tenth Amendment—Commerce Clause (Federalism)	The Court declared that Congress cannot use the Commerce Clause to declare that possession of a handgun at a school is a federal crime. The case was regarded as part of the "devolution revolution," in which the Rehnquist Court narrowed the definition of what constitutes interstate commerce and thereby restrained Congress' ability to regulate activities (in this case, the possession of handguns) more properly reserved to the states (see Chapter 4).	*United States v. Morrison* (2000). The Court ruled that parts of the Violence Against Women Act (1994) that gave women the right to sue their attackers were unconstitutional under the Commerce Clause.
McDonald v. Chicago **(2010)**	Second Amendment—right to keep and bear arms	The Court ruled that the Second Amendment right to keep and bear arms for self-defense is applicable to federal, state, and local governments (see Chapter 6).	*District of Columbia v. Heller* (2008). The Court held that the Second Amendment guarantees a person the right to bear firearms; this ruling struck down the strict gun control ordinance in the District of Columbia.
Citizens United v. Federal Election Commission **(2010)**	First Amendment—freedom of speech	The Court ruled that campaign finance limits were unconstitutional. The Court held that the government cannot prevent corporations, associations, and labor unions from contributing money to support (or denounce) candidates. The case law pertaining to campaign finance demonstrates the ongoing debate over the role of money in political and free speech as set forth in the Bipartisan Campaign Reform Act (2002), also known as the McCain-Feingold Act (see Chapter 8).	*Buckley v. Valeo* (1976). The Court held that the Federal Election Campaign Act (1971), which limited election contributions, violated the First Amendment provision of freedom of speech.